The Handbook of Online and Social Media Research

The Handbook of Online and Social Media Research

Tools and Techniques for Market Researchers

Ray Poynter

A John Wiley and Sons, Ltd, Publication

Library of Congress Cataloging-in-Publication Data

A catalogue record for this book is available from the British Library.

Poynter, Ray.
    The handbook of online and social media research : tools and techniques for market researchers / by Ray
  Poynter.
      p. cm.
    Summary: "Drawing together the new techniques available to the market researcher into a single reference,
The Handbook of Online and Social Media Research explores how these innovations are being used by the leaders
in the field. This groundbreaking reference examines why traditional research is broken, both in theory and practice,
and includes chapters on online research communities, community panels, blog mining, social networks, mobile
research, e-ethnography, predictive markets, and DIY research"-- Provided by publisher.
    Summary: "The book will become the key reference point for research practitioners and buyers as they
move from their security blanket of traditional research, with its outdated notions of science and reliability, into
the maelstrom that is unfolding in the post Web 2.0 world of Twitter, community panels, Facebook, and
YouTube"— Provided by publisher.
    ISBN 978-0-470-71040-1 (hardback)
      1. Marketing research. 2. Social media. 3. Internet searching. I. Title.
  HF5415.2.P66 2010
  658.8'3—dc22

2010026276

Typeset in 9.5/13 pt Gillsans-Light by MPS Limited, A Macmillan Company

Printed in Great Britain by CPI Antony Rowe, Chippenham, Wiltshire

Dedication

*To the memory of my parents
Bill and Mary (Florence) Poynter
who gave so much whilst asking
for so little for themselves.*

Contents

Foreword ix
By Finn Raben

Introduction xi

PART I
Online Quantitative Survey Research

1   Overview of Online Quantitative Research 3

2   Web Survey Systems 16

3   Designing Online Surveys 31

4   Working with Panels and Databases 66

5   Running an Online Survey and Summary 88

PART II
Qualitative Research

6   Overview of Online Qualitative Research 107

7   Online Focus Groups 116

8   Bulletin Board Groups and Parallel IDIs 132

9   Other Online Qualitative Methods and Summary of
       Online Qualitative Research 151

PART III
Social Media

10   Participatory Blogs as Research Tools 163

11   Online Research Communities/MROCs 176

12   Blog and Buzz Mining 221

13   Other Social Media Topics and Summary 243

PART IV
Research Topics

14   Specialist Research Areas.. 261

15   Website Research 282

16   Research Techniques and Approaches 322

17   The Business of Market Research...................................... 340

PART V
Breaking News!

18   New*MR*.. 367

19   Trends and Innovations 378

20   An Overview of Online and Social Media Research 391

Glossary 403

Further Information..417

References..421

Acknowledgements..427

Index 431

Foreword

By Finn Raben
ESOMAR Director General

The internet has revolutionized our world. It is at once a world-wide broadcasting capability, a mechanism for information collection and dissemination, and a medium for collaboration and interaction between individuals without regard for race, religion, political orientation, social strata or geographic location.

The internet has been the 'muse' of practically all technological developments of note in the past 20 years (laptops, smartphones, GPS systems), has breathed new life into many ailing industries (such as gaming, travel, and publishing), and has spawned entirely new industries centered around the establishment and management of online communities. Its influence now reaches far beyond its humble beginnings as a means of linking computers, into society as a whole.

As the internet becomes ubiquitous; faster and increasingly accessible to non-technical communities, social networking and collaborative services have grown rapidly, enabling people to talk, discuss, debate and share interests in many more ways than ever before. Sites like Facebook, Twitter, LinkedIn, YouTube, Flickr, Second Life, blogs, wikis, and many more, now let people of all ages rapidly share their interests of the moment with others everywhere . . . communication "of the people, by the people, for the people", to paraphrase Abraham Lincoln's Gettysburg address.

As 'muse' for the market research sector, the internet has been as successful as with other industries. 'Online' is now the most popular methodology used, and the online research market is currently valued in excess of $6 billion.*

Online research and online traffic/audience measurement now account for 10% or more of overall research spend in 22 countries, up from 18 countries in 2007.* As a (constantly evolving) sector of the MR industry, ESOMAR dedicates the majority of its resources to online, in order to ensure that practical guidelines, policy directives and legislative proposals remain in tune with current practices and applications.

Ray Poynter has long been an advocate and a proponent for embracing the internet both as an evolutionary – as well as revolutionary – tool, to the benefit of the industry. Ray has been a member of ESOMAR for almost 20 years and has been a respected speaker at ESOMAR conferences throughout that time, challenging conventional wisdom and urging people to move beyond traditional boundaries. He has consistently provided a thought-provoking alternative to the accepted modality wisdom, and with this book, now provides a real source of best practice guidance, for those wishing to adopt the internet and social media to a much broader extent.

Source: ESOMAR GMR Report, published September 2009

Exponents of market research – with Ray foremost amongst them – now realise that everybody is talking on the internet – often times without any restrictions whatsoever – about a vast range of topics. No longer is recruitment an issue; no longer is the phrasing of the question an issue; no longer is the duration of the interview an issue; and no longer is respondent fatigue an issue. If the topic is of interest, then the material is already there ... thus is born the 'Age of Listening' as opposed to the 'Age of Questioning'.

Putting to rest many of the urban myths, allaying many of the fears/phobias, but also highlighting the many evolving challenges that are associated with a greater utilization of the internet in market research (such as data quality, data protection and regulatory hurdles etc), this *Handbook of Online and Social Media Reserach* provides the first definitive guide to better understanding, and optimizing, your use of the internet and the social media.

In the context of the internet, we must recognize that as Heraclitus said in the 4th century BC: "Nothing is permanent, but change!", yet despite the pace of evolution, many of Ray's comments and suggestions made in this book will remain relevant for a long time to come.

I hope you derive as much value and insight from the book as we did; ESOMAR is honoured to be associated with this important reference document, and we look forward to continuing to monitor the internet (r)evolution in partnership with Ray.

Introduction

Welcome to the *Handbook of Online and Social Media Research*.

SHOULD YOU BUY THIS BOOK?

This introduction should help you know whether you have opened the right book. It first explains who the book is for and then it describes what is in the book and how it is organised.

WHO IS THIS BOOK FOR?

This book has been written with three groups of people in mind:

1. Market researchers who want to increase their knowledge and use of the internet and social media as a modality for their projects.

2. Experts in the field of online and social media research who want to compare their experience with an alternative view of best practice.

3. Buyers of market research who want to expand their understanding of what can be offered and also of the limitations implicit in the market research methods that are currently available.

Given the breadth, and indeed the length, of the book it is not envisaged that many people would want to sit down and read it from cover to cover. The book has been written as a handbook and each part, and each chapter within each part, is designed to stand on its own as much as possible.

WHY IS THE BOOK NEEDED?

The use of the internet is currently the most exciting and dynamically changing aspect of market research, and has been for the last ten years. However, despite the importance of this area, there are few books that specifically look at best practice in conducting online market research and, in particular, there is very little that looks at the use of social media to conduct market research.

This shortage of widely available, accessible material is in strong contrast with the content of market research conference papers, presentations, and workshops, where online market research and the use of social media are two of the most frequently discussed topics. However, conference papers, presentations, and workshops are not accessible to everybody and do not constitute an organised and convenient canon of knowledge for market researchers seeking to use the latest approaches. This book aims to provide a single resource for market researchers looking for best practice guidance in using the internet and social media.

HOW THE BOOK IS ORGANISED

The purpose of this book is to illustrate best practice in market research that uses the internet in general and social media in particular. The book is divided into five parts, each sub-divided into chapters.

The introduction sets the scene, covering a few key definitions and providing some information about what is already happening and where the trends are going.

Part I addresses the enormously important area of quantitative market research conducted via online surveys. This is already the most established aspect of online research and, in revenue terms, the online modality now accounts for a larger share of quantitative surveys than any other modality.

Part II focuses on established online qualitative techniques, such as online focus groups and bulletin board groups. Part III addresses the rapidly developing world of market research conducted via social media, for example online research communities, e-ethnography, and blog and buzz mining.

Part IV shifts the focus away from the modality issue and addresses topics of interest from the perspective of research needs. For example, techniques such as prediction markets, sectors such as public sector research, and broader issues such as international research are all discussed. Part V is called Breaking News and it addresses the emergent issues that researchers need to be aware of, but which are too new to be able to offer best practice advice. This includes philosophical issues such as NewMR and trending topics like Twitter.

The final section contains a glossary to help readers who may be looking for specific clarification of some of the terms used in the book. It also includes a remarkably long list of acknowledgements. This is because the book benefited from a large amount of collaboration in its preparation. Much of the material in this book was posted on the web and the contributions of the many people listed in this section have certainly made the book a better read and far better informed.

MARKET RESEARCH AND THE INTERNET

There follows a brief introduction to what is happening in terms of market research, the internet, and social media.

EVOLUTION AND REVOLUTION

This book covers both an evolution in market research and a revolution. The evolution relates to those established parts of market research, such as quantitative surveys, that have adopted online data collection as simply an additional modality. This evolution required some additional research techniques and the refinement of others in order to translate surveys from the high street, doorstep, and the telephone to the internet. Traditional market research skills have been expanded to deal with the new modality, and this book covers the skills and approaches that researchers need to master in order to optimise their use of this new medium.

There are two revolutions going on within market research and both are associated with the internet. The first is a quiet revolution, in which 75 years of basing quantitative market research on a paradigm of projecting the results of samples onto populations via assumptions of random probability sampling has been replaced by a willingness to use online access panels, which do not approximate to this model.

The second, noisier, revolution is the way that social media, and the philosophical challenge of Web 2.0, have created new propositions, new opportunities, and new rules for market research.

This book addresses both of these revolutions in terms of providing background, information, and advice on utilising the new opportunities presented to the market researcher. Looking forward, market researchers need to ensure that they master the tools and rules of both the evolution and the revolution, to ensure that they stay relevant and informed, and that is the mission for this book.

BACKGROUND TO ONLINE MARKET RESEARCH

The internet has been used as a medium for data collection since about 1995, although its rapid growth can mostly be identified as being from 1999 onwards, and its ascendancy in terms of quantitative data collection has only happened over the last three years.

Initially, the internet, and online data collection in particular, was seen as simply another modality, without any significant implications for what the research was or what it meant. However, the internet has led to changes in the nature of research, both in terms of challenging the assumptions that used to underpin market research (such as sampling theory) and in terms of opening up new possibilities, for example through the use of blog mining and online research communities.

This section brings anybody new to the topic of online research up-to-date with the key issues that are shaping online and social media research today. The next sections looks at the scale of online research, the reasons for its rapid growth, the specific role of online access panels, and the main concerns that buyers and providers of market research express about online research.

THE SCALE OF ONLINE RESEARCH

Data showing the scale of online research, compared with other data collection mediums, tend to be somewhat out of date by the time they are published, so the information shown in Table A.1 should be seen as indicative of the rate of change and the scale of the internet in market research, rather than as a definitive representation of data collection values.

Table A.1 Revenue share of all research, ESOMAR Global Market Research reports, 2006, 2009

	2005	2008
Online	13%	20%
Telephone	21%	18%
Face-to-face	24%	12%
Postal	6%	5%

Table A.1 shows data from two ESOMAR Global Market Research reports (2006 and 2009) showing the data for 2005 and 2008.

In 2008, about 55% of all market research revenue related to quantitative research conducted via surveys. In addition to this 55%, about 17% of market research revenues related to automated/ electronic data collection and 14% to qualitative research. In 2008, ESOMAR estimated that the global spend on market research was US $32 billion, which would make quantitative survey research worth nearly US $18 billion.

As recently as 2005, online data collection was a poor third to telephone and face-to-face in terms of global data collection modalities. However, by 2008 online had become the leading global modality for quantitative data collection.

The ESOMAR Global Market Research reports look at the differences in data collection modalities by country and these show some marked differences from country to country. For example, in 2008, over 30% of all research was conducted via the internet in Canada, Japan, and Australia. By contrast, the figure was 11% in China and Switzerland, and in Bolivia, India, and Portugal it was close to 0%.

The general assumption is that the share of research conducted via the internet will continue to grow, notwithstanding a number of concerns about online market research, which will be explored later in this book.

REASONS FOR THE RAPID UPDATE OF THE INTERNET BY MARKET RESEARCH

In terms of quantitative data collection, the internet is now the single most important global modality for data collection, according to the 2009 ESOMAR Global Market Research report. On a global scale, internet data collection has moved ahead of postal, face-to-face, and telephone data collection modalities in just a few years. The rapid rise of online data collection is well worth examining, partly to understand the key attributes of the internet modality, and partly to help assess what might happen next.

Compared with other data collection modalities, the internet has benefited from a number of modality-specific advantages, such as being able to reach hard-to-find groups and the provision of flexibility for respondents to take part in surveys at a time of their convenience. These advantages will have had some impact on the rapid uptake of the internet by market researchers, but they are not the main reason for its success in becoming the leading modality.

A more significant factor in the rise of online data collection was probably the increase in speed offered by internet, resulting in considerably faster project turnarounds. However, there is little sign that the reduction in product timings has led to any reduction in clients worrying that research takes too long and is too reactive.

However, the main reason the internet has been adopted so widely for quantitative research is the cost savings it has been able to offer compared with other data collection modalities. The ESOMAR Global Prices Study 2007 produced global figures and also compared face-to-face, telephone, and internet on like-for-like projects across several countries. The study showed that telephone tended to be about 40% cheaper than face-to-face, and online tended to be 40% cheaper than telephone in those markets where all three modalities were an option.

The push to realise the internet's potential cost savings took a special emphasis in the economic downturn following the collapse of the dotcom bubble in 2000, and has remained important.

Whilst cost was the main driver of the demand for online data collection, the key change that made it viable was the rise of online access panels.

THE RISE OF ACCESS PANELS

In the early days of online data collection there were no reliable methods of obtaining respondents for surveys. By comparison with other modalities, researchers were suddenly faced with a medium where there were no directories, no lists, and no RDD (random digit dialling). There were no simple options for identifying the population and no suitable methods for defining a sample.

The most frequent approaches, in those earliest days of online data collection, were to use advertising tools and client databases (for the small number of clients who had usable lists of customers' email addresses). The advertising route consisted of using invitations to surveys implemented via advertising mechanisms such as banner ads and pop-ups.

However, online data collection only took off as a major force when online access panels became widely available. Readers should note that as online access panels have become more central to research they are increasingly being referred to as, simply, online panels, or just panels.

Before the mid-1990s, panels had been fairly rare outside the USA, and they were usually reserved for specific purposes, such as retail audits. In the USA there had been a history of mail (postal) panels and this, to an extent, explained the more rapid development of online access panels in the USA. It has also been suggested that the more conservative nature of European research buyers and providers slowed down the development of online research in Europe.

The development of large scale online access panels became the key to unlocking the use of the internet for quantitative research. However, by adopting the widespread use of online access panels, market research has moved away from the ability to claim that it uses random probability sampling and that it can 'scientifically' project its findings onto the wider population – a fact and consequence that are covered later in this book.

There is a traditional saying in marketing that buyers tend to want things to be better, cheaper, quicker, but organisations can, at best, only offer two of these at any one time. By accepting the methodological limitations of panels, market research was able to make research both quicker and cheaper.

CONCERNS ABOUT ONLINE MARKET RESEARCH

Within just a few years of online research appearing on the scene, and certainly by 1999, most of the key issues and concerns surrounding it had been defined, and were being discussed at conferences and within research companies. These key concerns are:

○ **Representativity.** *Not everybody has access to the internet. Even amongst those who do have access, access is not equal. So, how can research conducted via the internet be representative?*

○ **Sampling.** *There is no list of who is using the internet and there is no agreed definition of the population of internet users, so how can samples be drawn?*

○ **Self-completion.** *Online respondents fill in the survey on their own, without an interviewer being present. Are these respondents who they say they are? Are they paying attention? Do they understand the questions? Do they have enough motivation to complete the project properly?*

○ **Technical limitations.** *Although these limitations have reduced considerably since the mid-1990s, the key limitations still exist. Smell and touch cannot be communicated via the internet, actual size is hard to convey, and the amount of stimuli that can be shown on a screen is still far less than can be shown in a photograph, on a real shelf, or in a magazine mock-up.*

○ **Loss of nonverbal contact.** *In a face-to-face situation, especially in a focus group, the researcher can watch the respondent and interpret nonverbal clues. This is not yet (and may never be) a convenient option via the internet.*

○ **Additional privacy concerns.** *The internet has introduced many new ways for information to be captured, stored, and shared. This has led to increased concerns about security and privacy, in terms of protecting both the respondents' and clients' interests.*

○ **Self-selection.** *In traditional research approaches the respondents were approached and asked for their cooperation. In most online research there is an element of self-selection, ranging from a small degree of self-selection through to it being the main route. For example,* *many people on panels have sought out the panel and applied to join it. This represents a very different approach to the traditional research method of inhibiting self-selection.*

○ **Professional respondents.** *Almost as soon as online surveys appeared on the scene, there were people actively seeking out the incentives that were being offered. This phenomenon has grown, especially with the rise of online access panels, to the extent where there is a concern that some/many respondents complete a large number of surveys and that they do it mainly for the financial rewards. There is a concern that the presence of professional respondents may imply one or more of (a) sensitised responses, (b) using false responses to complete more surveys, and (c) being less representative of the population.*

Since the 1990s, market researchers have found methods of living with the issues outlined above, without fully solving any of them. One of the reasons that a handbook of online market research is needed is to help those involved in the buying, specifying, or conducting of online market research to be aware of the limitations of the medium and the ways these limitations are typically addressed.

USING THIS BOOK

This section sets out some useful information on the best way to use this book, for example its conventions and clues.

ICONS FOR KEY NOTES

Given that there is a large amount of information in the book, it is important to highlight the most important items, to help ensure that the best practice guidance is accessible. In order to signpost the key notes, icons have been used to indicate points of special interest and these are shown in Table A.2.

Table A.2

Icon	Description
	Highlights warnings about topics that can be critical to research outcomes or quality/ethical issues.
	Summarised advice, such as check lists.
	Real world examples of how approaches have been applied.
	Lists of resources that the reader may find useful.
	Highlights that the next section is purely the opinion of the author.

REPETITION

Some of the issues covered in this book, such as the research implications of working with online access panels, are associated with several topics. This suggests that the book needs to adopt one of two approaches:

1.   Cover each issue once, in whatever depth is required, and in all other locations refer the reader to that section.

2.   Cover the same issue more than once so that the reader does not have to be diverted from the topic they are reading to review the issue.

Given that this book is designed to be a handbook and the focus is on making each topic as accessible as possible, the tendency is towards covering some key issues more than once. However, each time the issue is covered it is contextualised to the topic.

QUALITY AND ETHICS

One of the most dynamically changing parts of online market research relates to ethics and quality. The practical implications of this are changes in legislation, changes in respondent cooperation, and changes in regulations. This book visits the issues of quality and ethics in terms of most of the topics reviewed in the book.

CASE STUDIES AND INTERVIEWS

This handbook makes extensive use of case studies and interviews with industry leaders to show how the techniques and approaches being explored are used in the market place. This has been done with the kind consent of the many companies who have contributed case studies, information, and data. However, the reader should remember that case studies tend to represent 'good news' stories. A great case study illustrates how a technique has delivered insight or ROI – i.e. it shows that the technique can be useful; it does not show that it is always useful, in all cases and in all situations.

THE SPEED OF CHANGE

Because the medium being examined is the internet and because a large part of the book concentrates on leading edge topics, such as online research communities, blog mining, and e-ethnography, this book is a snapshot of a rapidly changing process.

Most of the observations in this book, and the guidance that accompanies them, will hold true for the next ten years. However, some may have changed within months, so the reader should complement

the reading of this book by following the key blogs, conferences, and thinking about onli
especially social media research (a list of resources is included at the back of the book).

There is also a website that accompanies this book which hosts extra material and an online discussion
about topics raised by the book. The website can be found at http://hosmr.com.

REFERENCES

Ethics, data protection, data security, and quality are important issues for market research, and there
are a large number of international and local regulations, guidelines, and initiatives. This book contains
specific sections where these issues are explored. Throughout the book the recommendations are
broadly based on the ESOMAR guidelines, as these guidelines are global and have been adopted in
association with a wide range of other bodies. However, the rules and guidance change rapidly, and
vary from country to country. Market researchers need to keep themselves acquainted with the latest picture in the markets they are operating in.

KEY TERMS USED IN THIS BOOK

In the world of market research, many different terms are used for the same thing in different markets,
and sometimes even by different market researchers within a single market. In order to aid clarity, the
key phrases that are in the book are outlined below. There is also a glossary of terms at the end of
the book which covers a wider range of terms and definitions.

Agency	A supplier of market research, which may also be called an institute or a vendor.
Client	A buyer of market research.
Client-side	Something which is done by or within a client company. For example, a market researcher employed by a client might be described as a client-side researcher.
Insight/research department	This term is used to denote a department within an organisation that buys research (i.e. a client), which is responsible for working with (amongst other things) market research information.
NewMR	NewMR is a term that has been adopted to group together those aspects of newly-developed market research that move away from two key tenets of traditional market research, namely the command and control model of researcher and respondents (towards a more collaborative model), and away from assumptions of random probability sampling to alternative models. Examples of NewMR include online research communities and prediction markets.

PART I

Online Quantitative Survey Research

The single biggest impact of the internet on market research to date has been on the collection of quantitative survey data. The chapters in this first part of the book address different aspects of quantitative survey research conducted via online surveys.

Part I covers

- Overview of quantitative online research
- Web survey systems
- Designing online surveys
- Online access panels
- Client databases
- In-house panels
- Running an online survey
- The online quality debate
- Summary of online quantitative research

Note, there are other forms of quantitative research that are not survey research, such as web analytics and scanner data. These are not covered in this part of the book.

Overview of Online Quantitative Research

The largest impact of online market research so far has been in the area of quantitative survey research, both in terms of volume and value. By 2008, according to the 2009 ESOMAR Global Market Research Report, the value of online quantitative market research was 20% of the global research total, which put it at about US$ 6.5 billion. By contrast, telephone quantitative accounted for 18%, face-to-face surveys for 12%, and qualitative research was reported as representing about 14% of global market research revenues.

It is important to note that the majority of quantitative research conducted via online data collection is not inherently different – in terms of the problems it is seeking to solve, the questions it asks, and the analysis that is conducted – from quantitative research conducted via other modalities, such as face-to-face or telephone.

This chapter is a high-level review of the key issues that confront market researchers and market research buyers when conducting online quantitative studies.

The topics covered in this chapter are:

- *Online survey process*

- *Surveys and the internet modality*

- *Finding respondents to interview*

- *Moving surveys online*

ONLINE SURVEY PROCESS

The typical process for the data collection phase for a project using online data collection is as shown in Table 1.1.

It is important to note that the timeline for an online survey is different from that of a telephone study, and even more so from that of a face-to-face study. In non-trivial cases, the total time required for an online survey will be shorter than that for a telephone or face-to-face survey, but this is not true of each individual stage. Compared with a face-to-face or telephone survey, Steps 2 to 4 of

Table 1.1

1	Create and agree with the client a draft questionnaire, often referred to as a paper questionnaire or a Word questionnaire (as in Microsoft Word).
2	Script the survey, i.e. create an online questionnaire, typically using one of the data collection systems.
3	Host the survey, i.e. install the questionnaire on a server attached to the internet and link it to a database to store the results.
4	Test and approve the survey.
5	Invite people to take the survey, for example send invitations to people on a database or to members of a panel.
6	Collect the data and monitor the progress of the survey, possibly tweaking elements such as quota controls.
7	Close the survey, download the data, remove and/or archive the online survey and data.

Table 1.1 tend to be slower for online projects, whereas Steps 5 to 7 tend to be faster (note, in a face-to-face survey Steps 2–4 would be the printing and dispatch of the questionnaires and Steps 5–7 would be the fieldwork and the data punching). Most of the time savings that are created by online surveys occur in Step 6.

In a face-to-face or telephone survey, the appearance of the questionnaire, which is dealt with in Step 2, is normally only a minor issue. Because the online modality is a self-completion mode, the layout, wording, and appearance of the survey are extremely important, as they are for postal surveys. Better designed, more carefully worded, more engaging surveys produce better data, but they also take longer to produce.

Step 3 in Table 1.1 is normally a quick process for online surveys and is analogous to the hosting of a CATI questionnaire for a telephone study.

Step 4 does not have a direct analogy in most face-to-face surveys; however, it can delay the online survey process. In all modalities it is a good idea to pilot a survey, but in online surveys the software and the layout have to be tested too, if major problems are to be avoided.

SURVEYS AND THE INTERNET MODALITY

The language of questionnaires and surveys tends to be derived from face-to-face research, with its references to questionnaires, pages, interviewers etc. However, each specific modality has its own features and characteristics that need recognising and utilising. This section reviews what we mean by different types of internet-related surveys.

WEB SURVEYS

In most cases, an internet survey is a questionnaire accessed via an internet browser (such as Microsoft's Internet Explorer or Mozilla's Firefox). This type of survey is commonly known as a web survey and is typically created and operated via specialist online survey software (such as the products from companies like Confirmit, Nebu, or Voxco). The survey can be provided via a range of tools, for example HTML, JavaScript, and Flash, and can appear as either one long page or as a number of screens, with each screen showing one or more questions.

Later chapters of this book cover the choice of web interviewing systems, the design of web surveys, and managing web survey projects.

There are alternatives to the web survey, but none of the alternatives is in widespread use. Examples of the alternatives include email surveys and downloadable surveys, which are covered in the sections below.

EMAIL SURVEYS

The term 'email survey' normally refers to a survey that is emailed to respondents. An email survey does not normally refer to studies where the survey is hosted on the web and an invitation is emailed to the respondent; this is normally referred to as a 'web survey'. However, email surveys have become much less common than they used to be and the term 'email survey' may have become more ambiguous.

In the very early days of online research, email surveys were popular because they did not require people to be online whilst they completed the survey. The internet at that stage tended to be very slow and most users were paying for access to it by the minute. Also, in those early days there were many people who had email access but who did not have access to the web, particularly from PCs they accessed whilst at work.

There are two ways to conduct an email survey. The first is to include the survey in the body of the email and the second is to send the survey as an attachment to the email.

Email surveys in the body of the email

Email surveys in the body of the email further divide into two main varieties, text emails and HTML emails.

A text email sets out the questionnaire as part of the email in the same way that a message is typed into an email. The respondent clicks 'Reply' and then scrolls down the email, entering their responses. The main drawbacks with this approach were that the survey tended to be boring, restricted, and respondents could miss questions, answer inappropriately (for example picking two options where only one should be selected), or even delete parts of the questionnaire. Interview software exists to draft these surveys, to conduct the mailing, and to interpret the replies.

An HTML email survey uses the power of HTML to create a more interesting survey. An HTML survey can look appealing. For example, it can use standard features such as radio buttons and check boxes, and can include a SUBMIT button at the foot of the email, making the survey more intuitive.

The main problem with HTML surveys is that many people's email filters will either prevent HTML emails from getting through, or they will convert them to plain text.

One area where email surveys have a specific benefit, compared with web surveys, is within a large organisation, for example when conducting a staff survey. In a large organisation a web-based survey can cause many recipients to log into the survey at the same time, potentially causing bandwidth problems. An email study distributed within a company will, in many cases, spread the load more evenly.

One special case of an email survey is where an email service is utilised to poll people's views, for example the voting buttons in Microsoft's Outlook can be used to gather people's views.

Email surveys as an attachment

In the early days of the internet it was quite acceptable to email a survey as a piece of executable code. These emails arrived on the respondent's machine, the attachment was opened, the survey completed, and it then emailed itself back to the project sponsor. The general reluctance to accept executable code via email has resulted in this form of survey becoming rare.

DOWNLOADABLE SURVEYS

A downloadable survey is one that is downloaded from the internet to a local device and the results are then sent back to the server at the end of the data collection process. Downloadable surveys tend to be implemented for mobile devices such as smartphones rather than for PC-based surveys.

One more recent innovation is to include a mobile, downloadable survey as part of a wider project, such as e-ethnography (a subject of a later chapter), but this remains relatively rare.

FINDING RESPONDENTS TO INTERVIEW

Initially, one of the main reasons that online data collection was held back was because there was no reliable and scalable method of contacting potential respondents. Face-to-face research was able to draw on sources such as electoral registers, postal address files and similar sources. Telephone was able to draw on directories and RDD (random digit dialling), but there was not (and still is not) a directory of who is on the internet.

However, through the 1990s and beyond, methods have been created that provide ways of finding respondents for online surveys. It should be noted that most of these innovations have required some changes in the assumptions about how sampling is conducted, a topic that is discussed later.

The key methods of contacting respondents are:

1. Online access panels
2. Client databases
3. Marketing databases
4. Client panels
5. Website visitors
6. River sampling

The following sections briefly define and outline these six approaches. The major techniques, and the implications of working with them, are dealt with in greater detail in later chapters. This section then finishes with a brief review of additional methods that have been used to find samples.

ONLINE ACCESS PANELS

The two big changes that facilitated the wide scale adoption of online data collection were the development of online access panels and the willingness of a large proportion of market research buyers to move away from the assumption of random probability sampling. This first of these two changes was obvious to both suppliers and buyers of research. It is less clear that the loss of the ability to claim random probability sampling was as widely understood.

Online access panels are also known as access panels, online panels, or simply just panels.

International online access panels, such as SSI, eRewards, LightSpeed, and GMI, are able to provide online samples for most of the developed markets (developed in terms of markets with a large volume of market research). In addition, in most developed markets there are a variety of local panels.

There are a number of different ways of working with online access panels, but the two most typical ways are:

1. The researcher provides the panel company with a sample specification and a link to a survey that has been scripted and hosted. The panel company then invites its members to take part in the survey.

2. The researcher specifies the survey and the sample specification and the panel company scripts the survey, hosts it, and provides the sample.

Because of the importance of online access panels there is a chapter specifically on working with them later in the book.

CLIENT DATABASES

Most organisations have some sort of customer database. These tend to vary from a very sophisticated CRM database of all customers (for example for an online retailer) through to a basic list of email addresses supplied by customers on an *ad hoc* basis.

The typical method of conducting research with a client database is to send a survey invitation to a sample of members drawn from the database. The most common way of sending the invitation is via email but there are other ways; usually the invitation will include a link to a web survey. There is more about working with client databases later in the book.

MARKETING DATABASES

There are a large number of organisations who hold databases for marketing purposes. The majority of the customers for these databases are direct mail companies, but they are sometimes used to provide market research samples.

The main concerns that market researchers have expressed about this approach are that: (1) there are few constraints about who is on these lists; (2) none of the quality guidelines which have been agreed by the research industry (see quality notes later) apply to these databases; and (3) the people on marketing lists may confuse marketing and market research, or competitions and market research.

Marketing database companies do not usually offer a scripting and hosting service for surveys, so the typical way of using them is that the database company sends out an email invitation to the survey, using an invite agreed with the researcher, including a link to the web survey.

Researchers who have used marketing databases have reported that they have experienced problems with duplicate responses (the same person answering the survey more than once, presumably because they are on the database more than once), and of a higher than expected number of people interested in prizes and competitions.

The key differences between an access panel and a marketing database are that:

(a)   the access panel is only used for market research, it is not used for marketing.

(b)   members of an access panel know they are on the panel and that they will only be contacted for market research purposes

(c)   most market research online access panels have signed up to guidelines, such as the ESOMAR guidelines

When using marketing databases, the researcher should make an effort to ensure that the people on the lists have given the appropriate permissions and that appropriate efforts have been taken to screen out children (or to obtain the relevant parental permission). The response rates from these lists tend to be lower than those from online access panels. Marketing databases have different pricing policies, with some charging by invitation, some by survey starts, and others charging only for completes.

Despite criticisms of marketing databases, they have been used in the past to help create online access panels.

CLIENT PANELS

A number of clients have created their own research panels. The key differences between a client panel and a client database are the same as the differences between an access panel and a marketing database.

Client panels vary in size from a few thousand members to tens of thousands of members. Some panels are managed in-house whilst others are managed by third-party companies. There is more about working with client panels later in the book.

WEBSITE VISITORS

The people who visit a website can be sampled for quantitative samples. For example, visitors to an online news service can be asked to do surveys about the website, the brand providing the news service, or the news service. This topic is covered in greater depth in Chapter 15.

There are two ways of soliciting the respondents: (1) using popups (or something similar such as overlays or pop-unders); or (2) by placing invites on the website.

Popups surveys can also be used to recruit respondents for general surveys, but this approach is better categorised as being a river sampling technique, especially if multiple sites are used.

RIVER SAMPLING

The concept behind river sampling (sometimes called real-time sampling) is to find and recruit respondents as and when they are needed, rather than keep going back to the same small sub-set of people who have chosen to join a panel or community.

Some of the proponents of river sampling claim that it more closely approximates to random sampling, compared with online access panels. However, most of the advocates concentrate on the 'freshness' of river samples, rather than any truer sense of representativeness. They point out that members of online access panels may complete upwards of 100 surveys a year. By contrast, fresh respondents, recruited by river sampling, are less likely to have had their responses affected by having completed large numbers of surveys.

The proposition that 'fresh is best' is one that has some face validity but the research conducted by the ARF's 'Foundations of Quality' project suggests that the number of surveys that somebody completes is not a problem. So a preference for a 'fresh' sample has to be considered a personal preference at the moment, rather than an evidence-based decision.

Examples of river sampling include:

- *banner ads*
- *popups*
- *interstitials*
- *overlays*
- *interaction devices within social networks*

River sampling represents a minority of all online recruitment, although some companies such as DMS Research in the USA have made a major feature of using it. River sampling is at its strongest when it can draw a sample (i.e. intercept people) across a wide range of sites, rather than concentrating on just one or two.

OTHER SOURCES OF SAMPLE

In addition to the methods outlined above, a wider range of alternatives have been trialled:

- *telephone recruiting*
- *SMS recruiting*
- *outdoor adverts, e.g. billboards*
- *ads in newspapers and magazines*
- *postal invites*
- *URLs posted on products or on receipts*
- *public access points, e.g. cyber-cafés or kiosks*

However, none of these has proved generally useful, even if they have proved useful in specific cases. Generally these methods produce low levels of response.

MOVING SURVEYS ONLINE

Moving a survey online describes the process of taking an existing study, for example one using face-to-face, telephone, or post, and moving the data collection to the internet. People have been moving surveys online since the late 1990s, so there is a substantial amount of learning that can be drawn on.

One of the implications of moving an existing survey online is the need to deal with legacy issues. Two common examples of studies with legacy issues are:

1. **Tracking studies**. For example, looking at elements such as brand, advertising, or customer satisfaction over time. Changing the data collection modality might result in a loss of ability to track changes.

2. **Studies that use norms or benchmarks to help interpret findings**. For example, concept testing, advertising pre-tests, and opinion polling often use weights or procedures based on historical projects. When a study moves online the weights or procedures might need to change.

 Advice

The key questions that need to be addressed when moving a survey online are:

○ *Can the right sample be contacted online?*

○ *Is the online sample large enough for the project?*

○ *Is the online sample different from the existing sample?*

○ *Are all the current questions capable of being asked online?*

○ *Would the current questions generate different answers online?*

○ *Should the new survey minimise the differences from the old study, or maximise potential improvements?*

○ *Can the new study be piloted or run in parallel with the old study?*

○ *Can any differences in the results be modelled?*

Taking all the points outlined above, it can be seen that when migrating a project from one modality to another there are three principal causes of changes to consider:

1. **Population effects**. The population that is available to an online research survey might be different from the population available to an offline survey.

2.   **Sample effects.** The sample of people who are likely to be attracted online might differ from the sample likely to be attracted offline.

3.   **Method effects.** The same person might respond in a different way to an online survey than to the way they would have responded to an offline survey.

The following sections address the points described above. When looking at potential differences the researcher should keep in mind that different does not mean worse. Different can be better, it can be worse, or it can just mean different.

CAN THE RIGHT SAMPLE BE CONTACTED ONLINE?

One key issue that needs to be addressed is whether the people who have been sampled in the past tend to be online and whether the proposed survey is likely to find them if they are. To answer this question the researcher may need to consider whether the sample is going to be sourced from an internal database or from an online access panel.

If the sample for the online survey is different from the previous sample (e.g. younger, richer, more likely to buy online, watching less TV), then it is likely that the results will be affected by the change to online.

One example of a case where online is not an appropriate modality is where the research objective is to estimate the usage of the internet. To find out internet penetration figures, another modality must be used. Even the scale of usage is hard to measure via online surveys, because the people who are reached will tend to be disproportionately and systematically heavier users of the internet.

Another example of a study that tends not to work online is a study looking at how people book flights from travel agents. The people online are likely to be much more likely to book flights directly and to potentially only use travel agents for complex journeys, whereas people without internet access may use travel agents for a wider range of services.

IS THE ONLINE SAMPLE LARGE ENOUGH FOR THE PROJECT?

If the study is a large tracking study, for example a weekly brand tracking study, the sample source needs to be large enough to be able to conduct the survey without re-sampling the same respondents too frequently and without having to shift to an alternative source. There are a wide number of studies showing that changing from one source to another, for example from one panel to another, is likely to produce changes in the results unrelated to changes in the population.

IS THE ONLINE SAMPLE DIFFERENT FROM THE EXISTING SAMPLE?

Even if the people who can be contacted online appear to be similar to those who were contacted previously, the people who agree to complete the survey might be different. The online sample, even if matched in terms of demographics, may show differences in terms of attitudes, beliefs, or experiences.

ARE ALL THE CURRENT QUESTIONS CAPABLE OF BEING ASKED ONLINE?

Some questions that are easy to ask in a face-to-face interview or over the telephone can be problematic to ask online. A very good example of this is the common research practice of asking for an unprompted list, followed by a prompted list, for example, an unprompted list of brands followed by the prompted list of brands. When an interviewer is present the unprompted list can be supported with probing. For example, if the question is something like 'Which soft drinks do you drink?', a respondent might say 'Coke', at which point the interviewer can probe by asking, 'What type of Coke is that?'

When conducting an online survey, an unprompted list has to be asked as a set of open-ends. This has several implications for the process. The first is that people do not type in names as accurately as a computer interprets them. If somebody types 'Coka-Cola' the computer won't necessarily recognise it as Coca-Cola, and the survey is very unlikely to probe for which variety of Coke. The problems are then compounded at the prompted stage. In a face-to-face or telephone interview the interviewer normally fills in the items that have already been spontaneously mentioned, and then prompts for the rest. In an online survey the respondent typically types in open-ended responses in the unprompted section and then has to answer the whole list, selecting again items mentioned in the unprompted question.

A researcher converting a survey online needs to review the current questionnaire to see whether changes are needed to accommodate the restrictions of the online medium.

DO THE CURRENT QUESTIONS GENERATE DIFFERENT ANSWERS?

Even when a question can be asked in the same way online, the answers may not be the same. It has been suggested that one of the differences between interviewer mediated surveys and self-completion is that in self-completion the respondent is more honest, which is often manifested as lower scores on questions such as likelihood to buy (Comley, 2002). It has been suggested that the absence of an interviewer results in respondents being less tempted to provide socially acceptable answers.

In some cases there may be data available to indicate whether a specific question and wording result in different answers online. However, in most cases it is necessary to conduct some sort of pilot or comparison.

SHOULD THE NEW SURVEY MINIMISE THE DIFFERENCES FROM THE OLD STUDY, OR MAXIMISE POTENTIAL IMPROVEMENTS?

Moving a survey to the internet often provides an opportunity to improve the results, for example by using better stimuli than is possible via telephone, by using better randomisation and complexity than face-to-face, or because of the increased honesty that results from not having an interviewer present.

However, better results are different results, which can be a problem. For example, if staff bonuses are linked to the results of a satisfaction study, changing the results (even if the new results are more reliable or valid) may have significant repercussions for the organisation.

One option that is often adopted when moving a survey online, is to accept that there will be a break in continuity and use the change to conduct a major review of the survey, removing redundant and less effective questions and possibly adding new questions.

CAN THE NEW STUDY BE PILOTED OR RUN IN PARALLEL TO THE OLD STUDY?

The best practice for moving a survey online is to pilot the new online survey in parallel with the previous study. This process can identify any problems with the online implementation and allow any differences in the results (including issues like response rates and respondent satisfaction) to be assessed. However, there is often a significant cost implication and it can delay the change.

CAN ANY DIFFERENCES IN THE RESULTS BE MODELLED?

If the new online survey is run in parallel with the previous study for a period of time, it may be possible to model the differences between the two studies. For example, if the online sample is 10% more satisfied than the offline sample, the old data can be modelled (by adding 10% to their satisfaction scores). Note, best practice is to model the old data, not the new data. Modelling the old data only requires one set of modelling, but if the new data is modelled (to make it like the old data) then the modelling has to be run on all new waves of the data.

HIGHLIGHTING CHANGES IN THE PARADIGM, CONFIDENCE, AND IMPLICATIONS

When the data collection modality for a project changes there may be obvious differences, for example differences in key scores. However, there may also be less obvious changes, for example changes in the underlying paradigm, or the level of confidence that users of the research can have in the findings, or the managerial implications of these changes for the client.

If the study to be migrated to the internet is currently based on the paradigm of random probability sampling, this may change when the study goes online (unless it is a customer database study and all/most of the customers are online). If the existing study is based on an assumption that a cross-section of the population is interviewed and that quotas are used to control the nature of that cross-section, then the online study may fit the same paradigm.

When moving a survey online it is a good idea to look at the claims that have been made about the reliability and validity of the study. It may well be that the current claims need modifying, irrespective of whether the survey stays offline or moves online. One change that might be helpful is to change claims about sampling error away from validity (i.e. actually represents the population) and towards reliability (i.e. if we asked this sort of sample the same questions again, this is how likely we are to get the same results).

2 Web Survey Systems

This chapter looks at the issues surrounding the choice of a web survey system. Online surveys are normally conducted by using one of the web survey systems, with the minor exception of email surveys. A web survey is one that is hosted on a website and is accessed via a web browser (for example Microsoft's Internet Explorer or Mozilla's Firefox). Web surveys are typically accessed from a computer, but it should be noted that increasingly they are being accessed from mobile devices such as a smartphones, for example iPhones.

There are a great many online survey systems, too many some would argue, ranging from low cost options such as Survey Monkey and Zoomerang through to large-scale products such as Confirmit and Nebu. Survey systems also vary in factors such as scale, power, their ability to create engaging surveys, and their integration with analysis.

One major difference between online survey systems is whether they are sold as software (which the buyer must install and host) or as a service (often referred to as SaaS or Software as a Service; they are also sometimes referred to as ASPs, Application Service Providers).

Because there are so many different web survey systems the choice can be daunting. One online resource for finding out about online survey systems (and other market research-related software) is the Research Central database provided by the UK consultancy Meaning. This can be found at http://www.meaning.uk.com/

The major considerations in choosing a survey system are set out in the sections below:

- O *Whether to have web survey system*

- O *Buy or develop a web survey system*

- O *Software or SaaS*

- O *Cost-related issues*

- O *System features*

- O *Capacity*

- O *Data protection and security*

    ○   *Data reporting/monitoring*

    ○   *Integration with other tools*

    ○   *Engaging surveys*

    ○   *Assessing the organisation and its potential*

The sections below look at each of these issues in greater depth.

WHETHER TO HAVE A WEB SURVEY SYSTEM

Small- to medium-sized research agencies have a choice about whether to have a web survey solution or not. Larger companies tend to need a solution. If a research agency does not have its own survey solution it will tend to use sample providers or other companies to script and host surveys as part of the service they buy.

The key benefits of not having an in-house survey solution are scalability (i.e. it is easier to deal with increases and decreases in the number of projects), and the ability to focus on the research and not the mechanics of the survey process. One potential limitation of not having an in-house solution is that the research design is limited to that which is offered to other agencies, i.e. there is little chance to add a unique element to the data collection. Most companies with a web survey solution would also tend to claim that there are cost advantages in having a system.

Andy Dexter, CEO of Truth, an innovative UK research agency, explains why his company does not have a web survey system:

> "Consulting versus data collection core business models are very different, so why get them mixed up? A business should focus on what it does best, and outsource the rest. We would rather access best in class data collection providers across all modes – online and offline – whenever we need to, rather than attempting to build our own solutions.
>
> To take a semi absurd example, we use PCs but I'm not about to start building them (although such devices would certainly be 'unique' . . .)"

BUY OR DEVELOP A WEB SURVEY SYSTEM

In the early days of online surveys, many researchers scripted their questionnaires in raw HTML. This was followed by a growth in both commercially-available products and in-house data collection systems. Since those early days, there has been an explosion in the number, range, and power of commercially-available systems.

For companies who have already developed an in-house solution there are legacy, efficiency, and cost issues in changing to a commercially-developed solution. The 2008 Confirmit Annual Market

Research Software Survey (Macer and Wilson, 2009) estimated that about 35% of research companies had internally developed web interviewing software, although about a third of these also used commercially-available software.

For companies who do not currently have an online data collection system there is little reason these days to create an in-house system, unless the organisation has very special needs.

One area where survey software solutions are still sometimes being developed in-house is that of online research communities. Companies running these online research communities want to integrate their discussions, polls, and surveys and are finding that this is difficult or impossible with many of the general survey solutions they use for regular web surveys.

SOFTWARE OR SAAS

In the past, users bought a copy of the software, installed it on their computers, and took it from there. In terms of online data collection this meant buying the software, installing it on servers, and being responsible for issues such as bandwidth, data security, reliability, and maintenance.

SaaS (Software as a Service) provides an alternative to buying and owning software. With SaaS web survey systems, the user pays for the use of the software from a company that provides the service over the internet. The provider of the web survey system hosts the surveys and provides access to the software, dealing with storage, backups, bandwidth, and upgrades. This approach is also known as ASP, the Application Service Provider model.

When people talk about SaaS they tend to describe it as a 'pay as you use' service, which could be taken to imply that if a user only makes minimal use of the system that they will have minimal charges. However, many of the larger, more complex, survey solutions have annual charges for accounts, the number of users, training, etc. This means their pricing model is more appropriately described as a fixed fee with variable usage. Indeed, Tim Macer has commented that 'Confusion pricing, worthy of the mobile phone networks, now stalks the online survey world.' (Macer, 2007).

Similarly, some software purchase options have maintenance costs based on numbers of surveys completed, giving their costs a variable element.

SaaS has become the standard for small- to medium-sized agencies, other than those who see controlling the data collection technology as one of their core competencies or who have chosen a specific package that does not offer a SaaS option.

○   *An example of the 'hands on' preference might be an agency that decided to use the open source web survey software platform LimeSurvey [http://www.limesurvey.org/].*

○   *An example of the choice being driven by the research needs might be an agency using Sawtooth Software's marketing science products (such as CBC) which are typically sold as software rather than as a service.*

Large agencies tend to go down the route of buying and hosting the software. This is for a variety of reasons including control, security, and contractual arrangements.

COST-RELATED ISSUES

Cost is usually a major driver in determining the route an agency takes in terms of its web survey solution. Indeed, cost is often **the** major driver. The price range for web survey systems is vast, from free at one end of the spectrum through to tens or hundreds of thousands of dollars at the other end. So, it is not surprising that the decision can be a complex one.

In general, the higher the cost of a system the more it provides. Although some cheaper systems have specific features that rival the more expensive products, the breadth and depth of the more expensive systems tend to make them more suitable for complex and commercial research situations.

When comparing one web survey system with another the buyer is confronted with a classic oranges and apples problem, i.e. the comparison is made difficult because the options between the systems differ and the way they are priced differs.

 Advice

In trying to understand what a web survey system will cost, a buyer will find it useful to construct a three-year, three-scenario matrix. Three years is a useful time frame as it is about as far ahead as most companies can be expected to form an estimate and it is as far ahead as most technologies can be expected to remain constant. Three years is also long enough for most start-up and training costs to work their way through and long enough for SaaS options to be fairly compared with software purchase options.

The three scenarios should be:

1. The most realistic estimate of what the business will need over the next three years

2. An upside estimate

3. A downside estimate

For each of the three scenarios it is necessary to estimate:

○ *the number of studies you expect to run per year*

○ *the number of interviews you expect to conduct each year, and ideally the number of individual questions answered per year, i.e. studies multiplied by questions multiplied by interviews. Some pricing models charge by number of interviews or questions*

○ *the maximum number of respondents who will be accessing your system at the same time (this has implications for bandwidth)*

○   *the number of employees you want to be able to use the system (many systems have a charge per user and may also require payment for training)*

○   *the number of different sites you want to use the system from (some systems charge by office, or sites as they are often called)*

○   *what additional services you might want to use, for example real time reports, dashboards, analysis, and online reports, and the scale of usage*

○   *the sort of access you might want to give to your clients, for example to online reports and analysis*

In addition to these details, the buyer also needs to define the features that they want their system to provide. A review of features is addressed in the next section.

At first this list will look very daunting and it will appear to be full of unknowns and even unknowables. However, the process of pulling this information together is essential if the options are to be properly assessed. If the estimates are considered to be very uncertain, then it will make sense to choose a web survey solution with plenty of flexibility, both in terms of scaling up and scaling back.

The easiest option to assess, against the matrix of estimates, is the SaaS option. Most providers will be able to take the answers from the questions above and produce an estimate of the three-year costs. The main costs in addition to the SaaS costs relate to training (including internal time) and interfacing to other systems, such as analysis and reporting packages.

In terms of buying (as opposed to renting) software, the matrix of answers will be an input to both the software provider and the IT advisor/provider. However, there are a number of issues to consider:

1.   What will the software costs be, including fixed and variable costs?

2.   Where will the software be installed, i.e. what type of server?

3.   What sort of security will the server be provided with?

4.   What sort of bandwidth will the server need?

5.   How will the server be backed up, what sort of disaster recovery will you need?

SYSTEM FEATURES

Web survey systems vary widely in the range of features they offer. Some of the key ones that should be kept in mind when choosing a web survey system are set out below:

○   *Questionnaire creation tools*

○   *Questionnaire testing facilities*

- Project management and monitoring
- Multimedia options
- Advanced graphical interface
- Panel management
- Project reporting
- Analysis options
- International options
- Mobile research
- Hybrid survey options
- Security options
- Marketing science modules
- Scalability
- Programmable script or language

Questionnaire creation tools

Most web survey systems allow users to create a survey by entering questions one at a time via the user interface. For very simple surveys, for example the sorts of surveys often programmed in a package like Survey Monkey, this is fine. However, for non-trivial studies, most users want more sophisticated options.

In many studies, a survey starts life as a 'paper' questionnaire, which is emailed backwards and forwards between the research buyer and provider. Good systems support this process, by both allowing a Word questionnaire to be directly read by the survey system and by producing a Word questionnaire from the web survey.

Other tools that are useful in the area of questionnaire creation are:

- libraries and templates to speed up production
- error checking at first entry point (spelling, grammar, and scripting logic)
- ability to change question types, especially multi to single and vice versa
- good cut and paste options
- multi-language facilities, including seeing languages side-by-side and the ability to export/ import questionnaires so that third parties can provide the translations

When surveys are entered into a system they are not normally WYSIWYG (what you see is what you get), so it is very useful to have a mode or button that allows the researcher to see the question and page as they will appear to the respondent.

Questionnaire testing facilities

Good systems provide a range of tools and options to help test an online survey. One powerful testing tool is the ability to run dummy interviews, e.g. creating a set of 5000 randomised dummy interviews.

A check list of things that a web survey system can provide includes:

- checking programming and logic steps
- checking how the survey is rendered on different browsers
- specification of the minimum configuration required by users to run the survey (for example does it need Flash, Java, or JavaScript?)
- tools to report on the accessibility of the survey

Project management and monitoring

There are a wide range of tools that a web survey system can provide to aid and improve the project management process. Key tools include:

- testing projects before launching them
- quota management
- monitoring and reporting response and completion rates
- paradata reporting, e.g. how long is each question taking, how many questions are being missed, number of back-ups or corrections
- top-line reports, reporting the responses to key questions, including filters and cross-breaks
- phased release of sample and invites
- email reminders

Multimedia options

The simplest multimedia, and one that most researchers will require, is the ability to show an image on the screen as part of the survey. As well as the ability to display an image the system needs to store the image or provide links to files. The best practice option is to store images in the same location as the questionnaire, to reduce the chance of problems when respondents load the survey.

Two more complex multimedia options are audio and video. As with images, the two issues are (a) can the system deliver the media to the respondent, and (b) where will they be stored. Because video files can be very large their storage can become a major issue, especially if your SaaS provider has high charges for storing and streaming video.

The most typical way of delivering video and audio is to stream them, in the same sort of way YouTube delivers video. This means the video is available for viewing more quickly, compared with options based on downloading and then playing. Streaming is also more secure than downloading, with respect to the respondents taking a copy of the file.

Advanced graphical interface

Researchers have become increasingly aware of the need to make surveys more engaging and this has increased the interest in using advanced graphical interfaces. These features include, but are not limited to:

- drag and drop
- sliders and other analogue scales
- using images as buttons
- images that can be rotated
- mock-ups of shelves or fixtures

The most typical way of offering these tools is via Flash. However, researchers should concentrate on what they need to achieve rather than the specific technologies used to deliver them.

Panel management

Panel management facilities are one of the biggest differences between the cheaper and more expensive ends of the market. The simplest web survey systems just provide a link which can be used to invite people to take the survey, via either email or a link. Simple survey systems often do not provide panel management facilities.

The most sophisticated web survey systems often include fully featured panel management services. Amongst the panel management services that a system can offer are:

- selecting randomised samples, using background variables
- survey invitations, including soft launches and phased releases
- handling sample reporting and reminders
- calculation and payment of incentives
- management information (MI) systems, reporting on who is in the panel, who has completed which survey, average response rates, total payments for incentives, etc

In addition, systems are increasingly adding community elements to panels, such as newsletters, blogs, discussions, and user initiated polls.

Project reporting

Project reporting can be divided into process reporting (which is covered in project management and monitoring) and results reporting, which is discussed here.

The results reporting can be as simple as providing on-screen counts or exports to Excel, or it can be a fully-featured reporting and cross-tabulation package. Anybody looking to choose a web survey system should decide on whether they want to do their reporting from the system, or from their preferred third-party package (or from an existing in-house system).

One key area of website survey reporting is that of online reporting and, potentially, of either dashboards or real-time reports. Dashboards simplify reporting, often with a simple green, orange, or red colour coding, so that the client is drawn towards key findings. Real-time reports pull key elements from the data and make reports of this data available to the researcher and optionally to the end client.

One key trade-off that usually has to be made is between simplicity and power. Most simple systems are quite limited in what they can produce, most powerful systems are difficult to use (or at the very least require a steep learning curve). There are no systems that are very powerful and easy to use.

Analysis options

Some aspects of analysis overlap with aspects of reporting, such as the ability to run cross-tabs, create derived variables, to calculate descriptive statistics such mean, median, and standard deviation, and conduct simple statistical t-tests.

Some web survey systems provide more advanced and/or specialised examples. For example, Sawtooth Software provides modules for conducting the analyses that underlie techniques such as conjoint analysis, DCM (Discrete Choice Modelling), and MaxDiff, along with advanced processing such as Hierarchical Bayes, and most recently their Adaptive CBC. However, most systems assume that advanced analysis will be handled by third-party packages such as SAS and PASW (which used to be known as SPSS).

International options

When looking at the features required for international surveys the picture resembles an onion, where one level sits on top of another. Starting at the centre the options are:

1.   Will the survey support the key Western international languages, such as English, French, and German (i.e. those using Roman characters)? In this context 'support' means (a) able to type questions in the relevant language, (b) the system commands that the respondent might see are in the same relevant language. System commands include phrases like "Next", "Back", and things like error messages and progress indicators.

2.   Can the system support non-Roman script, single byte languages such as Greek and Russian?

3.   Can the system support the full range of international languages, for example Chinese and Japanese?

4.   Can the system administer a single project with multiple languages?

Unless an agency is quite small or very focused on its domestic market, the ability to handle common double-byte languages, such as Chinese and Japanese, should be seen as a minimum requirement these days.

Mobile research

Mobile research is increasingly a term that covers two quite distinct aspects of market research:

1. Studies where people are using their mobile phone to respond to surveys, typically via SMS or voice.

2. Studies where people are using smartphones, such as the iPhone, to interact with conventional web surveys.

The first of these two options is covered below in the section on hybrid studies.

In terms of the second option, there are two areas where a web survey system can provide additional functionality for respondents using smartphones. The first area is to be able to render the survey so that it looks better on a smartphone's small screen than the default view intended for a full-sized screen. The second area is to have surveys that are designed specifically for smartphones, or specifically for a particular type of smartphone.

Unless a researcher knows they will be making use of mobile surveys in the next year or two, it is difficult to assess how much importance to put on mobile features. Mobile research has been talked about as being the next big thing for a few years now, but it may still be some time before it happens.

Hybrid or multi-modal survey options

In order to expand the reach of a survey, for example to make it more representative, some research projects use more than one modality, for example online and CATI.

A growing number of the more powerful survey systems are capable of handling multi-modal projects as a single integrated project, printing and scanning questionnaires for face-to-face, providing CATI for telephone, providing SMS for mobile phones, and providing web surveys for online.

Different systems vary in the number of different modalities they can handle and the degree of integration they offer.

Security options

Security, in terms of web survey systems, is a multi-faceted topic, covering protecting the client, protecting the respondents, protecting the researcher, protecting the system. Between malice and error there is a lot of work for security systems to deal with.

Advice

Security topics that need to be considered are:

- ensuring that the survey won't crash and cause inconvenience to, or even crash, the respondent's browser or the provider's website

- protecting the survey from respondents causing it to crash, for example by entering program code into verbatim fields

- protecting clients' intellectual property from theft or abuse by respondents, for example by making it harder for respondents to take copies of concepts

- controlling who can access the survey, for example by emailing unique links to each respondent and/or using passwords

- protecting the data transmitted from respondents to the survey, in sensitive cases this might mean using a secure protocol such as https (i.e. using Secure Socket Layer)

- keeping the agency and client data secure, which includes having back-ups, avoiding hackers, and having high reliability systems

It should be noted that a growing number of end clients are requiring ever higher specifications for the security of data collection systems. Key things on their checklist tend to be:

(a) location of the server, ideally in the same country as the client, in a secure building, with theft and fire mitigation measures

(b) continuity of service, including both the hardware and the connection to the internet

(c) level of protection from hackers and from unauthorised access

(d) detailed reporting requirements, for example which agency employees have access to a file and which ones actually access it

In some cases clients are employing third-party auditors to review the security of the agency's web survey systems.

Marketing science modules

Techniques such as DCM (discrete choice modelling), adaptive conjoint, brand price trade-off are all examples of marketing science techniques. A few web survey systems provide integrated solutions for advanced techniques, but most do not.

Many of the web survey systems that do not provide these advanced tools provide a method of running third-party software (for example Sawtooth Software products) as a module from their system. The strength of this approach is that most of the time researchers are creating surveys in their preferred system, assuming that most of the time they are not using marketing science options. The downside of this approach is that two data collection systems need to be used when using marketing science techniques, and may require a mixing of SaaS and bought software options.

Scalability

Scalability refers to the ability of a system to cope with changes in the number of interviews and projects that the system can handle; usually it refers to the ability of a system to handle increases. The sorts of issues that a system needs to be able to handle, if it is to provide a scalable solution, include:

- *the bandwidth to handle larger numbers of interviews, both in total and at any one time*
- *the ability for a study to handle larger numbers of respondents, from 100s to 1000s, from 1000s to 10000s, and from 10000s to 100000s or more*
- *the ability to handle more projects and more researchers*
- *more security, as the number of clients, projects, and researchers grow there is a need for enhanced security, along with issues such as permissions and archiving*
- *project management tools, along with more sophisticated reporting, become more important as the volume of work increases*

Programmable script or language

The simplest interview systems have a friendly graphical interface, but the user is limited to the options available in the pre-set list. More powerful interview systems are either built on scripting language or they allow a scripting language to be used in addition to a graphical interface, such as the way that Confirmit allows JavaScript to be used or Sawtooth Software allows CIW and other tools to be used.

Unless a researcher has very simple requirements, then some sort of scripting or language facility is needed.

CAPACITY

Web survey systems vary greatly in their capacity to handle different levels of demand. Capacity encompasses:

(a)   the number of interviews per year

(b)   the number of interviews at any one time

(c)   the demands the interview makes on the server*

There are many ways that a survey might make demands on the server, for example video, audio, Flash interactivity, large images and, in the case of adaptive surveys, the processing required to generate questions.

Many of the SaaS systems have acceptable use policies which, for example, limit the number of surveys, emails, and images that can be used within a specific time period.

DATA PROTECTION AND SECURITY

One of the main reasons for using a SaaS service is to outsource the data protection and security issues. The law, regulations, and clients are all becoming ever stricter in terms of what they expect market research agencies to do.

In many ways, the easiest option for an agency is to look for a SaaS provider who can meet the standards being set by clients, regulators, and legislators.

The two key issues are the security of information and the security of the service being provided.

The security of the information includes:

- *avoiding hacking and other attacks*

- *avoiding losing information, e.g. stopping people downloading it to data sticks*

- *avoid transfers being intercepted*

- *ensuring that information is encrypted*

The continuity issues include making sure that the service is robust in terms of possible interruptions, with factors ranging from maintenance through to fire and theft. It is increasingly common for clients to insist that key systems are in secure buildings with disaster recovery procedures in place.

The weakest links in most companies' security systems are the people, not the IT. This means that having well documented and implemented procedures is essential. However, some systems have better facilities for integrating companies' procedures. For example, an agency may want to specify separately and easily for every survey who has edit rights and who has read rights.

DATA REPORTING AND MONITORING

The first issue an agency needs to consider is what proportion of its reporting does it want to come from its data collection system and how much from its other systems. One of the key drivers of that decision is the extent to which an agency wants to work with, and distribute, real-time data. The more an agency wants to work with real-time data, the greater the pressure to use integrated reporting.

Simple data collection systems provide simple monitoring and very little reporting. At the other end of the spectrum there are end-to-end systems which provide sophisticated monitoring systems and reporting systems that include real-time systems, dashboards, and portals for combining reports.

INTEGRATIONS WITH OTHER TOOLS

The simpler data collection systems tend to stand very much on their own, with their integration being limited to exporting data in formats such as Excel. The more sophisticated systems have two ways of integrating other tools:

1. They include more tools within the data collection system, for example other data collection modalities, reporting, coding, and advanced analyses.

2. There are links to other third-party tools, such as text analytics, advanced analytics, and reporting packages.

The quality of integration with third-party tools is essential as there will always be cases where the data from the web collection system needs to be used in conjunction with other data or other processes. Systems that use non-standard formats and which do not have methods of reading or writing standardised files will normally prove to be a problem at some stage.

ENGAGING SURVEYS

One of the hot topics in market research at the moment, and one that will be discussed at various points in this book, is the desire to create more engaging surveys. Although there is no clear definition of what is meant by engaging, and there is some contradictory evidence about which innovations are actually helpful, there is a clear need for continued progress on this front.

Bad and boring surveys can be written on any data collection system, no matter how simple or sophisticated that data collection system might be. Indeed, it is probably easier to write boring surveys on the more complicated systems, particularly large grid questions.

One difference between data collection systems is whether or not they have engagement built in. Some systems have community elements and animated surveys (for example using Flash); others, however, require these to be added, either by buying additional modules or by using third-party options.

ASSESSING THE ORGANISATION AND ITS POTENTIAL

One of the key determinants of the best web survey system for an organisation is the skill base of that organisation and its potential to extend that skill base. For example, a software solution (as opposed to a SaaS solution) is going to require the organisation to host the surveys (either directly or via third-party hosting), to install the software and upgrades, to deal with technical issues. This, in turn, requires the organisation to have a significant IT capacity.

Web survey systems that depend on advanced skills such as scripting, programming, Flash, or marketing sciences, are going to make greater demands on the organisation than those with a simple, intuitive interface. However, as mentioned before, there tends be a trade-off between power and simplicity. The more powerful systems are less simple, and are more likely to require specialist staff.

One rule of thumb for small companies looking to provide specialist skills is that anything mission critical should be based on at least three people. This rule of thumb is based on one person to be on holiday, one to be off sick, and one to do the work!

3 Designing Online Surveys

This chapter reviews the principles of designing online surveys, particularly in the context of collecting survey data from samples that have been drawn from online access panels and client databases. Chapter 15, Website Research, covers some issues specific to survey design in the context of popup surveys.

Note that this book assumes that the reader is already aware of the fundamentals of research design, survey design, and questionnaire design. For further reading on research and survey design, the reader is referred to Naresh Malhotra's *Marketing Research: An Applied Orientation* (2007), and for questionnaire design the reader is recommended to refer to Ian Brace's *Questionnaire Design* (2008). Alternatively, the student could enrol on a programme such as the University of Georgia's online course 'The Principles of Marketing Research' [http://www.georgiacenter.uga.edu/is/mr/].

This chapter looks at the design of online quantitative surveys by first setting out the terminology that is used to describe and talk about such surveys, and then reviewing the key issues that researchers need to be aware of. However, one chapter of a book such as this can only go so far; indeed, there are whole books which are devoted to this topic and any researcher wanting to be actively involved in establishing the detailed design principles used by their company is strongly recommended to read Mick Couper's *Designing Effective Web Surveys* (2008) and Don Dillman's *Internet, Mail, and Mixed-Mode Surveys* (2009) and to access conference and white papers.

This chapter will therefore cover:

- ○ *Defining the terms used in online surveys*
- ○ *The self-completion paradigm*
- ○ *The overall structure of the questionnaire*
- ○ *The first and last pages*
- ○ *Improving the survey experience*
- ○ *Using multimedia and its implications*
- ○ *Accessible surveys*
- ○ *Surveys for online access panels*

○   *Surveys for client databases*

○   *Quality and ethical issues in survey design*

○   *Summary of designing online surveys*

DEFINING THE TERMS USED IN ONLINE SURVEYS

In order to write about online surveys it is necessary to establish a clear understanding of the terms that are used in this chapter and, indeed, in the rest of the book. The following terms are all in common use, but there are many variations that the reader may already be aware of. In most cases there are no rights or wrongs – they simply reflect the normal variability in the use of language. The terms used in this book are not necessarily the 'best' terms, but they are the ones that will be used consistently throughout.

This section only addresses those terms that need to be clearly understood in order to follow this chapter. In addition, a glossary at the back of the book covers a much wider range of online and social media market research terms.

Term	Explanation
Next/Submit button	In most online surveys, the respondent answers the questions on the page and then tells the survey system that they are ready to move on to the next page or, if it is the last page of the survey, that they are ready to finish the survey. In most cases, the respondent tells the survey software that they have finished a page by clicking a link or button on the page. This button will often say 'Next' or 'Continue' or 'Submit' or just '>>'. This book refers to these buttons as Next/Submit buttons.
Back button	Many surveys provide the respondent with the option to go back to the previous page. Again, the typical way that the respondent tells the survey software that they want to go back is via a button. This button may have text on it such as 'Back' or symbols such as '<<'. This book refers to these buttons as Back buttons.
Browser back button	Most internet browsers, such as IE and Firefox, have their own back button that typically takes the respondent to the previously-loaded page. In some cases (especially when the survey software is very straightforward), the browser back arrow will behave in a very similar way to a survey back button. However, in many cases, if the respondent uses the browser back button the survey software may become confused. Most surveys discourage the use of the browser back button.
Multi	A multiple-choice question where the respondent can select one or more answers.

Check boxes	By convention, check boxes are used for a multi, i.e. multiple-choice questions where a respondent can select more than one answer. Clicking a check box makes it selected, clicking it again de-selects it.
Single	A multiple-choice question where the respondent can select only one answer.
Radio buttons	By convention, radio buttons are used for a single, i.e. multiple-choice questions where respondents can only select one option. When a respondent clicks on a button it becomes selected, if another button is then clicked it is then selected and the previously selected button is unselected.
Screen	At the trivial level the screen is what the respondent is looking at. In the context of an online survey, the term 'screen' refers to that section of the questionnaire which the respondent can see in their browser window without scrolling.
Page	A page comprises all of the questions, text and images that in a paper questionnaire would be shown on a single page, and which in an online survey will be changed when the respondent presses the Next/Submit button. If the respondent's screen is smaller than the page, then the respondent will not be able to see the entire page without scrolling.

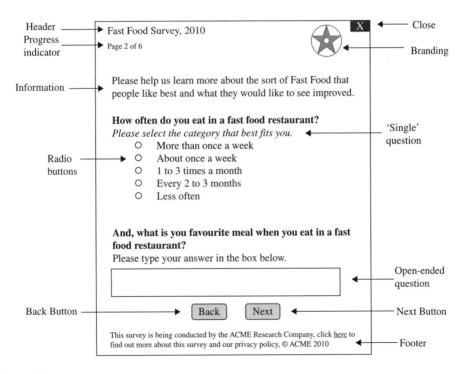

Figure 3.1

Figure 3.1 shows many of the terms used in online surveys. The whole of Figure 3.1 is a page from a questionnaire, the amount of it visible on a respondent's screen is the survey screen.

THE SELF-COMPLETION PARADIGM

The single most important difference between an online survey and a face-to-face survey or a telephone survey is that an online survey is a self-completion survey. Self-completion is something that online shares with mail (i.e. postal) surveys, and is a major difference between it and face-to-face and telephone.

The self-completion nature of an online questionnaire is a factor that needs to stay in the researcher's mind when designing online surveys. The survey has to be laid out so that the respondent understands what they are being asked to do. The design needs to minimise the chance of respondent errors and needs to engage the respondent. Remember, an interviewer can tell when a respondent is confused or needs motivating, and can provide direct assistance. With an online survey, the survey is all there is.

The disruptive impact of the self-completion process is increased by the variations in the way that the survey appears to different respondents. One respondent may have a large screen PC attached to a fast broadband connection; another may be looking at the survey on their iPhone and be dependent on a 3G mobile connection. Researchers spend a large amount of time thinking about the layout of the survey, but they can't guarantee how it will appear to each respondent.

 Advice

Because there is no interviewer present when somebody completes an online survey it is important that respondents are given a chance to pass messages back to the researcher. In particular, the researcher needs to know if something unforeseen, unexpected, or unplanned occurs. One very good way of doing this is to finish the survey with an open-ended question, asking if the respondent has any comment to make on the subject of the study and the survey itself.

KEY STEPS FOR A SELF-COMPLETION SURVEY

Because the respondent is completing the survey on their own the following steps should be taken:

1. Use language that is easy to understand and which is unambiguous. Use the smallest number of words consistent with getting the message across clearly.

2. Be polite and friendly. Remember respondents are doing researchers a favour, not vice versa.

3. Let respondents know where they are. Introduce sections, say what is coming next, say how far through the survey they are.

4. Make the survey as short and as pleasant as possible, consistent with meeting the research objectives.

5. Thank respondents when they finish or when they are screened out.

THE OVERALL STRUCTURE OF THE QUESTIONNAIRE

This section looks at the main structural issues in designing an online survey.

LAYING OUT THE QUESTIONS ON THE PAGE

The difference between online and interviewer mediated surveys is immediately apparent when we consider how to lay out the questions on the page. This is a very minor issue in an interviewer mediated survey, but is vital in a self-completion survey. How questions are laid out on the page, indeed the number of questions on the page, becomes a major issue.

PAGES AND SCREENS

Some researchers, when talking about online surveys, use the terms 'screen', 'page', and 'form' as interchangeable, but this can lead to design problems. Mick Couper, in *Designing Effective Web Surveys* (2008), defines these three terms as distinct concepts. However, he also points out that, for most purposes, market researchers can use the terms 'page' and 'form' as interchangeable, and should probably just concentrate on the differences between the terms 'page' and 'screen'.

A page is a reference that comes from both the world of 'paper and pencil' market research and modern web technology. In market research, the paper page was everything that could be seen by the interviewer or respondent without turning the page over, i.e. on one side of a piece of paper. By contrast, a web page, for example the Home Page, is everything that can be seen without navigating to a new page. However, on a web page the user may need to use the scroll bars in order to see everything, for example, the vertical scroll bar to move up and down and the horizontal scroll bar to move left and right. In online surveys, the term 'page' relates to all the questions and text that can be accessed without moving to the next page. However, the researcher should keep in mind that the respondent may have to use the vertical and/or the horizontal scroll bars to see everything on the page.

A screen is that proportion of a page that can be seen without using the scroll bars. The size of a screen is a function of three things: the size of monitor (in terms of pixels), whether the browser window is maximised or not, and the configuration of the browser (for example, if a browser has several rows of toolbars and a panel showing additional information, the effective 'screen' will be smaller).

In most survey situations, the page is the same for all respondents, but the screen is not. If the survey has been designed to fit in an 800 × 600 pixel window, most respondents will see the whole page but will also see great deal of space around the survey. If the survey is designed for a 1200 × 900 pixel window, then most respondents will see the whole page on their screen, but a significant minority will have to scroll to see the whole page.

Advice

There is general agreement that making a respondent use a horizontal scroll bar is worse than making him or her use the vertical scroll bar, in terms of completion rates and comprehension of the task.

Vertical scrolling versus multi-page surveys

Some surveys, particularly those written by non-researchers using low cost packages, put the whole questionnaire on a single page. In a single-page survey the respondent uses the vertical scroll bar to work their way through the survey down to the submit button (note, a single page survey does not have a Next button).

However, most market researchers have tended to shun the one-page survey (except where the survey is very short). A variety of reasons have been quoted for not using the single-page survey including:

- *it looks less professional*
- *it requires the respondent to use the vertical scroll bar*
- *the respondent can read ahead and may adjust their answers*
- *a one-page survey is less suited to routing, piping, or other adaptive and smart facilities of online interviewing.*

Many market researchers feel that multi-page surveys lead to higher quality data and that it is faster for the respondent. However, a review of comparative data suggests that the two formats produce very similar data and that in many cases the vertical survey is faster (Couper, 2008).

Although most market researchers seem to agree that multi-page surveys are best, there are several page- and screen-related issues they do not agree on. The key areas of debate are:

- *How many questions per page?*
- *How to handle pages that are too long for the screen?*
- *Whether to allow respondents to go back to an earlier page?*
- *Whether to use auto-advance?*

The next few sub-sections look at these points.

How many questions per page?

In the early days of online surveys there was a tendency to put as many questions on a page as would fit on the screen. This was because the internet was relatively slow and there were often delays between the pages. A respondent might click the Next/Submit button and then have to wait while the next screen loaded and appeared.

For most respondents in most markets and with most internet-connected devices, this problem has now disappeared and the number of questions tends to be a respondent-focused design issue.

If two questions belong together, and if they fit on the same screen (for example, household size and number of children), then it makes sense to put them on the same page. Putting questions on the same page can make the survey appear to take less time, and indeed it does reduce the number of mouse clicks (i.e. fewer Next/Submit clicks) and reduces the number of headings that the respondents have to read. This approach is sometimes referred to as 'chunking' (Couper, 2008).

However, if a survey has to be designed in a hurry, it is easier and relatively safe to simply put each question on its own page.

How to handle pages that are too long for the screen?

One way to reduce the risk that pages that are too long for a respondent's screen is to only put one question on each page. However, even this does not help if a single question is too long to fit on the page.

One reason a question might be too long is that a respondent's screen might be very small, for example if they are using netbook or a mobile device such as an iPhone.

In terms of survey features, three common reasons that a page might be too long include:

- *a large amount of text and/or images as part of the question*
- *a question with a very long list of choices*
- *a large attribute battery, for example, a grid with questions down one side and the scale across the page*

If the page contains a large amount of text and or images, then it is a good idea to tell the respondent at the top of the screen that they may need to scroll down the page to see the entire page and to reach the Next/Submit button.

 Advice

If the materials on the page are likely to require the respondent to use the scroll bars to see the whole page, ensure that the Next/Submit button is at the bottom of the page, below all the material the respondents needs to see and read.

If one question has so many choices that it is likely to be longer than the screen, there are several options the researcher can consider. One method of bringing a long list back onto the screen is to use two or more columns, if they are not likely to be confusing or to require horizontal scrolling. Another approach is to use a drop-down list, if the question is a single type question, but there is quite a lot of information suggesting that respondents do not like drop-down questions. Another option is to break the question into smaller parts. For example, if the question is asking respondents to indicate the make and model of their car, the survey could use one list to show only makes. The next question, on the next page, could then just show the models that relate to that make.

Whether to allow respondents to go back to an earlier page?

The early internet survey packages tended to be modifications of CATI packages (Computer Aided Telephone Interviews). CATI packages were written for interviewers to use as part of the telephone interviewing process. The CATI systems typically had a 'Stop' button and a 'Go Back' option. The Stop button was for stopping an interview (for example if the respondent hung up) and the Go Back button allowed the interviewer to correct something, for example if the respondent said something that made the interviewer realise that an earlier response was wrong.

Early versions of online survey software replicated both of these buttons. After many interviews were inadvertently lost, the Stop button was removed from survey software system. However, most survey packages retained the Go Back option.

Researchers have different views about whether they should put a button on the screen that allows (or possibly encourages) respondents to go back to see or change earlier responses.

Those in favour of the Back button refer to allowing respondents to be able to correct mistakes or the need to give them some sense of control.

The counter argument is that researchers often want 'top of mind' responses; they may not want considered views. There is also a concern amongst some researchers that respondents might use the Back button to change an earlier answer in a way that could shorten the survey. For example, if a question asks a respondent to select all the banks they have an account with, they might select four. However, when they then realise they will be asked five questions for each of these four, they might use the Back arrow to reduce the number of banks they use to only their preferred bank.

Another concern with the Back button is that in some non-trivial studies (for example, adaptive conjoint studies) it may not be possible to go backwards, because hidden calculated variables may have already been modified by the selections the respondent has made.

One special case, in the eyes of many researchers, is when auto-advance is being used (auto-advance moves a survey onto the next page as soon as a selection is made). When auto-advance is being used it is probably a good idea to provide a Back button for the respondent, to enable them to correct answers, or even just to check answers.

Forced completion

Most web survey systems can be configured to force respondents to answer every question, a process called 'forced completion'.

The argument in favour of forcing completion is that it means the researcher obtains the data they need without any missing fields. For some types of analysis, missing fields are a major problem, for example, cluster analysis and factor analysis. In these types of analysis, missing data requires either the estimation of data or the exclusion of some of the respondents.

The arguments against forced completion include the view that it can result in lower response rates, based on the opinion that some respondents might prefer to abandon a survey rather than be forced to answer a specific question they did not want to answer. Researchers have suggested that income is an example of a question that some respondents do not wish to answer. Equally, if a respondent feels that none of the answers are relevant to them they might abandon the survey.

A common practice is to take a middle line between the two extreme positions. Closed questions are often forced, but with a 'prefer not to say' option added to those questions deemed sensitive. Open-ended question are often not forced. Many researchers report, anecdotally, that when open-ended questions are forced the frustration of respondents is often expressed by what they type in these fields.

Website surveys are sometimes seen as a special case in terms of forced completion, with researchers such as Pete Comley of Virtual Surveys advocating the avoidance of forced completion.

The issue about forced completion is not yet fully resolved. Many of the online access panels prefer all of the closed questions on surveys to use forced completion. But, in contrast, many guidelines, such as the ESOMAR guidelines, stress that a respondent should not be unreasonably forced to complete each question.

Survey and progress information

This sub-section looks at letting respondents know what section of the interview they are in and how far through the survey they are. This process includes headings on the page, introductions to sections, and progress bars or indicators. This is done for several reasons, including:

- *as a courtesy to respondents*

- *to motivate respondents to keep going and finish the survey*

- *to help create a context for the questions currently on the page*

Headings and introductions

Most surveys have a section at the top of the page that can be used to set the context for the page. Researchers should keep in mind that headings are a relatively nuanced feature – some respondents will notice them but many won't.

Whenever a questionnaire changes context, it makes sense to alert the respondent to this change. For example, one section of a survey might be talking about what a respondent normally buys. After that section might be one looking at what they will do in the future. It is a good idea to precede the second section with some text saying something like '*Thank you for telling us about what you currently buy. Now we would like you to think about what you MIGHT do over the NEXT 2 MONTHS*'.

Progress bars and indicators

Most online survey systems have a method for telling the respondent how far through the survey they are. Sometimes these systems are graphical, such as a moving bar or a pie chart filling up. Sometimes they are numerical, such as X% complete, or they can be text based such as '*Page 4 out of 5*'.

Many industry guidelines recommend or require progress indicators, so they should be a default part of all online survey designs.

One frequent problem is when the progress indicator does not move smoothly through the survey. At worst, a survey progress indicator might move quickly up to, for example, 70% and then start crawling in 1% increments. The researcher should seek to use a progress indicator that is helpful and motivating to the respondent.

Whether to use auto-advance?

Most online survey packages have the facility to allow pages to auto-advance after the respondent has clicked on an appropriate answer.

This is only possible on those pages that contain single-choice questions. If there is an open-ended question, or a multi-select question, the respondent will still need to tell the system they are finished on the page, i.e. by clicking a Next/Submit button.

The main advantage of the auto-advance option is that it can create a sense of momentum which makes the interview seem shorter (which is good for the relationship with respondents). Also it requires fewer mouse clicks by the respondent which means it will possibly be quicker to complete.

However, if the study contains a mixture of pages that require the respondent to click a Next/Submit button and pages that do not, the end result can be disorienting for the respondent. So, it is probably best to consider auto-advance in surveys that only comprise single-choice and rating scale-type questions.

THE FIRST AND LAST PAGES

THE FIRST PAGE

The first page of a survey is the single most important page of a survey. This is the page where most respondents are likely to abandon the survey, followed by the second page.

The mission for the first page is to make the respondent feel welcome, to tell them anything they need to know, to tell them anything the law or the guidelines say they must be told, and to make them feel that the survey will not be an unpleasant experience (i.e. too boring, too long, too badly laid out, or too difficult).

There are two elements that all first pages should contain. These are the welcome and the terms and conditions. One element that is often on the first page is the first question or questions.

The welcome

The welcome will typically be at the top of the page and should reassure the respondent and provide a brief outline about the nature of the survey and the expected length of the survey. For example, a survey looking at advertising concepts for a soft drink might welcome respondents with something like:

Heading: The Soft Drink Survey – Listening to you!

Information: Thank you for agreeing to take part in this important survey about soft drinks. Today we will be showing you some new ideas and the survey should last about 10 to 12 minutes.

If the first question is on the first page, the welcome will ask respondents to answer it. If there is no question on the first page, the welcome will refer to the important information at the bottom of the page and encourage people to read it before going on to the next page to see the first question.

The terms and conditions

These do not need to be called terms and conditions. Different agencies use different phrases such as 'Read me', or 'Important information', or 'Important notes'.

This section should include anything that needs to be said to the respondent at the outset and the content of this information will largely be driven by the laws of the country where the research is taking place, the guidelines from the relevant research organisations, the research agency's house rules, anything the client's own rules require and, if the study is being conducted with the members of an online access panel, anything the panel company may require.

The sorts of things that might need to be declared in this section (depending on the criteria outlined above) include the following:

- *If a client database has been used to recruit the respondent, then this needs to be stated.*

- *If personally identifiable information is going to be collected, this should be declared before it is collected, ideally on the first page.*

- *If there is a prize draw or other remuneration, this should be stated on the first page and a link to the rules provided (and the rules should have a 'Print' button so that the respondent can make their own copy).*

- *If the responses are going to be used for mixed purposes, e.g. adding the data back into the client's database, then the respondent should be told this on the front page.*

- *If the survey is operated in accordance with specific guidelines (e.g. the ESOMAR guidelines) then many companies' house rules state that this should be mentioned on the first page. However, if the research is for mixed purposes (i.e. non-research purposes) then research bodies such as ESOMAR should not be mentioned.*

- *Who is conducting the research and how they can be contacted.*

- *Privacy policy, or even policies if both the client's and agency's policies are required. Note, in Europe (i.e. the EU) every survey is required by law to have a privacy policy.*

In non-trivial cases, the terms and conditions are not going to fit on the front page, so there are two main strategies that are commonly employed, and one approach that is nearly always used.

Most projects put the terms and conditions section below the Next/Submit button. This means the respondent is free to read it but is not forced to read it.

The two strategies that researchers often use are both based on the same principle. This principle is to look at the terms and conditions and identify the ones that are really important for people to see before they can reasonably be assumed to have given 'informed consent', and the items which a respondent might want to see but equally they might not want to bother with.

1.   The first strategy is to put the most important items at the top of the terms and conditions. This means they will be below the Next/Submit button, but visible on the page. The items that the respondent might also want to read are then in the text on the page, but below the essential ones.

2.   The second strategy is to put the important items on the first page and put links to the other items. These links are configured to open popup windows for those people who want to read them.

 Warning

Some clients ask if all the important notes can be dealt with by putting a link on the survey. The answer to this is whether the researcher honestly feels that this could be reasonably considered 'informed consent'.

Putting questions on the first page

Some agencies prefer to reserve the first page for their welcome and introduction to the survey. Others argue that the first page should be used as part of the evidence that the survey is straightforward and to get prospective respondents started quickly.

There is relatively little data on which approach leads to 'better' results. The differences are likely to be quite small when interviewing members of online access panels, who will be familiar with both approaches.

In terms of popup surveys, there are strong arguments that putting questions on the first page results in better response rates (Comley, 2000). However, many researchers still reserve the first page for a welcome, even on popup surveys.

In most countries, and under most market research codes of conduct, surveys with children require prior parental permission. For many studies this means that a question asking the age of the respondent should be one of the very first in the study, to help avoid accidently interviewing children. If the questions start on the first page, then in many of these cases age should be asked on front page.

THE LAST PAGE

The other special page of a survey is the last page. However, there are too many surveys where the last page is treated as being exactly the same as the previous pages. The key points about the last page include:

- ○   *Saying thank you*

- ○   *Providing information*

- ○   *Final comments*

- ○   *Including survey questions on the last page*

- ○   *Prize draw and opt-ins*

- ○   *Routing or closing*

Saying thank you

All surveys should finish with a thank you. This is a simple act of politeness. It is also a step towards persuading the respondent to do surveys in the future. Finally, it is also a clear signal to the respondent that the survey has finished.

Providing information

Once the respondent has moved past the last page they usually can't find out anything about the survey. For example, they might want to know the procedure to ask for their results to be removed, a rule that most research organisations require.

The last page is a good place to put information about the survey (either on the page or as a link) and to provide an explicit option to print the page.

Also, the last page should be used to tell respondents what will happen next. Are they going to be forwarded to the panel company, sent to the company website, or will the survey window close?

Final comments

It is a very good idea to end every survey with an open-ended question asking the respondents for any other comments about the subject of the research and about the survey itself. Because online surveys are self-completion, it is very hard for researchers to really appreciate how the survey is perceived by the respondents, and having a closing comment provides a channel for communication and can be an invaluable method of identifying problems with surveys.

The final comments question should either be on the last page, or immediately before the last page, depending on whether the researcher decides to have questions on the last page.

Including survey questions on the last page

Whilst there is a healthy debate about whether to include questions on the first page of the survey, there is no strong reason to put questions on the last page, and there are a couple of reasons why there should not be any questions on the last page (other than perhaps the final comment question).

When some respondents come to the last page they answer the questions on it and then close the window, which means their responses to the last page are lost. This only tends to affect 1% or 2% of people who would otherwise have completed the survey, but it can be avoided by not having any questions on the last page.

If there are questions on the last page, it reduces the standout of other material, such as information and the thank you message.

Prize draw and opt-ins

If the study includes a prize draw or if the survey offers respondents the chance to take part in some additional activity, for example joining an online panel, these are normally dealt with at the end of the survey.

If the survey is asking for contact details, then the respondent should have access to information about who is asking for it, what the details will be used for, how long the data will be stored, etc. This information is very similar to that which should be presented on the first page of the survey. The information will tend to be shown as a combination of links and text on the screen, and should include a print screen option to help respondents keep a record.

Note, if the last page of the survey asks for personal information to be handed over, then this should have been flagged in the survey invite and/or on the first page.

Routing or closing

When the respondent has finished the survey there are two options. Either the page will be closed, or the user will be forwarded, or routed, to another web page.

1. **Closing the survey window.** If the researcher wishes to close the survey window at the end of the survey there is a problem caused by the security settings of many browsers. An effort to close the screen by the survey software will often produce a system warning message saying that a process is trying to close a window. This message can be unsettling to some respondents, and they might press the cancel option. The two standard ways of closing survey pages are:

    (a) Put a message on the screen saying something along the lines of 'You may now close this browser window'. This means the respondent closes the window, and that avoids any disconcerting messages.

    (b) Put a message on the screen asking the respondent to click a link to close the window. This reduces the risk of a system warning message being served to the respondent, and even if a message is presented, the respondent is more likely to be happy with it, since they are the one closing the survey.

2. **Forwarding/routing the respondent.** If the survey window is not closed, the other main option is to forward, or route, the respondent to another web page. There are three typical destinations for this forwarding option:

    (a)   If the respondents came from an online panel, then in most cases they will be routed back to the panel at the end of the survey. Sometimes this is simply a courtesy, but it can also be integral to the process of the respondent being remunerated by the panel, for example, if the routing is part of the method of recording the completion of a survey.

    (b)   The respondent may be forwarded to a page on the research agency's website, perhaps to a page containing more information about the credentials of the research agency and information about the nature of market research. Sometimes this option is to forward respondents to a discussion page about the survey or topic.

    (c)   The respondent can also be forwarded to the website of the company who has commissioned the research. This option can seem very natural in projects conducted with people drawn from the client's database. However, some industry bodies consider this option to be a form of marketing and do not allow it within their definition of 'market research'.

ENHANCING THE SURVEY EXPERIENCE

In the early days of online surveys, particularly when respondents had been recruited via online advertising, there was a great deal of concern to make surveys as short as possible and to enhance engagement. Over the last ten years, and until recently, the trend has been towards online panels, longer surveys, and away from respondent engagement.

However, there has been a change of analysis over the last couple of years, with more people calling for improvements to the survey experience for respondents. There is a growing body of information that suggests that boring and poorly laid out surveys are contributing to the reduced levels of respondent cooperation, for example declines in both response rates and in the quality of responses. One example of the decline in quality has been the growth in the number of respondents who 'click through' a survey to get it finished, a phenomenon that is called 'satisficing'.

In many ways, the best people to speak to about how to improve online surveys are the people running the panel companies. They have a vested interest in making the survey process a more rewarding experience, in order to protect their investment in recruiting people and in terms of showing their contribution towards delivering insight. Over the last couple of years, panel companies like Survey Sampling International and GMI have been making presentations about the benefits of making surveys more engaging and the dangers of carrying on with 30 minute surveys full of boring grids.

Discussions about improving the survey experience include a wide range of activities, but key topics include:

- ❍ *Being better with people*
- ❍ *Improving surveys*
- ❍ *Quality and engagement initiatives*
- ❍ *Multimedia*
- ❍ *Measuring outcomes*

BEING BETTER WITH PEOPLE

Because online studies require the researcher to think about software and systems, and because researchers usually do not get to meet respondents, there can be occasions when researchers forget that it is **all** about people, and the people who are the most important to remember are the respondents. Research depends upon the goodwill of respondents. A satisfied respondent might do another 2500 studies over the next 25 years; an unhappy one could stop for ever.

Studies into the views and opinions of respondents make it clear what turns them off and what appeals to them. The key features that the researcher needs to consider include:

- ❍ *Asking for help*
- ❍ *Being screened out*
- ❍ *Being asked the same questions more than once*
- ❍ *Lack of honesty about how long the survey is*
- ❍ *The value/fairness of incentives*
- ❍ *Being polite*

Asking for help

Dillman et al. (2009) makes the point that cooperation rates tend to be better if the survey invitation and style are couched in the context that the brand and agency are asking for the respondent's help and advice. As part of this process, tell people why the survey is being conducted and how their help will be used.

Being screened out

Respondents hate being screened out, and this unhappiness occurs at two levels. The first is *any* screening out. The respondent receives an invitation to take a survey, makes the effort to go to the survey and is then rejected. Even if they still receive the incentive they feel their time has been wasted. Some panel members get screened out more than they get to complete surveys.

The second level of the screen out problem is when somebody is screened out of a survey after about five or even ten minutes. When this happens they are really sure that their time has been wasted. What's more, if they are panel members, doing 50+ surveys a year, they know enough about the process to realise that the reason, in most cases, is that the researcher has been too lazy or too thoughtless to make sure all the screening was dealt with near the start of the survey.

The two remedies that researchers need to adopt are:

1.   Improve the targeting of the invitations, so that fewer people are screened out. This means working with the panel companies, it means not asking for masses of invitations (which is quicker for the researcher but more likely to cause people to hit completed cells), and providing more information in the invitation to help people self-screen.*

2.   Ensure that questions that relate to screening are near the beginning. If, in a special case, there is a question which for methodological reasons needs to be eight minutes into a 15-minute survey, then accept everybody as a complete, but with some having a shorter survey, paying a complete incentive, and wording the survey for these people in a way they does not scream 'screen out'.

Being asked the same questions more than once

This response from respondents sometimes confuses researchers, especially when they go back and check the questionnaire and report that there are no questions which have been repeated. In most cases this arises because respondents consider many of the questions asked by market researchers too finely nuanced. For example, a marketer or market researcher might consider the questions:

How satisfied were you with the company's service to you on your last visit? ·

How satisfied are you with the company's service in general?

How satisfied are you with the company overall?

Researchers can easily see the difference when they are written down, side-by-side. But many respondents feel they are the same, especially when they don't see them side-by-side. Indeed, when market researchers check the data they usually find that for 95% of the respondents answers to the questions are the same.

Lack of honesty about how long the survey is

There is no excuse for not telling the truth. If you make a mistake, amend the first page to update the estimate. Also, think about the wording. If an invite says it 'should take about ten minutes', to the respondent reading the description that implies that it will be ten minutes. Saying the 'average length should be ten minutes' is more accurate and gives a better description of what the researcher probably means. Stating a range, such as 8–12 minutes is even better.

---

*There are concerns that putting too much information in the invite will result in people pretending to be somebody they are not in order to do the survey. However, it is not necessary to put all the information in the invite to help most people know that they are likely to be screened out. Also, it is not difficult to spot fraudulent interviews by putting a couple of validation/check questions into the survey. For example, in a 'Which products do you buy nowadays?' question, include a product that has been delisted for a couple of years. Anybody who picks it is either careless, confused, or fraudulent and all three groups need to be excluded in most cases.

The value/fairness of incentives

When panel companies, such as Toluna and OpinionsPaid, consulted their panel members, one of the first things that emerged were conversations about the incentives offered by the companies. By having a meaningful conversation with panel members it is possible to come to a solution that is acceptable to most people, but it will tend to increase incentives.

Being polite

'Manners cost nothing' is an old saying in many countries. Instructions in surveys should be couched in polite terms and should not generally tell the respondent they are wrong. For example, if a respondent misses a question on the page rather than saying:

'Error, answer all questions on the page!', in bright red text

consider something more like:

'Sorry, we need an answer to this question.'

At the end of the survey thank the respondent. If you have the respondent's email address (for example if the survey is being conducted via the client's database), email them a thank you and tell them that their data has been received.

IMPROVING SURVEYS

This section explores a number of different ways of improving how online questions are asked and provides advice on best practice. Some of the issues covered in this section are also important in the context of offline surveys, but they are particularly relevant in the context of online surveys and its self-completion modality.

As mentioned earlier, this section can only provide an overview and readers are referred to the books by Don Dillman et al. (2009) and particularly to the one by Mick Couper (2008).

The approaches covered in this section are:

- *Long and/or boring surveys*
- *Being asked questions that don't make sense, or have mistakes in them*
- *Grids and dropdowns*
- *Improving answer lists*
- *Making surveys easier to understand*

Long and/or boring surveys

In the early days of online surveys, when a survey was too long the dropout rate was very high and this tended to make surveys shorter. However, with the advent of panels and the growth of incentives there is an increasing trend for respondents to simply click through the survey once they reach a threshold of the survey being too long and too boring.

 Warning

Researchers should seek to ensure that their longest surveys are shorter than the median length for the source they are using. Ask the panel company or survey department about what the median is and then treat that as the absolute upper limit.

Being asked questions that don't make sense, or have mistakes in them

This should not happen! The next section looks at further ways of improving surveys, but two quick tips here are to pilot and soft launch surveys and check the verbatims to see if the respondents are querying anything.

Grids and dropdowns

Grids and dropdowns are not liked by respondents. Researchers tend to use them because they are trying to squeeze too many questions onto the page, and too many questions into the study. The best improvement a researcher can make is to reduce the list. For example, use statistical techniques such as factor analysis to understand which questions are redundant, or CHAID to identify which questions are associated with different outcomes.

Improving answer lists

One frequent complaint from respondents is there are problems in the answer list. These problems are an issue with both offline and online research, but the absence of an interviewer makes these problems more severe. There are three things that often cause problems for respondents:

1. **Ambiguous answers.** There are a wide range of ambiguous answers that occur in surveys, but 'classic' ones include:

    ○ *answers with two components, for example the answer 'Cheap and cheerful' is hard to interpret for a brand that might be cheap but not cheerful*

    ○ *overlapping categories, for example using age bands such as '18 to 30', '30 to 40', '40 to 50'*

    ○ *complex language, for example the use of technical terms, such as using the term 'syncope' instead of 'fainting', or 'microblogging' instead of 'Twitter'*

2. **Two or more suitable responses.** The question in Figure 3.2, as currently drafted, could present some respondents with more than one option and others with none. Many people have more than one computer, and these computers might use different operating systems. Which computer and which operating system should they think of when answering the question? Some people have dual-boot computers, running two or more operating systems, how should they answer the question? The respondent might not own a computer and is answering

Select the operating system that your computer uses?

O Windows XP

O Windows Vista

O Windows 7

O Mac OS

O Linux

O Other _____

O Don't Know

Figure 3.2

the survey on a smartphone (such as the iPhone) or from a games console – how should they answer the question? Depending on what exactly the researcher needs to find out, this question could be tidied up by first asking what device they are using to complete the survey on, and if they are using a computer, then asking which operating system they are using. Or, it could be changed into a multi question.

3.   **Leaving out a relevant code**. As well as reducing the quality of the data, leaving a relevant code out of an answer list is a cause of angst for respondents. Sometimes the missing code is simply a careless act, for example on a computer study forgetting that some people use Apple computers, or that in a car study some people use diesel, or even an electric or hybrid car. Leaving out a missing code is serious enough in a multi-choice question, but it can be a major source of error in a single. For example, a question asking respondents if they drive a petrol or a diesel car would oblige anybody who drives an electric or hybrid car to leave the questions blank, or if the question was forced, make an arbitrary choice between petrol and diesel.

However, the most common mistakes relate to not including an appropriate 'other', 'don't know', or 'does not apply' and, as just mentioned, these are most relevant when the question is a single. In the absence of interviewers to pass back information about the survey it becomes even more important to pilot the survey and ask respondents for feedback.

Making surveys easier to understand

The single best option is to make the survey shorter. The next best option is to at least make it seem short. One element of making a survey seem short is to make it intuitive and as straightforward as possible for the respondent.

1.   **Use language the respondent understands.** This is both a general point about research and a specific point about research with members of online access panels. Two common sources of problems in terms of the wording of surveys are using language which is too technical and, if the study is international, using terms that are less well understood in one area than another. For example, if respondents are from the UK or the USA, then terms which are neutral between the

two countries should be used, such as refrigerator instead of fridge, or compound descriptions such as boot/trunk and bonnet/hood should be used. In general, the language should seek to be as simple as that used in the popular newspapers. The researcher should aim to use short sentences, direct language, and structures that do not require complex punctuation.

2. **Use as many words as necessary, but no more.** Some researchers are tempted to use longer questions in order to be very clear about what they mean. Also, in some cases researchers also use long phrases for the answers, again in an attempt to make them clearer. However, in general, the more text there is on the screen, the fewer words respondents actually read. The best way for a researcher to investigate this is to review the time logs for surveys – most researchers are surprised at how little time the average respondent spends on each screen. This request to use as few words as possible might seem to conflict with the previous point about using language that the respondent understands. However, in practice these two points tend to be complementary. Do not worry about the nuances, most respondents will not see them and so you can't assume the data reflects them.

3. **Make the answer list self-explanatory.** Most respondents do many surveys. They broadly know what to expect and the wise researcher works with them to help make the survey easy to understand. For example, a question looking to find out whether people are male or female is often introduced with words such as "Which gender are you, please select the category that best applies?", followed by the two options 'Male', 'Female'. However, in most surveys it is quicker and easier for the respondent if the question is reduced to "*Are you?*", followed by 'Male', 'Female'.

4. **Use design elements to emphasise key points.** Where you need the respondent to pay more attention, for example if you had been asking a respondent about the **last time** they ate something and now you want to ask them about the **next time**, you should highlight this change by changing font size, or using colour or bold type, or in some other way. However, it is best to avoid underlining as this is a common visual clue for a hyperlink in online text.

5. **Organise the question and the responses to match the way respondents are likely to read the page.** The starting assumption in most Western countries is that the reader will read from left to right and from top to bottom – but note this is not true in all countries and cultures. Figures 3.3 and 3.4 show two different ways of laying out a MaxDiff question.

With the design shown in Figure 3.3 the researcher is asking the respondent to read the question from left to right, then to read down the left hand column to evaluate all four options, and then go back to the top of the page to find the most important, then back to the top again to find the least important – all the while scanning back to the left to check the text. Try it for yourself and think about how you are scanning the page.

By contrast, in the example in Figure 3.4 the respondent reads the question from left to right, then they read the four options from left to right, then they find the most important, then the least important, again from left to right.

The option in Figure 3.4 can be made even more intuitive by first asking most important, showing the four options, and only the buttons for most. Then asking least important as a second screen, with the option the respondent picked as most important greyed out or blanked (but keeping the other three options in the same position).

When choosing a skiing holiday, which of the items below is the most important and which is the least important?	Most Important	Least Important
The number of Black Runs and off piste runs available	○	○
The quality of the après ski, including the bars, clubs and restaurants	○	○
Whether key staff at the shops, restaurants and lifts speak English	○	○
The convenience of getting there, including flight times, airports, and connection to the resort	○	○

Figure 3.3

When choosing a skiing holiday which of the items below is the most important and which is the least important?	The number of Black Runs and off piste runs available	The quality of the après ski, including the bars, clubs and restaurants	Whether key staff at the shops, restaurants and lifts speak English	The convenience of getting there, including flight times, airports, and connection to the resort
Most	○	○	○	○
Least	○	○	○	○

Figure 3.4

Developing a narrative theme

Surveys make more sense to respondents and appear to take less time if they seem coherent and to have a direction. A survey should be laid out so that it moves naturally from one subject to another and in particular it should avoid doubling-back.

QUALITY AND ENGAGEMENT INITIATIVES

Over the last two years there has been a growing number of quality and engagement initiatives from a number of key players. Examples of these initiatives include improved interviewing options from some of the software vendors (especially approaches using Flash technology), actions by some of the panel companies (for example Toluna's community tools and Survey Sampling International's Respondent Preservation Initiative), and numerous discussions in groups in LinkedIn and on researcher networks such as Research Voice.

However, it should be noted that not all quality initiatives improve the respondents' survey experience. For example, accessibility initiatives, such as the WC3 Web Accessibility Initiative, tend to militate against the use of interactive media and even colour as these features reduce the total number of people who can use a website. Professional bodies' guidelines restricting the use of clients' products as incentives and not allowing respondents to buy products are not seen as respondent friendly by many respondents. Equally, some of the initiatives that are being put in place to reduce fraudulent behaviour are not likely to improve the respondent experience, for example repeating an earlier question to compare responses.

Multimedia

Some of the problems with traditional surveys, in terms of the respondent's experience, relate to the length of the survey, the wording of the questions, and the layout of the questions. However, some of the problems arise directly from the use of plain HTML, limiting questions to traditional web form tools such as radio buttons and check boxes.

Most of the interesting developments in the ways surveys are constructed currently use Flash, a technology from Adobe that facilitates animation and interactivity, or some similar technology. Flash can make surveys harder to script and it certainly requires the researcher to think more about the design of their surveys. However, the researcher needs to be aware that in creating a self-completion survey there is a strong need to make it both clear and engaging, and that it is a design process as well as a research process.

MEASURING OUTCOMES

Market researchers cannot simply move from traditional surveys to Flash enhanced, 2.0 style surveys and assume that they will deliver improvements. A number of comparisons have been run and the results show a mixture of good and bad news (Drolent, Butler and Davis, 2009; MacElroy and Malinoff, 2009).

Amongst the different effects that researchers have found when testing engaging questions, such as using Flash to provide sort tasks, sliders, and intelligent text boxes, are:

○ *surveys usually take longer*

○ *some data is better, e.g. sliders produce fewer straightliners*

○ *some data is worse, e.g. showing 10 empty text boxes usually collects more open-ended responses compared with text boxes that only reveal themselves when the previous one is used*

○ *some data is the same*

○ *some data is different, but it is unclear whether it is better or worse*

○ *most respondents are usually happier with the engaging surveys*

○ *some respondents do not understand the new question formats*

 Author's View

The pedant in me needs to point out that if two results produce different results it does not necessarily mean one is better than the other. The two results could be equally bad. For example, if the length of a pitch is 100 metres and one tape measures it as 90 metres and another as 110 metres, the two tapes are different, but equally wrong in that they are both 10 metres away from 100 metres.

USING MULTIMEDIA AND ITS IMPLICATIONS

Multimedia is a very broad term and one that is getting broader all the time. The default medium for a questionnaire is text, so at the most basic level anything that is additional to text implies multimedia. All of the following are to a greater or lesser extent multimedia:

○ *images*

○ *video*

○ *audio*

○ *dynamic components, for example using Flash to animate a section of the questionnaire*

· ○ *interactive components, for example using Flash to create drag and drop elements*

As well as being the default, text is also the simplest form of questionnaire component. Multimedia features add additional opportunities, but they also create additional challenges and risks. This section, and the sub-sections below, address each of the main areas of multimedia, looking at the theoretical and practical issues that surround the use of them.

Warning

With all multimedia there are two prime questions the researcher should keep in mind.

1. What will each individual respondent experience?

2. How will the experience affect the way the questionnaire functions?

Because people browse the internet using different platforms – for example different PCs, browsers, settings, operating systems – they will not all see and hear the same thing as each other. The researcher needs to ensure any multimedia used creates a better research instrument and check that it does not introduce so much variability that the research results are compromised.

What does the phrase 'better research instrument' mean here? Essentially, this means two things:

1. It captures a better and more accurate interpretation of the respondent's views and perceptions.

2. It provides a better experience for the respondent.

The second point is important for several reasons, including the need to maintain the cooperation of respondents, achieving a sample that is as representative as possible, and making it more likely that the respondent is paying sufficient attention.

IMAGES

Images are very useful in surveys to illustrate stimuli, for example showing pack shots, new formats, or logos. There are generally three types of use for images in surveys:

1. As the stimulus for one or more questions, for example when a new concept is shown to respondents, for them to rate and assess.

2. As an element of the question itself, for example brand logos can be used to make a grid question less 'boring' and easier to interpret.

3. As part of the design of the page, either to improve the branding of the survey or to improve its engagement.

What will the respondent see?

The first issue the researcher needs to assess is what respondents will actually see.

If the respondent is using a text-only browser they will not see any images. If they are using a screen reader (for example if they have a visual impairment) they won't see the image. If they are colour blind they won't see some or all of the colours in the image. If the images being used are there to improve the branding or engagement of the survey then any inability to see the images might not be a problem. But if the image is the stimulus for the question, or if the images are an integral part of the question itself, then not seeing the image is a major problem.

What will the image look like?

The next issue for the researcher to consider is whether the respondent can see the image in the way it was intended. If the respondent has a small screen, will they be able to see the whole image? For example, they may have a smaller screen because their computer screen is smaller, or because they are using a different device altogether, such as an iPhone. Similarly, if the colour scheme on the respondent's device is different, or the vertical/horizontal proportions are different, the image may appear different to the way the researcher intended.

Will the respondent look at the image?

The researcher also needs to consider whether the respondent actually looks at the image. For example, if the image is positioned at the bottom of the page (which means it may not be initially visible), will respondents actually scroll down and look at it?

The size of images

One limitation of browsers is that images cannot be very large or very detailed (researchers can't normally assume that images over about 1000 by 800 pixels will fit on a respondent's screen), so the researcher is often faced with a trade-off between making the image small enough to be visible and making it large enough for respondents to see the detail (for example, so the respondent can see the writing on a container in a pack shot image).

In the early days of online research, bandwidths were lower, and there was an issue about how much time would be required to download an image. This is less of an issue these days, in most cases, but if an image is very large or if somebody is connecting via a slower speed connection (such as some mobile and WiFi services), download times can still be an issue.

 Advice

Guidance for images

The following steps will make it more likely that images included in a survey will result in a relatively standardised appearance to respondents.

1. Check the screen size of the respondent's browser at the start of the survey. If it is smaller than the size you feel is appropriate, abandon the survey, perhaps offering them the chance to complete the survey at a later date from a different device.

2. Near the start of the survey, tell the respondent that the questionnaire will involve images and ask them whether their system will allow them to view images.

3.   Consider whether to show a test image near the start of the survey. A test image should be of a size that reflects the size you are planning to use. For example, you might show an image with, say, four cars on it and ask a question about what the respondent can see, with breaks for 1 car, 2 cars, 3 cars, 4 cars, 5, cars, 6 cars, and for 'Don't know', and 'No image visible'. Only those respondents selecting the correct answer are selected to continue with the survey.

4.   When showing images that you want the respondent to look at, ensure that they appear high enough on the page, certainly above the Next/Submit button.

5.   If the image being shown in the survey is too small to show some of the details (which some the respondents might want to see), then the researcher can provide a method for the respondent to see a larger version of the image. One way of achieving this is to create a popup of the image, i.e. if they click on it they see a larger image in a separate window. A more sophisticated alternative is to use interactive and dynamic tools, such as Flash, to create methods for the respondent to enlarge the image, or to enlarge part of the image.

AUDIO

Audio is used less often than images and less often than videos. However, it is particularly suitable for some situations such as testing radio ads or jingles.

Audio raises several more issues than images. Whereas most respondents will be able to see images, many will not be able to play audio, especially those who are using a PC or device at work or in a public place. Indeed, the researcher should keep in mind that a respondent might be putting their employment at risk if they take part in an online survey whilst at work, and playing an audio file might increase the risk of them being detected.

The two issues that the researcher needs to deal with are:

1.   Can the respondent hear the audio file?

2.   Will they listen to the whole file before they answer the questions?

Respondents might not be able to hear the audio because of one or more of the following:

○   *they do not have audio on their system, or their speakers are turned off*

○   *their connection is too slow to be able to play audio, for example if they are using a slow WiFi or mobile connection*

○   *their device configuration is not compatible with the format of your sound file. If this is the case, it is possible that they will download a suitable player, but it is also possible that they will be unable or unwilling to do so*

Advice

Guidance for using audio in a questionnaire

The following points will make it more likely that the inclusion of audio works in the way the researcher intends.

1. At the start of the survey tell the respondent that the survey will use audio, giving them a chance to quit if they do not have audio, or are using a very slow connection to the internet, or are in an inappropriate place to take part in the survey – ideally offering them a chance to take part in the survey at a later date.

2. Consider playing a test audio file at the start of the survey to check the respondent can hear the file. After playing the test file the respondent should be asked a question that tests that they have heard it clearly. If you are using images and audio, these can be tested with a single question that shows an image and the audio file.

3. On the pages that use audio, try to ensure that the Next/Submit buttons are not enabled until after the audio file has finished playing.

4. Consider giving the respondent a chance to listen to the audio file again.

VIDEO

As bandwidth has improved and software has become more powerful, the use of videos has become more common in online surveys. There are a variety of ways of delivering video in surveys, but the most common approach these days is to use the same sort of Flash technology that YouTube uses, which has the advantage of being compatible with most people's systems and of being relatively secure (but remember, nothing on the internet is truly secure).

As with audio, the use of video can be inappropriate for some respondents in some situations, for example when they are at work or in a public place. Like images, video can be a problem if the respondent has a small screen, for example if they are completing the survey on a mobile device such as an iPhone. The bandwidth requirement of video tends to be higher than that needed for both simple images and audio, so there will be more respondents whose bandwidth is insufficient to watch the video.

 Advice

Guidance for using video in a questionnaire

The following points, which are very similar to the audio guidelines, will make it more likely that the inclusion of video will work in the way the researcher intended.

1.   At the start of the survey tell the respondent that the survey will play a video, giving them a chance to quit if they do not have video, if they are using a very slow connection to the internet, or if they are in an inappropriate place to take part in the survey – ideally offering them a chance to take part in the survey later.

2.   Consider playing a test video file at the start of the survey to check the respondent can view the file. After playing the test video the respondent should be asked a question that tests that they have been able to view it OK.

3.   Try to ensure that the Next/Submit buttons are not enabled until after the video file has finished playing.

4.   Consider giving the respondent a chance to view the video again.

DYNAMIC AND INTERACTIVE COMPONENTS

The number of available components is increasing all the time, with most of them being scripted in Flash. Amongst the many elements that might be used are:

- *sliders, to enter rating scales*

- *drag and drop options, where respondents might drag images and drop them onto containers*

- *sort tasks, where respondents sort objects on the screen*

- *a wide variety of attractive buttons and check boxes*

- *3D viewing tools for pack shots*

- *books and magazines with turnable pages*

The two main questions the researcher needs to consider are:

1.   Will the respondent's device work properly with the components?

2.   Will the respondent be able to use the components?

If somebody has coordination issues, particularly if they are using a track-pad, then they may find it difficult to use tools such as drag and drop.

The best advice is to have a practice task near the start of the survey where the respondent is introduced to one of the potentially more difficult tools and the results checked. For example the screen could show a red car along with a red box, a blue box, and a green box, and the respondent be asked to drag the car into the box of the same colour.

ACCESSIBLE SURVEYS

Over the last ten years there has been a growing amount of interest, regulation, and legislation relating to accessible surveys. In the context of the internet, the term 'accessible' relates to websites, but in most cases online surveys are websites and often fall within the remit of accessibility concerns. The term 'accessible' has two key elements to it:

○ *helping people who have specific challenges to be able use the website, for example, people who have a visual impairment or missing limbs*

○ *allowing respondents to configure their browsers in any reasonable way, for example, in order to be fully accessible a site needs to be usable without requiring a visitor to use JavaScript*

Although different countries have different legislation (for example, Canada has its 'Common look and feel standards', the UK has its Disability Rights Commission, and the USA has its Section 508), the main reference point for accessibility is the W3C's WAI (Web Accessibility Initiative) [http://www.w3.org/WAI/]. Accessibility, as defined by the WAI, comes in a series of levels of conformance, from A through double-A, to the hardest level, triple-A. Most agencies take their lead from their clients in terms of the level of compliance they use for their surveys. In general, it is mainly the public sector which requires the highest levels of compliance.

SURVEYS AND ONLINE ACCESS PANELS

The design of any questionnaire needs to take the survey's context into account. When a study is being fielded via an online access panel this needs to be considered and factored into the design.

Online access panels tend to be used in one of two ways, either as full service providers (i.e. the panel company scripts and hosts the survey), or as the sample supplier. This section concentrates on this second case, where the agency scripts and hosts the survey (possibly via another third party or perhaps a SaaS system) and the panel company organises the sample source.

In general, designing an online questionnaire to be used with an online access panel is relatively straight-forward, certainly compared with options such as popup surveys; however it can also be more limiting.

In most cases the online access panel will be responsible for the following:

○ *sending an invitation to its members including a link to the survey*

○ *handling the respondent at the end of the survey, in most cases the survey forwards the respondent to an agreed panel page*

○ *offering incentives for the respondents, which means the process needs to feed information to the panel company's systems.*

The panel company may provide, or insist on, the following:

○   *a standard look and feel for surveys, possibly including a survey template and standard graphics*

○   *forced completion for closed questions (unless there is a good research reason to allow partial answers)*

○   *a maximum length for the survey*

○   *avoiding anything that might induce the panel member to approach the research company directly, to avoid members being poached*

○   *the panel company's privacy policy*

The questionnaire needs to be designed so that quota information is gathered in such a way that the researcher and the panel company can monitor the progress of the study in terms of recruiting the right people.

SURVEYS AND CLIENT DATABASES

The main design implication when using a client database is that in most cases the respondent will be aware that the survey is on behalf of the client, which rules out some options. This is because in most countries it is a legal and ethical requirement to tell somebody who is contacted from a database where the contact originates from.

The branding of the survey may be in the research agency's style or in the client's house style, or in some combination of the two.

In some cases the client will send the invitations to the people on their database but in most cases the research agency will draft and send the invitations to the potential respondents, using mailing information supplied from the client, subject to data protection legislation.

DRAFTING INVITATIONS

When working with client databases, and in other cases where the researcher may be responsible for drafting or helping draft the survey invitation, the appearance and the content of the survey invitation will have a marked impact on cooperation rates. In these cases, the design of the invitation is part of the survey design process and needs to be approached with the entire questionnaire in mind.

In most cases, the invitation will be sent as an email, and the first challenge is to get the prospective respondent to open the email. The second challenge is to entice the respondent to access the survey.

The following steps are all best practice in constructing an email invitation:

- *personalise the survey invitation and provide a simple link for the recipient to use*

- *make it clear from the outset that the email is inviting the recipient to take part in a market research survey*

- *say who the email is from and where you got their email address from*

- *say how long the survey will take, and be truthful*

- *provide a method for the recipient to request no further contact or unsubscribe*

- *describe the incentive, if there is an incentive*

- *if there is a closing date for the survey, make this clear*

- *provide a method for the recipient to find out more about the project and the researcher*

- *ensure that all relevant data protection requirements are met*

One area that requires balance is the extent to which the invitation reveals the topic and subject matter of the survey. Researchers are wary of saying too much, worried that some respondents may change their answers in order to avoid being screened out. However, numerous studies of respondents have shown that being screened out is a major complaint and has been cited as a contributory factor in people refusing to take part in future research. If a survey invitation discloses very little information about the survey, the number of respondents being screened out is likely to be higher, and the level of annoyance higher.

The balance the researcher is seeking to strike is to provide enough information to allow respondents to self-screen, but not enough information to enable rogue respondents to cheat. For example, a survey with housewives about buying bread from a leading store might disclose that the survey is looking for housewives who buy bread, but not disclose the store, or the frequency. The screening would then check gender, age, shopping role, bread buying, frequency, and store.

QUALITY AND ETHICAL ISSUES IN SURVEY DESIGN

There are a number of quality and ethical issues that relate specifically to the survey design, and a few of these have already been mentioned in this chapter. The key issues that the researcher needs to consider are:

- *Being honest with the respondent*

- *Not collecting unnecessary information*

- *Controlling access to surveys*

- *Testing surveys*

BEING HONEST WITH THE RESPONDENT

The principle of informed consent requires research to '*say what you are doing*' and to '*do what you say*'. For example, if a project is described as being purely for market research purposes, then the individual information must never be used for marketing purposes and must not find its way into clients' databases. If one of the objectives of the project is to enrich the client's database, then the respondent should be told this at the earliest possible stage, for example in the invitation and/or on the first page of the survey.

Two areas of honesty that respondents often complain about are the estimated length of the survey and the accuracy of the progress indicator.

NOT COLLECTING UNNECESSARY INFORMATION

In most cases, the longer the survey the lower the quality of the information, and in particular the lower the quality of the information collected in the latter part of the survey. Therefore, unnecessary questions should not normally be included in a questionnaire. Indeed, the best practice is to review a survey to check that every question relates to one or more of the project's objectives.

Unnecessary information can also compromise the privacy and data security of the respondent. For example, asking them to enter their postcode will, in some countries, identify them as an individual, especially in combination with, say, age and sex data.

CONTROLLING ACCESS TO SURVEYS

Researchers only want respondents to answer a survey once and in most cases want to restrict surveys to only those who have been specifically invited.

Generally, access to surveys is controlled by the use of passwords, unique links, or cookies. The use of a unique ID and password is a secure method of running surveys, but it can be seen as unfriendly and there can be problems with users forgetting their ID or passwords.

A more flexible route, compared with the ID and password route, is to create unique URLs, one for each respondent invited. These unique URLs are then emailed to the respondent. In many cases, these unique URLs are in fact a generic URL combined with a username and password, a process that the better survey systems can automate.

Cookies, and similar techniques such as recording IP addresses, only tend to be used where self-selection is more of an issue, such as when links are posted on websites.

TESTING SURVEYS

The survey design process should include allowing time for testing surveys. The testing of surveys is a process that should ideally include reviewing the questionnaire, test interviews, machine testing, and reviewing the user process once the survey is live.

The design of a questionnaire and the complexity of testing it are directly linked. As surveys become more complex, the testing becomes more difficult. The sorts of problems that may confront the researcher include:

- ○ **Null and single lists.** *In many studies respondents pick a subset of items based on some point of saliency, for example they pick the brands of toilet cleaner they would consider buying from a long list of cleaners. This list may then be fed into other questions, such as a choice task or brand image arrays. However, what happens if a respondent picks none of the items – will the survey crash, or show an empty fixture? What about a respondent who picks just one item – will they see a competitive array with just one item in it?*

- ○ **Errors in rotations and cells allocations.** *Do all of the items and questions appear as often as they should? Are respondents being allocated to the right cells correctly?*

- ○ **Incompatible combinations.** *Some combinations of questions do not make sense to the respondent, for example in a conjoint study looking at drinks, a question about the colour of the glass should not be asked in combination with a question about whether the drink should be in a bottle or can (because a can does not have a glass colour).*

- ○ **Inconsistent responses from respondents.** *For example in a PSM (i.e. a van Westerndorp Price Sensitivity Meter) pricing study, if a respondent says $10 is cheap, should the system stop them from saying that $8 is expensive?*

- ○ **Logic errors.** *These are amongst the hardest to test. Does the logic keep working irrespective of the answers the respondent might enter? Auto-running a large number of dummy randomised interviews is an essential element to the testing of non-trivial surveys.*

- ○ **Back-arrow issues.** *If a survey has a back arrow (allowing respondents to go back to the previous page), the researcher needs to check that this will not interfere with the logic and/or the storage of the survey's variables.*

The testing of complex surveys needs to focus on two elements:

1. Does the survey look right? This includes sub-questions such as: does it show the right questions to the right respondents and does it crash when more 'unlikely' responses are entered?

2. Is the survey storing the right values, including working and hidden values?

SUMMARY OF DESIGNING ONLINE SURVEYS

The key point to keep in mind is that the respondent is on their own, there is no interviewer to explain how to answer questions, and nobody to encourage them to keep responding to the survey. All the respondent sees is the survey, so it needs to be self-explanatory and engaging.

Two key sources for any researcher looking to learn more about self-completion surveys, for example mail, internet, and online surveys in general are Dillman et al.'s *Internet, Mail and Mixed-Mode Surveys* (2009) and Mick Couper's *Designing Effective Web Surveys* (2008), and the reader is recommended to consult these if they want to take their knowledge of the design of online surveys further.

KEY TAKEAWAYS FOR DESIGNING ONLINE SURVEYS

The following points are the key items covered this chapter.

- ○ *Online surveys are self-completion surveys; this is the single most important design consideration.*

- ○ *Surveys should be designed to be clear to the respondent and to make it more likely that the respondent completes the survey and stays engaged throughout the process. This includes:*

    - ○ *making the survey as short as possible*

    - ○ *using the minimum number of words that explains what is needed*

    - ○ *using question types that are 'respondent friendly'*

- ○ *The survey should be designed around what most respondents will be able to see, in terms of screen size and browser facilities.*

- ○ *The first page of the study needs to deal with all the key information and permission issues.*

- ○ *The last page of the survey should thank people and ask whether the respondent has any comments they want to make about either the subject of the research or the survey.*

- ○ *The more complex the survey, the more it needs to be tested before being launched.*

- ○ *The two aims of any survey should be (a) to answer the research questions, and (b) not turn the respondent against market research surveys.*

 # Working with Panels and Databases

This chapter looks at working with online access panels, client databases, and client panels. The key thing that these three (and some similar options such as communities) have in common is that people have agreed to join them (to a greater or lesser extent) and tend to be familiar with surveys. However, there are also differences between these three options which are covered in this chapter.

The chapter reviews three key methods of working with organised collections of potential respondents. These three methods are:

○   *Online access panels*

○   *Client databases*

○   *In-house, or client, panels*

ONLINE ACCESS PANELS

Online access panels are the main reason why online quantitative research has become the leading global data collection modality. They are also the cause of a fundamental shift in the underlying market research quantitative paradigm of producing projectable results based on random probability sampling.

An online access panel (increasingly commonly known as an online panel or just a panel) is a collection of potential respondents who have signed up to an organisation which provides people for market research surveys.

Although online access panels exist in a number of varieties, they tend to have the following in common:

(a)   The members of the panel know they are on a market research panel and have opted in to it.

(b)   The panel is used solely for market research. If a collection of people is used additionally for other purposes, such as marketing, it is not an online access panel (it could still be useful, of course).

(c)   The panel operator keeps some information about the respondents in their database enabling them to draw samples, for example by age or gender.

(d)   The survey invitations sent to the panel members and the incentives are dealt with by the panel company. Panel companies tend not to pass on contact information to their clients.

In addition to online access panels there are also online panels that are operated by market research companies but which are not offered as a free-standing service to other market research agencies. These are similar in most ways to online access panels.

This chapter looks at the following aspects of online access panels:

- ○   *Choosing an access panel*
- ○   *Working with a panel provider*
- ○   *Improving response rates and survey quality*
- ○   *The panel paradigm – the loss of random probability sampling*
- ○   *Panels and quality*
- ○   *Creating an online panel*

CHOOSING AN ACCESS PANEL

The first step in conducting most online quantitative surveys is to select an online access panel to act as the provider of the sample. In most cases this will be a default process, and the panel chosen will be the one that the researcher normally uses. However, initially – and periodically thereafter – a decision has to be made about which panel to use. This section sets out the key issues that the researcher should consider:

- ○   *Sample or full service*
- ○   *Quality*
- ○   *Cost*
- ○   *Capacity*
- ○   *Database variables*
- ○   *Customer service*

Sample or full service

Some sample companies only offer sample, i.e. they will send respondents to a survey created by the researcher. However, many panel providers also offer a service where they script and host surveys.

In many cases, the prices from a panel company for sample only and the script and host service are similar. From the panel company's point of view the cost of scripting is often offset by the savings generated by not having to check the researcher's survey and implementation.

The reason that many researchers continue to script surveys is to create unique or branded surveys.

Quality

Comparative studies have shown that different panels tend to produce different results, which may imply that there are quality differences between panels. There is ongoing research to identify the impact of different panel characteristics, such as how the members are recruited and how duplicate and fraudulent respondents are detected.

 Resources

One of the key reference points in terms of quality are ESOMAR's 26 Questions, which can be found online at http://www.esomar.org/index.php/26-questions.html. The questions were first published in 2005 and have been periodically reviewed since. The questions are presented as those that buyers can or should ask panel companies to answer. The 26 Questions include topics such as data quality, multiple panel membership, sample measurement, panel recruitment, and sample source.

Cost

When two products are equal in other ways, the obvious answer is to choose the cheapest; similarly, if the better panel is the cheapest the obvious answer is the right answer. However, when choosing a panel company it is not always easy to see the quality difference (see previous section) and the researcher needs to be careful in how they collect quotes to ensure that the relative costs can be easily compared.

 Advice

When requesting quotations from panel companies there are two key guidelines:

(a)   Give the panel company as detailed and accurate a specification as possible. If the survey ends up being 15 minutes instead of 10 minutes, or if the incidence ends up being 5% instead of 20%, the final cost is likely to be higher than the original estimate or the number of completed surveys lower.

(b)   Ensure that the quotation from the panel company provides a total price, including any incentives and handling charges.

In terms of combining quality and costs the four steps below will balance quality and cost:

1.   Rule out any panel that does not meet a quality threshold.

2.   Request quotations from the panel companies in the consideration set, or a subset of them.

3.   Review the feedback from the panel companies. They may be recommending changes to the project specification and it is worth considering their suggestions.

4.   The final decision lies somewhere between choosing (a) the cheapest of the suppliers who meet the quality threshold, and (b) the best sample the project can afford.

Because a research agency is the intermediary in the research process, the final arbiter of the trade-off between benefits and costs is the end client.

When assessing the cost of working with a panel company the researcher should consider how easy the panel is to work with. If the panel company is responsive and deals with things without being chased then they are cheaper to work with than a provider who needs constant chasing and whose work needs constant checking. Panel prices of $1 more per respondent may not cost more if the service level is much higher.

Capacity

When choosing a panel company it is important to assess their ability to handle the whole project, particularly if the research is likely to consist of more than one wave.

At the time of securing the quotation, ensure that the panel company declares whether they outsource any of their recruiting to other panels — it is not unusual for panel companies to source additional sample from other panel companies if they run into capacity issues. If the panel company outsources some of its recruiting to a third party there are two possible problems for the researcher:

1.   The risk of duplicate respondents increases when more than one panel source is used because many panel members are on more than one panel.

2.   There is considerable evidence that shows different panels can produce different results for the same survey. If one wave of a study comes mainly from panel company A and the second wave comes from panel company B, the differences between the two waves may be caused by genuine differences or just by differences between the two panels.

Databases variables

All online access panels store some background information on their members. If they don't have this sort of information then they are not an online access panel, they are a database or list. However, the panels differ in how much background information they hold. Background variables have two key implications:

(a)   Having more background variables can allow survey invitations to be better targeted, which can reduce costs and also the nuisance suffered by panel members (respondents tend to hate being screened out and better targeting reduces the number of screen outs).

(b)   If variables are stored they can be passed to the researcher, meaning they do not have to be asked of the respondent. Passing stored variables means not asking respondents the same questions in every survey, which shortens the interview.

Customer service

Like any service, one of the key features of working with a panel provider is partly a function of their product and partly a function of their customer service. Key actions that mark out good customer service are things like staying late when a project needs it, volunteering suggestions for improvements, responding quickly and accurately, and working hard to eradicate errors.

WORKING WITH A PANEL PROVIDER

Most research companies tend to work with a small number of panel companies and this allows them to optimise the relationship. The following steps outline processes that represent best practice in working with a panel company and are predicated on developing an ongoing relationship. If a project with a specific panel provider is a one-off project then the steps are similar but they need to be taken more slowly and with more double-checking, to ensure that both parties understand what is wanted.

This section on working with panel companies looks at the four key elements of working with a panel company:

- *The quote*
- *Booking a job*
- *Organising a timeline*
- *Monitoring a survey*

The quote

The first step of any project is to get a quote from the panel company (or the panel companies in the consideration set). The more accurate the quote, the less likely there is to be a problem later on. The researcher should clearly describe the project, stating the sample specification, the length of the survey, any special scripting requirements, and the likely timeline.

This stage should clarify whether the panel company is providing just the sample or the scripting and hosting as well. Notes on scripting/hosting issues are covered in Chapter 5, Running an Online Survey.

Booking a job

The job should be booked with the panel company as soon as the end client commissions the project. The earlier it is done, the less chance there is of a problem later on. Find out who the project's exec will be at the panel company, find out if they are in the same time zone as you. Talk to the panel company and check if they have training days, public holidays, or planned maintenance scheduled for the fieldwork period. At this early stage the fieldwork can often be tweaked to avoid known problems.

It is a good idea to get the mobile phone number of the panel exec at this stage, to expedite matters if a crisis occurs. If the panel exec has holidays booked for part of the project timeline, consider asking for an alternative exec.

Organising a timeline

Key dates to agree in the timeline are:

1. Finalising the sample specification.

2. Sending a link of the questionnaire to the panel for them to sign it off (unless the panel company are scripting the survey).

3. Soft launch of the survey.

4. Start of fieldwork proper.

5. Target date for end of fieldwork.

6. Feedback of problems and comments to the panel company.

Projects do not always run to time. This means that timelines need to be revisited and checked. If the client authorisation of a questionnaire slips by one day it does not mean that the fieldwork will necessarily slip by only one day. If there are backlogs in the system a window might be missed and the delay could be longer.

Monitoring a survey

The researcher needs to monitor the study and check for the following:

○ *progress towards quotas*

○ *completion rates*

○ *the number and profile of screen outs*

○ *problem respondents*

○ *any problems reported by respondents*

○ *whether cells are closing properly*

○ *whether the survey closes properly*

Warning

It is never too early to send the panel company information about progress against quota targets. The longer a problem is allowed to run the harder it will be to rectify.

High screen outs, low completion rates, and high numbers of respondent problems are indications of potential problems that the researcher needs to look into:

(a) Is there a problem with the survey – for example, are there errors, or a lack of clarity, or is it too long?

(b) Is the panel company sending the wrong sort of people to the survey?

As quota cells are completed (including any overage that the researcher has requested) the survey needs to ensure that any future respondents are screened out. If this does not happen there will be extra costs.

As a quota cell completes, it is a good idea to let the panel company know so that they can avoid inviting anybody else who matches that specification and thereby avoid alienating panel members. Similarly, when the survey has collected enough interviews in total, ensure the survey is closed at the researcher's end and that the panel company is told.

 Advice

The following three checks will all help the project run more smoothly:

1. Make sure that the panel company does not send a large number of invites before the soft launch has been assessed.

2. Watch out that the invites from the panel company are balanced, i.e. it would be a bad idea to invite mostly young people, or mostly people in the South in the first wave of invitation, otherwise the easy quota cells will be filled up with these people, potentially creating spurious results.

3. Check that the panel company does not close the study at their end before you have enough interviews.

IMPROVING RESPONSE RATES AND SURVEY QUALITY

All of the discussions about quality and response rates elsewhere in the book apply to panel surveys, for example keeping the survey short, easy to understand, and engaging. So this section simply adds a couple of points relevant to working with panels.

The first point is that panel companies tend to know more about improving the respondent experience than anybody else. Ask their advice and use it whenever possible.

The second point is that panel respondents tend to finish surveys rather than dropping out half way through, but they will often just 'click through' the latter half of a boring survey. The panel member needs to finish to be rewarded and to avoid being flagged as somebody who often drops out. When fielding a long survey, check the data near the end of the survey, for example the number of items known and the number of open-ends to see if respondent fatigue/disinterest is a problem.

THE PANEL PARADIGM

This is covered elsewhere in the book but it is important to keep stressing it.

 Warning

In almost all cases, a survey conducted via an online access panel cannot be treated as being representative of the wider population in the way a true random probability sample can be.

This does not mean that online access panels should not be used, it does not mean they are necessarily misleading, but it does mean that what researchers say and do has to be modified.

The key reason a sample from a panel is not an approximation to a random probability sample is that there is usually no way of knowing whether a representative sample of the wider population exists within the panel. If a representative sample does not exist within the panel, then no amount of weighting or sub-sampling will produce a representative sample.

Strategies for sampling from panels

This section looks at some strategies for dealing with samples and panels.

Complex weighting. If the researcher has good information about the population then it might be possible to weight the data to make it much more like the population. One method, made popular by Harris Interactive, is propensity scoring (Terhanian, 2008), and another is to use CHAID to assign weights (Fine et al., 2009). However, both of these routes require time and high quality information about the population.

Quotas. The most common way of working with panels is to match a small number of key demographics to the target population, for example age, sex, and income. This approach is based on an assumption that the responses to the object of the research are relatively similar for all people in the target population who share the same quota variables. For example, if a new cereal is being tested the assumption is that if young wealthy females on the panel like it, then young wealthy females who are not on the panel will also like it.

Benchmarking. One approach is to keep the sample specification constant and then to assume that changes over time amongst people who meet this specification will be matched by changes in the target population. This approach is the basis of most ad and brand tracking. The absolute values produced by the tracking may or may not reflect the wider population, but it is the changes in the tracking lines that are monitored and reported.

Modelling. Modelling is a more sophisticated variation of benchmarking and seeks to link the output from a panel survey to the real world. For example, a series of product tests might be conducted with samples from an online panel, with the specification of the sample held constant. Over time the company will acquire market feedback and can attempt to model what a survey score of X means in terms of market outcomes.

Potential sampling problems with panels

Whilst there is no formal basis for sampling from panels it tends to work most of the time. The reason is that most market research studies are looking at questions where the responses tend not to be correlated with the differences between the panel and the target population.

Problems tend to occur when the nature of the panel is likely to be correlated with the subject under examination. Online panels are not suitable for evaluating services that are used as an alternative to the internet, for example surveying usage and attitudes towards holidays of people who tend to use traditional travel agents (people who mostly use traditional travel agents are unlikely to be on an online panel).

Should significance testing be used with panel samples?

Significance testing, for example, assessing that the error term in a sample of 1000 people is +/–3%, is based on an assumption that the sample is drawn randomly from the population. When using a panel the sampling statistics do not say anything specific about the validity of the results.

However, the sampling statistics do have a role in terms of assessing the reliability of the findings. When using a panel the population is not the whole country, it is the whole panel. The error statistics indicate how likely it is that another sample from the same panel will be different, which is a valid and relevant measure of reliability.

So, yes! Researchers should use significance testing with panel data to ensure that the differences being reported are likely to be big enough to matter and big enough to be reliable. But researchers should avoid implying that they are estimates of the population sampling error.

PANELS AND QUALITY

Concerns about the quality of online panels came to the fore in 2006. Speaking at the Research Industry Summit on Respondent Cooperation in the USA, Kim Dedeker (who was then Procter & Gamble's

VP Global Consumer Market Knowledge) revealed a range of problems that her company had faced with online access panel reliability. The main example Dedeker quoted was a study that Procter & Gamble had fielded twice with the same panel and where the results pointed to two different business conclusions. Although other people had been raising concerns before (and since) this was the speech that is generally considered as sparking a raft of initiatives to indentify and confront the quality issues surrounding the use of online access panels in market research.

One of the largest quality initiatives was the ARF's Online Research Quality Council. It pulled together leading industry figures and spent over US$1 million researching the current state of play, issuing its report in late 2009. Amongst the findings from this research were that different panels did indeed produce different results (some of the time), that panels tended to be internally reliable (the same study fielded twice with the same panel tended to produce the same result), and that people who did large numbers of surveys (e.g. 100 a year) did not produce results that differed from those who only did a few studies a year.

The ARF process has also produced the Quality Enhancement Process (QeP) which aims to provide a framework for improvements.

The ESOMAR 26 Panel Questions has already been mentioned in this chapter, but it is worth noting that ESOMAR, the ARF, and other bodies are increasingly working together to address quality issues.

Another important initiative, which is also working with the others mentioned in this chapter, is the creation of an ISO standard for access panels in market, opinion, and social research. ISO 26362 is available online at the ISO website http://www.iso.org/iso/iso_catalogue/catalogue_tc/catalogue_detail.htm?csnumber=43521.

Response rates

When working with online panels, response rates are measures of quality, and have very little to do with how representative the survey is of a meaningful population (the population of an online access panel is a tiny percentage of the total population within a country). The difference between a 50% response rate of a non-representative sample and 10% of a non-representative sample has little measureable impact on how representative the research is.

In general, two factors tend to cause response rates to differ between the same survey being run on two different panels:

1. If one panel contains a large number of people who are inactive – i.e. who rarely or never respond to invitations – then its response rates will be lower than a panel which tends to clear out inactive members.

2. If one panel has background variables that allow it to target the survey invitations to people who are likely to match the screening criteria, its response rate for that survey is likely to be higher than a panel that does not have its panel members profiled on the key questions needed to target the invitations.

CREATING AN ONLINE PANEL

In the more developed research markets there is no pressing need to create new online access panels, but the process is still going on in the developing markets. In addition to online access panels, there is a substantial amount of interest in niche or brand panels, although to a growing extent these are being superseded by community enhanced panels.

In the ESOMAR *Market Research Handbook*, industry guru Pete Comley provides a range of tips for anybody looking to create a panel, and these remain relevant today (Comley, 2007). For example, Comley talks about using a variety of sources to recruit the panel, having a good profiling study, and ensuring that new panel members receive surveys soon after registering.

CLIENT DATABASES

Most client companies now have one or more databases of their customers. These databases typically range from little more than a list of email addresses through to fully integrated and sophisticated CRM systems. In most cases, these databases were created and are owned by the company's marketing or sales function.

Client databases can be a really useful way to contact a client's customers to conduct market research. Most of the material covered in this online research part of the book is relevant to research conducted via client databases, but there are some special considerations and these are dealt with in this section.

Many of the special conditions that relate to client databases arise because of legislation and industry regulations, and therefore the conditions differ from country to country. As shown elsewhere in this book, the guidance is loosely based on the ESOMAR guidelines and a legislative framework that could be described as mid-Atlantic, i.e. combining Europe and North America. Individual researchers will need to check the conditions that relate specifically to their market and their regulatory bodies.

This section looks at the following aspects of working with client databases:

- *Types of databases*

- *Factors that limit the use of client databases*

- *Drawing samples*

- *Inviting respondents*

- *Dealing with complaints*

- *Mixed-purpose research*

- *Response rates*

- *Summary of client databases*

TYPES OF DATABASES

Client companies hold a wide range of different databases including:

- *customers*
- *prospects (especially in business-to-business research)*
- *people who have complained*
- *people who have taken part in competitions and/or promotions*
- *people who have registered through a website*
- *people who have connected via social media, e.g. fans of a Facebook Page or Twitter followers*
- *people who have taken part in previous research and said that they are happy to be contacted for further research*

Each of these types of database has different characteristics and this will have an effect on their suitability for market research. Equally, different companies maintain their databases in different ways. Some companies have sophisticated systems and are on top of all the relevant data protection guidelines and laws, some are not.

FACTORS THAT LIMIT THE USE OF CLIENT DATABASES

There are a number of factors that can limit how a client database can be used for market research. These factors include:

- *The permissions that exist for the data*
- *Disclosing the client*
- *Limitations imposed by marketing priorities*

The permissions that exist for the data

In most countries, contact information can only be used for purposes that the individual has consented to, usually at the time the information was collected. Many databases are organised with a set of permissions that people on the file may have opted into. (Note, in some countries is it OK to use the lower test of 'have not opted out of'.) For example, many organisations collect and record three types of permission:

1. Can the company contact you for marketing purposes?
2. Can third parties contact you for marketing purposes?
3. Can you be contacted for market research?

In these and similar cases, customers can only be contacted if they have said yes to the market research option. To the surprise of some market researchers, there are people who say yes to marketing and no to market research.

When working with a client database the researcher should satisfy themselves that adequate permissions exist.

Disclosing the client

When using a database to email people, it is usually a requirement (in most countries and under most guidelines) to disclose the source of the contact as part of the email. This means that when using a client database for a project the client will be disclosed. Disclosing the client is OK for some research, such as customer satisfaction, but it is less suitable for other types of research such as brand comparisons.

Limitations imposed by marketing priorities

Because most client databases are owned and managed by marketing there are often a number of limitations placed on how they can be used for market research. These limitations include restricting the number of emails sent to the database, which means that research has to compete for a scarce resource.

DRAWING SAMPLES

Some databases have systems for drawing a random sample but many others struggle to perform this task. The researcher should check that a sample supplied from a client database is not systematically skewed, for example the first 5000 records might mean the newest 5000, the oldest 5000, or even the first 5000 alphabetically or all drawn from the same region or category.

Similarly, clients vary in the degree to which they conform to legal data protection requirements. Some are very good and ensure that data is properly protected and does not include inappropriate fields. However, some send lists without encrypting them and with fields that ought not to be included (e.g. financial data). If data is received inappropriately the researcher should ensure that it is immediately sorted out, for example, inappropriate fields deleted, the data encrypted, and all copies except the encrypted/edited data removed (for example deleting attachments to emails that have been received). The problems with the data should also be highlighted to the client in a way that can be confirmed, such as sending them an email.

INVITING RESPONDENTS

The invitations to the potential respondents are typically sent in one of three ways:

○   *From the research agency, using email details supplied by the client and subject to data protection guidelines*

◯   *As emails from the client*

◯   *As survey links in some other client communication, such as a client e-newsletter*

From the research agency

The key to success in emailing a client's database is honesty, brevity, and clarity. The invitation should make it clear that the email is an invitation to take a survey and should make it easy for the recipient to click the link which ideally is fairly high up the page. Some people will be happy to click it as soon as they realise it is a survey, others will read on for more information.

The invitation needs to say who it is from, the details of the survey (how long it is and roughly what it is about), how they were selected (at the minimum the source of their email address), details of any incentive scheme, and a note of how the respondent can find out more about the research agency.

When the agency is sending the emails there are two choices: as a plain text email or as an HTML email. The benefits of the HTML option are that the email is more attractive, for example it can include company logos. The disadvantage is that many email systems either block or strip HTML emails. Some email systems have an option to send emails in parallel as both plain text and HTML; if the HTML version is going to fail the plain text version is promoted.

In most cases, the web survey system handles the emailing and creates a dynamically assigned unique URL for each respondent to control access to the survey.

Emails from clients

If the client is handling the emails the issue of how to protect access to the survey needs to be addressed. One option is to create unique URLs and pass these to the client to use. Another option is to create user names and passwords; however, this sometimes leads to people forgetting their usernames or passwords, or failing to type them in properly.

Survey links from client

Using a generic link to a survey is the least satisfactory option for securing interviews and results in the lowest response rate. As well as attracting a low response rate, it makes it more difficult to control access to the survey, for example to prevent people completing the survey more than once.

Two methods of controlling access are (a) using cookies, or (b) asking the respondent to enter some unique piece of information that can be verified, such as their customer ID.

DEALING WITH COMPLAINTS

Customers who have been contacted to conduct surveys sometimes raise questions relating to some unrelated topic (such as a product or service complaint) or request that they be removed from the company's mailing list.

Most research codes of conduct have provisions that complaints from customers can and should be passed on to the client. The best way of handling these complaints are to strip them out from the survey and forward them to the client, with an email message sent to the customer to say that their message has been forwarded to the client.

If a respondent asks to unsubscribe, then, in most cases, there is a legal requirement for them to be unsubscribed from the client's database. This tends to be handled in one of two ways. The best way is to forward the request to the client for them to unsubscribe the person, but what sometimes happens is that the customer is emailed a link to an unsubscribe page, which allows them to unsubscribe themselves.

MIXED-PURPOSE RESEARCH

When working with client databases there is a frequent temptation to use projects for both market research and other purposes, for example to increase the amount of information in the client's databases. This used to be impossible under most codes of conduct. However, more recently codes of conduct have permitted this provided that it is categorised as 'mixed purpose' or 'non-research purposes'.

Mixed-purpose research, where it is allowed, must ensure that it does not portray itself as being market research, it must not make any reference to research codes of conduct, nor to anonymous research, and must abide by relevant legislation (e.g. data protection legislation) and relevant codes of conduct (e.g. direct marketing codes of conduct).

RESPONSE RATES

One of the most common questions – and one of the hardest to give a definitive answer to – is the one that asks 'What sort of response rate should a survey using a client database achieve?' The first thing that complicates the answer is that it depends on the type of survey, whether the invite comes from the client or the agency, and what sort of relationship the people in the list have with the client. The second complication is that the response rate is not altogether defined in the context of a client database.

High and low response rates

As a very rough approximation the range of response rates runs from 5% to 25%. The lower end of this range tends to arise when the people on the database have a poor, or almost non-existent, relationship with the company running the research. The higher end of the scores (and a few are much higher than 25%) tend to occur when the people on the database have a very strong and positive relationship with the brand, where the survey invitation is attractive, and where the survey is short and engaging. Higher response rates also tend to be associated with databases that are up-to-date with dead records removed.

If a project achieves a response rate of less than 5% then it is worth investigating the following:

○ *Does the database contain a large number of dead or dormant records?*

○ *How many of the invitations bounced back?*

○ *How many of the invitations were opened?**

○ *Was the problem a low number of people clicking on the survey or was it that too many abandoned the survey?*

○ *Can the wording of the invite be made clearer or more appealing?*

○ *Can the survey be made easier, clearer, or more engaging?*

Calculating the response rate

The first step in calculating the response rate is to add up the number of people invited to take the survey. At first glance the researcher might think this was simply the number of invitations emailed out, but this ignores two issues:

1. How many of the listed email accounts are still active?

2. How many of the invitations were seen?

The first step in calculating the base is to discount any bounce backs (emails that were rejected by the domain or email system). The second step is to discount any 'Out of Office' messages that indicate that the recipient is likely to be away until after the close of the fieldwork date. However, it should be noted that the base will still be an overestimate since not all systems generate bounce backs, and it does not account for those people who are away and who do not set an out of office message.

As mentioned above, some researchers attempt to estimate the number of invitations that were opened (and which therefore had a chance to be read) by enclosing a web bug as part of the email.

---

*Some emailing systems can provide statistics on whether the emails were opened. They do this by including a web bug with the email. A web bug is typically a 1*1 pixel transparent image that is downloaded from a server as part of the email. The act of downloading triggers a counter in the email system. This approach is not foolproof and may have some ethical issues involved (at the very least the email should mention the use of it), but it can provide guidance on whether the email invitations are even being opened.

Once the base has been estimated, the calculation can move on to the outcomes. The three calculations that are normally made are:

1. **The invitation response rate**. The number of people who started the survey divided by the number who received the invitation.

2. **The survey response rate**. The number of people who finished the survey divided by the number who received the invitation.

3. **The completion rate**. The number of people who finished the survey divided by the number who started it.

In terms of assessing projects, the survey response rate is indicative of how likely the study is to be representative of the population (i.e. the whole database). The completion rate is a good indicator of how good – or bad – the survey is from the respondent's perspective. The invitation response rate is a combined indicator of the quality of the invitation and of the relationship between the client and the people on their database.

SUMMARY OF CLIENT DATABASES

Client databases can be an excellent and cost effective way of conducting a wide range of market research projects and can be far more representative than online access panels for some types of study, such as customer satisfaction and media tracking (if only the brand's media is being tracked). However, there are other types of study that are not suitable for client databases, for example those that compare the merits of a range of brands.

The key driver of the response rate of studies conducted via clients' databases is how good the relationship is between the client and the people on the list. If the list is used for a variety of contacts, and if it is easy for people to remove themselves from it, then the responses and the response rate will tend to be good. If the email addresses have simply been accumulated over time and are rarely used, then the responses are likely to be poor.

Private lists are in some cases morphing into either internal panels (panels owned by a client company and managed by them or a third party) or into online communities. In a few cases these panels have been expanded beyond being used by just the client, for example P&G's Tremor Panel which has become a leader in word of mouth marketing and is available to other companies.

IN-HOUSE PANELS

In-house panels are panels of people who have been recruited specifically to help a company or organisation improve the service it gives to its customers. These panels vary greatly in terms of size, sophistication, and organisation. Some panels have fewer than 500 members whereas many others are much larger. For example, Australian telecommunications company Telstra has 18 000 members on its MyTelstraExperience panel.

In-house or client panels differ from client databases in the following ways:

1.   They are owned by the research/insight function rather than the marketing/sales function.

2.   The target size for an internal panel is typically much smaller than the target size for a market-ing/sales/customer database.

3.   The members of a panel should know they are on a panel and will be approached for market research/insight/consultation/advice purposes

In-house panel members are described in lots of different ways. For example, they may be called members, advisors, consultees or a number of other names. Some panels are only used for internal research, i.e. research conducted by internal researchers; other panels are used by the agencies offer-ing research services to the company.

The primary drivers for companies creating in-house panels are cost savings, speed, and a sense of being more in control of insight generation.

The main downside of an in-house panel is that the panel will usually not be typical of the broader customer population. Members of an in-house panel may become identified with the brand and sen-sitised to research approaches. Other potential downsides to in-house panels include the workload in managing a panel, the cost of managing a panel, and the risk of setting panel member expectations too high.

The following sections look at some of the key issues that face organisations that operate an in-house panel, including:

  O   *How sophisticated?*

  O   *Who will manage/operate the panel?*

  O   *Not just surveys!*

  O   *Tips for using an in-house panel*

  O   *Summary of in-house panels*

HOW SOPHISTICATED?

At one extreme, an in-house panel might consist of little more than a list of people, a simple survey option (such as Survey Monkey), an email package, and a method for members to unsubscribe. More sophisticated panels use specialist panel management software.

The more sophisticated solutions have systems to handle sign-ups, unsubscribes, survey invitations, incentives, and panel management functions. Beyond this level of sophistication there is also the client online research community and client community enhanced panels, which are covered later in the book.

Simple options

If an organisation has a very small budget, or if the project is a low key or exploratory idea, then a simple approach may well be suitable. The implications of the simple approach are that surveys are likely to be very straightforward, drawing sub-samples (for example by demographics) will not be easy, and somebody will need to take care of the logistics, such as making sure that people who have requested an unsubscribe or who notified the panel of a change are dealt with.

One very important detail that will need attending to is data protection and security, for example, making sure that personal data is secure, encrypted, and only accessible to people authorised to access it and for purposes that have been authorised.

More sophisticated options

If an organisation wants to do more than send simple surveys to all of the members of its panel, then it is likely they will need a more sophisticated option. Such systems can offer the following features:

  ○   *ability to draw sub-samples, both randomly and to meet specific criteria*

  ○   *the handling of incentives*

  ○   *handling sign-ups to the panel, for example allowing sign-up links to be posted on websites*

  ○   *handling unsubscribe requests automatically*

  ○   *a range of services for sending invitations, reminders, messages, and newsletters to panel members*

  ○   *quota controls on the surveys*

  ○   *management information systems, for example reporting on response rates, average numbers of surveys per member, and payment history*

  ○   *qualitative options such as online focus groups and bulletin board groups*

  ○   *community features such as blogs, friends, user polls, and discussions*

Many of the leading web survey systems provide some or all of the features outlined above.

WHO WILL MANAGE/OPERATE THE PANEL?

The two main options are to either run the panel internally or commission a third party to run the panel on the company's behalf.

Running the panel internally

The main potential benefits of running the system internally are:

- ❍ *the cost savings, at least in pure cash terms*

- ❍ *the possibility of being more responsive to requests*

- ❍ *in some cases, providing more data security compliance*

Some of these benefits depend on whether the internal solution is going to be run by an IT/operations department or by the insight/research team. If the insight/research team runs the system then the costs are likely to be lower and the panel is likely to be responsive to its members. However, the panel is likely to be more limited and, if it is successful, then the research/insight team could easily be swamped by work and feedback.

Using a third party

If the panel is run by a third party, either a full service agency or a panel company, then the potential benefits include:

- ❍ *the ability to handle more work without overloading the insight/research team*

- ❍ *access to people with a strong background in panel management*

- ❍ *access to the latest thinking and the 'best in class' approaches*

However, the costs of third-party managed panels tend to be higher.

NOT JUST SURVEYS!

Until the late 1990s, in-house panels were mainly postal panels and the tendency was to use them in a very one dimensional way, i.e. to complete standard questionnaires, perhaps with some product placement or service experience. Online in-house panels open up a range of additional options, including:

- ❍ *online focus groups (or bulletin board groups), allowing topics to be explored more deeply*

- ❍ *photo projects, where a group of panel members are asked to use their mobile phones to take pictures and upload (or MMS) them*

○   *co-creation projects, which can range from simply voting on the name for a new flavour through to suggesting names and ideas to full-blown co-creation, either via collaboration systems such as wikis, or by getting a group of panel members together in a specific location*

○   *fun polls, i.e. single question surveys which display the answer as soon as a panel member has voted. In general, these are used more as a method of generating engagement for the panel members, but they can be also be used to provide almost instant answers to questions of the moment*

  Advice

TIPS FOR USING AN IN-HOUSE PANEL

Most of these points are the same issues as those for running an access panel, but in a few cases they are nuanced differently:

1.   Manage the expectations of the panel members from the outset. If you are only going to use the panel for quant surveys, and only about four times a year, do not sell the panel as a great fun-packed experience!

2.   Let the panel members know you value them and that they are making a difference. At the very least thank them for every contribution they make. Make sure that you are responsive to any contact panel members make with you and that you are prompt in your replies.

3.   Remember that the panel will, in most cases, tend to be skewed in favour of people who are knowledgeable, interested, and disproportionately attracted to the company's product. This means that the results are not directly projectable to the wider customer base. Many companies use their panels to generate and screen ideas, trusting the panel to reject poor suggestions. However, these companies will often test positive results with a more independent sample, particularly if the initiative involves risks, such as spending money.

4.   Even if you are using conventional incentives (e.g. cash or prizes), make sure you complement these extrinsic rewards with intrinsic rewards. Examples of intrinsic rewards are things like: information about upcoming events (e.g. TV advertising, product launches, sponsored events), visits to significant places (e.g. factories or breweries producing the product), and samples of new products before they hit the general market.

SUMMARY OF IN-HOUSE PANELS

In-house panels are such a good idea that it is surprising there are not more of them. The key benefits are that they can lower costs and speed up feedback loops. One major limitation of in-house panels is that they can consume large amounts of internal resources to manage, or require a contract to be placed with an external provider.

In-house panels are good for some research, such as idea screening, but unsuitable for other research, such as comparisons between brands.

Panels that are managed in-house tend to be smaller and less sophisticated. As panels become larger and their use more sophisticated, the benefits of having an external agency run the panel become larger.

The general trend in in-house panels, as with many forms of panels, is towards a greater community/ social nature, for example towards an online research community or a community enhanced panel.

SUMMARY OF WORKING WITH PANELS AND DATABASES

Most quantitative online research is conducted via online access panels, client databases, and in-house panels. Other options exist, but they represent a smaller proportion of quantitative surveys. Given that online quantitative is the leading modality for quantitative research, panels are becoming a core part of quantitative research and an essential tool for most market researchers in most markets.

Online access panels and in-house panels represent a major shift in the research paradigm, away from an approach based on random probability sampling towards one which is essentially convenience sampling.

Because of quality concerns an enormous amount of work has been put into improving the research industry's knowledge about how panels work and into finding the best ways to operate them. Key initiatives in this area include the ESOMAR 26 Questions, the ARF online quality initiative, and the new ISO standard for online access panels.

The key change that is happening in the area of panels and databases is towards an increased social or community focus. This trend tends to have two objectives, namely to increase panel member engagement (to help retain and motivate panel members) and to access a wider range of insights from the panel members.

5 Running an Online Survey and Summary

This chapter looks at the process of running an online quantitative research project. The main focus will be on market research projects using online access panels, although most of the material will be equally applicable to studies utilising client databases or other sources. The steps reviewed in this chapter are:

1.   Determining whether online is a suitable modality for the project

2.   Sourcing the sample

3.   Designing the survey

4.   Scripting and testing the survey

5.   Launching the fieldwork

6.   Monitoring the fieldwork

7.   Closing the job

8.   Analysis and reporting issues specific to online research

Note that this chapter does not review in any great depth those research steps which are common to all modalities, such as creating data tables and presentations. This chapter refers to some material dealt with in greater depth elsewhere in this book, for example questionnaire design.

After the steps above there is a brief summary, highlighting the key issues for researchers running online surveys.

DETERMINING WHETHER ONLINE IS A SUITABLE MODALITY FOR THE PROJECT

This step should apply equally to any data collection modality, but it is a topic more frequently discussed in the context of online research. In markets where online research is already established this step tends to operate as a negative test. Because online research is typically faster and cheaper, the question often becomes 'is there a reason *not* to use an online modality'.

Warning

Possible reasons not to use online are when:

- ○ *Online is slower or more expensive*

- ○ *The stimuli can't easily be rendered online*

- ○ *The study is highly confidential*

- ○ *The target sample is not online*

- ○ *The research topic is likely to interact with the online medium*

- ○ *There are comparability issues*

- ○ *The study requires a random probability sample*

These reasons are expanded on below.

ONLINE IS SLOWER OR MORE EXPENSIVE

Generally online modalities are cheaper and quicker than other modalities, but there are exceptions. The main exception is where a survey is very short and simple, and where the sample size is very small. For example, 100 interviews with housewives, asking 10 simple questions, might be faster and quicker via telephone. In some markets, even face-to-face might be cheaper and/or quicker.

THE STIMULI CAN'T EASILY BE RENDERED ONLINE

There is a wide range of stimuli that are not suitable for online surveys, such as taste, touch, and smell. Most sensory testing still has to be conducted face-to-face. Some research organisations have, however, had substantial success with posting products and other test materials to respondents, especially to panel members.

Over time the number of things that can be rendered online has increased, although this sometimes has implications for the sorts of PCs the respondents need to have and the bandwidth available.

THE STUDY IS HIGHLY CONFIDENTIAL

There are steps that can be taken to make it harder for respondents to download and share material from the survey. However, the risk cannot be completely removed. For example, somebody can always use their iPhone or similar to record what they see on the screen.

Equally, it should be kept in mind that even face-to-face interviews are not 100% secure, especially with the growth of smartphones.

THE TARGET SAMPLE IS NOT ONLINE

Even in markets where the internet penetration is very high (such as the Scandinavian countries where penetration is close to 90%), there are systematic differences between those who are online and those who are not. Generally, the people who are not online tend to be older, have lower incomes, and be more disadvantaged in terms of features such as housing, employment, and education opportunities.

If the purpose of the research is to explore a group that tends not to be online, then the online modality will tend to be unsuitable. For example, research amongst disadvantaged groups, such as the homeless, would not be suitable for an online survey.

THE RESEARCH TOPIC IS LIKELY TO INTERACT WITH THE ONLINE MEDIUM

Some topics are too closely associated with the internet as a medium to be researched via the internet. For example, a study of how people buy music CDs in stores is likely to be distorted by the fact that people who are not online buy all of their CDs in stores, whilst people online are likely to buy some or all of their CDs online, as well as download music and compare stores with online purchases.

COMPARABILITY ISSUES

The issue of moving a study online and possibly losing comparability is dealt with elsewhere in the book, but the loss of comparability with previous studies can be a reason why a study should not be conducted online.

If a study is being run in more than one country, online may not be available in all of the markets, so a decision might be made to use a methodology available in all the markets. However, it should be noted that in many cases there is no single modality that is suitable and available for all of the countries in a multi-country study. When conducting a general consumer study, online and telephone are not suitable for India, and door-to-door interviews are not suitable in Australia or the USA, so compromises often have to be made, especially to minimise costs.

THE STUDY REQUIRES A RANDOM PROBABILITY SAMPLE

Unless the whole population has internet access and the whole population can be identified then a random probability sample cannot be drawn. Examples of where these conditions are met include undergraduates at many universities (where the students all have email address with an academic domain, e.g. .ac.uk or edu.au), and visitors to a specific website or online service – eBay could sample eBay users, for example.

Public sector work sometimes requires that random probability sampling is used, as does some work designed to be used in court cases. However, even in these cases the researcher should remember that many authorities believe that if the response rate to a survey is below 70% the study does not meet the criteria for a random probability sample, even if the initial sample was adequately defined.

SOURCING THE SAMPLE

In most cases, the question is whether to use a client database or an online access panel. Both of these options are covered in depth in the previous chapter, so this section only briefly reviews the topic.

As a generalisation, if the client has a database, if it is suitable, and if it is available, that will be the best option. The database route will tend to be cheaper, will tend to avoid professional and highly sensitised respondents, and will directly reach customers.

However, for many types of studies a client database is not suitable, even if it exists and is available. Projects where it is inappropriate to reveal the sponsor of the research and projects where it is necessary to interview a cross section of consumers are both examples of surveys that are normally unsuitable for conducting via client databases.

The key to working with online access panels is to first rule out any that can't provide the right level of quality and service and then give the rest a very clear specification for the project in order to get accurate quotations.

DESIGNING THE SURVEY

The design of web surveys is dealt with in greater depth in Chapter 3. The survey should be designed to answer the research questions in the shortest and most engaging way consistent with the requirements of the project.

Very simple studies may be drafted online in the web survey system. However, most studies are drafted as a paper copy first and only scripted once the paper copy has been agreed. The paper copy may be drafted in a specialist package, but is often written in a word processor package such as Microsoft Word.

The design of an online survey is composed of two elements, both of which are important to get right. The first element is the same as face-to-face and telephone, i.e. designing an overall structure and specific questions that will answer the research question. The second element is the way that the survey appears on the respondent's screen to make sure it is clear and conveys the questions in the right way.

Many research agencies have quality procedures that require evidence that the client has 'signed off' the paper question.

SCRIPTING AND TESTING THE SURVEY

Online web surveys differ in their complexity. This variation stretches from the simplicity of a system like Survey Monkey through to more powerful systems such as Sawtooth Software's SSI Web product. Although there is no right or wrong way to organise scripting of surveys, in projects where the research company is scripting the survey in-house there are tendencies for:

(a)   larger companies to be more likely to have a dedicated scripting team, and

(b)   companies using less complex products, such as Zoomerang, are more likely to ask researchers to script their own surveys.

The mechanics of scripting the survey are largely dependent on the characteristics and features of the survey system being used and the way it is organised within a specific organisation. The two parameters that make scripting take longer are length and complexity (for example, logic and adaptive scripts). Of these two, complexity is more important than sheer length in terms of making the project take longer to script.

Once the scripting has been done the testing becomes the main issue and the following questions should be asked:

O   *Does the survey look right? This means, does it look right to the researcher, client, and ideally to some test respondents?*

O   *Is the logic of the survey correct? For example, are the right questions asked to the right respondents, with the right rotations, and with the correct selection of cells and concepts?*

O   *Is the survey storing everything that needs to be saved, and in the right format?*

Two steps that are useful in the testing process are:

1.   Print out a hard copy of the survey and go through the interview, crossing out each question on the paper survey when it appears and is checked. This will normally require several passes through the survey to check all the branches and adaptive options. Note this is a minimal check not an exhaustive one. It checks that every question appears and is *capable* of being correct, not that it will *always* be correct.

2. Many of the more sophisticated web survey systems have a method of generating randomised dummy interviews. Effectively, the software runs the survey repeatedly, picking responses at random, but within the ranges allowed by each question. After running a reasonable number of test interviews (for example, 5000) the collected data can be inspected. The first thing to check is that every break of every question has some data in it, and that the bulk of the data is where you would expect it to be. This system will also identify some types of logic and scripting error.

Many research agencies will have a quality gate or procedure that requires a formal sign-off by the client that the survey is correct. This is potentially unfair as the client can only test a few variations of the survey (there are many routes through a non-trivial survey, because of piping, randomisation, adaptive scripting, etc.), and a client would be advised to only sign off that they had checked the general 'look and feel' of the survey, but not that they had checked beyond that.

In projects using an online access panel, it will usually be necessary to get the panel company to review the survey and agree that it conforms to both their guidelines and the agreed specification for the project. Where the project is well designed, this is little more than a formality. However, if there are issues with the survey that require amendments, a three-way loop of client, agency, and panel can be created which might delay the start of the fieldwork.

LAUNCHING THE FIELDWORK

Once the testing process is complete and all the quality forms have been signed and filed, the fieldwork begins. When working with an online panel company this usually means asking them to send the invitations, but there can be a gap of several hours between requesting the launch and the first respondents arriving at the survey (indeed, sometimes there can be a gap of several hours between the panel exec authorising the launch and the first surveys arriving).

One key issue for the researcher is the phasing of the fieldwork. If the researcher (or panel company) were to send a large number of survey invitations it might be possible to conduct the fieldwork in a very short time, even in less than an hour. However, in most cases there are two good reasons why a researcher would avoid this.

1. The type of people who are online at the time the invite is sent may share some characteristics with each other that might also make them different from other people. For example, if the invitations are sent at, say, 3 pm on a mid-week day, the people who respond quickest to the survey are likely to include people who work (people do cyber-skive) and to exclude mothers of young children who are on the school run. Best practice is to ensure that the fieldwork is phased to include some weekdays and at least one weekend, for example, by running the survey from a Thursday through to a Tuesday.

2. If the survey contains an error, and if the fieldwork is completed very quickly, the researcher will have no chance to spot the problem and fix it. Therefore the best practice is to use what

is called a soft launch. A soft launch is where a modest number of invites is sent, with a view to collecting perhaps 20 to 50 completed interviews. These interviews (and the screen outs) are then reviewed to check whether everything seems to be working before a larger number of invites are sent out.

The timing of the project launch can have an impact on the response rate and on the ability of the researcher to deal with problems. The general consensus is that the best time to launch a survey is between 10:00 am and midday on a Tuesday, Wednesday, or Thursday. Mondays tend to be a busy day, with people tackling tasks and emails that came in over the weekend, and Friday runs into the weekend too easily. The mid-to-late morning is considered good because it is after most people have emptied their inboxes, and provides a chance for people to do the survey during their lunch hour.

Launching a survey in the late afternoon may result in a survey not being adequately monitored by the research team for the first few hours it is in the field, which is not a good idea. Launching a survey late on Friday is considered the worst time of all. First, it means that the survey has to be monitored on Friday evening and Saturday to see if anything goes wrong and therefore any problems will need to be put right on a Friday evening or on a Saturday. Also, if an email is not opened on Friday afternoon, it may remain in an inbox until Monday and then be lost with all the other emails received over the weekend.

 Advice

MONITORING THE FIELDWORK

One of the many ways that online research differs from face-to-face research, and even to CATI to some extent, is the degree to which the researcher can and should monitor the fieldwork. Amongst the things that the researcher should be monitoring are:

Errors. Does the survey crash? Have respondents sent in emails or other messages to say the survey has crashed or hung their machine?

Problems. These are often harder to spot than errors. One way to spot problems is to read the open-ended responses. Respondents will often mention problems in the open-ends; this is particularly true if the last question in the survey is something along the lines 'Is there anything else you would like to tell us about XXX or this survey? If so, please type your comments in the box below', (where XXX is the subject of the survey).

Paradata. Paradata refers to data about the process, as opposed to the data that is the subject of the process. The paradata for a project includes things like the length of the survey, the number of questions not answered, the average length of the open-ends and, crucially, abandonment rates and the questions at the point where the survey tends to be abandoned.

Quotas. Ideally, the quotas should complete at an even rate. If the easy quotas are being filled more quickly than the harder ones, the project can end up struggling to fill the harder quotas and potentially having to make compromises.

The data. By monitoring the data the researcher is looking to gain an understanding of the main issues being revealed and to assess whether the research is likely to answer the research questions. Examination of the data may also highlight areas where the survey can be improved. For example, if a noticeable number of respondents pick 'Other' for a specific question the researcher may consider adding additional pre-codes, based on the typed-in responses.

Analysis ideas. At the start of the project the researcher will usually have an idea how the data is going to be processed – for example, they will often have an idea of how the tables should be laid out. By using these ideas to shape the top-line reports the researcher can verify their ideas and improve the specification of the analysis.

REAL-TIME REPORTING AND MONITORING

In addition to monitoring the job from a project management point of view, many projects now enable real-time reporting for the client. This has two major implications for researchers:

1.   If the client is reading the data in real-time, the researcher has to either (a) monitor the live results, or (b) look ill-informed when the client notices some interesting dip or turn in the data. This is a lose–lose scenario for the researcher, because one option costs money and the other reduces the perception of 'value added' service.

2.   The assumption underlying real-time data reporting is that the data as collected is correct. However, at the processing stage the data is often tidied up, for example by removing suspect respondents and weighting the data – which can result in important differences between what the real-time reporting shows and what the final reports show.

Given that providing real-time reporting can involve higher costs, it would make sense that it was wanted or needed before including it in the design for a research project.

CLOSING THE JOB

Compared with most other data collection modalities, the closing of an online job contains more steps, the key ones being:

1.   The web survey system needs to be told the survey is closed, which will in turn cause it to present a 'survey closed' message to any potential respondent who tries to access it.

2.   The panel company needs to be told that the survey is closed so that they do not send any more invitations and remove it from any internal listing that might be forwarded to respondents to the survey.

3.   The data should be cleaned to remove or separate any personally identifiable information. For example, it is not unusual for respondents in an online study to type their name and/ or contact information into open-ended fields as part of a request for help or assistance (especially if the survey has been conducted via a client database).

4.   The data for analysis is locked down (to avoid accidental edits), archived, and made available to whoever is conducting the analysis.

5.   If incentives are being used, and if they are being handled by the research agency (which is often the case with client databases but is not often the case with online access panels), these need to be actioned, in accordance with the terms and conditions of the incentive procedure.

ANALYSIS AND REPORTING ISSUES

This section covers those analysis and reporting issues which are either unique to online research or which are particularly relevant to online research. The items covered in this section are:

- *Editing, coding, cleaning, and statistically adjusting*

- *Analysis*

- *Reporting*

EDITING, CODING, CLEANING, AND STATISTICALLY ADJUSTING

The first stage of the analysis is the classic process of editing, coding, cleaning, and statistically adjusting the data, but without the transcribing process that is typically associated with postal and face-to-face surveys. In terms of traditional research methodologies, these processes are well described by Malhotra (2007).

In terms of online data collection, the specific implications of these four phases of the initial data analysis are set out below.

Editing and cleaning

In classic market research, for example face-to-face, paper-and-pencil data collection the editing phase relates to processing paper questionnaires and the cleaning stage relates to processing computer files. In an online modality there are no paper questionnaires, so it makes sense to think of combining the editing and cleaning processes into one. It should also be noted that some of the steps that some authors would ascribe to the data analysis phase are often conducted during fieldwork in an online survey.

Issues that relate particularly, but not uniquely, to online surveys are:

Missing data. If the survey did not use forced completion, it may contain missing data, i.e. there are respondents who reached the end of the survey but who did not answer every question. If this is the case, the researcher needs to decide which respondents to keep and which to discard, for example by specifying a minimum percentage of questions that must be answered or by specifying key questions that must be completed.

Incomplete surveys. In most cases market researchers use only completed surveys for their studies, rejecting those where the respondent did not finish the survey, i.e. incomplete surveys. However, there are cases where the researcher may choose to include incomplete surveys. One special case is where some of the respondents appear to have closed their browser on the last page, rather than clicking the Next/Submit button, resulting in their answers for the last page being lost (ideally the design of the survey should prevent information being lost in this way). Another special case, in the eyes of some researchers, are surveys such as website satisfaction studies where the less satisfied respondents are less likely to bother to finish the survey. Ignoring these less satisfied respondents might introduce a larger bias than including the incomplete responses.

Rogue respondents. Some respondents may have completed the survey too quickly, some may have 'straight-lined' the survey (i.e. simply clicked straight down the page to complete the survey quickly), some may have answered questions inconsistently, and some may have typed comments into the open-end questions which indicate that they did answer the survey in good faith. Rogue respondents require identifying and deleting from the data. If the study was conducted via an online access panel there may be a protocol for reporting rogue respondents back to the panel, which may in turn result in them not receiving their incentive and potentially being removed from the panel or even blacklisted across a number of panels.

Back filling. Depending on how the survey has been scripted, there may be inconsistencies in the responses caused by confusion with the interface and questions. For example, if somebody picks an item as their 'most frequently bought' item they may not have also selected it on their list of 'ever heard of', or 'buy occasionally'. Ideally, these problems should be avoided by the use of adaptive scripting. Back-filling or back-coding is the process of editing the data to ensure that people's responses are consistent.

Coding

Coding the open-ends from an online survey is very similar to completing the same task with other modalities. Two differences worth mentioning, however, are that (a) the task can be distributed, potentially around the world, via the internet and (b) sometimes the coding can take place during fieldwork.

Statistically adjusting

The processes for statistically adjusting the data from online surveys are similar to those for other modalities. Typically they include weighting the data, and occasionally processes such as the standardisation of rating scales or advanced analytics such as the calculation of conjoint utilities.

ANALYSIS

There are a number of analysis options that can be integrated with online data collection tools, as described in Chapter 2, Web Survey Systems. But in most cases the analysis of the response data from an online project does not differ from those of other methodologies.

One area where online modalities create an extra dimension is paradata, i.e. data about the process. The paradata from a project can include a wide range of information and a cross-section of the possible data is shown in the list below:

- *day and time that the survey was conducted*

- *the length of the survey, in terms of minutes taken to complete it*

- *the type of browser and operating system the respondent was using*

- *the screen size the respondent was using*

- *the number of characters typed into open-ended response questions*

These variables may be associated with differences in the data and it is usually worthwhile checking for their impact during the analysis of online data. For example, do daytime people have different views to people who respond at night, or are people who complete the survey quickly different to people who take longer?

REPORTING

There has been a growth in online reporting systems, as described in Chapter 2, Web Survey Systems. However, in most cases the reporting of online data collection is very much the same as for other modalities, since offline data can also be reported via online reporting systems.

The main additional reporting element that online surveys have introduced is real-time reporting.

SUMMARY OF RUNNING AN ONLINE SURVEY

This short section pulls together the key points made during the chapter.

The key step is checking that online is a suitable modality for the project. Because it tends to be cheaper and faster in most markets it is the default decision, but there are plenty of situations where it is not appropriate, for some topics, for some products, for some target groups, and in some countries.

The key to success in working with the people supplying your sample, especially if the sample is coming from an online access company, is to contact them early, tell them everything that might help them do their job, and listen to what they say and suggest.

Keep the survey design as short and engaging as possible, consistent with meeting the aims of the project. If the study is non-trivial, try to get as much detail as possible agreed between the client and the researcher before the scripting starts.

Use a variety of approaches in the testing process, including creating randomised respondent responses. Use a soft launch to check that the survey is functioning as expected.

Spread the fieldwork over, at least, the weekend and some weekdays, for example starting the study on a Thursday and finishing the following Tuesday to mitigate biases.

Actively monitor the job whilst it is in the field. For example, check whether the easy quotas are filling up much more quickly than the harder ones, and if they are talking to the sample provider. Check the open-ends and the paradata for indications of errors or problems. Monitor the data to help better specify the analysis.

From the start to the finish of the job, keep an eye out for data protection and privacy issues.

SUMMARY OF DATA COLLECTION MODALITIES

This final section about online quantitative survey research looks across the key modalities used to collect quantitative data and highlights their key differences and implications. This approach helps set online in a clear context, highlighting what is the same and what is different.

In 2008, according to the ESOMAR Global Market Research 2009 report, it was estimated that quantitative survey research accounted for about 55% of all market research. Of that 55%, online accounts for about 39% (i.e. 20% of all research spend), with telephone just behind at 33%, face-to-face at 22%, and postal at 9% (i.e. 5% of all research spend).

The three things that the share of quantitative research data highlights are:

1.   Online quantitative research, especially via online access panels, has become the largest single modality of data collection.

2.   Online quantitative research is still growing as a share of all quantitative research, partly within countries where it is already strong, partly as new countries catch up.

3.   The majority of survey research is not conducted online; the total of face-to-face, telephone, and mail is larger, globally, than online.

The implication of these three points is that most researchers need to master online techniques but they can't yet disregard other data collection modalities. Indeed, if and when new approaches develop – such as mobile research – online may never be the only approach that researchers need to understand.

INTERVIEWER

The main issue that divides the modalities is the presence or absence of an interviewer. This difference is crucial in many ways. Respondents tend to prefer surveys with an interviewer, especially when the interviewer is physically present as in a face-to-face survey (note, this does not mean that *all* respondents prefer interviewer moderated surveys, simply that research has shown that most do).

When using interviewer moderated methods, one advantage is that, if there are problems with the survey, the interviewer can explain, help, probe, and ensure that messages about problems are relayed back to the project team.

With self-completion modalities (for example, online and postal) nobody sees the respondent. Are they who they say they are? Are they concentrating appropriately? Are they confused? However, on the other hand, there is considerable evidence that people are more honest when there is not an interviewer present and, of course, the cost is less without an interviewer.

SAMPLING

The key historic issue about sampling was whether it approximated to random probability sampling. Random probability sampling is based on an assumption that the population is known and that every member of the population has a known, non-zero, chance of being selected. If a sample is a random probability sample (or could be made to behave like one through the use of techniques such as weighting) then, subject to sampling error, results from the sample could be projected to the population.

If a sample is not a random probability sample then the results cannot be projected to the population directly. With non-probability sampling the researcher has to adopt an alternative strategy, such as one of the following:

(a)   Use an alternative technique to link the sample to the population, for example propensity weighting (for more information see http://www.schonlau.net/publication/03socialscience computerreview_propensity_galley.pdf), or by establishing a modelled link, for example experience may indicate that a score of X in the sample equates to a Y share of purchase in the real market.

(b)   Assume that the movements in the sample, from one wave to another or from one test to another, reflect changes in the population, even if the absolute values may not reflect the population. Much brand and ad tracking is based on this assumption.

(c)   Assume that the sample is a reasonable proxy for the population. Quite often the face validity of this approach is improved by using quotas to make some key characteristics of the sample match the population, for example age, gender, and income.

(d)   Adopt alternative sampling approaches, borrowed from qualitative research, such as triangulation, confirming and disconfirming cases, and maximum variation sampling.

(e)   Use techniques that are not based on sampling at all, such as prediction markets.

Although traditional market research has, since the 1930s, been built on an assumption of random probability sampling, in most cases the reality has been very different. If there is a significant proportion of people who can't be reached by whatever medium has been used for the research (for example people who do not have a landline, or who tend to be out a lot), or if there is a significant proportion of the population who decline to do a survey, then non-response bias can render random probability sampling, and its implications for representativeness and projectability, worthless. Views differ, but it is safe to assume that if the response rate is less than 70%, then the study is not approximating to a random probability sample. This means that most face-to-face and telephone commercial research has not approximated to a random probability sample for many years.

Most online research is conducted via online access panels, and online access panels are clearly not a method of random probability sampling. The shift by market research to using panels is a shift from a claim of using random probability sampling to using convenience samples.

It is worth noting that online research conducted with client databases (or via visitors to a website) might approximate to random probability sampling if (a) the database or the website visitors are the relevant population, and (b) if the response rate is high enough.

Face-to-face data collection tends to come in two main varieties, door-to-door and central location. In some countries both methods are prevalent, in other countries only one will apply. For example, in North America and Australia, face-to-face is very rarely conducted door-to-door. Door-to-door studies can be constructed so as to approximate to a random probability sample, if the response rate is high enough. Central location testing is not capable of approximating to a random probability sample, and usually relies on the sample being a reasonable proxy, e.g. by quota controlling for variables that are felt to be key.

For a while, and in some markets (such as Australia and the USA), telephone research was able to claim a semblance of random probability sampling. In markets where more than 90% of households had a telephone, and as a result of the development of RDD (Random Digit Dialling), only response rates stood between the researcher and a credible claim of random probability sample. However, due to the growth of mobile (cell) phones telephone research has lost its ability to assert that it is representative, except in those cases where it is able to include mobile phone users as well as the users of fixed lines (a growing number of companies are reporting that they can survey mobile phones as well as fixed lines).

Postal research has declined in importance over recent years and the ESOMAR Global Research figures for 2008 show it as accounting for only a quarter as much spend as online. In most markets it is possible to construct a sample frame for postal research that would be representative of the general population. The key limitation in terms of achieving a representative sample is non-response, which in most market research surveys result in fewer than 70% of surveys being returned (usually a lot less than 70%).

STIMULI

The four data collection modalities being reviewed here have very different implications for the kind of stimulus material that can be used.

In the early days of online research most surveys were restricted to simple text, some colour, and perhaps a low resolution graphical image or two. The limiting factors were the software being used and, even more critically, the speed of most people's connection to the internet. With the advent of widely available broadband (in many markets), good software, new options (such as Flash), the range of stimulus material that can be used includes pictures, audio, movies, and interactive tasks. In terms of what cannot be used online, the most notable are smell, taste, touch, and detailed pictures (for example, an A4 photo can clearly show twenty cars on a show card, but most screens struggle to show more than eight, because of size and definition. A computer screen rarely shows more than 100 pixels per inch, a photo will typically have many more pixels per inch).

Two limiting factors in terms of stimuli for online surveys are:

(a)   people who complete the survey whilst at work, where both sound and movies may be inappropriate, and

(b)   the rise in the number of people who are completing their surveys via smartphones (such as iPhones) and who therefore have smaller screens.

Face-to-face data collection, particularly central location testing, presents the widest range of stimuli that can be used. However, it should be noted that some face-to-face formats are quite limited, for example when conducting in-street interviewing using a clipboard, paper and pencil. In terms of face-to-face interviewing, the introduction of CAPI (Computer Aided Personal Interviewing) extended the range of stimuli that could be used in face-to-face interviewing, for example by making it easier to show media files.

Telephone surveys have the most limited range of stimuli that can be readily used. In a typical survey the interviewer reads the questions to the respondent, who then gives their answer. This means that the questions and prompts cannot be too complex, which is why conjoint analysis is normally considered unsuitable for telephone research. Audio files (for example a radio advert) are suitable for telephone surveys.

Most postal surveys are very limited in the stimuli they use; they tend to be a printed questionnaire, possibly with an image or two. However, some researchers have used postal surveys with much more complicated stimuli, including scratch and sniff cards, DVDs, and products to use and test.

ADAPTIVE

Survey modalities vary in the degree to which the survey can 'adapt' to the respondent. The most adaptive interviews are those computer administered surveys which are scripted to adapt the lists, stimuli, and questions based on earlier responses. Computer administered surveys can be online, telephone (in which case it is CATI – computer aided telephone interviewing), and face-to-face (in which case it is CAPI – computer aided personal interviewing).

Online surveys can be, and often are, adaptive. Unless face-to-face surveys are computer administered the degree of adaptivity is limited to procedures such as skip patterns and rotations.

When telephone surveys are computer administered they can be adaptive. If a telephone survey is not computer administered then the adaptivity will be limited to simple options such as skip patterns and rotations.

Postal surveys represent the least adaptive modality. Surveys may contain instructions such as "If yes, skip to question 12 on page 3", but respondents are often poor at complying with these instructions.

SUMMARY OF DIFFERENCES

Table 5.1 summarises the key differences between the leading data collection modalities for quantitative research.

Table 5.1

	Online	**Face-to-face (paper & pencil)**	**Telephone**	**Postal**
Interviewer	Self-completion.	Interviewer mediated.	Interviewer mediated.	Self-completion.
Sampling	Tends to be via access panel, hard to claim random probability sampling, subject to response rate concerns.	Door-to-door may be able to claim random probability sampling. Central location cannot claim random probability sampling	RDD may be able to claim random probability sampling, subject to response rate and coverage concerns.	Can claim to use random probability sampling, subject to response rate concerns.
Stimuli	Video, audio, medium resolution images, interactive materials.	Can include video/ taste/smell/high definition images.	Just that which can be conveyed by the spoken word, plus recorded audio/music.	Usually just text or text and photos, however, can include products, scratch'n'sniff, DVDs etc.
Adaptive	Scripts can be adaptive.	Not adaptive.	If computer aided then scripts can be adaptive.	Not adaptive.

PART II

Qualitative Research

For most of the last fifteen years, and for most researchers, the term 'online qualitative research' has meant online focus groups and, to a lesser extent, bulletin board groups, with a modest nod towards email groups and online depth interviews.

More recently, since about 2006, there has been an explosion of interest in the use of social media for market research and much of this interest uses techniques or methods that are wholly or partly qualitative, including e-ethnography, text analysis, and online research communities (also known as MROCs).

Social media is the subject of Part III of this book. Therefore, this section focuses on online qualitative research from a pre-social media perspective. The term 'pre-social media' has been taken to include online focus groups and bulletin board groups, along with a number of other approaches such as the remote viewing of focus groups and the qualitative enhancement of online quantitative research.

This part of the book is structured into the following four chapters:

- Overview of online qualitative research
- Online focus groups
- Bulletin board groups and parallel IDIs (in-depth interviews)
- Other online qualitative methods and summary of online qualitative research

6 Overview of Online Qualitative Research

This chapter provides an overview of what online qualitative research is, who is using it, its strengths and weaknesses, and why it has not taken off to the extent that online quantitative research has. The chapter is divided into the following topics:

○ *Defining qualitative and quantitative market research*

○ *The growth and scale of online qualitative research*

○ *Introduction to online qualitative techniques*

○ *Synchronous and asynchronous approaches*

○ *International projects and differences*

DEFINING QUALITATIVE AND QUANTITATIVE MARKET RESEARCH

For most of the history of market research, the difference between qualitative and quantitative research has been a bit like good art – hard to put into words but usually easy to recognise when you see it. However, the internet is beginning to challenge the old certainties. Quantitative studies are becoming more collaborative, qualitative projects are beginning to generate vast amounts of data (where the term 'data' is used in its broadest sense to include text, pictures, video, speech, objects etc).

Traditionally, researchers have taken the process of enumerating as quantitative and the processes of talking, listening, watching, and reading as qualitative. However, it is increasingly useful to be more precise about the definitions of qualitative and quantitative, particularly when dealing with internet-related approaches.

The key differences between quantitative and qualitative methodologies can be defined as follows:

(a) If an analysis **should** produce the same result when two trained practitioners apply the same method to the data, with the same processing steps, then the method is quantitative. The significance of this is that the results depend on the data and the method, not the operator.

(b)   If (a) is not true, but the analysis is based on an accepted theory of investigation or knowledge, then it is qualitative. The results depend on the data, the method, **and** the interpretation of the researcher.

(c)   If neither (a) nor (b) is true, then it is neither a quantitative nor qualitative method and should not be treated as market research.

To take an analogy from medicine: determining somebody's blood pressure is a quantitative process, deciding if they have a specific psychiatric condition is qualitative, and hanging a crystal over their head to check that their aura is healthy is just mumbo jumbo, it is neither qualitative nor quantitative.

The definitions above allow the following research approaches to be defined as qualitative:

○   *focus groups, including both offline and online focus groups*

○   *depth interviews, often referred to as IDIs (in-depth interviews), conducted face-to-face, via telephone, or online*

○   *bulletin board groups, an asynchronous technique that does not have a close equivalent in offline qualitative*

○   *semiotics, the study of signs and symbols, which applies equally to the offline and online worlds*

○   *observational qualitative research: offline this approach includes accompanied shopping and online it includes accompanied browsing. By contrast, observational quantitative research includes scanner data, counting footfall, and website analytics*

○   *ethnography, i.e. observing people's lives. Offline, ethnography is increasingly being associated with video ethnography. Online, the term 'ethnography' is morphing to include watching what people do in social media, virtual worlds, and in their real life as captured by a variety of devices, such as webcams, mobile phones, and PDAs.*

○   *blog and buzz mining, i.e. searching the discourse that people have posted on the web. Until this can be fully automated these techniques are mostly qualitative. The only aspects that are quantitative are the very simple approaches, such as counting the frequency of words, or enumerating the use of a set of emoticons, which are quantitative, but limited*

○   *online discussions, for example in online communities, are qualitative, but there are also quantitative activities associated with online communities, such as surveys.*

At present, very large amounts of qualitative data, for example the hundreds of thousands of discussions that can be investigated via blog mining, are still qualitative. The only quantitative use of this data at the moment is very limited in scope, for example word counts and tag clouds.

THE GROWTH AND SCALE OF ONLINE QUALITATIVE RESEARCH

When online qualitative first broke onto the scene in the 1990s, there was widespread discussion about the merits of online focus groups and very different views about the likely uptake of the use of online qualitative. The picture has become clearer over the past 15 years and the growth of online qualitative research has not matched the growth in online quantitative research.

Quantitative research has increased from its first stirrings in the late 1990s to become the dominant global modality in just ten years. By contrast, online qualitative, in all its different forms, is still only a tiny percentage of the total of qualitative research although, as Part III will explain, this may be about to change.

One indication of the scale of online qualitative was given in May 2009 in a press release from Itracks (a leading player in the world of online qualitative research), which announced that they had recently conducted their 10 000th online focus group (and by November 2009 the number had passed 11 000). Whilst this is a large number in absolute terms, it is small compared with the number of conventional, face-to-face focus groups conducted over the same period of time.

Looking at the available data, for example from ESOMAR, it is unlikely that, globally, online qualitative accounts for more than about 4% of all qualitative research. By comparison, online quantitative research accounts globally for more than a third of all survey research.

The situation can be summarised as being one where there is a lot of online qualitative research going on, but it is a very small part of the qualitative total, and an even smaller part of the online research total (which is mostly quantitative).

REASONS FOR LACK OF GROWTH

The reasons for the lack of growth in online qualitative research are dealt with more fully later in the next section on specific techniques. However, there are two key reasons that are worth listing at this stage which help explain why online qualitative research has grown so much less than online quantitative during the last 15 years.

1. The cost and speed benefits of online qualitative were not as big an advantage in online qualitative as they were in online quantitative. Before the widespread adoption of online data collection, the cost of quantitative research was largely about the cost of surveys. Making surveys cheaper provides a major benefit. However, qualitative research is mostly about the researcher, so making the respondents cheaper does not provide as much benefit as it does in quantitative research.

2. Very few leading qualitative researchers embraced online qualitative. Indeed, many were hostile to it because they felt the absence of the non-verbal and physical side of focus groups was too big a loss. By contrast, online quantitative had key opinion leaders and clients promoting it.

The evidence

The evidence about online qualitative is covered more fully in Chapters 7 and 8. However, it is important to note that where comparative studies have been conducted they have generally found that online qualitative research produces similar business findings to conventional qualitative research. This clearly only applies to types of research that can be conducted online, i.e. not including those requiring taste, touch, smell, etc.

However, the evidence appears to have had little impact on many of the people arguing against online qualitative research, who have mostly based their arguments on theoretical rather than experiential positions.

It is also worth noting that many of the key benefits highlighted by the advocates of online qualitative research are not seen as core issues by many of their opponents, for example geographically dispersed respondents, immediate and complete transcripts, and the ability to exclude problematic respondents.

INTRODUCTION TO ONLINE QUALITATIVE TECHNIQUES

The next three chapters look at specific techniques in online qualitative research, so this chapter serves as an introduction and overview. This section sets out some terms and definitions so that we can move ahead with an agreed understanding of the language employed.

Online focus groups. Online focus groups, also known as OLFGs, are the internet equivalent of traditional offline focus groups, using specialised chat software to bring people to a designated website to conduct discussions. The paradigm for an online focus group is very similar to that of face-to-face groups, albeit with the loss of the physical contact and without the intimacy of a face-to-face group.

Bulletin board groups. Bulletin board groups (also known as bulletin board focus groups – BBGs, and BBFGs) take place over time and are therefore based on a different paradigm than focus groups, more considered thoughts and less top of mind. In bulletin board groups people make their comments when it suits them and with the benefit of more time, i.e. more time to think and more time to reflect.

Email groups. Email groups (also known as moderated email groups or MEGS) are group discussions conducted via the simple mechanism of email. Email groups were the first online qualitative research to appear, but they are now quite rare.

Virtual worlds. Virtual worlds, such as Second Life, create some interesting possibilities for virtual research. However, these developments have been somewhat held up by the failure of virtual worlds to take off amongst mainstream internet users.

Parallel IDIs. These online in-depth interviews (often referred to as IDIs) are a method of conducting multiple depth interviews in parallel. Typically, parallel IDIs are conducted using bulletin board software, modified so that the respondents cannot see each other's contributions. The moderator of parallel IDIs can speak to all the respondents, and read what all the respondents are saying, without the respondents being aware of the other respondents. Conventional depth interviews can also be conducted via the internet in the same way as they can via the telephone, for example using online chat, Skype, or instant messaging.

- **Qualitative explication of quantitative surveys.** Although quantitative research has included open-ended questions from its inception, the internet has enabled a wider range of qualitative feedback and explication to be added to quantitative surveys. These extensions to quantitative surveys include tools such as allowing users to annotate online images, capturing comments via webcams, and using post-survey portals.

- **Remote viewing of physical groups.** The internet can be used to stream video from a conventional face-to-face group to observers who can be anywhere around the world using broadband internet connections, supplemented with systems for tagging and archiving.

SYNCHRONOUS AND ASYNCHRONOUS APPROACHES

When reviewing online qualitative research, many researchers draw a major distinction between synchronous and asynchronous approaches. In synchronous techniques (also known as real-time techniques), the researcher and the respondents are online at the same time. An online focus group is an example of a synchronous technique. Synchronous techniques are the closest analogy that online has for the way that most qualitative research is conducted offline, which tends to be via face-to-face focus groups and physical and telephone depth interviews.

Asynchronous techniques are those where the researcher and the respondents do not need to be online at the same time, for example bulletin board groups or email groups. Diaries are an example of an offline research technique that is asynchronous, but offline is overwhelmingly synchronous.

Asynchronicity has become one of the key trends of modern society, far beyond the world of just market research. For example, asynchronicity underpins 24-hour shopping, disintermediation (for example, the way that ATMs have replaced bank tellers, and websites have replaced travel agents), time-shifted TV viewing, and the shift from broadcast to podcast. Citizens increasingly want to do things at a time that suits them, not at times that suit others.

The first online qualitative technique that arrived on the scene was the introduction of email groups, which was an asynchronous technique but only occasionally used. The next was the development of a synchronous technique, the online focus group. This was followed by the asynchronous bulletin board group, which in many ways was the forerunner of the online research community (also known as an MROC).

Although there will always be a role for both synchronous and asynchronous techniques, the strongest market research developments over the last few years, in both quantitative and qualitative research, have been in asynchronous approaches, and this is expected to continue in the foreseeable future.

One of the key differences between synchronous and asynchronous qualitative approaches is the shift from top of mind to considered responses. Asynchronous approaches allow researchers to tap into consideration, reflection, and maturation.

INTERNATIONAL PROJECTS AND DIFFERENCES

One of the attractions of online research is its ability to work across international borders and to improve the central administration of projects. However, as well as solving some issues the internet introduces additional challenges. Some of the issues that need to be considered are:

O   *The loss of local partners. Even in studies where there are no apparent language issues, there can be cultural or generational issues that are not apparent when viewed from afar.*

O   *The translation costs for online qualitative projects can be very high, especially for asynchronous projects where the translation process tends to be small and often.*

O   *There can be a temptation to use English for too many projects. In most countries there are some people who speak English, or who can read and write English. It is often possible to run an international online qualitative project in English, but it is not always a good idea.*

On the other hand, the cost and time savings in conducting international online qualitative research can sometimes be large enough to make a project viable, i.e. it could be the difference between doing or not doing the research.

KEY COUNTRY AND CULTURAL DIFFERENCES

The notes below are based on generalisations. This means that there is enough truth in them to make them of value, but there are enough exceptions to make them dangerous! Most of these observations relate to traditional qualitative research as much as they do to online qualitative research, but they tend to be more important online as there may not be a local partner 'educating' the international researcher. The context of this section relates to what an online researcher needs to be aware of, especially as the internet creates the illusion that research can easily and safely be conducted internationally without the involvement of local researchers and without specialist knowledge.

Issues that are tackled in this section include:

O   *Europe and North America*

O   *Recruiting participants*

O   *Online versus offline honesty*

○   *Size of groups*

○   *Conformity to a plan*

○   *Counting and voting in groups*

Europe and North America

Although concentrating on Europe and North America is a simplification, it can be justified in terms of the proportion of market research currently conducted in these two regions. The data collected by ESOMAR in the 2009 Global Market Research report indicated that 49% of the global research total (in terms of value) is conducted in Europe, with a further 30% conducted in North America. The next highest total, at the moment, is Asia Pacific with 11%. Not only is the total in Asia Pacific much smaller, but the countries and cultures are much more differentiated than they are in Europe or North America, i.e. it is even more unsafe to generalise about Asia Pacific.

Therefore, the notes below focus on differences in conducting online qualitative between Europe and North America, with references to other markets where available.

Recruiting participants

The big demarcation in the recruitment of participants (i.e. online respondents in qualitative projects) is whether or not they tend to be recruited from panels (either online access panels or specialist qualitative panels). The alternative is to recruit participants via recruiters or from a client's customer database.

As a generalisation, North America is more willing to accept recruitment from panels and Europe is less willing, but there are North American researchers who reject it and there are European researchers who are happy to recruit from panels.

The willingness to recruit qualitative participants from panels has a direct impact on the attractiveness of online qualitative research. Online qualitative, when combined with recruitment from online panels, is more likely to generate speed and cost advantages. Online qualitative when combined with traditional recruiting practices, for example free finding sample, tends not to show significant cost and speed advantages.

Online versus offline honesty

Although there are plenty of researchers who have wondered aloud about whether respondents online are more inclined to fib, there is little support for their concerns from the studies that have been conducted. Some studies suggest that, for some topics, people may be willing to be more honest online, and that some age groups may be more willing to be honest online (Herbert 2001).

A study in 2009 investigated the views of online community participants in Australia, New Zealand, China, and Japan, and in both China and Japan the view from the participants was that it was easier to be honest online because they were less subject to social pressures (Poynter et al., 2009).

Size of groups

There is no agreed consensus for how big an offline or online focus group should be. The span seems to run from about four (sometimes called mini-groups) through to about fourteen.

As a generalisation, offline (i.e. face-to-face) focus groups in North America tend to be larger than those in Europe. Wendy Gordon refers to ten to twelve participants as being common in the USA, with six to eight being more common in the UK (Gordon, 1999). Gordon also highlights that the USA offline model is more likely to be round a table, whereas in the UK it is more typical to see soft chairs or sofas.

Hy Mariampolski refers to USA offline groups as likely to comprise eight to ten participants, and refers to European groups as being more likely to have six to eight members (Mariampolski, 2001). Mariampolski also draws attention to differences in the length of focus groups, with a typical offline group in the USA being two hours, whereas in Europe the groups tend to be longer, perhaps two to three hours. Gordon highlighted that the UK also had shorter (two hour) groups and that an individual moderator running two groups in one evening was not uncommon.

However, despite there being little agreement about the size and length of offline groups, there is a general view that online groups should be smaller than offline groups, both in Europe and North America, and that online groups should be shorter, typically about one hour.

Conformity to a plan

Qualitative researchers differ in terms of how closely they stick to a specific plan or discussion guide. For some researchers the discussion guide is a short list of topic headings and perhaps some prepared stimuli. For others, the discussion guide can be a multi-page document, potentially including the complete wording of questions.

As a generalisation, qualitative research in North America tends to stay closer to the plan, whereas many qualitative researchers in Europe adhere to the plan more loosely (but there are plenty of counter examples, both ways).

In most cases, online qualitative research, especially online focus groups, tends to stick relatively closely to the plan or discussion guide. The words on the screen are all that the participants see, the text has to do all the work that the face-to-face moderator would aim to achieve with voice, body, intonation, and situation. Similarly, when the analysis of an online group is conducted, it is done so in terms of the specific words used by the researcher/moderator. Many online qualitative researchers write every question and probe they expect to use as part of the session in the discussion guide.

Counting and voting in groups

One phenomenon that is very rare in European face-to-face qualitative, but which is not uncommon in North America, is the practice of asking a question to the group and asking them to vote (for example by raising their hands), and then recording the answers.

Fully-featured online focus group and bulletin board group software tends to have built-in features that allow participants to vote and answer surveys, and this reflects the fact that some researchers want to include this voting as part of their research method.

It is perhaps interesting to note that, although the issue of voting in online focus groups and bulletin board groups is still considered divisive, there is broad agreement that using polls and surveys within online research communities is a useful feature to have available.

7 Online Focus Groups

Online focus groups (also known as OLFGs or OFGs) are the online equivalent of traditional face-to-face focus groups (also known as in-person groups). As in a traditional focus group, a small number of people are pre-recruited and meet in a nominated (online) place; the moderator leads the discussion, using a discussion guide, with a view to drawing insight from the interactions and contributions of the members of the group.

This chapter runs through the following topics:

○ *Introduction to online focus groups: the characteristics of an online focus group and how they differ from face-to-face focus groups*

○ *Running an online focus group: what needs to be prepared and the moderator's role*

○ *Choosing an online focus group solution: looking at the issues that should be taken into account when choosing a system*

○ *The arguments for and against online focus groups: why they have not been more successful, why some people dislike them, and why some people like them*

○ *Resources for online focus groups: a range of resources for online focus groups*

○ *A summary of online focus groups: a guide to the key characteristics of online focus groups and some key points for using them*

INTRODUCTION TO ONLINE FOCUS GROUPS

Online focus groups are the online equivalent of traditional, face-to-face focus groups, replicating many of the features familiar to qualitative researchers.

In the early days of conducting online focus groups, for example the mid-1990s, there were no bespoke solutions for online focus groups and the pioneers tended to use standard chat software. However, most people running online focus groups for the last ten years have used specialist software and systems, i.e. systems that were designed specifically for market researchers and focus groups. Most of the online focus group software available today has a wide range of features that have been developed to make it more suitable for market researchers. The key features are listed below and then outlined in the following sub-sections.

- *Modes*
- *Discussion guide*
- *Multimedia*
- *Participant handling*
- *Polling software*
- *Webcams*
- *Management information systems*
- *Analysis options*

MODES

Online focus group software provides for people to attend focus groups in different modes, for example as participant, moderator, admin (administrators), and observer.

A **participant** shares a chat space with the other participants and the moderator. In a typical configuration, the participants have no direct contact with the observers or the admins.

The **observers** might, for example, be clients. They are able to see what is happening, but normally don't interact with the participants.

The **moderator** (or moderators) interact with both the participants and the observers, and have access to a wide range of extra functions, such as directing the participants to a particular image or website, looking at activity records for the participants, posting new topics, and probing responses.

The **admin** function is used to create the chat room, and to enable it to function well. In a typical project the admin function will only interact with the other parties during the focus group if there is a problem. Admins may liaise with respondents and clients before the group starts to check whether there are any systems issues and to help people get online for the focus group.

The more developed systems also have a **project manager** role, created for systems that can hold and store a number of projects. The project manager might need to look after several jobs, whereas moderators may only be granted access to a specific job, and only for the lifespan of the job.

DISCUSSION GUIDE

A typical online focus group system has the facility to upload a discussion guide before the session commences. The discussion guide will generally include the text of all the questions and probes that the researcher expects to use during the session. The uploading of the discussion guide reduces the workload, as the researcher then only types unforeseen questions and probes. Some systems allow the researcher to upload notes with the discussion guide to act as reminders during the session.

The discussion guide will also include all the media, or the links to the media, that the researcher plans to use during the focus group.

MULTIMEDIA

Online focus group systems normally have a range of multimedia facilities, such as the ability to show images or videos to the participants. Indeed, any form of media that the internet can display is available to the online focus group moderator.

Some systems also have a facility to allow some forms of interaction, for example drawing/writing on a shared area or appending notes to an image.

As well as displaying stimuli, one particularly useful facility is being able to force all of the participants' browsers to display a specific image or video (as opposed to simply enabling the participants to view the stimuli); this ensures that all members of the group are sharing the same experience. Equally useful is the ability to remove something from all the respondents' screens. For example, an image may be displayed, and then removed, allowing it to be discussed in the knowledge that none of the respondents can still see it.

PARTICIPANT HANDLING

There is a variety of participant handling tools that can make the researcher's life easier. For example, some online focus groups have a waiting room, where participants can be marshalled ready for the focus group; some have the ability to send questions or tasks to participants for them to complete before attending the group. During the focus group session, the moderator usually has the ability to send messages to individual participants or even to exclude them from the group if their behaviour is problematic.

The participant handling software typically has a facility to send participants an email before the group, giving them a reminder about the timing and a unique login/password combination. Respondents use the link to log into the focus group using a standard browser, but they are sometimes required to download applications from the server as part of the log-in process.

One useful facility offered by some of the platforms is the ability to remove a post from the discussion. This is useful if somebody says something inappropriate, although it can also be useful if the moderator clicks on the wrong post or probe.

MULTIPLE ROOMS

As well as a waiting room where respondents can be assembled, and the main discussion room, more advanced options may provide additional or side rooms. For example, a moderator might split the men into one room and the women into another, allowing separate tasks to be completed before bringing the group back together again.

POLLING SOFTWARE

Some of the online focus group systems have facilities to poll the attendees, for example, to ask questions such as 'Having now discussed this new product, would you buy it?'

In some circles the idea of asking polling or survey questions in a focus group is considered inappropriate. However, perhaps those researchers who think this sort of question should never be asked in a focus group should remember they don't have to use the facility; it is there for those who do wish to use it.

WEBCAMS

A number of systems have the ability to allow the moderator and the participants to see video images of each other using webcams and microphones. However, it should be noted that the use of live video is much less common than text only groups, even when available.

MANAGEMENT INFORMATION SYSTEMS

Management information systems (MIS) can make the researcher's task much easier. Before the group starts, the MIS can tell the researcher who is there and their answers to any pre-group tasks. During the session, the MIS can tell the researcher how long it is since each participant last made a contribution. Researchers generally want to ensure everyone is encouraged to join in and need to check that somebody has not disappeared to make a cup of coffee. Good MIS makes this monitoring much easier. Ideally the MIS should be able to tell you who is logged in and who is currently typing, which helps keep the moderator in control.

ANALYSIS OPTIONS

Focus group systems typically include analysis options, such as the ability to export the verbatims (with links to who said what and in response to what), the ability to generate tag clouds and, in many cases, image-based outputs relating to tasks, for example heat maps where participants have been able to click on stimuli to say which bits they like and don't like. It is likely that one of the key changes over the next few years will be the integration of more analysis tools within online focus group systems.

Advice

RUNNING AN ONLINE FOCUS GROUP

It should come as no surprise that there is no clear agreement about the best way to run an online focus group, since there is little agreement about the best way to run face-to-face groups. For example, traditional groups might be comprised of 14 people, asked direct questions, and asked to raise their hands to allow the moderator to record how many voted each way, or they could comprise six people encouraged to draw dream diagrams and act out personification fantasies.

The notes in this section reflect the views of a number of moderators, but they should not be interpreted as representing a settled consensus.

CHOOSING TECHNIQUES

Some offline techniques work just as well online, some work better, some need changing, and some tend not to work as well (Sweet, 2001). The online researcher needs to think through the tasks that they want to use and review how they will translate online.

Table 7.1 shows a view of how offline techniques tend to translate online, based on the work of Sweet (2001) and online discussions with a range of experienced qualitative researchers.

CREATING FOCUS

Do not expect a coherent and tidy conversation to naturally occur in an online focus group. Online respondents often talk (i.e. type) at the same time as each other, and the moderator needs to be aware of what everybody is saying. Often, respondents will not read whilst they are typing, meaning

Table 7.1

Opinion	Description
Better online	Factual lists, e.g. what is in your refrigerator, what products do you use?
Same online	Word associations Lists of ideas
Needs changes online	Brainstorming Annotating images
Less good online	Picture or product sorts. Paired tasks

they may miss what another participant is saying. However, most participants read what the moderator says, so the moderator should periodically paraphrase or recast what has already been said.

Sometimes, somebody will spend a few minutes typing in a response, which may be interesting but relates to a point that the rest of the group have moved on from. The moderator will need to decide whether to reply one-on-one or, if it is revealing, to move the conversation back to that point.

Online focus group attendees often say more than face-to-face respondents, but they may not be in synch with each other or the moderator.

If more than one client is attending, it might make sense to ask one client to act as a coordinator, and ask that coordinator to be the one who passes ideas and comments to the moderator (Sweet, 2001).

FEWER RESPONDENTS

An online focus group uses fewer members than a face-to-face group (for example six to eight instead of eight to twelve). The smaller number of respondents is partly to compensate for the expectation that they are likely to be talking at the same time, and also because it is generally harder to form a discussion online than face-to-face.

Opinions differ about what size an online group should be, just as opinions differ for offline groups. However, the general view is that online groups should have fewer attendees than offline groups. For example, Naresh Malhotra (2007) recommends four to six for an online group and eight to 12 for an offline group, whereas Casey Sweet (2001) suggests six to eight participants for online groups. In a review of literature on the subject Elisabeth Brüggen and Pieter Willems (2009) suggest three to five attendees are recommended.

The number of groups, and also the number of moderators, is not just a matter of preference, they may also be a matter of experience. Online focus group veteran Doug Bates from Itracks says: 'When a researcher first starts using online focus groups they may find it is really useful to have two moderators, and perhaps fewer respondents. However, with experience they will find they can do more. These days I find that I tend to prefer eight to ten respondents for both offline and online focus groups.'

SHORTER

Just as there is no agreement about the number of attendees at an online or offline focus group, there is no unanimity about how long an online focus group should be. The consensus tends to be that online groups should be shorter than offline groups. This is partly because online groups are very efficient, but it is also because it is very hard to hold somebody for a long time when they are at home. Visitors, telephone calls, children, and pets can all cause the sort of distractions that do not normally occur in a face-to-face focus group.

Sweet (2001) describes 90 minutes as a typical length, and this is supported by other experts such as Doug Bates from Itracks.

TWO MODERATORS

Consider using two moderators. When two moderators are used, one can pursue the discussion guide whilst the other can concentrate on the respondents, dealing with queries and off-agenda comments.

In an Itracks case study, Teresa Capeling makes the case for co-moderation of online focus groups, with the second moderator dealing with client-related issues as well as dealing with 'vague' and 'reluctant' respondents.

CHOOSING THE RESPONDENTS

Consider screening the respondents in terms of comfort in a chat room. At the very least the respondents should know about their browser and be able to type. Although many users are now far more familiar with the internet than they were five years ago, there are some groups, demographics, and countries where that is less true.

LANGUAGE

Unless the entire group is using online slang (for example lol, 'sup, IMHO) ask participants to avoid it, and also avoid using UPPER CASE typing.

MONITORING THE RESPONDENTS

Keep checking that all the participants are still there. For example, send a private message to people who have not contributed for a while.

CHOOSING AN ONLINE GROUP SOLUTION

There are a number of different possible solutions available for companies looking to select a system for conducting online focus groups. The key issues that should be considered are:

- *Finished package or raw tools*
- *Rent or buy*
- *Complexity versus power*
- *Reporting tools*

- ○ *Integration with other tools*

- ○ *Multimedia facilities*

- ○ *Languages*

- ○ *Cost*

FINISHED PACKAGE OR RAW TOOLS

The simplest way to run an online focus group is to use specialist software and have the focus group set up on somebody else's server, with their IT staff looking after it. This is, of course, the second most expensive way to run a focus group (the most expensive way being to do it wrong and then having to put it right or suffering the consequences). If you are running a small number of online groups, and if you can charge your costs to a client, then using finished packages, such as the products from Itracks or others, is likely to be the best option.

Using raw tools, for example chat software, or adapting web meeting services (such as Webex or GoToMeeting) is more relevant if an organisation is either (a) looking to reduce costs across a number of projects and/or (b) looking to create a non-standard application. The potential long-term benefits (i.e. potential for lower marginal costs and bespoke offer) of a company writing/commissioning their own bespoke solution are even higher, but the risks and the short- and medium-term costs are much higher.

It should be noted that a few people still use general chat software to facilitate online discussions, particularly when conducting discussions within online communities. One of the main concerns about these cheaper, chat room solutions is whether they adequately deal with privacy issues for clients and respondents.

RENT OR BUY

Renting the software is a reference to SaaS (Software as a Service), i.e. the user pays to use the system when they use it and the system is hosted on the provider's computers, such as with companies like Itracks. As with other SaaS areas, occasional and/or less technical users are likely to be better off with a SaaS solution. Users who conduct many studies and/or who have more IT sophistication are more likely to want to have their own system, so they can both tailor it and benefit from lower per project costs.

COMPLEXITY VERSUS POWER

Unlike most types of software, online focus groups do not provide a clean trade-off between complexity and power. Some systems that are complex to use lack power; some systems that are powerful can be relatively simple to use. This lack of a clear trade-off means that organisations should review as many systems as possible and be looking to maximise both simplicity and power.

The sorts of power that systems can offer include participant management, management information, the manipulation of discussion guide and prompts, and interview modes (e.g. moderator, admin, observer, and participant).

REPORTING

At the very least the system needs to be able to export the transcripts of the focus groups. Ideally, the reporting should have a range of export facilities, allowing the comments to be linked to the participants, the prompts, and with notes made by the moderators during the group. Some systems provide a range of tools that can help with the analysis without having to export the data, for example the creation of tag clouds.

INTEGRATION WITH OTHER TOOLS

If the online focus groups are likely to be run with panels, customer databases, or online communities, then it will be useful to use tools that can fully integrate with these panels or communities. For example, the online focus group can appear in the community and the moderator can access previous posts and surveys conducted as part the community.

MULTIMEDIA TOOLS

If the researcher wants to use advanced media then they will need a service or platform that will support it. In particular, if the intention is to use webcams to provide audio-visual groups, the software must be able to support this. One issue to check is the amount of material that can be stored. If a focus group is going to use images and video as stimuli, then this has to be stored somewhere and streamed when it is needed.

LANGUAGES

If all the focus groups are going to be run in English, then most of the chat systems will be able to handle the discussions. If other languages are going to be used then all of the system elements need to be able to display prompts in the correct language. Key areas to check are things like whether the login screen will be in the local language, whether system messages and error messages will be in the appropriate language, as well as any buttons, links, and help notes.

COST

Cost is clearly a major issue and it needs to be addressed in one of two ways. If the researcher has a specific plan to conduct a small number – say one to six groups – then the software and support costs for these projects need to be estimated and covered by the total price of the research project which is charged to the client. If the research company's plan is to provide online focus groups as a regular part of their service they should attempt to calculate the total three-year costs for each system and any alternative that is being considered, including training costs, IT costs, and any software fees or usage costs.

THE ARGUMENTS FOR AND AGAINST ONLINE FOCUS GROUPS

This section looks at reasons why the take-up of online focus groups has been so much less than the take-up of online quantitative research. This is then followed by a brief review of the debate about the merits of online focus groups.

WHY ONLINE FOCUS GROUPS HAVE NOT BEEN MORE SUCCESSFUL

As outlined above, online focus groups have not taken off to anything like the same extent as online quantitative research. There are several reasons for this which are explored in this section, along with the benefits. The topics covered are:

- *Cost*
- *Quality*
- *The client's role*
- *Comfort with the medium*
- *Reach*
- *Speed*

Cost

The main driver of growth in the use of the internet in quantitative research was the cost saving it offered, and was largely facilitated by the expansion and acceptance of online access panels. The cost saving argument for focus groups is much less clear.

The main factor that determines whether online groups are likely to save money is geography. In countries where distances between locations are small, the financial savings are likely to be small, and it is rare for an online group to be substantially cheaper than a conventional group. A typical scenario in a relatively small country, like the UK, is that the researcher might leave the office just after lunch, travel two or three hours to the groups' location, conduct two groups, one after the other, then travel home on a late train (often listening to a recording of the groups on the train and starting the analysis), finally arriving home between ten and twelve at night. Most companies using their researchers in this way will let them start late the next day, perhaps 11:00am. The cost to the research agency is just the travel. All the rest of the cost is the impact on the researcher (a type of cost that economists call an externality, because it does not fall on the company). In this small-country context, online focus groups might improve the lifestyle of the researcher, but they do not generate significant cost savings for agencies.

By contrast, in countries like the United States where distances are greater, moderators often have to stay overnight when conducting face-to-face groups, and it is not unusual for online groups to offer significant cost savings in these situations – although even these savings are disputed by some.

Although online groups reduce travel costs, they can increase moderator costs if two moderators are used per group. Also, online groups tend to be smaller, so it might be deemed necessary to conduct more groups to reach the same level of client comfort – e.g. six groups of eight participants has the same number of participants as eight groups of six participants.

One of the key costs with online groups is the cost of recruiting the participants. This can be reduced if the sample is recruited from a panel and there are a number of vendors who provide this service. However, there are many qualitative researchers and buyers of qualitative research who refuse to consider recruiting groups from panels (for both online and offline research) – despite their widespread adoption by quantitative researchers.

The net cost position for online focus groups is that they can be cheaper, but they are not so much cheaper, nor so systematically cheaper, that they have induced the industry to make a large scale switch to the online method.

Quality

Quality is usually the key concern expressed by people who are uncomfortable with online focus groups, particularly if they have never had any direct experience of an online qualitative project. The essence of the dissatisfaction to date is twofold:

1.   It is much harder to generate genuine interaction between online participants.

2.   The moderator loses all the non-verbal elements that are an essential part of their normal process.

Most of the 'leading' qualitative researchers (e.g. the industry gurus, the major speakers at conferences, and the writers of the books and therefore the people who need to 'sell' online groups to the industry), did not believe that online groups were as good as face-to-face groups. They did not feel that they could extract as much meaning, because of the loss of the physical presence and the dependence on typed responses to typed questions. Indeed, many of these leading figures would describe language as being too limited in its ability to truly interpret people's feelings and meanings, never mind language in typed format.

Historically, there have been counter arguments. For example, people put forward the view that because gender, ethnicity, and disabilities were all invisible in an online group, it was now more possible to mix people together in new and better ways. Vendors pointed to the benefits of having complete, error free, transcripts immediately after the groups are finished. The ability to combine people from very different geographies was also held up as a benefit.

A number of comparison studies have been conducted, directly comparing online focus groups with 'real' groups, and generally they showed that the business advice that resulted from online focus groups was similar to that from conventional groups. However, despite what some of these studies found, the consensus of most of the buyers and providers of qualitative research is that face-to-face groups should be preferred to online focus groups.

 Author's View

Perhaps the quality issue should more properly be called the quality perception, since it does not appear to be based on any facts.

The client role

When online focus groups first appeared on the research scene a number of potential client benefits were advanced. Clients would be able to take part in more groups, because they could do it from their office or even from home. Another advantage, it was thought, was the opportunity for clients to send messages to the moderator during the group.

However, many researchers and research buyers commented that one of the benefits of 'real' groups was the time that the client and the researcher spent together at various facilities around the country, talking to each other about the project (and about much more). The online environment tended to remove this casual conversation element, and possibly appealed less to the very social nature of many qualitative market researchers.

For example USA qualitative research Susan Sweet commented:

> 'Most clients are willing to give up the travel/in-person experience of observing every type of qualitative research EXCEPT for "live focus groups." I have had more than one client in the past year explain that they get much more from the experience of being together in the back room, hearing consumers and strategizing together, than they can ever get while watching online. Brand teams feel they coalesce while sitting in that darkened room eating M&Ms together, and they are unwilling to give it up. '

Comfort with the medium

There is a widespread view in the qualitative research industry that many qualitative researchers are not comfortable with the level of technology that online focus groups require. Against that, there are some people who feel more comfortable online, but these people tend not to have an established voice within the qualitative industry.

This area is another example of a difference, over the last fifteen years, between the qualitative and quantitative worlds. Amongst quantitative researchers there was a critical mass of researchers who actively wanted to be involved in online research because they were attracted to the technology, which was already a familiar part of their toolkit for areas like statistical analysis.

Reach

One of the benefits of online research is that it is not limited by geography. Offline focus groups are limited to those who live within easy access of the selected locations. However, this ability to reach more areas is only a benefit where the people the researcher wants to reach are geographically spread.

The concept of reach has a lot of salience for quantitative researchers who are looking for a sample that is representative of a whole country. By contrast, a qualitative sample rarely sets out to be fully representative; it is more likely to represent key sub-groups or archetypes. Having the focus groups more geographically spread out does not necessarily make a qualitative sample better in any meaningful sense.

Speed

Under certain specific situations, online groups can be faster, for example when talking to people who are in an online community or from a panel, or where physical groups would require significant amounts of travel. However, under normal research circumstances, the key driver of how long a qualitative project takes is the recruitment of the groups and finding time in the researcher's diary.

The recruitment of the group is much faster if they are being recruited from a panel or an online community. However, if respondents are recruited in the traditional way, the process is no faster than offline.

If the size of a country or the research schedule require a substantial amount of travel for the moderator, then it is easier to fit an online group into a busy schedule. However, this is less true in countries where the travel to and from a group is typically achieved in the same day as the groups.

SUMMARY OF THE DEBATE ABOUT ONLINE FOCUS GROUPS

There are strong positions for and against online focus groups, which have to an extent coloured the whole debate about online qualitative.

The case against

From the earliest days of online focus groups there has been a significant group of practitioners who have cast doubt on the technique, and even whether it should be called a focus group at all. One example of the criticism came from Thomas Greenbaum (2001). The points made by Greenbaum and others (Brüggen and Willems, 2009) include:

Group dynamics. The face-to-face nature of the traditional group allows the moderator to create group dynamics that rely on all the participants being together in the same place.

Depth of insight. Because of the lack of personal contact, moderators find out less about online participants than they would in a face-to-face group.

Non-verbal information. People give a large number of non-verbal clues, which the moderator can use as part of the development of insight and also as a method of improving the way they run the group. For example, people's faces and body language readily convey excitement or boredom.

Typing skills. The ability of participants to contribute to the group is limited by their ability to type, which is quite different from a face-to-face group where most people have the skills required.

Limited stimuli. A face-to-face group can use a much wider range of stimuli than can be conveyed by the internet, for example, taste, touch, and smell.

The case for

Other commentators have responded by highlighting the benefits of online focus groups for example, the points made by Friedman (2001), Yardena Rand (2003) and others include:

Candid response. Because people are anonymous they may be more honest, particularly for some sensitive topics.

Uninfluenced responses. Because people tend to all respond at the same time, their responses are less influenced by what others are saying.

Efficient. Respondents tend to answer questions more directly and are less likely to 'chatter'; moderators feel more able to ask very direct follow-up questions.

More representative. Online groups can be more representative, particularly when researching hard-to-reach groups or groups that cannot normally attend a central location for a focus group.

Controlling the group. In an online group it is easier to avoid one participant dominating or disrupting the group.

Convenience and cost. Online groups can be cheaper and can deliver a faster turnaround from commission to results.

EVIDENCE ABOUT ONLINE FOCUS GROUPS

Colin Cheng, Dennis Krumwiede and Chwen Sheu (2009) reviewed much of the evidence about the difference in the findings produced by online and offline focus groups. They found that the research done by various authors suggests that:

○ *online tends to be better in terms of equity of participation and in self-disclosure*

○ *less information is produced online, because there is less incidental and anecdotal conversation*

- ○   *the results about the quality of the findings are not consistent, some finding online and offline to be the same, others reporting differences*

- ○   *it is likely that the skill of the moderator is the single largest determinant of the quality of the insight produced, rather than any difference between online versus offline.*

Other authors have also spoken about the self-disclosure aspect of online groups, suggesting that the anonymity and lack of personal interaction facilitated people being more honest (Sweet, 2001; Rand, 2003).

 Warning

In short, the evidence is somewhere between neutral to positive in terms of whether online focus groups work. However, this evidence appears to have little effect on the views of many researchers and research buyers. This was the phenomenon that Amy Yoffie (2002) was writing about when she wrote: '*Even though online groups have been available for at least seven years, there is still a vehement prejudice against this methodology . . .*'

 Resources

RESOURCES FOR ONLINE FOCUS GROUP

The list of resources shown here is not exhaustive; it is a cross-section of well-known leading players, along with one or two newer entrants.

Itracks, full service and DIY, http://www.itracks.com

Artafact, full service and DIY, http://www.artafact.com/

My Virtual Focus Facility, DIY online focus groups, http://www.myvff.com

ChannelM2, includes audio/visual groups, http://www.channelm2.com/

Polimetrix, full service and DIY, http://www.polimetrix.com/services/qualitative.html

QualMeeting, from 2020 Research, http://www.2020research.com/qualmeeting.html

WebEx, sophisticated web meeting and webinar service, http://www.webex.com

GoToMeeting, sophisticated web meeting and webinar service, http://www.webex.com

SUMMARY OF ONLINE FOCUS GROUPS

Online focus groups work well for the people who use them, but they represent a very small part of the total number of focus groups conducted each year, most of which are traditional, face-to-face groups.

Research into online focus groups suggests that they can often provide business insight which is very similar to the business insight delivered by researchers using offline focus groups, in those situations where both online and offline are suitable modalities. However, despite the evidence, many qualitative researchers and qualitative research buyers believe that online focus groups are inherently less good.

The people who favour online focus groups often talk about features – such as transcripts, geography, representation – that are not seen by the resolutely anti-online qualitative researchers as being major benefits.

Online focus groups tend to be more competitive, in terms of speed and cost, when the attendees are recruited from panels, and they have less of a competitive advantage where the attendees are recruited conventionally.

Much of the interest in qualitative online research to date has been directed to the asynchronous approaches. For example, interest was initially directed more towards bulletin board groups and recently more towards online research communities. This may have been because these techniques are seen as offering something different to that which can be achieved offline, whereas online focus groups are not seen to offer much that is different. Bulletin board groups are covered in the next chapter and online research communities are discussed in Chapter 11 in Part III.

8 Bulletin Board Groups and Parallel IDIs

This chapter looks at bulletin board groups and parallel IDIs (multiple, online, asynchronous in-depth interviews) and the way they are being used by market researchers.

Bulletin board groups (also known as bulletin board focus groups, BBGs, and BBFGs) use modified bulletin board software to conduct online qualitative projects. Bulletin board groups are an example of an asynchronous technique, i.e. the participants and the moderator do not have to be online at the same time. Bulletin board groups are not simply a translation of an offline technique, they are a method that has grown out of the online modality and have tapped into new areas, in particular reflection, consideration, and maturation.

Parallel IDIs are a form of online, asynchronous in-depth interview. Offline depth interviews are conducted one-on-one between an interviewer and a subject, either face-to-face or on the telephone. A typical offline depth interview is conducted in one session, with the interview lasting anything from 15 minutes to two hours, depending on the project requirements. Parallel IDIs, by contrast, are a set of simultaneous in-depth discussions taking place over a period of time, for example over several days or even several weeks.

Note that traditional in-depth interviews can also be conducted via the internet, either through online focus group software or one of the many ways of connecting over the internet, such as Skype, instant messaging, chat, or specialised meeting software such as GoToMeeting.

Bulletin board groups and parallel IDIs are both covered in this chapter as they are both asynchronous qualitative techniques and are usually conducted using the same software platform. In most cases, parallel IDIs are conducted using bulletin board group software.

This chapter is divided into the following sub-sections:

- ○   *Introduction to bulletin board groups*

- ○   *Running bulletin board groups*

- ○   *Introduction to parallel IDIs*

- ○   *Running parallel IDIs*

❍   *Resources for bulletin board groups and parallel IDIs*

❍   *A summary of bulletin board groups and parallel IDIs*

INTRODUCTION TO BULLETIN BOARD GROUPS

A bulletin board group (also known as a bulletin board focus group, BBG, and BBFG) is a group discussion that takes place over an extended period of time (from days to months). The discussion is led by a moderator who posts discussions, prompts, replies, and tasks on a specially configured bulletin board. The respondents, or participants, log into the bulletin board, read the latest posts, complete any tasks set for them, and add their comments.

A bulletin board group is referred to as an asynchronous approach, because it does not require the moderator and the participants to be online at the same time. It is a qualitative technique because the focus is on the conversations that happen, even though polls and surveys can also be used. The difference between a synchronous technique (such as a focus group) and an asynchronous technique (such as a bulletin board group) is potentially profound. A synchronous technique can elicit top of mind reactions, group dynamics, and rapid conclusions. Asynchronous techniques give the participants and the moderator time to think about answers, to be reflective and introspective, and for views and reactions to mature.

There are concerns that there are occasions in a focus group where the researcher asks questions that respondents struggle to answer because of their imperfect memory, for example what they have bought or used recently (Towers, 2005). In a bulletin board group the participant can provide an accurate answer, for example by checking what is in their closet or garage.

CHARACTERISTICS OF BULLETIN BOARD GROUPS

Whilst bulletin boards vary, the sub-sections below cover their main characteristics.

Appearance

The earliest bulletin board groups of the late 1990s looked very much like those used by hobbyists and techies, i.e. text heavy sites with complex lists of discussions and threads. Since then, however, the software options for online discussions have improved almost out of all recognition. Some of these changes have been driven by the needs of market researchers, others reflect the sorts of discussions that internet users expect to have in other forums, such as in social networks. A typical bulletin board will tend to follow one of three styles.

The first style is to create a very professional and independent feel that aims to convey an unbranded professionalism, in the same way that in the offline environment many focus group facilities convey an unbranded and professional impression.

The second style is to create a bulletin board group themed around the sort of people being invited to take part. For example, if the group is made up of mothers of young children, the styling (and the name of the discussion) might reflect 'moms'. Similarly, a group assembled to discuss sports-related issues might be named and styled around sports.

The third style is the branded group, where the group is typically created from customers of a particular product or service, and is overtly being run on behalf of that product or service. In this case the branding and the name of the group would reflect the brand's house style.

In most cases, the term 'styling' relates to the elements surrounding the discussions and threads, for example the home page and the banner and footer of the page. The discussions themselves tend to be styled relatively consistently from one project to another.

Number of participants

A typical bulletin board group has between 10 and 30 participants, but smaller and larger groups (sometimes much larger) are not uncommon.

In this chapter, the term 'participants' is used to refer to the respondents who are recruited to take part in a bulletin board group. These participants could equally be called respondents, informants, subjects, or even cases. Although the choice of a term can be quite revealing, it is an arbitrary choice and is likely to change with fashion.

Short term and long term

Most bulletin board groups are short term, i.e. they tend to run from a few days to three weeks (Schillewaert, De Ruyck and Verhaeghe, 2009), but longer durations are not uncommon. Long-term bulletin board groups are much longer, for example three months, twelve months, or even ongoing.

Short-term bulletin board groups tend to be very active, with participants expected to take part at least once a day, or at least to try to. For example, QualBoard provider 2020 Research describes the typical group using their software as lasting three to seven days, with participants logging in two to three times a day, and the typical number of participants as ten to thirty.

Long-term bulletin boards tend to be run in one of two ways. The frequency might be relatively relaxed, for example weekly, with conversations tracking projects over long periods of time. The alternative approach is to run the bulletin board group with periods of high activity (e.g. daily), mixed with slower periods, with no activity being required for two or three weeks.

Short-term groups tend to be very task focused, i.e. they are created to specifically answer a particular research or business question. Long-term groups are occasionally task focused if they are following some activity that takes a long time, such as the purchase of a new home, but more often they are created as a resource, allowing the client to research a wide range of specific questions and topics.

Recruitment

The participants in a bulletin board group are generally recruited and rewarded much like the participants in offline and online focus groups. However, there is a trend towards recruiting the participants from online access panels or client databases.

When recruiting participants for a bulletin board group it is important to ensure that they understand what is expected of them. For example, if the group is going to last two weeks and if they are expected to log on to the group at least once a day, they need to understand and agree to that. If being a participant in a group involves undertaking tasks, for example visiting a store, playing a game, or visiting a website, this level of commitment should be made clear to participants when they are being recruited.

The recruitment process should also check that the participants have access to suitable hardware. For example, if they are going to view streamed video, they need to have sufficient bandwidth and the ability to hear and see video files. This tends to mean the ability to access the bulletin board group from home, since most employers and schools are not keen on people watching videos on their machines!

Access to the group

Participants are given their own secure login to prevent non-members from joining or viewing the group. Because participants will need to log into the group on a number of separate occasions, some of them will forget their username and password, so the system should ideally have an automated method of reminding and resetting passwords.

Multimedia

Bulletin board group systems normally allow a range of stimuli to be used, including images, video, and links to websites. Some systems allow the media files to be stored and served from the bulletin board group system, others require the media files to be stored elsewhere.

Modes and moderator facilities

One of the key things that differentiates systems created for market research bulletin board groups and general bulletin boards is the provision of facilities specifically crafted for market researchers. Amongst the facilities that are specifically relevant to market research are:

- *modes; the minimum number of modes offered by bulletin board groups is two, the moderator (i.e. the researcher) and the participant but there may also be an observer and a separate admin mode*

- *discussion guide options, allowing a series of questions to be uploaded with the option to time release them*

- *discussion controls, allowing the researcher to determine what different people can see; for example, the moderator may determine that a participant cannot see the next question until they have replied to the current question, or that they must post their reply to a task before they can see other participants' posts*

❍   *admin privileges, allowing the moderator to manage the group, for example being able to send private messages, edit or remove other people's posts and, if necessary, remove a participant*

❍   *MIS (management information systems) to allow the moderator to receive detailed information about what is happening, for example which participants have logged on, the number of posts per participant, the length of posts, and which topics are being discussed the most*

❍   *reporting and analysis tools, including the ability to export all the conversations, to produce tag clouds, and to follow conversation threads*

Bulletin board tasks

'Tasks' is a generic term that embraces all the various things a bulletin board group moderator asks the participants to do. The key tasks that are typically used are listed below.

Questions. The most frequent tasks conducted via a bulletin board are questions. The moderator posts a question and the participants post their answers. In bulletin board language, a question and its responses are called a thread. Having posted a question, the moderator may need to post follow-up comments or explanations to keep the thread moving or to probe responses.

Polls and surveys. Depending on the nature and size of the group, polls and surveys can be a useful way of gathering profiling information or of gaining an overview of people's attitudes to a topic. For example, if a project is exploring gift giving, a simple survey asking people to fill in a grid of types of gifts against occasions might help the moderator shape the discussion and avoid missing some key issues. Polls and surveys can easily be run via third-party systems, but some bulletin board group systems have facilities to run integral polls and surveys.

Multimedia tasks. Participants can be asked to view an image, listen to audio, or watch a video as part of a task. This type of task is usually associated with a request for participants to add their comments after completing the tasks. The multimedia can be provided via third-party services, but it is more secure if the bulletin board group software allows them to be integrated and served from the board itself.

Collaborative tasks. All of the discussions that happen on a bulletin board are collaborative, but beyond this level of collaboration there are a number of other tasks that can be conducted. Some systems have a white board where participants can write, draw, append pictures, or type. If the participants are relatively tech savvy then a project wiki can be created and used as a collaborative tool.

Off-board tasks. One of the key benefits of a bulletin board group is the power of time, which allows off-board tasks to be set and completed. Examples of off-board tasks include asking participants to watch a TV show, visit a retail outlet, engage in a sporting activity, visit a website, or play a game. Generally, this activity is followed by a period of conventional discussion on the board, with the moderator posting questions for the members to respond to.

Upload tasks. Participants can be asked to upload images or videos as a specific task. For example, participants may be asked to take a photo showing the contents of their refrigerator and upload that. This can then lead to discussions about the differences in what people have in their refrigerators and in how they arrange them. Care should be taken in terms of copyright and intellectual property rights, so the participants must be reminded to only upload images and videos they have a legal right to upload.

BULLETIN BOARD GROUP BENEFITS

Bulletin board groups are not simply an online equivalent of an offline technique; they are a new method for researchers to gain insight. The major benefits of bulletin board groups are as follows.

○   *They allow participants to reflect about their answers and can therefore explore issues more deeply than a one-off approach allows.*

○   *They provide time for the moderator to build up an understanding of what is motivating participants and to revise the discussion guide to gain better insight.*

○   *They provide time for participants to undertake tasks, such as to visit a store or review what is in their refrigerator.*

○   *They are cost effective in that neither the moderator nor the participants need to travel.*

Bulletin board groups are not usually seen as simply an online substitute for conventional, offline qualitative research; rather, they are offered as a method of accessing experience, reflection, and maturation.

ARE BULLETIN BOARD GROUPS REALLY GROUPS?

Even many of the researchers who find bulletin board groups useful have highlighted the limited group dynamics that take place between the members (Turner, 2008). The majority of interactions in a bulletin board group are between the participants and the moderator. However, the process is clearly different from an exercise where participants are absolutely unaware of each other's contributions, and bulletin board groups raise the possibility for moderators to benefit from participants being informed by other participants' views and to encourage collaborative exercises.

BUSINESS-TO-BUSINESS

Researchers have found that bulletin board groups are particularly relevant in B2B (Business-to-Business) research, both as a group activity and as a series of parallel IDIs (IDIs are covered more fully later in this chapter). Peer group interaction is often seen as a motivating feature of bulletin board groups in B2B research; however, this sort of interaction can raise anonymity issues.

ANONYMITY

Most market research is undertaken under strict rules of anonymity. These rules mean that clients do not know the identity of the respondents, and respondents do not know the identities of other respondents. In a bulletin board group there is an increased risk that this anonymity will be accidently breached. If a bulletin board group participant uses their real name and/or their real photo there is a risk that other participants, the researcher, or the clients will recognise them. Also, as a dialogue builds over a period of time it is possible for the content of a discussion to reveal too much information about a participant, for example, if they talk about a club or society they are a member of, or their local store, or their street.

Researchers using bulletin board groups need to be aware of these potential problems with anonymity and take steps to protect the participants.

BULLETIN BOARD GROUPS IN ACTION

This section looks at how different researchers have put bulletin board groups into use.

Product placement and BBGs

In this example from the USA, Campbell Research used bulletin board groups to test and refine materials for their client. The online part of the project comprised in-home product placement with two bulletin board groups, each made up of about 40 respondents and each lasting 14 days. The projects were conducted using Itracks software (Itracks use the BBFG abbreviation for bulletin board focus groups). Campbell Research combined face-to-face focus groups, bulletin board groups, and a quantitative mail survey to gain a complete answer for their client. More details are available at http://www.itracks.com/LinkClick.aspx?fileticket=qUZy3ooGGqU%3d&tabid=99.

THE LINK BETWEEN BULLETIN BOARD GROUPS AND COMMUNITIES

To a considerable extent, the difference between bulletin board groups and online research communities is simply a generational one. When bulletin board groups were first developed they reflected current practice in terms of how the internet was being used to create discussions, i.e. bulletin boards. Although some natural bulletin boards and forums still exist on the internet, they are increasingly being replaced by online communities in general and discussions within social networks (such as Facebook) in particular.

It is possible that bulletin board groups will be replaced by online research communities (also known as MROCs) over the next few years. At the moment, bulletin board groups have the advantage of being quicker to create, of currently having more research functions, and of being more suitable for parallel IDIs. By contrast, online research communities are more intuitive for the participants and more attractive to many clients.

Researchers who currently use both online research communities and bulletin board groups tend to see little reason for bulletin board groups to be superseded by online research communities. But newer entrants to the field appear to take communities as their starting point. Another factor in the convergence is that most bulletin board group software is perfectly capable of running online communities.

Given that the leading providers of bulletin board groups also provide online research communities, the change from bulletin board groups to online research communities may be more of a drift, with the platforms morphing together, rather than any distinct transition from one to the other.

Online research communities are covered in Part III.

RUNNING BULLETIN BOARD GROUPS

The following steps outline the key tasks that are common to most bulletin board group projects. These notes focus on short-term groups, with a slight digression into long-term groups. The steps in a bulletin board group are laid out below, followed by further notes for each of the steps:

1. Design the bulletin board group

2. Create the discussion guide

3. Recruit the participants

4. Moderate the groups

5. Extract and report insight

6. If there is more time, revise 2 and repeat from 4

7. Close the group

DESIGN THE BULLETIN BOARD GROUP

The term 'design' covers a wide range of tasks, including both research elements and the way the bulletin board group should appear to the participants and the client.

The look and feel of the bulletin board

If the software allows the look and feel to be customised, the researcher needs to determine what these should be, typically choosing from one of three distinct styles:

(a)   Use a neutral and independent look, in the same way that offline focus group facilities tend to be styled. For many bulletin board group software systems this is the default option.

(b)   Create a theme for the board associated with the topic. For example, if the board is talking to people about savings and pensions, then the URL and the theme might reflect the topic of pensions, and perhaps a title such as 'When you retire'.

(c)   Theme the board around the brand under investigation. For example, if the board is to be run amongst the customers of a fast food chain, it could be designed to reflect the colour scheme, logo, and general style of that brand.

Routes (b) and (c) take longer to achieve and are usually more expensive, so they tend to be used for the larger or longer projects, with option (a) being preferred for many projects.

The number of participants

When determining the size of bulletin board group, the key question is how many active members does the group need? Some groups of 30 participants have 28 active members. Other groups of 30 participants might have only eight active members. The benefits delivered by a bulletin board group are a function of their active members, with less benefit being accrued from the less active members.

The best practice is to recruit and motivate participants such that most members of a bulletin board group are active, even at the risk of losing the less active participants. Methods of achieving this are covered later, but the three key points are good recruiting, appropriate incentives, and managing the bulletin board group in an engaging way.

The typical number of participants, in a bulletin board group, ranges from 10 to 30, but smaller and larger numbers are not uncommon.

There are three factors that tend to push towards a smaller number of participants:

1.   **Cost.** The larger the number of participants, the higher the recruitment costs and the higher the incentives that may need to be paid.

2.   **Workload**. The more participants a group has, the more material they will produce, requiring larger amounts of processing. It should be noted that more material does not necessarily mean better answers; once there is enough feedback to answer the question, further material will add only marginal value.

3.   **Group dynamics**. If a group is too large, participants can become demotivated because their comments and contributions might seem insignificant, particularly if many others are also commenting and posting. Indeed, when larger groups are required, it is not uncommon for researchers to break them into smaller sub-groups, running in parallel.

There are also factors that push towards larger numbers of participants:

1.   A larger group is more capable of surviving problems, for example, if some participants turn out not to be active.

2.   If the researcher wants to use polls or surveys to assess the frequency of some activity, then a larger number of participants is going to deliver more credible results.

3.   If some topics that are going to be discussed are of more interest to some group members than others, then a larger total number of participants will lead to a more acceptable number of comments per topic.

4.   If the researcher has a large number of sub-groups to investigate, then the total number of participants will need to be larger.

In designing a bulletin board group the researcher needs to balance these factors against each other to select the number of participants.

The duration of the project

Given that time is money, bulletin board groups usually run for long enough to deliver the required insight and answers, but no longer. In general this tends to be one to four weeks, but longer and shorter groups are not uncommon.

In terms of length, the exception is the long term or continuous group. These groups are usually treated as a resource rather than as a means to a specific end. Often a long-term bulletin board group will be positioned as an advisory board, or mentors, or innovators, indicating to the members that they are special, and justifying a usage pattern that will tend to alternate from slow to busy.

Activity cycle

One of the keys to moderating a bulletin board group is the activity cycle. In a bulletin board group, the activity cycle is the frequency that the moderator will post a question or other task. The activity cycle also determines how often the researcher expects the participants to visit the board.

The combination of the duration of the project (how long the board will run for) and the activity cycle (how often a new question or task is posted) determines how many questions or tasks can be conducted via the bulletin board group. For example, a one week (five day) bulletin board group might use an activity cycle of two tasks per day, allowing ten tasks in total. This would require participants to log on to the board at least twice a day or to complete more than one task per visit. It should be noted that participants are usually expected to respond to other posts as well as the moderator's tasks, so they may be logging on to the board more often than the activity cycle might imply.

In most cases, the activity cycle is based on a five day week, i.e. Monday to Friday. However, in special cases it may be desirable to run the activity cycle over the weekend, if it meets the needs of the project and the nature of the participants.

The terms and conditions

The starting point for the terms and conditions for a specific project should be the research company's standard terms and conditions. However, these should be reviewed for each project to check whether they need extending and to make them particular to the end-client for that project. In most cases the terms and conditions should include the following:

(a)   The moderator has the right to amend the terms and conditions.

(b)   All intellectual property resides with the end-client, or the research agency and the end-client, to avoid later disputes.

(c)   The participant recognises that the research is confidential and agrees not to disclose anything they see without prior permission.

(d)   The participant agrees to use their best endeavours.

(e)   An agreement about the scale of contributions that the participant is expected to make, and that failure to contribute regularly may result in the participant being removed from the project

(f)   Any rules and procedures involved in the incentive scheme.

The incentive scheme

There are a range of possible incentive schemes, such as pay per post, pay per week, and prize draw. Bulletin board groups tend to be intensive and the participants need to be motivated. Part of the motivation can be provided by the way the group is moderated, but in most cases incentives will be necessary.

A typical approach to bulletin board groups is to use incentives similar in size to face-to-face focus groups, and make the payment contingent on the participants' contributions. So, for example, if a bulletin board group is scheduled to last two weeks, the incentive might be paid in three parts: one part after the registering and profiling process; one at the end of week 1 if the participant fulfils minimum criteria; and the final third when the tasks in week 3 are adequately completed.

The interaction framework

The researcher has to decide which bulletin board group facilities to enable for the participants. For example, can participants post their own questions and threads? Can participants send each other private messages? Can participants comment on each other's posts?

Traditionally, and across a range of research techniques, market researchers have adopted a controlling style that Brunswick's Graeme Trayner has called a 'command and control mindset'. More recently, market researchers have realised that they need to adopt a more collaborative mindset, something which has been called Research 2.0 and NewMR. Consequently, the best practice advice is to start by assuming that the participants will be able to use all of the available facilities of the group, and then remove those facilities that might compromise the research or distract the respondents.

Many researchers find it useful to restrict participants so that they can't see the later tasks until they have read, or possibly completed, the current task. Also, it may be useful to restrict a participant's ability to see other participants' comments until they have first entered their own comment.

CREATE THE DISCUSSION GUIDE

There is a paradox at the heart of a bulletin board group discussion guide. At one level it needs to be a finished document, capable of being posted on the board according to a previously agreed timetable. However, at the same time the discussion guide needs to be treated as work in progress, informed by the discussions taking place on the board.

The shorter the timeframe for the group, the more detailed the discussion guide should be. For example, if a project is scheduled to run for one week, the discussion guide should include every question and task, fully written out in every detail. However, if the project is scheduled to run for three weeks, the discussion guide for the first week might be fully finished, but be in draft form for the last two weeks.

Regardless of how finished the discussion guide might appear to be, the researcher needs to be prepared to amend and update it if the contents of the participants' comments and posts require it.

RECRUIT THE PARTICIPANTS

In addition to the normal recruitment issues, the researcher needs to ensure that the participants:

- *are able to use the bulletin board software*

- *agree to the Terms and Conditions*

- *are available during the project*

In terms of participants being available, a short-term group might be looking for most members to log on at least once a day, possibly more often. Longer-term boards are often based on the participants logging on two to three times a week.

In the early days of bulletin board groups, the tendency was to recruit the participants in the same way as for face-to-face qualitative research. These days the participants are often recruited from online access panels or from the clients' databases.

MODERATE THE GROUPS

The first step of the moderation process is to post a task. This might be a question, or it might be a video to watch, a website to visit, or some domestic task such as checking the contents of the family's refrigerator.

When posting a new task it is a good idea to initiate a message to all the board members to let them know it is there, subject to not overloading them with messages. Depending on the construction of the group, the message might be sent via email, instant messaging, SMS, or some other alternative.

After a task has been posted the moderator needs to monitor the board to see if the participants have any problem with it. Once the feedback on a task starts, the moderator needs to check that the discussion is going in a useful direction (useful in terms of the project's research objectives). Sometimes a discussion will become distracted by some side issue. In such cases, the moderator needs to move the conversation back to the research agenda.

Many bulletin board group systems allow the researcher to lodge tasks in advance which can then be auto-posted at a specific date and time – gaining the researcher some free time. However, whilst this facility is useful, the researcher still needs to monitor the responses and to probe participants as and when necessary, so the time gained by the auto-post can easily be lost again.

In some bulletin board groups, and on some topics, the conversation amongst participants may be self-sustaining, and sometimes on topic. However, in many cases most of the interaction is between the moderator and the participants. For example, the moderator may post a question, and this might be followed by five responses, all of which address the moderator's post, rather than each other's posts. Whilst it is rewarding when real interaction happens, the researcher should accept that often it will not happen and that they will need to play a very active role in the discussions.

When using a bulletin board group the analysis of the topic does not wait until the end of the project; it begins during the moderator's monitoring and responding to the discussions. The researcher should be following the texts to see what theories they suggest. As theories are being generated by the texts, the researcher should be seeking to validate and explore them via additional questions and probes.

As well as pursuing the current task, the moderator should be using MIS (management information systems) reports to check:

     ⃝   *who is taking part and who is not*

     ⃝   *what posts and activities are taking place and on which threads*

     ⃝   *if any surveys or polls are being used, what the response rate is, what the results are*

     ⃝   *whether the rate of engagement (e.g. logging in, reading, posting, task completion etc) is staying at an acceptable level or is dropping*

EXTRACT AND REPORT INSIGHT

The extracting of insight from discussions is probably the least developed part of online qualitative market research. In many cases the reports presented to clients spend too much time restating what participants said, too little on suggesting what the participants meant, and too little on providing actionable findings and recommendations for the client.

Where the amount of text is modest, the analysis normally consists of carefully reading the texts and thereby identifying concepts, relationships, and motivations. Sometimes tools like word clouds are used to reveal patterns in the text to help explain meanings.

Where the amount of text is larger, tools such as Leximancer and NVivo can reduce the time required to analyse it. However, it should be noted that, at present, there are no automated text analysis programs capable of processing texts and producing insight without substantial interventions by an analyst or researcher. At the moment, good software can make an analyst more efficient, but it can't replace the analyst.

CLOSE THE GROUP

Once the project is completed, the project needs to be closed, all of the participants thanked, any remaining incentives paid, and the information archived. As part of the closing process, the board should be archived, both in terms of the information and the look and feel.

INTRODUCTION TO PARALLEL IDIS

Another use of bulletin board group software is to conduct parallel IDIs (in-depth interviews), an online technique derived from face-to-face and telephone depth interviews, utilising the software platform provided for bulletin board groups.

Depth interviews are a longstanding feature of offline qualitative research, but there are key differences between traditional depth interviews and parallel IDIs. Depth interviews are conducted one at a time, with the interviewer finishing one interview before moving on to the next. Typical depth interviews last anything from 15 minutes to two hours. By contrast, the parallel IDIs are held side-by-side, with the researchers talking to all of the participants at the same time. A parallel IDI is conducted over days, weeks, or longer, allowing the participants and the researcher to benefit from consideration, reflection, and maturation.

It is also possible to conduct live depth interviews using the internet, i.e. synchronous, one-at-a-time depth interviews. These live interviews can be conducted using a range of internet tools, including focus group software, Skype, chat, instant messaging, or specialist meeting software such as GoToMeeting. Many of these synchronous options also have the option to use audio and sometimes video connectivity.

THE LOGISTICS OF PARALLEL IDIS

Parallel IDIs are typically conducted using bulletin board group software. However, unlike a conventional group, the board is configured so that each participant is unaware of the other participants, i.e. they can't see the posts and responses of the other participants.

The researcher is free to create and use most of the tasks that can be used in bulletin board groups, other than the collaborative ones.

The main limiting factor with parallel IDIs is the quantity of discourse that the researcher can cope with, in terms of both reading the posts and of responding to queries and points raised by the participants. Twenty participants in parallel IDIs will often generate more text than 20 participants in a bulletin board group.

The typical number of participants in parallel IDIs is between 8 and 30, but smaller and larger (sometimes much larger) numbers are not rare.

RUNNING PARALLEL IDIS

The logistics of creating and running parallel IDIs is very similar to the process for bulletin board groups.

Designing the parallel IDI. The board can be configured as brand themed, topic themed, or neutral, in the same way as bulletin board groups. The design process for a parallel IDI defines the duration of the IDIs, the activity cycle, and the number of participants.

Creating the discussion guide. Although the researcher needs to be prepared to be flexible, they should start with a clear and detailed discussion guide, setting out the tasks, the text of questions, and the initial timeline.

Recruit the participants. Participants can be recruited in a variety of ways, for example traditional qualitative recruiting, recruiting from clients' databases, and recruiting from access panels. Because the analysis in parallel IDIs is often intended to be deeper than is the case with bulletin board groups, many researchers are reluctant to recruit IDI participants from online access panels.

Conduct the interviews. The starting point for the researcher is the discussion guide, with its previously described questions and tasks. The researcher will typically need to chase some participants to reply and respond to queries and responses from other participants. This process is made much easier if the software being used has good MIS.

Extracting the insight. The analysis of a parallel IDI project does not start when the last task is completed; it starts during the first tasks. As the data begins to emerge the researcher should try to form theories based on it, identifying questions that can confirm, refine, or refute these theories. At the end of the project tools such as tag clouds and text analysis software can be employed to analyse the data more thoroughly.

Closing the project. At the end of the project the participants are thanked and any incentives paid. The project is then archived and removed from the internet.

Similarities with Email groups and eDelphi

Parallel IDIs share some key features in common with email groups and eDelphi techniques. In all three techniques the research acts as the centre point, talking to all of the participants, synthesising the learning from each round of communication, and using some of it as the stimuli for the next round of insight generation.

The key difference between parallel IDIs (at least when conducted via a sophisticated bulletin board group system) and email groups and eDelphi approaches, is that the researcher has many more tools available in the parallel IDI context, whereas the email groups and eDelphi exercises are dependent on the limited communications of email.

RESOURCES FOR BULLETIN BOARD GROUPS AND PARALLEL IDIS

This section reviews a range of resources that facilitate bulletin board groups and parallel IDIs, along with a listing of further information and resources.

SOFTWARE AND SERVICES

This particular section looks at the issues surrounding the choice of software and services.

Bulletin board group software and services

There are three main options available in terms of bulletin board groups:

1.   A fully featured bulletin board group solution from a provider such as Itracks.

2.   A bulletin board solution, such as phpBB or vBulletin.

3.   An online research community.

Fully featured services. The fully featured bulletin board group solutions tend to be run as a SaaS (Software as a Service) solution, i.e. research agencies pay to use them, rather than buying a copy of them. The company providing the service will, typically, script and host the bulletin board group and provide the researcher with the technical support needed to run the group.

Bulletin board systems. There are a large number of bulletin board systems available. Many of these systems are free, like phpBB, or very cheap, like vBulletin. However, most of them require significant technical knowhow, especially if they are to be sufficiently robust and secure to use for a commercial research project.

Online research community. The online research community option is explored fully in Chapter 11.

Parallel IDI software and services

Although it is possible to run parallel IDIs using systems configured from bulletin board tools such as phpBB or vBulletin, this route requires significant technical competence. Most parallel IDIs are conducted using the facilities provided by fully featured bulletin board group systems.

  Resources

SOFTWARE AND SYSTEM SOLUTIONS

Note the list of resources shown here is not exhaustive, they are a cross-section of well known and leading players and should provide a good entry point into this area.

Itracks, full service provider, http://www.itracks.com

Artafact, provide bulletin board groups, http://www.artafact.com/

ChannelM2, includes audio/visual bulletin board groups, http://www.channelm2.com/

QualBoard, from 2020 Research, http://www.2020research.com/qualmeeting.html

Focus Forums, provides bulletin board group facilities, http://www.focusforums.net/

vBulletin, bulletin board software, www.vbulletin.com/

phpBB, bulletin board software, www.phpbb.com/

A SUMMARY OF BULLETIN BOARD GROUPS AND PARALLEL IDIS

Bulletin board groups were the first form of online qualitative that added something quite new to the canon of techniques available to market researchers. Indeed, it could be argued that bulletin board groups were the first genuinely new technique that was introduced because of the adoption of the internet as a medium for market research. By contrast, most online quantitative techniques at that point were simply the application of existing techniques via a new modality. Online focus groups offered the online equivalent of a technique that was already being conducted online, albeit with some differences.

Bulletin board groups provide the researcher with a window into people's lives through the medium of an ongoing conversation. Because bulletin board groups allow reflection, maturation, and deliberation they can follow changes over time.

Parallel IDIs provide a way of holding multiple one-on-one discussions, breathing new life into the email group idea.

Although both bulletin board groups and parallel IDIs have added something new to the range of techniques available to market researchers, they are clearly qualitative techniques and tend to compete for existing qualitative budgets.

DIFFERENCES IN DEFINITIONS

Because the field of online qualitative research is relatively new and dynamically changing, many of the terms currently being used lack precision in terms of their exact definition, with some software vendors, service vendors, and researchers using terms in different ways.

For example, Channel M2's multimedia bulletin board groups could be described as being a technique somewhere between a conventional online focus group and a conventional bulletin board group. The focus of these multimedia boards appears to be such that the moderator and at least one participant tend to be online at the same time, allowing the participant the choice of using voice, instant chat, or posting comments to communicate, although the boards can also be used in asynchronous mode.

Several of the vendors in the online qualitative space use the term IDI to mainly refer to synchronous conversations, where the internet has simply replaced a face-to-face or telephone depth, whereas others use it for asynchronous or parallel depths.

These differences in terminology are to be expected in such a rapidly developing field, but they do mean that researchers should check and clarify the definitions that both suppliers and clients are using.

THE FUTURE?

There are some signs that bulletin board groups may be superseded by online research communities (MROCs) over the next couple of years. This is for a number of convergent reasons.

The first reason is that the software for bulletin board groups has become significantly better over the last few years and in most cases is capable of being run as an online community rather than just as a bulletin board group. The second is that many potential participants are more familiar with the conventions of online communities than those of bulletin boards.

However, the main reason may simply be that the term 'community' is much more fashionable than the term 'bulletin board group'. Online research communities have shown that they appeal to both qualitative and quantitative researchers. Although most aspects of online research communities are essentially qualitative, they are not restricted to competing for just qualitative budgets.

The counter argument offered by some researchers is that bulletin board groups can be run in a more tightly focused way than communities, creating time and cost savings. Indeed, some researchers point out that they currently run bulletin board groups with sub-sets of members from their online research communities.

The future of parallel IDIs is much less clear. They may end up being subsumed into two trends. The first is the growing use of new communications channels for synchronous conversations, including the use of SMS, chat, video, instant messaging, VOIP, etc. The second is the use of e-ethnography and the recruitment of participants as self-reporting amateur market researchers – a topic reviewed in Part V.

Other Online Qualitative Methods and Summary of Online Qualitative Research

In addition to the two major online qualitative techniques already reviewed in this section, i.e. online focus groups and bulletin board groups, there are a number of other online methods that fit the description of 'pre-social media'. These methods are reviewed in this chapter, and are listed below.

- ○   *Email groups*

- ○   *Depth interviews via the internet*

- ○   *Viewing focus groups remotely*

- ○   *Virtual words and virtual qualitative*

- ○   *Qualitative explication of online quantitative studies*

There is also a wide range of qualitative methods and approaches that has been developed in conjunction with social media, such as blog mining and online research communities. These are covered in full in Part III, Social Media.

This chapter provides a summary of online qualitative research, bringing together the threads covered in the previous chapters.

EMAIL GROUPS

Email groups are now fairly uncommon, but they were one of the first methods that used the internet to conduct qualitative research and they may still have some relevance in the future. Moderated email groups (MEGs) were first developed by UK researcher Pete Comley (Eke and Comley, 1999) and are an example of an asynchronous approach. In an MEG the researcher communicates with the participants via email, i.e. no special software is required.

Although email groups are now relatively rare, it may be worth researchers keeping them in mind because they may re-emerge in a slightly new form as a result of the development of social media.

For example, it may be that the email group could be revamped in the context of Twitter, Instant Messaging, status updates, writing on walls, SMS, or Google Wave. Another use of moderated email groups is in eDelphi projects (Brüggen and Willems, 2009).

A typical MEG is conducted over the course of about two weeks with approximately 15 to 20 participants. The researcher breaks the discussion guide into several pieces to spread the communication over about five to ten emails. The participants are expected to reply to each email, which means responding to an email every one to two days.

The main reason that MEGs only last for a couple of weeks, and the reason why the number of participants is kept fairly small, is the workload created for the researcher. The researcher needs to reply to all emails promptly and some of the replies from the participants can be very long, sometimes several pages from a single respondent.

Moderated email groups engender very limited group dynamics, because participants don't normally interact directly with each other. The researcher summarises the responses and uses the summaries as part of the stimulus material for the next wave of prompts, probes, and questions.

Moderated email groups were felt to be suitable for those occasions when the researcher was willing to trade-off breadth for depth. They work better when the researcher is looking at a single idea or topic. Because an MEG is asynchronous and takes place over several days, it also allows respondents to reflect on their opinions and for their ideas to evolve over time.

A moderated email group study conducted in the UK at the time of the 2000 Olympics illustrates the power of the asynchronous approach (Quigley and Poynter, 2001). The study looked at British attitudes to a number of phenomena, including the use of sponsorships paid to athletes to allow them to concentrate on their training. At the start of the Olympics the attitude of most members of the group was negative towards sponsorship. However, as the UK's tally of medals, especially gold medals, grew, the attitude towards sponsorship swung round. By the end of the Olympics the views were strongly in favour.

VIEWING FOCUS GROUPS REMOTELY

Over the last 30 years there has been a developing business in video-casting focus groups, allowing people who are not present to view them. Two of the biggest names in this area, in market research, are FocusVision [https://www.focusvision.com/] and ActiveGroup [http://www.activegroup.net/].

The basics of remote focus groups are very straightforward, at least they are these days. A focus group is held in a location which has both video recording and streaming facilities. Basically this means one or more video cameras and a good internet link. The locations also need the appropriate services to make this stream available to the authorised viewers. These facilities can be set up on an *ad hoc* basis, but it is easier, cheaper, and quicker to work with facilities that already have the remote technology in place and tested. Both ActiveGroup and FocusVision have partners in about 30 countries, which means that this route is a viable option in most of the places where there is significant market research spend.

BEYOND STREAMING

Remote focus groups have created more opportunities than simply allowing people to watch live transmissions of focus groups. Amongst the sorts of resources offered by the service providers are:

○ *archiving the storage of streamed focus groups*

○ *tagging and searching. Systems can allow researchers and clients who view focus groups to tag items, either live or when viewing archived material. The tags allow researchers and clients to search archived material and to create meta analyses*

○ *transcripts, allowing conventional analysis, and the linking of transcripts to tags and clips*

PRIVACY AND DATA SECURITY ISSUES

The remote viewing of focus groups introduces a number of additional concerns about privacy and data security. The most important thing to remember for researchers involved in the remote viewing of focus groups is that in most countries people's faces count as personally identifiable data. Most countries have legal restrictions on what can be done with personally identifiable data, and many of them have limits on what data can be transferred abroad and what procedures and permissions are required.

Each agency and each country has their own detailed policy and guidelines, but the following points should provide a useful guideline.

1. Gain informed consent from the people being recorded. This means telling them who will watch the material (the types of people and their locations, not their names), where the material will be stored, how long it will be stored, how it will be used, and how the person can contact the company at a later date if they want to remove their permission for its use.

2. Ensure that anybody viewing the material knows that if they find they know or recognise one of the respondents attending a group they should stop viewing that material.

3. Ensure that anybody who can access the material is aware of the limitations to its use. For example, most recorded focus group material can't be used for internal training or marketing purposes, but this means that everybody who can access the recordings has to know this.

4. Ensure that when the material is erased all copies are removed. Note, many countries' data protection laws have strict rules about the destruction of personally identifiable information.

Given that privacy can be a tricky area, most researchers need to seek advice, especially on ensuring that the initial permissions are sufficiently robust. Quite often the company supplying the streaming service will be able to help with advice.

THE FUTURE OF REMOTE VIEWING

The growth in the streaming of focus groups depends on three key criteria:

1. That there is continued and widespread interest in conventional focus groups.

2. That the costs of the services manage to provide sufficient return on investment (ROI) in terms of the benefits of remote viewing and of the enhanced archiving facilities.

3. That legislation about personal data does not become too onerous (people's faces and voices are personal data and the default in many countries is that they are protected).

At the moment there are major changes taking place in mobile technologies, with devices like Flip cameras and iPhones, along with faster and cheaper mobile internet access. It may be that the convenience of setting up *ad hoc* and informal remote viewing may significantly improve; including depth interviews and self-reporting. If this comes to pass then the key benefit that major companies will offer will be the archiving, collaborating, tagging and remixing of the recorded/streamed material rather than the capturing of the material itself.

VIRTUAL WORLDS AND VIRTUAL QUALITATIVE

In the early days of Second Life, the virtual world created by Linden Labs, a number of researchers experimented with conducting qualitative research in this virtual world. These projects included virtual focus groups, one-on-one depth interviews with avatars, and even an enterprising project which used sofas that were programmed to ask questions of the people who sat on them (Derval and Menti, 2008).

However, the growth of Second Life has stalled (or gone into reverse, it depends on whose figures you use). According to Linden Labs' own figures, on 5 October 2009 slightly fewer than one million users had logged in during the previous month. This means the scale of Second Life is insignificant at both the global and local levels. Therefore it is unlikely that Second Life will play any significant role in the future of market research, but that does not mean virtual worlds have gone away and they may become very relevant in the future.

THE FUTURE OF VIRTUAL QUALITATIVE

The interest that Second Life generated, and the scale of virtual worlds such as World of Warcraft (which has about 5 million active users), suggest that the concept of virtual qualitative research – i.e. based on people interacting via avatars in virtual worlds – will make a reappearance.

The key driver of the future of virtual worlds is likely to be dependent on them being easier to use and ideally adding some elements of asynchronicity. At the moment one of the main limitations of virtual worlds is that one hour of fun in a virtual world requires one hour of real time, and that time has to coincide with other people being there for the same hour – in a time-poor world this can be a major limitation.

One possible use for virtual qualitative research might be in evaluating designs, for example for apartments, holiday destinations, bars, retail locations, and office accommodation. These assessments could be based on actual locations or designs/concepts for locations. However, the interfaces for virtual worlds will need to improve substantially for this to happen.

QUALITATIVE EXPLICATION OF QUANTITATIVE STUDIES

One of the weaknesses of quantitative research is that whilst it might produce results that are statistically significant they may be hard to interpret in terms of why respondents give the scores they give. A traditional way to ameliorate this problem has been to add open-ended questions to quantitative surveys. For example, if somebody in response to a satisfaction scale question says they are dissatisfied with the service they have received, they might be asked why, via an open-ended question.

When market researchers use online quantitative questionnaires to survey people, there is a greater danger that the respondents may not fully understand the questions they are being asked. This risk arises primarily because there is no interviewer present to help interpret the questionnaire and to pass back queries to the researcher.

In response to these perceived weaknesses, and as an opportunistic use of the medium, a number of approaches have been developed to add an explicative qualitative element to online quantitative studies.

One innovation that some researchers are using in quantitative studies is the addition of a 'call me' button which facilitates Skype or telephone conversations with an interviewer. However, this does require interviewers to be available and assumes that the number of calls will be relatively modest. A similar approach is taken by iModerate [www.imoderate.com] which enables an online chat to be initiated between respondents and a moderator.

Some researchers have combined qualitative and quantitative approaches by interviewing a quantitative sample simultaneously. For example, the sample of 100 to 200 is assembled online and they are all taken through the survey in parallel (Comley, 2008). The researcher and the clients can review the results and probe key groups to expand on their answers via both closed and open-ended questions. These approaches can be created using adaptations to online focus group software, quantitative packages such as Confirmit, or via bespoke solutions such as Invoke [http://www.invokesolutions.com/].

POST-SURVEY QUALITATIVE EXPLICATION

Historically, when a quantitative study has finished, especially an *ad hoc* study, all contact is ended between the researcher and respondent. The respondent does not find out what happened, they can't contribute additional thoughts or comments on the survey, and the researcher can't ask for further clarification from the respondents. However, a growing number of researchers who conduct online quantitative surveys are adding a qualitative component to the end of their surveys. These vary from one-off elements such as the use of a webcam to leave recorded comments, through to mini-communities.

Webcam comments. A number research companies, such as UK agency Virtual Surveys, have promoted the use of finishing online surveys by asking respondents if they have a webcam. If the respondent has a webcam or even just a microphone they are invited to leave a comment about the topic of the research. The power of this approach is that the video clips can often communicate the findings from the quantitative research far better than traditional tables or charts.

Post survey discussions. Another approach is to route people who have finished to an online discussion where respondents can post their comments and see what other people have said. This method can be particularly powerful when utilised by an online access panel, as has been shown by Australian panel OpinionsPaid [http://www.opinionspaid.com/op/blogs/].

Post-survey portal. An extension of the post-survey discussion is the post-survey portal. A typical portal runs for the length of the fieldwork and for a short while afterwards. The portal serves several purposes, trying to meet the needs of client, researcher, and respondents. The portal provides a place where results and further questions can be posted by the client and the researcher, and where respondents can post comments on the survey or other comments such as their post survey experience.

SUMMARY OF ONLINE QUALITATIVE RESEARCH

This final section pulls together the threads explored in this and the previous three chapters. It highlights the main issues confronting researchers using online qualitative research, and looks at the implications for the future.

PRE-SOCIAL MEDIA QUALITATIVE RESEARCH

This section has looked at online qualitative research, from a pre-social media context. The main reason for this was to separate the relatively defined techniques of online qualitative from the very undefined techniques that are emerging from social media. However, the advent of social media in market research is likely to represent a disruptive change, not just in terms of online qualitative but also in the divide between qualitative and quantitative research and the relative status of the two. Over the last few years, about five times as much money has been spent on quantitative survey research as qualitative research. Indeed, qualitative research accounts for just 14% of the total of all research, according to estimates from ESOMAR.

Before the advent of social media, as a research phenomenon, online qualitative research was quite distinct from online quantitative research. In most cases, online qualitative research competed against offline qualitative proposals just as online quantitative research tended to compete against offline quantitative proposals. In the pre-social media context, online qualitative has mostly meant online focus groups and bulletin board groups, with a small number of other approaches also being in the mix.

 Author's View

WHY ONLINE QUALITATIVE HAS NOT DONE BETTER

One major difference between online qualitative research and online quantitative research is the difference in their relative success. Online has become the largest single modality for quantitative research, whereas online qualitative has remained a very small proportion of qualitative research.

To some extent the reasons why online qualitative have not been more successful have to be conjecture, but here are some that seem to have widespread currency.

Looking back at the success of online quantitative it is clear that it was able to offer research that was cheaper and faster, but in terms of quality it was no better and sometimes clearly not quite as good. However, many buyers and vendors of quantitative research were happy to compromise on quality to get the cost and speed benefits (or perhaps in some cases did not fully understand the compromises they were making).

By contrast, online qualitative has not, in most cases, offered big speed and cost savings, and there is a widespread perception that there is major quality difference between face-to-face qualitative and online qualitative, despite the evidence of most comparative studies supporting the quality of the results from online qualitative research.

With online quantitative research there was a critical mass of innovators and key opinion leaders who pushed the idea of online data collection, for example researchers like Pete Comley and Gordon Black, and clients like General Mills. Qualitative has not had the same critical mass of key opinion leaders pushing for the adoption of online qualitative techniques. However, towards the end of 2009 General Mills announced that they were going to move most of their qualitative research online, albeit mostly via online communities.

THE KEY ETHICAL AND QUALITY ISSUES

The last ten years have seen online quantitative research being beset by quality and ethical issues on all sides, particularly related to its uses of online access panels. By contrast, online qualitative research has only faced the same sort of issues as offline qualitative research.

There has been some concern about the remote viewing of focus groups, but to a similar extent there have been concerns about using the output from video ethnography and creating DVD reports including edited images.

The main ethical issues for online qualitative researchers are to:

○   *ensure they operate within informed consent, and*

○   *protect respondents and participants, particularly their anonymity and privacy.*

THE FUTURE OF ONLINE QUALITATIVE

It is unlikely that the forms of online qualitative research being used before the advent of social media (for example, online focus groups and bulletin board groups) will suddenly take off and become a dominant feature of market research. However, the advent of social media may change the whole picture.

Online research communities already appear to be a larger part of the global total of research spend than all pre-social media online qualitative techniques combined. Some of the work of online research communities is clearly quantitative in the way it is described, and to some extent marketed. However, a large part of what online communities (and other social media) are used for is clearly qualitative and this appears set to grow.

In the future, we may see growth of online focus groups as a method of communication between researchers and community members, providing an alternative and quick method of gaining insight. Bulletin board group methods may become integrated within both short- and long-term communities.

The future of most online qualitative research may be subsumed into the market research use of social media. If this proves to be true, then online qualitative research will no longer be competing for just qualitative budgets. A short-term online research community is just as much a competitor for an *ad hoc* quantitative project as it is a competitor for an *ad hoc* qualitative project.

Buzz and blog mining, online research communities, e-ethnography, the semiotics of the web, and the use of respondent blogs are all new and exciting developments in market research. They are all associated with social media, and they are all, to a greater or lesser extent, qualitative.

One of the challenges that may face qualitative research in the near future, as it becomes ever more associated with social media, is how to make sure that 60 years of knowledge, developed by qualitative market researchers, is not disregarded as new researchers, many with quantitative backgrounds, start using qualitative techniques in social media research.

Social media is the topic of the next part of the book.

PART III

Social Media

The chapters in this part of the book look at how market research has started to embrace and utilise the disruptive change of social media; a phenomenon that stretches from blogs to wikis, from communities to YouTube. As mentioned at the start of the book, the use of the internet for market research represented a major evolutionary change in the way that market research is conducted. By contrast, social media potentially represents a revolutionary change. As Mark Earls and John Kearon have said, it can be thought of as a change from ME-research to WE-Research (Kearon and Earls, 2009).

This section starts with a brief introduction and consists of the following chapters:

- Participatory blogs as research tools

- Online research communities

- Blog and buzz mining

- Other social media topics and summary

INTRODUCING SOCIAL MEDIA

Over the last few years the largest change that has affected the internet has been the rise in the use of social media and the development of something that has been dubbed Web 2.0. This introduction briefly looks at what we mean by social media and Web 2.0 and sets the scene for their impact on market research.

The next four chapters then look at how market researchers have been meeting the challenges and opportunities created by developments in the internet, such as blogs, online research communities, and e-ethnography.

SOCIAL MEDIA, HARD TO DEFINE, EASY TO RECOGNISE

Social media is a very broad term and no two commentators seem to define it in exactly the same way. However, the core element of the definitions of social media is the way that the internet and other new technologies are being used to move away from media that was essentially a one-to-many model, for example broadcast, towards a many-to-many model, such as Facebook.

Examples of social media include blogging, micro-blogging (e.g. Twitter), social networking (e.g. Facebook, Mixi, Cyworld), Wikis (e.g. Wikipedia, the collaborative encyclopaedia), social bookmarking (e.g. Delicious and Digg), photo sharing (e.g. Flickr), video sharing (e.g. YouTube), voice networking (e.g. Skype), music sharing (e.g. Last FM), product and service reviews (e.g. TripAdvisor), virtual worlds (e.g. Second Life and World of Warcraft), and multiplayer games (e.g. Farmville).

The term 'social media' is useful because it groups together much of the new phenomena of the internet in a relatively value-free way. The term does not imply that social media is better than other media, or that it will necessarily replace old media, it is simply a description of media based on the paradigm of many-to-many.

USER-GENERATED MEDIA

One of the key developments, both in technology and behaviour, relates to UGM, or user-generated media. For most of recorded history only the few were able to produce media, for example books, newspapers, records, and films. Even the advent of the box Brownie camera did not really change the balance – most photos were destined to remain in albums and shoe boxes in people's homes.

Social media has changed the rules and the barriers for entry have dropped massively. For example, anybody can blog, for free. Anybody can share their photos, for free. Anybody can share their videos, for free. This ability to create and share content, this UGM, is a key part of the social media revolution.

WEB 2.0

The term 'Web 2.0' was first coined in 2004 and by 2009 was already appearing dated. The concept of Web 2.0 embraces two elements: the first is the emergence, growth, and popularity of social media; the second is a change in the paradigm of how control is shared between providers and users. The adoption of the idea of Web 2.0 reflected the evidence that users were taking more control of their interactions with media, with organisations, and with each other. This change has been described in transactional analysis terms by Pete Comley (2006) as a shift from an Adult<>Child model to an Adult<>Adult model.

The term 'Web 2.0' was adopted by many other fields of endeavour, for example Law 2.0, Government 2.0, and Marketing 2.0. It was also adopted in market research, with Martin Oxley probably being the first to refer to Research 2.0 (Oxley, 2006). The concept of Research 2.0 was quickly taken up by a wide range of market researchers and became very popular with conference organisers. The term 'Research 2.0' soon became particularly associated with the rapidly growing use of online communities for market research, and to a lesser extent with the use of blogs and blog mining. During late 2008 and early 2009 'Research 2.0' was beginning to be seen as dated and the term 'New MR' was beginning to supersede it, even though the two are not exactly the same.

10 Participatory Blogs as Research Tools

Blogs were one of the first of the social media tools to be adopted by market researchers as a tool for market research. Their use divides neatly into two groups: as an input into observational techniques such as blog mining, and as an active tool where respondents are recruited and asked to record a blog as part of a research project, i.e. participant blogging.

The topic of blog mining is covered in Chapter 12, Blog and Buzz Mining.

This chapter focuses on participant blogging, i.e. using blogs as an active research tool, where respondents are recruited to use them as part of the research process. The chapter is divided into five parts:

- ○   *Introduction to blogs*

- ○   *Participant blogs as a research tool*

- ○   *Running a blog project*

- ○   *Issues to consider*

- ○   *Summary of participatory blogs*

INTRODUCTION TO BLOGS

'Blog' is a term that has become so common that it can often be assumed that everyone is blogging, that everyone is reading them, and that there are agreed definitions of what a blog is and how blogging can be used in market research. However, nothing in social media is that clean or simple.

The first part of this chapter reviews the concepts and terminology associated with blogs and establishes a framework to move forward.

WHAT IS A BLOG?

No two definitions of a blog are exactly the same but the essential element is a website organised as a set of chronological posts by an author or authors. The term 'blog' is a shortened version of the term 'weblog'.

Examples

Sometimes the easiest way to understand a concept is to look at a variety of examples, so here is a cross section of popular blogs:

○ **Seth Godin's Blog**, *http://sethgodin.typepad.com/. The regular musings and observations of marketing guru Seth Godin. One of the controversial aspects of Godin's blog is that it does not facilitate comments from readers.*

○ **My Boyfriend Is A Twat**, *http://www.myboyfriendisatwat.com/. A blog revealing extracts from the life of Zoe McCarthy, a Britain who lives in Belgium. Her regular rants are often humorous and have led to McCarthy being voted European blog of the year on three occasions, enabling her to monetise her site as a book and via merchandising.*

○ **Blog Maverick**, *http://blogmaverick.com/. This is a CEO blog, written by Mark Cuban, owner of USA basketball team the Dallas Mavericks. One of the things that makes this blog interesting is that most CEO blogs are written by people in IT-related companies, whereas Cuban's roots are in sport.*

○ **Guido Fawkes Blog**, *http://order-order.com/. A political blog authored by a right-of-centre writer in the UK. The blog has been responsible for breaking a number of stories which have caused problems for leading figures.*

○ **Huffington Post**, *http://www.huffingtonpost.com/. Strictly speaking, the Huffington Post is more than just a blog, as it aggregates information and includes a news service. Nevertheless, this left-of-centre website which concentrates on politics and current affairs is often cited as being one of the internet's most influential blogs.*

○ **BoingBoing**, *http://www.boingboing.net/. This blog is a stream of curious clippings from the internet. A great source for the weird stuff that helps its readers seem well informed and connected.*

○ **Vovici Blog**, *http://blog.vovici.com/. An influential market research blog written by the well informed and prolific blogger Jeffrey Henning.*

○ **The Future Place**, *http://thefutureplace.typepad.com/. A blog written by the author of this book, mostly market research, with a dash of futurology and personal opinions thrown in.*

Blogs can be written using a wide variety of platforms and systems, but many of them use Wordpress, Typepad, or Blogger.

TWITTER AND MICROBLOGGING

There is a section on Twitter in Part V, Breaking News, so the notes here are simply an introduction to and clarification of Twitter and where it fits in the blogging picture.

In theory, Twitter is an example of microblogging. But, at the moment that definition is almost back to front, i.e. microblogging is probably best described as being Twitter. This is because the other microblogging platforms have far fewer users and a much lower profile than Twitter. Indeed, most people who use Twitter would not know that it is called a microblogging service.

Twitter users post short updates of up to 140 characters, which are stored chronologically in their account, just like a regular blog. However, these posts, or 'tweets' as Twitter calls them, are also broadcast to everybody who has chosen to follow that person.

 Examples

Examples of people using Twitter are:

- **Guy Kawasaki**, *http://twitter.com/GuyKawasaki. Guy Kawasaki is a venture capitalist and IT industry pundit. He uses Twitter to keep people in touch with what he is doing and to market some of his ideas.*

- **Kevin Rudd**, *http://twitter.com/KevinRuddPM. Kevin Rudd is the Prime Minister of Australia and uses Twitter to provide a window into his personal and family life and also to highlight things he has done politically.*

- **Ashton Kutcher**, *http://twitter.com/APlusK. Actor Aston Kutcher has over four million followers, and is an example of a celebrity tweeter.*

- **ZebraBites**, *http://twitter.com/ZebraBites. Katie Harris is a market researcher based in Australia whose tweets combine market research, networking, and general chatter.*

- **Ray Poynter**, *http://twitter.com/RayPoynter, the tweets of the author of this book.*

Although Twitter has attracted media attention because of the well-known people who tweet, such as Oprah Winfrey, most people use it to follow people rather than to create their own stream of news, views, and thoughts.

At the end of 2009 Twitter was much bigger in English-speaking countries than in the rest of the world, and was actively blocked in some countries, particularly those who try to repress dissent.

Twitter is also a social network, although it has the unusual feature in that its 'friend' relationships are not reciprocal. For example, just because I might choose to follow Stephen Fry does not mean that Stephen Fry will choose to follow me.

OTHER VARIETIES OF BLOGGING

In addition to blogs and Twitter, there are other internet-related activities that are blog-like. For example:

- *Social networks. Many social networks provide a method for members to comment on what they are doing, for example, by providing status updates, lists of activities, or walls to write on. All of these can provide a chronological list of postings and many also allow other people to comment on them.*

○   *Some communities explicitly provide their members with a section to use for blogging. One platform that provides blogs as a default is Ning [http://www.ning.com/] and an example can be seen at the location-based community site HarringayOnline [http:// www.harringayonline.com/].*

○   *Multimedia services such as Flickr and YouTube can be used in a blogging sort of way, for example using images or videos instead of text.*

PARTICIPANT BLOGS AS A RESEARCH TOOL

Blogs are typically used in research projects when the researcher wants to explore some aspect of participants' lives in more depth than would be the case with more traditional forms of research. The general approach is to define a specific topic and then to recruit participants to blog about that topic during the course of the project. Whilst there is a wide variation in how blogs have been used in research, participatory blog research projects tend to have several elements in common, for example:

○   *In a typical configuration, each participant (a term that is often preferred to respondent for these types of projects), is given their own blog to maintain.*

○   *Participant blog projects are normally qualitative in nature. The participants are sometimes asked to fill in a survey as part of the exercise, but this tends to be for background and segmentation purposes as opposed to feeding directly into the insight process. The core of the insight normally comes from qualitative analyses of the blogs' content.*

○   *In a typical project, the participants are recruited in the same ways that are used for other qualitative projects and online research communities. Any incentives used tend to be quite high compared with both quantitative research and online research communities, reflecting the scale of the contributions that the participants are expected to make.*

○   *Blog projects tend to last for more than four days but less than three months (although some run longer). The drivers of the timeline usually include the client's desire to get an answer quickly, the cost of incentivising participants, and the difficulty of keeping the participants blogging over an extended period of time.*

○   *The number of participants tends to be modest, compared with quantitative studies and online research communities, typically ranging from about eight to about sixty participants.*

In addition to these common elements, there are a wide number of things that can vary from project to project, either based on the requirements of the project or the preferences of the researcher. The items that may be part of a blog project include whether or not participants:

○   can see and comment on each other's blogs

○   are asked to code their posts or other people's posts

○   are allowed (or encouraged, or required) to upload videos, images, and links

○   are able to use their mobile phones to post to their blog. Indeed, in some cases this may be the key aspect of the study

Where participants are able to see each other's blogs, and possibly encouraged to comment on other blogs, the research is sometimes referred to as Blog Groups.

   Advice

RUNNING A BLOG PROJECT

This section looks at the issues that confront a market researcher conducting a blog project, or a project with a blogging component, i.e. participant blogs or blog groups. The steps in running a project are first listed and then expanded on below:

○   *Scoping the project*

○   *Designing the blogs*

○   *Anonymity and data security*

○   *Terms and conditions*

○   *The activity cycle and intensity*

○   *Creating the research plan*

○   *Recruiting and training the participants*

○   *Managing the blogs*

○   *Extracting insight from participant blogs*

○   *Finishing a blog project*

SCOPING THE PROJECT

The scope of a project is a description of what the project is designed to answer, how long it will run for, how many participants will take part, and what features are essential to the project.

A participant blog project tends to use significant resources (e.g. time and/or money) at several key stages. These stages are:

○   *the creation of the blogs*

○   *recruiting and training the respondents*

○   *managing the project*

○   *extracting insight*

Of these steps, the resource implications for both the recruiting/training and extracting insight stages are a function of the number of respondents. The more respondents there are, the greater the costs of recruiting and training them and the longer the insight extraction will take. Managing the blog only tends to be affected if the number of participants is quite large or if they have problems.

The amount of resources required for the creation of the blogs is largely determined by how sophisticated the functionality of the site is required to be and the amount of styling that is applied, but it is not normally greatly affected by the number of respondents. Because the costs of a participant blog project can be significant, the duration of a project and the number of participants should be sufficient to answer the research questions but no greater.

A typical participant blog project lasts between one and four weeks and involves between eight and 60 respondents, but both smaller and larger projects are not uncommon.

DESIGNING THE BLOGS

The two main issues in designing participant blogs are:

(a)   making them simple to use, and

(b)   providing the facilities that the project needs, but not more

 Warning

In terms of making the blog easy to use, the researcher should keep in mind that most participants will not be active users of a blog. Even those who do blog are likely to be familiar only with their own system. So the design needs to be simple, and the recruitment/welcome process needs to include sufficient support to get each participant online. This point is explored more fully later in the chapter.

 Advice

Most projects need to enable the following features:

1.   Participants are able to post (i.e. write) blogs.

2.   Participants are able to send messages to the moderator.

3.   The moderator is able to send messages to all participants or to an individual participant.

4.   The moderator is able to edit or delete blogs.

5.   The moderator is able to delete participants.

The following features are ones that the researcher might want to include:

1.   Participants are able to view other participants' blogs.

2.   Participants are able to comment on other participants' blogs.

3.   Participants are able to upload images and/or videos.

In most cases, the researcher probably does **not** want to enable the following:

1.   Participants sending each other private messages.

2.   Participants friending each other.

3.   Participants sharing their posts with non-participants.

4.   Participants suggesting new members.

Many forms of participatory research, such as online research communities, are often heavily themed, either in terms of the client's branding or the topic under investigation. This reflects the focus of those techniques in trying to develop a sense of community. However, participatory blogs are not community focused and in most cases their design simply needs to convey a clean and professional image that is consonant with the aims of the project.

ANONYMITY AND DATA SECURITY

As with other market research, the participants' anonymity, safety, and data security is an issue of the highest importance. One of the key issues in terms of protecting the rights and safety of participants is to ensure their anonymity.

Many researchers now configure their participant blogs (and other social media projects) so that participants are discouraged from using their real name and photograph as their avatar. Ideally, participants should use an image of their choice and an alternative name.

As part of monitoring the project, the researcher should be vigilant to check that people are not inadvertently posting things which reveal too much about themselves, for example photos of their front door along with comments about where they live.

Advice

TERMS AND CONDITIONS

Most social media projects require terms and conditions that are more substantial than traditional face-to-face research projects, and this is true of participatory blogs. The terms and conditions need to cover:

- ❍ *recognition that the moderator can change the terms and conditions*

- ❍ *a definition of unacceptable behaviour (e.g. cyberbullying and xenophobia)*

- ❍ *confirmation that the intellectual property generated by the project belongs to the end client, or the research agency and the end client*

- ❍ *the rules that relate to any uploaded material, including copyright issues*

- ❍ *details of the project's privacy policy and what will happen to the data*

- ❍ *the scale of commitment that is expected from the participants*

- ❍ *the details of the incentive scheme, if there is one*

ACTIVITY CYCLE AND INTENSITY

One of the main differences between blog projects and most other forms of market research is the degree of intensity that is required of the researcher and particularly of the participants. In a short-term blog, participants might be expected to blog daily or more often. For example, in a travel to work study the participants might be expected to blog about every trip to and from work, and possibly to review the posts by other travellers. In this scenario the researcher is likely to need to be commenting and messaging the participants frequently in order to keep the activity levels high.

Some projects require the respondents to post their blogs via mobile phones several times a day, for example each time they experience a particular phenomenon, and then to expand on these posts in the evening, typically using a computer to log onto their blog.

Alternatively, a participatory blog project may follow some aspect of people's lives that changes slowly, for example looking for a new house or the way that a new marketing campaign unwinds over a period of weeks. In these cases, the participants might be blogging one to three times a week and the researcher might be restricting the messages they send to one or two a week.

The activity cycle of a project is the frequency with which tasks occur within it. If participants are posting daily and the researcher is commenting or messaging daily then the activity cycle is daily. If a project requires one post a week, with one main message or post from the moderator per week, then the activity cycle is weekly.

CREATING THE RESEARCH PLAN

The research plan – similar in concept to a discussion guide – should be written before the participants are recruited. It should include the tasks and questions that are going to be asked, along with a timeline for these tasks and the messages to participants.

However, as Ralph Waldo Emerson said, 'A *foolish consistency is the hobgoblin of small minds*'. As a participatory blog proceeds, the researcher must be prepared to update the research plan. This might mean adding elements to probe further or to clarify issues, which in turn may require other elements to be dropped from the plan.

RECRUITING AND TRAINING THE PARTICIPANTS

Participants can be recruited in any of the normal ways for a qualitative project, e.g. via online panels, client databases, or recruiters. In most cases the incentives for a participatory blog project are going to be at least as large as they are for a focus group. When recruiting the participants it is important to be very clear about the scale of commitment required, to help ensure a good rate of cooperation during the project.

As part of the welcome to the project, the participants will need to be trained in how to use the blogging platform. At a minimum this should include telling the participants how to post to the blog, perhaps setting them the task of introducing themselves. It may be useful to provide the respondents with a telephone number which they can use to call for advice.

MANAGING THE BLOGS

Managing a participatory blog is a combination of dealing with the planned activities, as laid out in the research plan, and responding to what the participants are posting. The researcher needs to be in relatively frequent contact with the participants. This can be by email or by comments added to their blog posts, for example probing for extra information.

The researcher also needs to monitor any lack of action by a participant, contacting them promptly to see if there is a problem.

EXTRACTING INSIGHT FROM PARTICIPANT BLOGS

As with other asynchronous qualitative projects, the analysis begins as soon as the respondents start posting. The researcher should be looking to develop theories grounded in the data and then seek to develop or refute those theories during the project, adjusting the questions and tasks to provide greater illumination.

At the end of the project the detailed analysis should seek to isolate the key themes, separating the noise from the signal.

FINISHING A BLOG PROJECT

Participants are generally aware of the end date of a project when they start, but they should be reminded periodically. Indeed, if they are beginning to flag a little, reminding them of the impending closing date is one way of encouraging them, for example '*Just two more days left, this is really useful information.*'

It is often useful to keep the blogs accessible for a few days after the end of the project to allow participants to catch up with any outstanding posts or uploads.

ISSUES TO CONSIDER

This section looks at some of the issues that market researchers need to consider when using participant blogs.

WHEN IS A BLOG NOT A BLOG?

Some uses of the term 'blog' by market researchers and others do not match most of the common definitions of a blog. For example, enabling people to post their point of view in a general discussion is not what most people mean by a blog, nor is a facility allowing people to leave an audio or video comment, for example at the end of a survey. Just because a research company has a technique that uses the term 'blog', it does not mean that it is actually based on blogs.

Most terms in social media are a bit vague, but a blog can be defined as:

1. A website accessed via an internet browser or a mobile device.

2. Having an author (either a person or a company); occasionally a blog has more than one author.

3. Having posts which are added sequentially. Most blogs allow readers to sort the posts by topics or tags, but the default is chronological.

Where a blog has conversations they tend to be between the author and reader, rather than between readers.

Warning

PARTICIPANTS AND THEIR FAMILIARITY WITH BLOGS

As mentioned earlier, researchers should not assume that the participants they recruit for a participatory blog project are already familiar with blogs, unless they were recruited and screened for those characteristics. Even if a participant is a regular blogger, they may not be familiar with the way the researcher has configured the project's blog.

As a rough guide to the sort of challenge that researchers can expect to face, the author commissioned an experiment, asking potential respondents in the USA about their blogging activities. The results of the experiment are shown below, followed by some notes about the experiment.

Table 10.1 looks at whether most people in the sample read blogs. Just under a third of the sample never read blogs. This indicates that a researcher should not assume potential participants are familiar with blogs, unless they plan to screen out people who never read blogs.

Table 10.1

Do you read blogs?	%
Often	17%
Sometimes	54%
Never	29%
Base	151

Table 10.2

Do you write a blog yourself?	%
Yes	13%
I have one, but I don't post these days	14%
No	73%
Base	151

Table 10.2 looks at whether people actively blog. The data indicates that amongst this sample less than one-third blog, and only a small proportion actively blog. This reinforces the point that the researcher will have to train participants. If the project used screening to only recruit active bloggers the sample would run the risk of being too biased for most purposes.

Table 10.3 looks at Twitter, another popular area with researchers. The data suggests that about half of this sample have not used Twitter, and only a minority use it.

Table 10.3

Do you use Twitter?	%
Yes	20%
I have an account but I don't login	27%
No	53%
Base	151

So, what is the sample? The data was collected from the USA DIY research provider AskYourTargetMarket, in December 2009. The logic of using this is that it is a good indicator of the sort of sample that ought to be relatively heavy internet users. The respondents are likely to be members of several panels and the fact that they are available to complete surveys quickly indicates that they are typical of people more likely to be found when recruiting participants for a project. If this hyperactive sample is not blogging and Twitter friendly, then it is unlikely that other samples that market researchers are likely to attract will be competent blog and Twitter users.

Given that this sample shows such low levels of blogging and Twitter usage, it is fairly safe to conclude that most researchers using participatory blogs should assume that a large chunk of their participants are inexperienced with blogs and Twitter.

ETHICAL CONCERNS

Most of the ethical issues raised by participatory blogs should be familiar to most qualitative researchers, for example ensuring that the client is aware of the projectability of the results and the need to ensure that participants are not led towards a particular finding or conclusion.

Similarly, the online ethical implications of participatory blogs should be familiar to most researchers who use online techniques, such as the need to protect data and to verify who the participants are.

The main additional area of concern is the need to ensure that participants' anonymity is protected, i.e. protected from each other and from the clients and the research team. In addition, participant safety should be protected by making sure that they do not develop inappropriate relationships with each other or with the researcher and client.

SUMMARY OF PARTICIPATORY BLOGS

Participatory blogs are a very powerful way of gaining insights into people's lives. They make use of one of the leading ideas in NewMR, namely working collaboratively with participants to conduct the research, using what Mark Earls and John Kearon have termed as the shift from ME-researcher to WE-Research (Kearon and Earls, 2009).

Participatory blogs can be quite onerous for both participants and researchers. Participants are expected to make frequent contributions, researchers need to support the participants, to develop the conversations, and extract the insight. The amount of time that the researcher is required to commit is a major driver of costs.

In most projects the participants will not be experienced bloggers, so the systems used must be intuitive and, in addition, good training and support must be offered.

Participatory blogs are a good way to get under the skin of a topic. By exploring participants' day-by-day experience of a topic, the picture begins to emerge and makes the extraction of insight easier.

Typical projects involve eight to 60 participants and last from one to four weeks, but exceptions to these parameters are not uncommon.

Online Research Communities/ MROCs

Online research communities are those created specifically to facilitate market research and are quite distinct from other online communities, such as natural communities (for example Facebook) or brand communities (for example Starbuck's MyStarbucksIdea). There is ongoing discussion about the best name for online research communities and they are also known as MROCs (Market Research Online Communities), private branded communities, and insight communities.

This chapter looks at the following topics:

- Overview of online research communities/MROCs

- A taxonomy of online research communities/MROCs

- Online community tools

- Designing an online research community

- Moderating and managing communities

- The theory of research communities

- Examples of communities

- Resources

- Quality and ethical issues

- The future of online communities

- Summary of research communities

OVERVIEW OF ONLINE RESEARCH COMMUNITIES/MROCS

For most market researchers, online research communities represent a new topic, but one that has recently been gaining traction right across the market research industry. Whilst a few agencies, such as Communispace (a USA agency running MROCs globally), have been offering research communities since around 2000, they did not really break onto the wider scene until about 2006, and have been growing rapidly ever since.

Online research communities/MROCs are carving out a new space that crosses the qualitative/quantitative divide. The majority of research communities have a few hundred members, which suggests quantitative research, but most of the insight from communities is gathered via discussions, which suggests qualitative research.

In terms of other techniques, online research communities fit between bulletin board groups (a qualitative technique) and community-enabled panels (which tend to be quantitative in nature, often with tens or hundreds of thousands of members).

Research communities are typically used in one of two quite distinct ways.

1. They are created as a solution to a specific research problem, for example, the design of an advertising campaign, or exploring customer usage issues with an aspect of a service, or the testing of a new design for a website. These communities, dealing with specific problems, tend both to be short term (i.e. less than three months) and to compete directly with other *ad hoc* research techniques, both qualitative and quantitative.

2. Other research communities are used as an ongoing resource, allowing an organisation to research a wide range of topics in a responsive and cost-effective way. These communities are more usually long term (six months or more).

Research communities typically comprise a collection of customers who have agreed to work with an organisation to improve its services or products, although there are some communities that focus on a topic or other shared characteristic rather than being customer focused. Community members tend not to be representative of the wider population of customers and, over a period of time, will tend to become increasingly aware of and interested in the brand. These community characteristics create biases and skews in the research, a phenomenon that needs to be taken into account. Rather than being representative, the aim is usually to make the community 'typical' of one or more customer groups, in a similar way that focus groups are often recruited to be typical of specific groups.

The reasons that research communities seem to be attracting so much interest are that they:

○ *allow companies to access the authentic voice of the consumer*

○ *go beyond just numbers*

○ *produce much faster research with a very low marginal cost (in the case of ongoing communities)*

○ *provide an insight into how most brand communications might operate in the future*

○ *allow customers to actively engage in discussions with brands and services, letting them 'make a difference'*

There are other ways of using different types of online communities, for example using existing networks such as Facebook and Twitter. However, at the moment none of these alternative approaches produce the sort of focused and actionable research that online research communities are producing.

A TAXONOMY OF RESEARCH COMMUNITIES

Because the field of online research communities/MROCs is developing so rapidly it is important to create a structure to help researchers understand the options that they must consider when using this tool. This section describes the different characteristics of online research communities by looking at the following topics:

- *Short-term communities*

- *Long-term communities*

- *Open versus closed communities*

- *Agency versus client moderated*

- *Research or hybrid communities*

- *The right number of members*

- *The balance between research and member agendas*

SHORT-TERM COMMUNITIES

A short-term, or project, community runs for the length of time required to meet the needs of a specific *ad hoc* research project. The length of a typical short-term community varies from about three days to three months, and will usually have between 30 and 500 members (although there are exceptions to these parameters).

Unlike continuous communities, short-term communities are likely to be conducted as an alternative solution to a traditional *ad hoc* research problem. A small community, for example 30 to 80 members, is likely to be seen as a replacement for a qualitative project. A larger community can be an alternative to both qualitative and quantitative projects.

Examples of short-term communities include:

- *developing a communications programme*

- *evaluating the needs of a target group of users or customers*

- *testing a product or service, for example testing a website for a financial service*

- *understanding customers' relationships with a product or service*

Warning

A short-term community is unlikely to develop a true sense of community between the members nor between the members and the brand. This means short-term communities usually need to be incentivised. This is especially true if the timeline for the project is short and the workload for the members is relatively onerous. However, if the brand has a very strong relationship with its customers, extrinsic incentives might not be needed.

Short-term communities are normally created and moderated by a research agency rather than being developed in-house by clients. This is because a short-term project is normally associated with a limited amount of time and money, and creating an in-house solution from scratch is likely to be too expensive, time-consuming, and too risky. For research buyers, there are speed, cost, and risk avoidance benefits in using an agency, provided that the agency already has a solution which only needs to be tailored to the buyer's specific requirements.

In a typical short-term community, say one to three weeks in duration, the members are expected to contribute to the community on a daily basis, with new tasks (e.g. discussion and polls) being set daily. In the context of research communities, the term 'daily' normally refers to Monday to Friday; members often continue to take part at weekends but it is rare that the weekend is used for core research activities. The frequency of new tasks is often referred to as the activity cycle of the project.

Because of the compressed timeline available to a short-term community, a moderator plan is normally created for the whole project at the outset, at least in outline form. In many ways, the moderator's plan is like the discussion guide used in a depth interview or focus group. The moderator's plan will be modified during the project in response to the inputs from the members, but there should normally be a draft written before the start of fieldwork.

LONG-TERM COMMUNITIES

A long-term or continuous community is typically one that addresses a series of research topics rather than one specific project. A long-term community tends to operate as a research resource for the organisation that has commissioned it. In most cases, there is little difference between a long-term community (which usually means six months or more) and a continuous community.

A typical long-term community has more members than a short-term community, for example 100 to 1200 members, but there are a wide range of exceptions. There is an interaction between the number of members in a community and the level of incentives being used. If large incentives are used with a community, then it will tend to have fewer members, to avoid costs escalating.

The activity cycle of a long-term community is slower than that of a short-term community, typically weekly instead of daily. The activity cycle with a long-term community is normally evenly spaced, i.e. it does not typically alternate between periods of high activity and lulls of inactivity (but again there are exceptions). The key to a well functioning long-term community is engagement, and that in turn depends upon regular contact and the provision of a range of activities.

OPEN VERSUS CLOSED COMMUNITIES

Most online research communities are created as closed, or private, communities, which are also referred to as walled gardens or gated communities. The members of these closed communities are recruited by invitation only, which reduces the risk of inappropriate people being part of the project. A closed community is normally protected by a login and password, which means that it is hidden from view.

An open community, by contrast, has members who will typically have joined from a variety of sources, including self-selection routes. For example, members of an open community may have responded to advertising, they may have joined as a result of initiatives such as 'member find member', or they may have responded to links on a brand's website.

It should be noted that even an open community can have some restrictions on who can join it. For example, an open community may screen potential members on criteria such as whether they are customers or users of some specific product or service. Alternatively, an open community may screen members by age, location, or some other characteristic. For example, in 2008, the British Government decided to use an online research community as part of its programme of research into the implementation of its proposed ID Card scheme. The community was open for anybody to view, but only people aged 16 to 24 years, who lived in the UK, and who were willing to abide by the terms and conditions of the community were allowed to join.

 Advice

The key reasons why most communities are closed are:

1.   To control the size of the community. Most communities are designed to have a specific number of members, for example, 50, 500, 2000. Their size tends to be limited because of views about the optimum size for a viable community and because of cost-related issues, including the cost of recruiting, incentivising, and analysing.

2.   To facilitate a community being targeted at a specific group of people, for example only customers who have used the service at least twice in the last six months.

3.   To allow incentives to be used without attracting the attention of professional respondents and of sites such as paidsurveysites.net.

4.   To increase the security of the community, making it less likely that competitors and the media are aware of ideas being tested and of the conversations being held. However, it should be remembered that nothing on the internet is truly safe and secret.

5.   To offer more reassurance to community members in terms of privacy.

Communities tend to be open when one or more of the following apply:

○   *the research is more about involvement than insight*

○   *the aims of the community are wider than just research, for example including word of mouth advocacy*

○   *the organisation is trying to maximise the size of an online community*

○   *the organisation needs to demonstrate characteristics such as openness, transparency, and particularly that it is listening*

A closed community and a completely open community are simply two ends of a continuum. There are many points between these two extremes – for example, a community may have a waiting list that prospective new members could apply to be on, or it may operate a 'member find member' approach, where community members are encouraged to recommend and vouch for new members.

INCENTIVES

Most online research communities use some form of incentive, but there is a wide variation in what companies do. The key questions are:

(a)   Should a community use incentives?

(b)   If incentives are used, what form should they take (for example, should they be cash, points, or prizes)?

(c)   If there are incentives, what should they be linked to (for example, should they be linked to work done or quality)?

Discussions about incentives often tend to focus on extrinsic incentives, such as cash, points, and prizes. However, intrinsic rewards are just as important, i.e. the emotional and psychological rewards that community members gain from making contributions that are welcomed, acknowledged, and respected.

The main argument against paying extrinsic incentives is that they can change the relationship between the community and its members. If there are no extrinsic incentives, the community will only function if its members feel they are doing something that is enjoyable or rewarding. If members are being paid, there is a risk that the metaphor will become one of paying somebody to do something they don't want to do. If a community is delivering true engagement and value to its members, it should not be necessary to pay incentives, and the absence of extrinsic incentives will make the team running the community try harder to develop the engagement.

One practice which balances the intrinsic and extrinsic rewards is to run the group in a sufficiently engaging way that the intrinsic rewards are a sufficient incentive, and the extrinsic rewards are then clearly positioned as an additional thank you. However, it is not uncommon for communities to be incentive driven, sometimes with relatively high levels being paid. There are occasions where the rules or conventions of the organisation running the research inhibit or prohibit the use of incentives. This is often true for organisations funded by public money or by charitable contributions.

There are two counter arguments that people make in favour of incentives.

1.   The first argument relates to fairness. If companies are making money from people's views, surely it is only fair to reward the time and effort members are contributing. This point of view suggests that a community shouldn't be based on the client always 'taking' and never 'giving'.

2.   The second argument is related to the practicalities of getting the necessary responses to the programme from the community. In some communities, particularly short-term, highly tasked ones, incentives may be the only way to persuade enough people to take part, particularly at the required level of activity.

If a community is going to be incentivised, it needs to define what the incentives are and how they will be distributed.

Types of incentives

A very common form of incentive in online research is cash (often paid as online vouchers or as points that can be converted into cash or products). However, many researchers worry that this is the incentive most corrosive to the concept of a community of interest, and the one most likely to create an employer/employee mentality.

Many communities offer rewards linked to the reason why people have joined the community. For example, the airline easyJet offers its members the chance to win flights. However, this approach is frowned on by some research bodies (such as the UK's MRS) who feel it is too close to marketing. On the other hand, it seems to be what members want.

Many communities offer intrinsic rewards, such voting on the 'post of the week'. Many communities seek to make members feel they are special, for example by sending advance information about new products, services, or upcoming adverts, or by inviting members to events such as a tour of a factory or location.

Allocating incentives

If a community is using incentives, it has to decide on how to allocate them. Currently common options include:

○   *An incentive allocated to every member, regardless of what they contribute. This is simple, and if the reward is just a thank you it might be OK, but it does not incentivise activity. If the amount is small, it may not even be seen as much of a thank you. If it is large, it will drive costs up without necessarily increasing the quantity or quality of contributions.*

○ *An incentive paid to every member who makes some contribution during a relevant period of time, for example a month or three months (a contribution might be classified as a post, answering a poll, or perhaps uploading a photo). This method does incentivise activity but it can be expensive. These incentives can be quite high for short-term communities, for example US$50 per week for two weeks for everybody making at least three contributions during the week.*

○ *A prize draw, offered either to everybody in the community or to those who have contributed in the relevant period. This method allows for a larger incentive whilst controlling costs, but not every potential community member finds prize draws a motivating incentive.*

○ *An award paid to the 'best' contribution in the relevant period. Some communities allow their members to choose the best contribution; others prefer the moderator or the end client to make the choice. One problem with this approach when used with long-term communities is that a small number of members can end up winning most of the prizes if they are the best and/or the busiest contributors.*

Many communities which use incentives use a combination of the techniques outlined above.

 Warning

One trap that some new communities fall into is that they offer very large incentives initially, in order to 'get it going'. However, this approach usually leads to high expectations amongst community members, which can result in large incentives always being necessary, or to a drop in activity as members realise the big incentives were just to get them interested and they are now being asked to 'work' for much less.

AGENCY VERSUS CLIENT MODERATED

One area that is widely discussed is the issue of who should provide the day-to-day management of a community. There are some who argue that once a research community is created it should be owned and run by the brand, not by a third party such as a research agency. This view recognises that most members who join a community do so because they want to speak directly to the brand; members want to feel that the community has the potential to directly drive the brand's development.

However, the majority view at the moment seems to be that online research communities should be managed on a day-to-day basis by a third party, often a research agency. This view is based on the following perception:

○ *Looking after a community can be very time consuming. Ideally, a community should be moderated and managed by a team and this scale of resource is often unavailable within client companies. On a week-to-week basis a client might require its resources to be used elsewhere, forgetting that community members expect to be responded to promptly.*

O   *Knowing the best way to run a community and the tools available requires modera-tors to stay in touch with a wide variety of sources. New tools and approaches are being developed all the time, with papers and conferences being produced around the globe. Companies who run communities invest time in R&D and in keeping up-to-date with the latest thinking and the latest guidance; this can be harder for client companies to do.*

O   *The onerous reporting cycle, implicit in most research communities, can result in pressure to report only the obvious findings and for analysts being too willing to sacrifice objectiv-ity by accepting what community members are saying. Contracting a research agency to extract and report the insight from a community can be a useful discipline and helps ensure that the analysis is conducted sufficiently robustly. Whilst this can be done in-house, it is often easier to create a reporting mechanism with a third party, particularly one that can be audited, reviewed, evaluated and, if necessary, fired.*

However, even in those cases where the community's day-to-day management is provided by a third party, the brand or organisation needs to commit to being involved. When community members ask questions they want to hear answers, they want those answers to correctly reflect the brand's views and plans, and they want those answers promptly. Community members tend to join communities to speak to the brand, not the agency, they want to know that the brand is listening to them and that they are being taken seriously.

RESEARCH OR HYBRID COMMUNITIES

Communities come in many shapes, sizes, and forms. Most communities provide some potential for market research, but those whose main focus is market research tend to differ from communities which have some other primary focus. Within their own spheres of competence, these other types of communities have their own names and terms, but from a research point of view we can consider them all as hybrid communities. The term 'hybrid' indicates that they are used for research and some-thing else, often marketing.

Research communities typically are much smaller and more likely to be closed than hybrid commun-ities. Research communities are also likely to avoid actively asking members to engage in marketing-related activities.

Examples of hybrid communities

The following panels are all examples of hybrid communities when viewed from the perspective of market research. These examples illustrate some of the different ways that non-research communities can lead to insight.

Examples

VocalPoint

VocalPoint [http://www.vocalpoint.com/] is a community of some 500 000 USA 'moms', owned by P&G and used as an integral part of P&G's Tremor service. VocalPoint is used for both market research (quantitative and qualitative) and for word-of-mouth marketing.

Tremor's integrated approach to research and marketing is highlighted by the case studies presented on its website. One of the case studies relates to the toothpaste brand Crest [http://www.tremor.com/Revealing-Case-Studies/Crest-Weekly-Clean/ viewed 11 December 2009] and talks about how qualitative and quantitative research were used to develop a positioning for a new product, Crest Weekly Clean. After the positioning was created, the VocalPoint community was used to create trial and word-of-mouth advocacy in a campaign that included a microsite on the community and direct mail. The direct mail included product information, a free trial voucher, and four vouchers to be given to the recipients' friends.

Because neither VocalPoint nor Tremor are heavily branded as P&G they can be used to research and market a wide range of products and services.

MyStarbucksIdea

MyStarbucksIdea [http://mystarbucksidea.force.com/] is a brand community operated by Starbucks using a platform provided by SalesForce. Although the community has a USA focus, it clearly has thousands of non-USA members (by March 2009 Starbucks was quoting a total membership of over 150 000 members).

MyStarbucksIdea is basically a vehicle for customers to suggest ideas to Starbucks and to vote and comment on other ideas. MyStarbucksIdea won a Forrester Groundswell award in 2008, announcing that in the first six months it had received 75 000 ideas. It is not necessary to join the community to view the site, but it is necessary to join before being able to post ideas or comments.

WePC.com

WePC.com is an ideas community jointly owned by Intel and ASUS (a Taiwan-based manufacturer of netbooks and computer components). In some ways the WePC.com and MyStarbucksIdea communities are quite similar in that they are both ideas focused. But whereas the MyStarbucksIdea is very brand focused, the WePC.com community is much more focused on general issues, such as the ideal size and shape for a netbook. Despite its niche position, WePC.com regularly gets thousands of people viewing a single discussion.

 Advice

Why have research-only communities?

Hybrid communities have some very significant strengths. Because they might generate sales they can be more directly cost effective than something which is purely research; the ROI for research communities tends to be indirect or deferred. Indeed, it is possible for a community based on word-of-mouth marketing to offer research as a free service as part of marketing projects. Hybrid communities are usually much larger than research communities, which opens up the chance to find special interest groups within the community, or to use larger sample sizes (which may appear to some buyers as more representative).

However, there are a number of advantages in using a research-only community to gather research insight:

○ *The community is small enough for a real and productive sense of community to be developed (although similar ends might be achieved by taking a sub-group from a larger hybrid community).*

○ *Members may be more willing to be open and honest if they do not think they are being 'sold' to.*

○ *If the community is seen as a marketing asset, its use can become a battle between the marketing director and anybody wanting to use it for non-marketing purposes. This is a common problem with in-house databases, where the priority is to use them for marketing and there is a perceived need to limit the number of emails and requests, which often squeezes out other activities such as market research.*

 Advice

THE RIGHT NUMBER OF MEMBERS?

The number of members in a research community is one of the key determinants of the nature of the community and also of its cost. Or, to put it another way, the size of a community is determined by the nature of the community and the budget.

The larger a community, the more expensive it is to recruit, the more expensive the incentives might be, and the more time it takes to analyse the data.

Projects with a large number of members often struggle to create a meaningful sense of community. In general, a community that is attempting to build a sense of belonging and interaction will be limited to perhaps 300 active members, so perhaps 300 to 1200 members in total (different communities have a wide variation in their ratio of active members to total members). When a project uses a larger number of active members, and if the intention is to develop a close sense of community, strategies such as sub-groups need to be adopted.

Table 11.1 indicates typical sizes for different communities.

It should be noted that the key issue is how many active members a community has. One of the differences between agencies is whether they restrict the membership of their communities to active

Table 11.1 Typical number of members by type of community

Type of community	Middle Range*
A short-term community, lasting two weeks, engaged in a qualitative exploration of a service feature, conducted with regular service user.	30 – 90 members
A short-term community, lasting four weeks, using both qualitative and quantitative techniques to explore new menu options for a fast food restaurant, with sub-groups of personal and family users.	100 – 250 members
An ongoing community, looking at different aspects of alcohol consumption at home, using both qualitative and quantitative techniques.	100 – 1200 members
A brand panel, utilising community techniques to increase engagement and panel retention, representing users of a specific brand of personal care product. The panel is used to provide a source for *ad hoc* quantitative projects and also for some qualitative projects during the year	5000 – 50 000 members

*The middle range is an intuitive estimate of the middle 80%, i.e. 10% of communities might be smaller and 10% might be larger

members (in which case they typically have higher incentives and fewer members), or whether they have larger total numbers and accept that some of their members will not be active.

THE BALANCE BETWEEN RESEARCH AND MEMBER AGENDAS?

One challenge for an online research community is to determine the optimal balance between running it to maximise the results the client needs and running it in a way that allows community members to express their views and concerns.

In the early days of Web 2.0, and in the early days of the development of online communities as a resource for market research, there was a realisation that market researchers needed to move away from what Brunswick's Graeme Trayner has termed the '*command and control*' mindset and cede some control to respondents (Poynter, 2007). Although this represented a major change for market researchers, it was simply part of a much more general trend in the relationship between brands and customers and between services and users, as shown by the comment by P&G's CEO A. G. Lafley who, at the Association of National Advertisers Conference 2006, called for brands to cede control to their customers.

One insight into why market researchers needed to change their model was provided by Pete Comley (2006) who suggested that we needed to think about market research in transactional analysis terms. Comley's observation was that Web 1.0, the traditional form of brand and customer relationship and the standard market research relationship with its respondents, was predicated on a Parent-to-Child relationship. As Comley pointed out, Parent-to-Child relationships are perfectly stable, provided that both parties accept their role. However, the Web 2.0 phenomenon and the way that brands were beginning to change their relationships with their customers reflected an Adult-to-Adult relationship. Comley's point was that market research also needed to adopt an Adult-to-Adult approach, or risk a crossed relationship where researchers were using an Adult-to-Child metaphor whilst respondents were expecting to engage in an Adult-to-Adult discourse.

However, even amongst those market researchers who are keen to give up some control in order to engage with respondents to achieve the benefits that can be delivered by working in more collaborative ways, there is no clear consensus about how much control to cede. At one extreme, the ceding of control might only apply at the periphery of the process, for example by letting respondents choose their own avatar or the colour scheme for their home page. At the other extreme, communities could operate like natural communities, creating their own agendas and policing the community themselves, according to their own guidelines.

During 2008, the ceding control picture became clearer (Poynter, 2008) and the consensus appears to be a recognition that there is a fundamental difference between natural communities and research communities. A natural community only exists if its members want it to exist, and it exists for whatever purpose that community deems appropriate. A research community is a purposeful community. The function of a research community, in the eyes of the organisation paying the bills, is to deliver insight. If a research community is not performing, the moderation of the site (and possibly the recruitment) needs to be changed to ensure that a productive community is created. In essence, this means that the company moderating the community cannot cede so much control that it prevents value being delivered to the end client.

  Advice

At a minimum, a company running an online research community will probably want to reserve the following powers to itself:

- ○ *The ability to close the community, especially relevant if the funding is removed.*

- ○ *The ability to change the terms and conditions. This implies that the original terms and conditions specify this provision from the first day.*

- ○ *That all intellectual property created by the community is owned by the client (not the agency and not the participants) unless it has been explicitly agreed otherwise.*

- ○ *That the community has the right to ban members and their posts if the moderator believes that those members are: (a) inclined to act against the client's long-term interests; (b) if the member is so reckless as to create an unreasonable risk of damage to the client or other community members; or (c) if the member is doing anything illegal, liable to civil action or, in that favourite phrase of lawyers, 'bringing the community into disrepute'.*

Note the points above are general advice about the approach a company might wish to take, they are not specific recommendations for the wording of terms and conditions, and they are certainly not 'legal advice'.

 Warning

The reference to the long-term interests of the client in the last clause in the list above is very important. A community should not seek to stifle all negative comments. If a community member is interested in helping the client, but is very angry about some specific incident, then it is important they can talk about it. However, if a member has no interest in helping the client, they do not normally have a role in a brand focused research community.

ONLINE COMMUNITY TOOLS

An online community presents an almost limitless array of techniques and approaches that can be deployed to enhance the community, to increase engagement, and to deliver insight. This section looks at the key techniques and approaches that can be used, including:

- *Discussions/forums*
- *Polls and surveys*
- *Blogs*
- *Online chat*
- *Photo and video uploads*
- *Collaboration tools*
- *Member personalisation*
- *Entertainment*
- *Offline activities*

DISCUSSIONS/FORUMS

Discussions and forums are the most basic and central element of online communities. They are the primary mechanism by which community members express their views and the main way that researchers ask their questions.

The standard way to organise a discussion or forum grew out of the conventions of online bulletin boards and have been developed more recently in step with changes in social media. For example, many research community members will already be familiar with the conventions of discussions through their use of social networks such as Facebook.

There are a variety of ways of laying discussions out, which can lead to researcher/member disputes about the 'best' or even the 'right' way to proceed.

Generally, a discussion starts with a post, possibly including links or multimedia. The post often starts with an introduction and goes on to ask one or more questions. Contributors then post their comments, which are displayed in one of the following ways:

- *oldest comment at the top*

- *newest comment at the top.*

- *comments embedded next to the comment they were replying to*

Figure 11.1 shows a simplified discussion with the oldest comment first, Figure 11.2 shows the same conversation with the newest comment first, and Figure 11.3 shows the same discussion with comments embedded next to the item they were replying to.

When the oldest comment is at the top, the flow of the comments tends to be relatively natural, but the latest comments may require a reader to scroll through several pages of comments before seeing them.

When comments are sorted with the newest entries at the top, it is easy for readers to see the latest ones, but the discussion flow is less natural to read.

What is the best food to take on a long walk?
I always like to take an apple, cheese and bread.
Starman, 5 December 2009, 12:15
I think nuts are a great food when out for a walk.
HappyGal, 5 December 2009, 14:21
What about if somebody on your walk is allergic to nuts, might it be dangerous?
FreeBird, 5 December 2009, 19:42
I think it depends on the time of year. In the winter I always take a flask with hot soup in it. But in the summer I am more likely to have something like fruit.
WanderFull, 5 December 2009, 20:22
Hmm, that's a good point I had never thought about before
HappyGal, 5 December 2009, 21:51

Figure 11.1   Oldest comment first

What is the best food to take on a long walk?
Hmm, that's a good point I had never thought about before <div align="right">HappyGal, 5 December 2009, 21:51</div>
I think it depends on the time of year. In the winter I always take a flask with hot soup in it. But in the summer I am more likely to have something like fruit. <div align="right">WanderFull, 5 December 2009, 20:22</div>
What about if somebody on your walk is allergic to nuts, might it be dangerous? <div align="right">FreeBird, 5 December 2009, 19:42</div>
I think nuts are a great food when out for a walk. <div align="right">HappyGal, 5 December 2009, 14:21</div>
I always like to take an apple, cheese and bread. <div align="right">Starman, 5 December 2009, 12:15</div>

Figure 11.2   Newest comment first

What is the best food to take on a long walk?
I always like to take an apple, cheese and bread. <div align="right">Starman, 5 December 2009, 12:15</div>
I think nuts are a great food when out for a walk. <div align="right">HappyGal, 5 December 2009, 14:21</div>
What about if somebody on your walk is allergic to nuts, might it be dangerous? <div align="right">FreeBird, 5 December 2009, 19:42</div>
Hmm, that's a good point I had never thought about before <div align="right">HappyGal, 5 December 2009, 21:51</div>
I think it depends on the time of year. In the winter I always take a flask with hot soup in it. But in the summer I am more likely to have something like fruit. <div align="right">WanderFull, 5 December 2009, 20:22</div>

Figure 11.3   Replies embedded

When replies are appended to the comment they refer to, the overall flow is very easy to read. However, it can be hard to see where the latest comment is.

Comments in discussions and forums are normally moderated, i.e. they are assessed to see if they conform to the terms and conditions of the site. If a comment is deemed unsuitable it will either be edited or rejected.

Items can either be post- or pre-moderated. In a pre-moderated forum the moderator assesses each item before it is visible to other community members. Pre-moderation is safer in terms of avoiding abuse, but tends to kill the flow of dynamic discussions. Post-moderation allows the discussion to flow more naturally and potentially reduces costs. In a closed community, where rogue posts are less likely to be a problem, post-moderation will normally be the best option. In an open community, particularly one where the views can be more contentious, pre-moderation may be the better option.

POLLS AND SURVEYS

Superficially, polls and surveys might appear to be the quantitative tools of online research communities. However, polls are often used to create engagement and as a stimulus for a discussion, as opposed to deliver quantitative findings. This approach might then use surveys to supply quantitative information.

Polls

In social media, the term 'poll' refers to a single question survey, usually organised such that once somebody votes they then see the results of everybody who has already entered their response, or 'voted' as it is often called.

Although polls can be used to create counts, they are more often used to help create engagement or as an entry point into a discussion. In this second usage, one good way to gain engagement is to use a poll linked to a discussion (for example, the way polls are conducted in LinkedIn). The community member votes in the poll and is then shown the current results. The member is also shown the comments made by previous voters and is presented with a chance to add his or her comment. Figure 11.4 shows an example of a poll with an attached discussion.

Surveys

Surveys provide a method of gaining quantitative data from an online research community, including background and segmentation information. Surveys can be integral or external to the community and can be organised either to keep the results private or shared with the community.

An integral survey runs inside the community, i.e. a member has to be logged into the community to complete it. An external survey is normally triggered via a link which is sent to the member (for example, in an email or SMS) or via a link within the community. In the author's experience, emailing the link to a member usually results in the highest response rate and placing a link in the community the lowest response rate.

Although some communities are set up so that the results of all (or sometimes most) of a survey are shared with community members, it is more usual to keep the detailed results private, and perhaps share a brief summary with the community.

Even though a survey within a community is quantitative it is not representative of anything other than the community. If the community is typical of specific groups of customers, then the survey

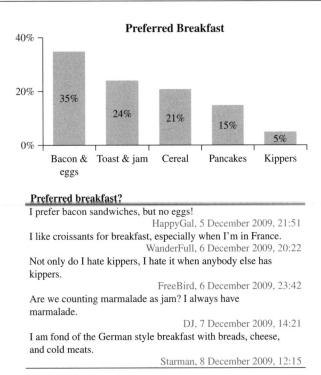

Preferred Breakfast

Bacon & eggs	35%
Toast & jam	24%
Cereal	21%
Pancakes	15%
Kippers	5%

Preferred breakfast?

I prefer bacon sandwiches, but no eggs!

> HappyGal, 5 December 2009, 21:51

I like croissants for breakfast, especially when I'm in France.

> WanderFull, 6 December 2009, 20:22

Not only do I hate kippers, I hate it when anybody else has kippers.

> FreeBird, 6 December 2009, 23:42

Are we counting marmalade as jam? I always have marmalade.

> DJ, 7 December 2009, 14:21

I am fond of the German style breakfast with breads, cheese, and cold meats.

> Starman, 8 December 2009, 12:15

Figure 11.4   Discussion linked to a poll

results will be typical of those groups. The term 'quantitative' here should be taken in its epistemological sense of measuring the views of community members, not in the casual way that market research sometimes uses it to imply representativity.

BLOGS

Many community platforms allow members to maintain their own blog. Whilst this can seem attractive, it is unlikely that most members will use the blog, especially if it is not visible to the wider internet. However, if the blog is an integral part of the project then it can add real value. For example, if the intention is for community members to keep some sort of record or diary, then a blog can be the natural way to facilitate that.

If the community is mostly about discussions and collaboration, then blogs are likely to be a distraction. As mentioned elsewhere, when designing a community it is a good idea to create and enable only those features that are going to be helpful; this helps make the system easier for the members to learn and easier for the moderators to manage. However, Paul Child from UK agency Virtual Surveys makes the point 'We've found blogs also give a different type of insight. The stream of consciousness structure means you get afterthoughts and peripheral issues coming through, which not only help with context but can often uncover issues that have not been considered.'

When using blogs in communities, the researcher has a number of options to consider. The most important issue is whether to allow other community members to see each other's blogs or to keep them as private to the blogger and the researcher. The general advice is to only keep the blogs private if there is a good research reason. If blogs are going to be open to all community members to view, the researcher needs to decide whether to make it an optional or a required aspect of the project, i.e. should participants be pressed to view each other's blogs.

When using blogs to capture aspects of participants' lives, researchers will normally need to monitor the usage of the blogs by participants to ensure that they are keeping up-to-date with their posts and uploads. Regular messages can help participants keep up-to-date and reassure them that their work is being read and appreciated.

ONLINE CHAT

Online research communities have reintroduced the idea of online focus groups, but often in a relatively low key way which is why they are often referred to as online chat or as a real-time discussion when conducted in the context of a community.

Within an online community an online chat session can be used to create more engagement and to gain some quick insight into a topic of interest. Most online focus groups use quite-sophisticated applications, with a range of modes, discussion prompts, and management information tools. However, this is less true in online communities, where the online chat is often more like a traditional web chat, but this may change as more tools become available and integrated with community solutions.

PHOTO AND VIDEO UPLOADS

Photo and video uploads can be used to allow members to personalise their space, but can also be used as a central element of the research, for example when participants taking part in an e-ethnography project might be asked to capture images of their daily life.

The main decisions/variations in how multimedia is used are:

○   *Does all the multimedia get uploaded to a single area, or does each participant get their own space?*

○   *Are participants expected to add comments to their photo and video uploads?*

○   *Are participants able/encouraged to comment on other people's uploads?*

○   *What are the limits, in terms of file sizes, for uploads?*

○   *What guidelines need to be put in place about the ownership of uploaded materials?*

❍ *What guidelines need to be put in place about the appropriateness of uploaded materials?*

❍ *What permissions need to be put in place about using uploaded materials?*

Analysing video is a much slower process than analysing text or images as it has to be viewed in real time. This means that most projects that collect video tend to be constrained in size, in terms of number of participants and in terms of time span.

One of the great impacts of uploaded video is its ability to convey messages to the recipients of the research insight. There is an adage that a picture is worth a thousand words. In research it is often the case that one customer making their point clearly on video can have more impact than a chart based on a thousand people.

Some researchers have highlighted occasions where members have been concerned about invasions of privacy. Whilst this appears to be rare at the moment, it makes sense for researchers to think clearly about why they want photos and videos, convey this clearly to community members, and reassure them about how their information will be used.

COLLABORATION TOOLS

Collaboration tools are less well developed than many of the other popular features of research communities and can often be relatively confusing for participants. Amongst the tools being used at present are the following:

❍ *Whiteboards. A whiteboard is an area where people can collaboratively write, draw, and post images. Whiteboards can be used to create 'sort and describe' exercises. They are typically only suitable for relatively small groups of people, for example two to four at the same time.*

❍ *Wikis. Wikis are perhaps the most powerful way of collaborating (for example, think of Wikipedia), but they can be off-putting for novice users. Wikis tend to suit larger numbers of participants, with no practical upper limit in terms of how many can collaborate.*

❍ *Post-it or sticky notes. Post-its can be used to allow participants to add comments to topics of investigation. For example, new outdoor or magazine ads can be displayed and partici-pants can add their comments via sticky notes.*

One of the key ways that collaborative tools are being added to communities is via third-party widgets and services, such as Huddle (which includes whiteboards, file collaboration, and wikis), http://www.huddle.net.

When using approaches based on collaboration it is even more important than usual to ensure that all intellectual property rights reside with the end client. This means having clear terms and conditions and making sure that all participants know what is happening.

MEMBER PERSONALISATION

A natural community usually provides a wide range of tools so its members can personalise their presence. The methods of personalisation include features such as profiles, wallpaper, and the creation of friends. These features can be provided in an online research community, and some of the key ones are outlined below:

○ *Avatar. An avatar can consist of just the name the member wishes to be known by in the community, or it can include an image as well as a name. In an online research community the safety of members is of paramount importance, so members should be encouraged (some say forced) to use names and images that do not reveal their true identities to other members (remember the moderator will usually still know who people really are).*

○ *Public profile. In natural communities, profiles are almost ubiquitous, i.e. showing details such as gender, location, interests, etc. However, in an online research community their role is more open to discussion. The general advice is that public profiles – i.e. those profiles visible to other community members – should not be detailed enough to reveal the true identity of the individual, but facts such as gender, favourite brands, location (at some broad level), and things like favourite movies and books can all add to members' engagement. If any of the community members are 'young' (however defined in your market, often this means under 18 years), it is important that their ages are not displayed as part of their public profiles, in order to reduce the risk of abuse.*

○ *Home or personal page. Many community platforms provide a home or personal page for community members. A home page may contain one or more of the following: list of friends, photos, videos, a profile, a blog, a wall (where others can write comments), a status field (like Facebook status), wallpaper, and widgets. A researcher designing a community needs to think about whether a home page is likely to be relevant. If the project is a short-term community, without blogs, friending, and photos, then a home page is likely to be a distraction.*

○ *Friends. A natural community normally has a method of creating friends/buddies/contacts/followers, and therefore most online research community platforms can add this functionality. The researcher needs to decide on a case-by-case basis whether 'friending' is a relevant part of how they want a particular community to function.*

The debate about whether to allow participants in a research community to personalise their experience and, if it is allowed, what features to include tends to centre on the role of the community. At one extreme, if the community is highly focused and short-lived then personalisation is largely irrelevant. At the other extreme, a long-term community might seek to mimic a natural community and build up friend networks, including groups that involve both participants and clients. This second extreme is probably best considered a hybrid community (i.e. going beyond just research) and great care must be taken over the security of participants, clients, and colleagues.

ENTERTAINMENT

One of the keys to creating a successful community is to generate a sense of engagement on the part of the participants. As part of the engagement process, some researchers have looked at a range of approaches that can be broadly referred to as entertainment.

At one end of the spectrum, entertainment might be provided by adding videos, for example a range of TV commercials or a news feed relevant to the topic being explored by the community. For example, in the UK the magazine *The Grocer* has an online site with a news feed that could be piped into a community.

Moving further into the entertainment field, a site might include humorous videos, typically as links to YouTube, perhaps with an invitation to members to nominate other videos to include on the site.

At the top end of the spectrum might be the addition of online games, either single player games such as Tetris or multiplayer games, such as Scrabble or Farmville-type games.

The key issue for the researcher to consider is whether these techniques improve or potentially distract from the research. The issue of copyright also needs to be considered.

OFFLINE ACTIVITIES

Some researchers have found that they can substantially improve the engagement of members with the community by creating offline events. Examples, offline events include face-to-face focus groups, meetings with executives from the client, and even trips to locations such as a factory making the biscuits of the company sponsoring a community about snack food.

Another offline option is to conduct tele-depths with community members, which can be a very fast way of getting a deeper understanding of a topic in a more conventional way.

The evidence about these offline events is anecdotal at the moment, but they do appear to improve engagement. Care should be taken of the security of members, reminding them not to share personal details, and generally avoiding 'young people' (i.e. people whose ages requires special consideration in the relevant market, often this means under 18 years old).

DESIGNING AN ONLINE RESEARCH COMMUNITY

This section focuses on the process of designing an online research community. In a typical research project this is a two stage process, with the initial design typically written as part of the proposal for research and the detailed design being completed when the project is confirmed.

The design of a community has to be scoped and considered in the context of the client and their objectives. An assessment of what the client is able to bring to the table is an important element in the scoping of a community. For example, are they able to be very open or is their culture risk-averse?

The design process starts with the strategic issues, such as whether to use a short-term or long-term community and whether to use an open or private community. The design then moves on to the detailed issues such as which community tools to deploy.

The section looks at the following topics:

- *Which type of community is best*
- *Look and feel*
- *Community tools*
- *Recruiting the members*
- *Terms and conditions*
- *Privacy and safety*

 Advice

WHICH TYPE OF COMMUNITY IS BEST

There are a number of questions to be considered when determining which type of community to choose when designing a community. The key options are outlined in the taxonomy of communities discussed earlier in this chapter.

The main drivers of the design decision are the research needs of the organisation and the resources available, including time and money.

Short-term or continuous?

In many ways this is the most fundamental question that the researcher needs to consider when designing a project. If the research relates to a single research need, something that is often referred to as 'ad hoc', then a short-term community is likely to be the solution.

A long-term community usually represents a decision by the client to either create a resource to facilitate a wide range of cost-efficient research or to start working with its customers to tap into the power of discussion and of crowdsoucing innovation.

Sometimes a short-term community is commissioned as a pilot for a long-term community. These pilots tend to be at the longer end of short-term communities, for example three to six months.

If an organisation is nervous about being able to integrate research communities into their processes, then this can be a sensible approach.

Open versus closed?

In most cases, the default option is to use a private community, i.e. closed. Open communities tend to be more expensive (in terms of moderation costs) and are more limited in terms of the research that can be conducted. Therefore, open communities tend to be selected when the benefits they offer, such as the sense of involving anybody who wants to be involved, outweigh the disbenefits, e.g. cost and loss of privacy.

Number of members

When considering the size of a community the key issue is the number of active members, not the total number of registered members. The analysis needs should drive the decision about the number of active members. If the project is highly qualitative and likely to generate a lot of material, then the size of the community should be smaller. If the project is likely to use quantitative tools then the community size will need to be larger.

Longer-term communities will usually need more members than short-term communities, to deal with attrition and fluctuations in levels of member interest. Communities with a high level of incentives will tend to be smaller than communities that are less incentivised.

LOOK AND FEEL

There are two extremes in terms of the look and feel of online research communities. Some providers tailor every community so that it matches the client branding exactly and choose the configuration of tools and functions to match the needs of the specific project. The other extreme is a provider who uses the same format for every client with just a small amount of tailoring to add – perhaps a corporate colour, a logo, and the text describing the site.

Although some people are emotionally very attached to bespoke designs, there is little evidence that they make much difference to community members, and they can take a lot longer to implement. The main benefit of standardised designs is that they are faster and cheaper to create, which makes them particularly attractive for short-term communities.

An open community is likely to be seen by more people than a private community, so an organisation may feel that it is more important for these types of community to be more closely aligned with its corporate look and feel.

COMMUNITY TOOLS

When considering the specific tools and features to include in a specific research community, the researcher should seek to include only those functions that are needed for that community.

If too many unnecessary features are included, there is a risk that members may be confused about what they are supposed to be doing. For example, if online chat is not in use then it should not be visible (note, just greying out the chat option is not as good as removing it when it is not needed).

In a short-term community, the researcher should have a good idea at the outset of the project of all the tools they expect to use and of those that are unlikely to be needed. For example, if a short-term community is going to be used to test a series of ideas about changes to a service, then it is unlikely that blogs, friends, or entertainment options would be relevant.

In a long-term community, most platforms allow tools to be introduced when necessary, so the key design issues need to focus on those issues that need to be there from the outset in order to set the tone and character of the community. For example, if personalisation is going to be part of the community then it should be enabled from the start.

RECRUITING MEMBERS

Most online research communities are recruited in one of two ways: either from the client's customer databases or from online access panels. If a community is intended to be focused on customers, then the client database option is generally the best option (if a suitable database exists). If there is not a suitable client database, or if the community is not intended to be based solely on customers, then the most appropriate method in most cases is an online access panel (many of the leading panel companies are happy to quote for this sort of project).

Other recruitment methods that are sometimes used include:

○ *buying online advertising, either on the 'traditional' internet or on social networks such as Facebook*

○ *placing adverts or links on the client's website*

○ *using an email marketing database*

○ *offline advertising, including TV, newspaper, outdoor*

○ *postal recruiting – this is particularly relevant when forming an online community to represent a specific geographic community, for example, creating an electronic town hall.*

 Warning

If an advertising route is chosen then the community will essentially be self-selecting. Iin this case, it is usually advisable not to mention incentives, otherwise the community may attract a disproportionate number of professional respondents. Indeed, the message conveyed by the adverts will to an extent determine the 'type' of members recruited, so care should be taken to set the correct expectations. When signing up members the key steps are:

- *Have criteria for screening people out. For example, ask if they work in an inappropriate industry, if they are outside the age ranges, or outside the right region/country.*

- *Ensure that people are aware that there are terms and conditions and that they have agreed to them.*

- *Gather some profiling information, but do not put people off with a large boring survey. Remember a community is not an online access panel!*

- *Have something for the new members to do. If you sign people up and do not send them anything for a month, then you will lose quite a few of them and demotivate some of the others.*

Once a community is up and running another recruitment option is the 'member-get-member' method, where existing community members are encouraged to recommend other potential community members and they can be asked to vouch for them to help avoid abuse.

 Advice

TERMS AND CONDITIONS

One of the most important and least sexy aspects of an online research community is the terms and conditions. The list below is not exhaustive (you will need to take professional advice), but the key issues that a researcher needs to consider are:

1. **Who owns the intellectual property created by the community?** The client sponsoring the research needs to be sure that they will end up owning the ideas created by the community. Ambiguity on this point could result in real problems. It should be clear to everybody involved in the community that any intellectual property generated by the community does not belong to the members or the research agency, but solely to the end client.

2. **What do you expect the community members to do?** Many communities specify that they will remove members who are not active within a specified period (typically three months or a year). If you expect members to keep your secrets, you should say so. If you expect your members to *use their best endeavours* to answer questions honestly, you should say so.

3. **What activities are not allowed?** Most communities ban cyberbullying and the posting of offensive material (particularly racist, sexist, or homophobic content). Many communities ban people from contacting other community members or from revealing their personal details (to protect members from harm).

4. **Anti-community behaviour.** Whilst most moderators and operators of communities believe that it is important to hear negative views about the brand or organisation being researched, a community does depend on there being some degree of cohesiveness. If a

member does not have a common interest with the rest of the community then it makes sense to have the power to remove them.

5.   **Rules for the incentives.** If a community uses incentives, the procedures for determining who gets what should be in the terms and conditions.

6.   **Eligibility.** The terms and conditions should specify who is qualified to be a member. This element will often cover such issues as the location members must come from (national versus international), demographics (e.g. sex, age, family profile), and whether or not they need to be a customer or user of the sponsor's products or services.

7.   **Data protection and privacy.** The terms and conditions should be integrated with the privacy policy and cover issues such as where the data will be stored, who can see it, what use the information will be put to, and a description of what sort of contact the community member is agreeing to.

8.   **The power to change the terms and conditions.** This is probably the single most important thing to include in the terms and conditions. The first draft of terms and conditions is unlikely to prove suitable for the whole life of the community. Therefore, the terms and conditions should specify that the organiser can, from time to time, update, amend, and vary them. In general, the rights of the members are protected by their right to withdraw from the community, plus rules and laws relating to data protection and privacy.

In addition to having comprehensive terms and conditions, the community should take steps to ensure that the key messages are actually communicated. Different communities deal with this in different ways. One way to highlight the implications of the terms and conditions is to present a summary to new members; another method is to highlight different features of the terms and conditions on a week-by-week basis, perhaps as a short article on the main page of the community.

  Advice

MODERATING AND MANAGING COMMUNITIES

This section looks specifically at the process of managing and moderating a community (including both short-term and long-term communities) along with the issue of producing insight and delivering ROI for the organisations buying the research. It addresses the following topics:

  ○   *The community moderator/manager*

  ○   *Managing a short-term community*

  ○   *Managing a long-term community*

  ○   *Dealing with negativity*

  ○   *Creating engagement*

- ○ *Creating a sense of community*

- ○ *Improving communities*

- ○ *Delivering insight*

THE COMMUNITY MODERATOR/MANAGER

The term 'moderator' in online research communities combines two previous uses of the term. Market research has used it for many years to describe the person running a focus group (along with other terms such as 'facilitator'). The focus group moderator is responsible for leading the discussion and interpreting the findings, and a community moderator fulfils a similar role.

The term 'moderator' has been used for many years by online forums, bulletin boards, and natural communities to describe the function of looking after the integrity of the discussions – for example, by removing rogue members, dealing with queries, and deleting abuse. The moderator of an online research community also fulfils this second role, a combination of policeman and help desk.

Different organisations use different titles for persons or people running their communities, so a moderator in one company may be known as a community manager in another. Some organisations have moderators who deal with both research and technical issues, others sub-divide the roles. In this book, the term 'moderator' is taken to be synonymous with the lead researcher, i.e. the person who is leading the community engagement, producing the insights, and dealing with any technical issues. This is for reasons of clarity and simplicity. However, in many situations the moderator role, as described here, will actually be performed by more than one person.

Many organisations have found that a moderator team of three people per community is useful, typically with three levels of seniority. This enables cost-efficient processes to be developed where the bulk of the day-to-day work can be completed by a more junior member of staff, but with more senior members involved to provide cover, direction, and help with insight. This system is particularly cost efficient when the organisation is running several communities. The more senior members of team might be looking after several communities at the same time, with the most junior moderators working on just one to three communities.

Mixing community moderation and other research

Many researchers have commented that it can be difficult to combine community moderation with traditional research projects. Traditional research projects (for example, an ad test, a customer satisfaction tracker, or a pricing study) typically have phases of high activity (including visits to the client for briefings and debriefs) and lulls in activity. When working with traditional research projects, the researcher attempts to match the lulls in one project with the peak activity on another, creating the space to handle more projects.

However, communities are 'always on' and require daily moderation from the researcher. The members of the community need to feel that they have the attention of the moderator at all times, making it difficult to deal with a conventional project and a community project at the same time. In general, it is best for community moderators not to be running conventional projects at the same time.

COMMUNITY PLAN

A community plan is the research community's equivalent of a focus group's discussion guide. Just as different qualitative researchers use discussion guides with differing degrees of detail (from broad topic headings for some to specific questions and phrases for others), so community plans differ in terms of their level of detail. A community plan will typically include:

○   *emails/messages that will be sent to community members, along with any news and updates that will be posted on the site*

○   *topics for discussion, along with notes about what the topic is intended to deliver in terms of meeting research objectives*

○   *polls and surveys, detailing the questions and the objectives they are going to meet*

○   *tasks that the respondents will be asked to complete, including online tasks such as online chat sessions, or offline tasks like watching a specific TV programme or visiting a particular shop.*

The community plan for a short-term community should contain details about handling the closing of the community.

MANAGING A SHORT-TERM COMMUNITY

The shorter the timeline for a community, the more intensive the management needs to be and the more onerous the requirements for the members. For example, if a short-term community is designed to last three months then the cycle of activity is likely to be weekly (i.e. similar to a long-term community). On the other hand, if a community is scheduled to last two weeks then the activity cycle is likely to be daily.

One of the key aspects of managing a community is to manage the expectations of its members. If the community is going to run for one week, with new tasks/questions being asked daily (daily tends to mean Monday–Friday), perhaps with daily emails/messages being sent to members, then this should be made clear at the recruitment stage. Members need to understand what they are being asked to do and to know what they are going to get back from their involvement, for example, recognition, thanks or cash.

The shorter the cycle of activity, the more detailed the community plan needs to be. For example, if a community is scheduled to run for two weeks, i.e. ten days of activity, the community plan for the first few days should be complete in every detail, and exist in some detail for every day of the project.

The analysis of a short-term project is also related to the activity cycle for a community. For example, if a project lasts two months and has a weekly cycle of activity, the analysis might take place weekly, with a weekly teleconference with the client to pass on findings and to refine the research plan for the following week. If the project lasts just one week, with a daily cycle of activity, the analysis will typically happen on a daily basis, with client input being sought on the Tuesday, Wednesday, and Thursday.

DEALING WITH NEGATIVITY

One of the issues that can make some clients anxious, if they are new to research communities, is a concern about negative comments made by participants. Clients' worries about negative word of mouth includes: will the negative views affect other participants, will the comments leak onto the wider internet, and will the comments upset internal stakeholders.

To some extent, the issue of negativity is a key example of the sort of change that NewMR is asking market researchers and clients to confront. The key point to understand is that a community is not creating a chance for people to say negative things about a product or service. Consumers already have many ways to be negative, both online and offline. A community provides a chance for the company to hear what their customers are saying, including the negative things that are already being said. This is one of the most important aspects of an online research community/MROC.

Whilst there are communities that are heavily moderated and where most negative comments are removed, and there are some which look like 'free for alls' which abound with negativity, most online communities have a system of managing negativity. Dealing with negativity tends to fall into two issues: dealing with inappropriate comment and dealing with inappropriate community members. A community can only function if there is a community of interest. In the case of a brand-related community, the minimum requirement for members is that they are interested in telling the brand things that could result in the brand being 'better'. If a member has no interest in helping the brand, then it is better that they should not continue to be a member. What a community is looking for are people who are willing to be 'critical friends', people who will help the brand improve its performance.

If a member makes a comment that is inappropriate (or perhaps has a photo or avatar that is inappropriate), then the moderator needs to contact them to explain why the post is inappropriate and either remove or edit it, taking care not to demotivate the member.

However, most negative comments that occur in an online research community are not inappropriate. One of the most important services the researcher can provide for the research buyer is to explain why most negativity should not be edited, removed, or discouraged. Indeed, in many cases there is more to learn from friends being critical than there is from friends being nice.

CREATING MEMBER ENGAGEMENT

In general, engaged members are productive members. Even if extrinsic incentives are being used, the community members will only deliver the maximum value if they are fully engaged, which usually means that they enjoy being involved in the community.

The first step in creating member engagement is to know what is happening. Ideally, the management information systems will tell the researcher who is logging on, who is posting comments, and who is completing polls and surveys. There is an old maxim that says 'if you can't measure it, you can't manage it', and this is certainly true about engagement.

 Advice

There are many ways of creating member engagement, and no two moderators will run their communities in exactly the same way. However, the following points are elements that have been used to create engagement:

○ *Keep members busy. Nothing loses engagement faster than gaps in the level of activity.*

○ *Use direct language and avoid compound questions. Remember that a community is an ongoing discussion; there is time to work through a sequence of questions rather than asking all the questions in one go.*

○ *Use language that is appropriate to the audience. Some communities are informal, some are technical, and some business communities are relatively formal. There is no one style of language that suits all communities.*

○ *Avoid making everything seem like 'work'. In order to improve engagement it is sometimes necessary to create tasks or topics that are more about catching the interest of the members rather than answering a specific research question. Polls can be a useful way of asking something that might be more interesting than commercially useful.*

○ *Feed back to the respondents. Many of the people who join communities do so to make a difference and they will be more engaged if they are told what has happened to their input. One of the most powerful forms of feedback is when the end-client provides the feedback. Other forms can be as simple as the moderator posting comments such as 'Great comment, please tell us more'.*

○ *Target individuals. Using the management information systems the moderator can target people who are not currently being engaged – for example, by emailing them to ask why (or phoning them and having a chat). When somebody who has not been recently active makes a contribution, the moderator can make sure they are acknowledged, perhaps asking for a follow-up comment.*

○ *Cede control. Topics and discussion suggested by members should be followed up wherever possible and the originator of the suggestion recognised.*

The dating metaphor

One way to think of a community is to compare it to a couple on a date (this metaphor was originally suggested by UK thought leader Pete Comley). If we could see inside the minds of the two people out on their first date we might find out that one of them might be thinking '*Will he/she sleep with me?*', the other might be thinking '*Will she/he marry me?*' However, if either of them asks this as their first question, it is unlikely that the evening will develop into an ongoing relationship. So they might start with simple, safe questions such as '*Do you come here often?*' or '*Do you like the band?*'

Similarly, in the early days of a community it makes sense to ask easy questions about things that people are very willing to share, for example favourite colour, happiest experience, favourite ad, etc. Once a community is established, the more difficult topics can be addressed.

When some clients first start working with communities they might bring with them approaches and mindsets they have developed using conventional research approaches, particularly quantitative surveys. A quantitative survey is the 'one night stand' of market research. If you don't ask all your important questions during the survey, then you have missed the chance.

By contrast, a community is a relationship. Researchers are able to use communities to ask the difficult and important questions, but it is usually best not to rush things.

 Advice

Creating a sense of community

Whilst it is possible that an online research community will form itself into a natural community, this does not normally happen. In most cases, the community moderator needs to assume the responsibility for converting the people recruited for the project into a community. There is no simple blueprint for creating a community, but the following steps are all worth trying:

○ *As moderator, ensure you use a suitable image as your avatar and a 'real' name. Do not simply be called 'Moderator' or 'Admin'. One way of balancing the desire to make the avatar image 'friendly' and avoid compromising your privacy is to use a cartoon sketch or image of yourself.*

○ *Welcome people when they first join the community, tell them that if they have any questions to contact you.*

○ *Have some easy tasks for people to do when they first join. Fun polls are great, especially if the community's polls are linked to follow up discussions where people can leave comments.*

○ *Keep an eye out for people who start posting less often, send them an email to see if everything is OK.*

○ *If somebody who has not posted for a while suddenly posts, make a point of following it up with a moderator post saying something like ' That is a great point, has anybody else thought anything similar?' – but make sure the moderator contribution matches the post.*

○   *Have a section where people can contribute suggestions for further discussion. When possible adopt some of these suggestions and announce that this topic was suggested by that member.*

However, most communities never become communities in the way that natural communities do. Most of the communication and bonding in the community is likely to be between the members and the moderators. This is not necessarily a problem provided that the community continues to function.

HANDLING LULLS IN CLIENT ENGAGEMENT

One problem for research communities, especially for long-term or continuous projects, is that there may be times when the client buying the research is simply too busy with other priorities to be properly engaged with the community. In an extreme case this might result in the client not supplying research topics for a period of time. During these lulls the researcher needs to ensure that there are regular topics for the community. One strategy is to use topics that have previously been suggested by community members. Another is to trawl the relevant trade press for stories that can then be turned into topics.

The key determinant of success in handling client lulls is whether or not the members of the community feel there has been a problem. The aim is to keep members unaware that the direction for the community has come from the agency instead of the client.

FINDING AND DELIVERING INSIGHT

For any research technique to deliver ROI it first has to find and communicate relevant insight and, second, it has to do it faster, cheaper, or better than other available techniques. This section looks at the challenges of finding and delivering insight from communities.

 Advice

Finding the insight

Although there is a growing body of knowledge about how to create and moderate communities, there is much less agreement and evidence about the best process of extracting insight and this is currently one of the greatest challenges.

Amongst the strategies currently being employed are:

○   *Tagging conversations as they occur. Since moderators should be reviewing all posts and comments as they are being made it is little extra work to ask them to tag the comments at that point, enabling the text to be analysed later.*

○   *Asking members to tag their own comments and posts. This can be done with tags in the form of text or by utilising emoticon type tags. Communispace is one agency that has pioneered the practice of requiring members to use emoticons to help interpret their contributions.*

○   *Asking members to interpret each other's comments. Some researchers have reported success by asking community members to provide a summary at the end of a project. For example, at the end of one short-term community in the UK the members were asked to produce a 200 word summary of what they thought had been uncovered by the discussions. These were used as one element to feed into the final analysis, along with the weekly summaries that the researchers had produced.*

○   *Using text analysis software, such as Leximancer. However, it should be noted that, at present, whilst text analysis tools make human analysts more efficient, they can't replace the human element.*

○   *Keeping the size of communities small. One of the reasons that has been advanced for keeping the size of communities small, in some cases to about 50 members, is to keep the amount of text down to a level that can be readily processed.*

  Advice

One complaint that clients have expressed about online communities is that some agencies are inclined to report what members have said, as opposed to either (a) what members meant, or (b) what clients should do as a result of what members are saying.

Delivering the insight

In traditional market research projects, most clients are only loosely involved during a project's fieldwork and analysis stages, one exception being those clients who tend to view their focus groups. This procedure has been dubbed the 'commission and forget' syndrome.

By contrast, in most online research communities the client is likely to be involved throughout the fieldwork and analysis phases and this has an impact on how the insight is communicated. Additionally, the client's input is vital in the development of the community plan, both in the generalised long-term shape of the plan and the specifics of the next few activities.

Many clients and agencies work on a reporting schedule that is tied to the activity cycle of the community. If the community is a long-term community, with a weekly cycle of activity, the reporting will tend to be weekly. If the community is a short-term community, with a daily activity cycle, the client should ideally be involved in a daily feedback loop. Frequently, these daily or weekly sessions are held as tele-conferences.

The 'end of project' report – or periodic report in the case of a long-term or continuous community – becomes the point at which the individual components of learning are pulled together to create a strategic whole, as opposed to the tactical insights that have been delivered during the regular reporting of the project.

THE THEORY OF RESEARCH COMMUNITIES

Although online research communities are relatively new, there has already been an extensive amount of research into how they work. This has focused on topics such as why people join them, how they vary by country and culture, and the way that communities are viewed by the participants. This section draws together some of this information and the latest thinking about the role of communities in market research.

WHY DO PEOPLE JOIN COMMUNITIES?

As the use of online research communities grows and becomes more central to how organisations are getting closer to their customers, there is a growing need to find out more about why people join communities. What are they are looking for? What sort of people join? What sort of people do not join online research communities?

An important study of community members was conducted in 2009 by a team from the University of Salford who looked at the membership of an online research community and the experience of the moderators of that community (Ferneley and Heinze, 2009). The project used United Biscuits Snackrs community and the interviews took place with both community members and moderators from Virtual Surveys (the agency operating the community for United Biscuits).

Ferneley and Heinze (2009) highlighted similarities and differences between online research communities and naturally occurring online communities (about which there is a much wider body of information). For example, in a naturally occurring online community the recruitment and the communications are normally peer-to-peer. In an online research community the moderator is the key point in both recruitment and communication.

Ferneley and Heinze proposed an emergent segmentation with seven segments, based on the motivations of the members. These segments were:

- *social engagement seekers*

- *power seekers*

- *freebie seekers*

- *information seekers*

○ *information hungry*

○ *hobbyists*

○ *geeks*

The different segments all had different combinations of motivation, relating to community involvement, trust between members, intrinsic and extrinsic motivation, the degree to which they wanted to influence the brand, the receipt of information and the extent to which they wanted information for their own interest or to gain influence amongst their own peer groups.

The key lesson for any researcher who is seeking to maximise the benefit of a research community is to recognise that the communities comprise different sorts of people and should seek to meet these different needs. Ferneley and Heinze also raised suggestions about how members are recruited. For example, if the intention is to minimise the number of freebie seekers, then the extrinsic rewards should not be stressed in the original invitation.

RESPONDENTS' VIEWS OF COMMUNITIES AND OTHER RESEARCH

There are two ways that online research communities can be compared with other more established research methods. The first is from the position of the client and researcher, in terms of what the community can deliver. This perspective is one that has been widely discussed in articles and at conferences, and is touched on at various points in this chapter.

The second, and much less discussed, perspective is how online research communities are perceived by their members. There has often been an assumption that communities are good for their members, because it is widely alleged that communities empower members, allowing them to make a difference and to get their point across in a convenient way.

A study of Australian respondents drawn from an online access panel compared the views of participants of online communities with online surveys, face-to-face surveys, telephone surveys, and face-to-face focus groups (Cierpicki et al., 2009). The conclusions were a moderate, but not unqualified, success for online research communities. Key findings included:

○ *Focus groups are more likely than online communities to be seen as enjoyable. Online communities scored about the same as online surveys and face-to-face surveys, although communities were seen as more enjoyable than telephone surveys.*

○ *Having an interviewer or moderator physically there, as in the case of a face-to-face interview, makes the respondent more likely to feel that they are getting their point across, which puts online communities at a disadvantage compared with focus groups and face-to-face surveys. However, communities do a better job than telephone surveys and online surveys.*

○ *Communities are not seen as being as convenient to participate in as online surveys.*

○ *People who have taken part in communities are less likely to say the effort was worthwhile than people who had attended a focus group. But online communities were ahead of telephone and online surveys in being worthwhile.*

○ *People were most likely to say that they were completely honest in online surveys, with online communities having a very similar score to focus groups and face-to-face surveys.*

Two key observations from this research are:

1.   Some communities work their members quite hard, for example expecting them to log on several times a day. This will not necessarily be seen as enjoyable and convenient.

2.   The more discursive/welcoming an environment becomes, the more the member will feel they can get their point across but the less honest they will feel they can be (presumably because of the need to provide socially acceptable responses).

An earlier study looked at the reactions to online communities in Australia, China, Japan, and New Zealand (Poynter et al., 2009). This study found that members in all four countries welcomed the chance to answer questions in their own words, rather than predetermined lists. The study highlighted one potentially important difference between cultures. In Australia and New Zealand, members indicated they were similarly honest in face-to-face and community situations. However, some of the respondents in China and Japan indicated that they were more likely to be honest online, because they felt less requirement to conform to what others might expect them to say.

The lessons so far are that researchers should:

1.   Keep exploring the views and opinions of community members and ideally benchmark these views against other techniques.

2.   Make contributing to a community more convenient for members, by offering more channels and by making it possible to do more things quickly and easily.

3.   Prove to members that they have got their views across, for example by spelling out outcomes but also by echoing points back to members.

EXAMPLES OF COMMUNITIES

The following case studies highlight different online research communities, illustrating some of the points discussed earlier in this chapter and showing the value that organisations are getting from online research communities.

 **Examples**

easyJet Online Research Community

easyJet is a European low cost airline (a type of airline that is also known as 'no frills'). It is characterised as being 'cheap and cheerful', and in its markets it is known for its bright orange colour scheme and for not being stuffy (as evidenced by its willingness to be the subject of a UK reality show, 'Airline UK').

easyJet have an online research community operated by UK research agency Virtual Surveys, which has been running for an extended period. When easyJet first decided to commission a research community their key priorities were:

○ *a community grounded in research expertise rather than technical expertise*

○ *a method of getting closer to the customer in a way that fitted with the key aspects of easyJet's existing research programme*

○ *a community proactively managing to keep members engaged, replacing non-participating members as and when needed*

○ *a moderated community to ensure that conversations were developed and insight generated*

○ *to create an open channel of two-way communication between customers and easyJet*

○ *a longer-term objective of co-creating the future for easyJet*

The easyJet community was created in the summer of 2008 and has been running continuously ever since. In the language of the discipline, it is a continuous, agency moderated, closed (i.e. invitation only), online research community.

The community was created with 2000 members, from people who had flown with easyJet over the previous 12 months, and the membership has been periodically updated since. The community is incentivised by putting members into a monthly prize draw to win a pair of easyJet tickets to a destination of their choice.

New topics are researched in the community each week. The members are emailed by the moderator to alert them to new tasks, such as discussions and polls. easyJet estimate that during a six month period they are able to explore about 80 topics. The key agency/client link is a weekly teleconference where the topics and discussions are discussed and future actions agreed.

easyJet use the community to research the following areas:

○   *advertising and brand communications, including radio ads and the ads on the back of seats*

○   *brand strategy, e.g. brand personality and pricing*

○   *concept testing, including in-flight catering and entertainment*

○   *customer experience and service delivery, for example punctuality and airport security*

○   *network developments, e.g. destinations and schedules*

○   *customer understanding, including insights into summer holidays and car hire*

○   *website, looking at personalisation issues and assessments of competitors*

easyJet see their community as a method of testing issues earlier in the pipeline than they would have previously been able to, but also to produce findings more quickly than with other research techniques, with the typical turnaround from business question to analysis being just one week.

Sophie Dekkers, the Customer Research Manager at easyJet described the community in the following way: *'We were able to conduct more research, for more areas of the business, in a faster timeframe, but within the same budgetary constraints. It will be the blueprint for easyJet customer interaction and research moving forward.'*

The easyJet case shows how an online research community can be integrated within a service company. Once the community research programme is in process a company becomes aware that they don't need to guess what customers think, they can ask them and get a rapid feedback. The key thing about the community is that it is positioned as a resource for research rather than as an answer to a specific problem.

 Examples

CDW, Long-Term, B2B Research Communities

CDW [http://www.cdw.com] is a leading USA-based provider of technology solutions to business, government, and education and they have been using private online communities since 2004. CDW have three communities, each built and managed by Communispace.

The three communities each consist of about 300 members who are makers or influencers of IT decisions. As well as providing feedback to CDW, members interact with each other, providing a place to network and to seek and offer support.

In late 2008 and through early 2009 the three communities worked with CDW to improve how prospects experience the early sales process. For example, the communities helped CDW understand and improve the cold call process from the recipient's perspective. The community members highlighted the increase in calls they were receiving and the lack of definition and differentiation this was creating. CDW and their communities then went on to look at the whole process, from first early sales contact to recommending initial solutions – for example, reviewing and discussing the different ways IT decision makers source information and make decisions.

CDW took their learnings from the communities and created new procedures and training programmes for their Account Managers. CDW estimate that these new approaches and systems have driven average customer value 17% higher than the previous year, before these best practices were implemented.

Scott Harrison, Director of the CDW Sales Academy put it this way:

> 'As the economy grew more uncertain over the last two years, we knew that we were going to have to provide an even higher level of service to our current and future customers. In order to demonstrate our commitment to helping them run their businesses, we listened, learned, and implemented key suggestions from our Communispace community members into our training programs at the CDW Academy. As a result, these best practices provided our Sales Account Managers with the opportunity to generate more sales leads, build stronger relationships, and help customers re-focus their priorities on what's important now, while developing their business.'

The CDW case, and the community provided by Communispace, highlight several aspects of a long-term community in the context of Business-to-Business research. Their case study shows how a long-term community can be used to work collaboratively on a major project to develop a specific project. Whereas the easyJet case identified the quick hits of an 'always on' community, the CDW case shows how communities can also be used in a more deliberative way to co-create solutions.

 Resources

RESOURCES

A book on online research communities can only be a snapshot of progress. In order to keep in touch with a changing field like this, a researcher needs to follow the latest thinking and investigate new options as they emerge on to the market. The list below is a cross-section of blogs that provide useful information on the subject of online research communities. More information is available on this book's companion website, http://hosmr.com/

BLOGS WITH SIGNIFICANT CONTENT ABOUT ONLINE RESEARCH COMMUNITIES

Communispace. A blog from leaders in communities, edited by a team including Diane Hessan, http://blog.communispace.com/

Forrester. Forrester host a blog specifically for 'Consumer Market Research Professionals', edited by a team including Tamara Barber, which often includes useful information on online research communities, http://blogs.forrester.com/consumer_market_research/mrocs/

FreshNetworks. A blog focused on communities and Web 2.0, edited by a team including Matt Rhodes, http://blog.freshnetworks.com/

InSites Consulting. A leading edge market research agency from Belgium, the blog is edited by a team including Anke Moerdyck, http://blog.insites.be/

PluggedIn. A blog subtitled 'About MROC Talk', edited by Matt Foley and Ben Werzinger, http://www.pluggedinco.com/blog/

The Future Place. A blog looking at future related issues with a significant amount related to online communities, edited by Ray Poynter, http://thefutureplace.typepad.com/

Virtual Surveys. Produces a general online research and online communities blog, edited by a team including Paul Child, http://www.virtualsurveysdiscussion.com/vslblog/

Vovici. A blog about online and New MR topics, edited by prolific blogger Jeffrey Henning, http://blog.vovici.com/

QUALITY AND ETHICAL ISSUES

In addition to the quality and ethical issues addressed in other parts of this book there are issues that are specific to online research communities and these are covered in this section.

ABSENCE OF A FORMAL METHOD

In theory, if not in actuality, traditional quantitative market research is based on a scientific method of random probability sampling. This method suggests that by taking measurements from a randomly selected sample the results can then be projected onto a population. Established quantitative analysts can point towards a canon of knowledge addressing sampling methods and analysis. In addition, both buyers and vendors of established research can point to a large amount of empirical evidence supporting the value of research.

By contrast, there is no broadly accepted body of information that underpins the use of online research communities. To put it bluntly, there is neither established theory nor empirical data to underpin the use of online research communities.

This absence of any formal theory does not mean that clients should avoid online research communities. But it does mean that vendors should be careful to ensure that clients are not over-sold the credentials of research communities, at least not until more work is done on establishing either a theory or good empirical support.

QUALITATIVE NAIVETY

Online research communities have attracted many quantitative researchers into areas of qualitative research with which some of them are unfamiliar. This has led some researchers to simply treat the communities as if they were representative samples, which is clearly wrong, and has led others to oversimplify the analysis process. For example, it is not uncommon to hear some researchers talking about numbers of words in comments and word clouds as if they were key issues as opposed to interesting additional facts.

PRIVACY AND SAFETY

Compared with most other forms of market research, online research communities provide more opportunities to compromise people's privacy and, potentially, their safety. The key reason for this is that, compared with other research techniques, the participants are more focused on each other than they normally would be, and there are more methods for participants to identify other people involved in the community, including other participants, moderators, and potentially even clients.

David Stark (2009) highlights the risk of people involved in identity theft or social network scams becoming involved in research communities and then preying on other community members. For example, a criminal could collect email addresses from community members and at a later date send a survey invitation which appeared to come from the community. Stark points out that the risk of abuse is actually increased by some legislation. For example, in the USA researchers offering rewards of more than $600 must collect Social Security Numbers, so respondents are used to handing them over when asked by appropriate market research companies. However, this would be a potential disaster if the request actually came from a criminal pretending to be the community moderator.

Best practice for research communities is to advise members to adopt a name and image for their avatar that does not reveal their actual identities. Indeed, many agencies actively police avatars to check that they are not revealing people's identities.

A similar concern arises on behalf of moderators and clients. Many employers feel that it is inappropriate to ask their staff to use their true image in a research community as they may meet community members out in the street, and these days there are concerns about phenomena such as stalking. However, it is usually appropriate for moderators to use their real names, or at least a version of their real name, in closed or private communities. The situation is more complex in open communities where a moderator's private life and their role in a project could clash. For example, a respondent could search for aspects of a moderator's private life in areas such as Facebook or Twitter. There is currently no clear guidance on how social media researchers should separate their work and private life.

The privacy and safety issue is the reason why many researchers choose not to enable 'friending' and one-to-one messages between participants in online research community projects. This is especially true in cases where some or all of the respondents might be classified as 'vulnerable', a term which includes children, people with some disabilities, people with learning difficulties, oppressed groups, etc.

ABUSE

The best way to avoid abuse is to set clear guidelines about what is acceptable and what is not from the outset. Researchers should note that people who spend a lot of time on forums and bulletin boards may be used to a more 'robust' level of discussion than the community is prepared to endorse. In many ways, the least problematic participants in a research project are those with relatively little previous experience of online communities and forums.

The terms and conditions of the community should clarify what is meant by abuse and should specifically refer to cyberbullying. One useful link to borrow ideas from is the UK Government's DirectGov site on cyberbullying [http://yp.direct.gov.uk/cyberbullying/], with its strap line *'Laugh at it, and you are part of it'*.

David Stark (2009) has warned of the risk to the researcher if actionable material is posted on a community website, quoting a case in Italy where four Google executives are being prosecuted because of a video that was hosted on YouTube. Stark advocates pre-moderation of all posts as a remedy. However, other researchers have found post-moderation to be more appropriate in closed/private communities because it does not slow down the natural conversation.

However, while abuse and privacy concerns are real worries, problems tend to occur only rarely and a researcher can run several projects without encountering any unacceptable behaviour.

THE FUTURE OF ONLINE RESEARCH COMMUNITIES/MROCS

The future of online research is hard to define due to the rate of change in the world of social media and the number of forces at play that might impact on online research communities. Amongst the factors influencing the market research context for online communities are:

- *Market research regulations. Most research organisations ban activities that are known to change the attitude and/or behaviour of respondents. There is a widespread view that members of a well run online research community become more identified with the brand and more likely to become brand advocates. This may lead to online research communities being considered by trade bodies as 'not research'.*

- *Scalability. Most market research is conducted by large international agencies and for international clients. If online research communities can be scaled up to compete with core research categories such as ad testing, ad tracking, customer satisfaction, NPD, etc, then their future role could expand beyond the niche that qualitative research has historically been confined to.*

- *Respondent fatigue. Over time, online research communities may become of less interest to their members. As the number of communities grow, it is possible that customers will become members of several online research communities. But perhaps it is more likely that some communities will prosper whilst others struggle to find and engage members.*

O   *Alternatives. Online research communities have succeeded so far because they deal well with two current limitations of other types of market research, namely the difficulties researchers have in dealing with large groups of people and the problems with trying to conduct research in a public forum or community. However, alternatives may appear and provide a better solution. Two possible alternatives are (a) very large communities, operating as both a marketing and a market research resource, or (b) new ways of tapping into the communities that people are already members of.*

If online research communities do develop into a major component of market research (for example more than 10% of total global research revenues), it is likely to result in changes in the structure of market research. The first change relates to the absence of fieldwork. This shrinks some aspects of the research organisation and changes ratios of costs. This would continue a process first started by the adoption of internet fieldwork for quantitative studies. The second change is the modification in the workflow of an online research community. Traditional research comprised periods of high activity, such as the design phase, with periods of low activity, such as during the fieldwork. Research communities, in contrast, produce a much more even flow of work, making it hard to deploy researchers across both traditional research and online research communities.

SUMMARY OF RESEARCH COMMUNITIES

Online research communities (or MROCs) are one of the hottest topics in market research, with a large number of both research buyers and vendors rushing to utilise them. By some accounts, they are the fastest growing technique within the world of market research and are already larger (in research revenue terms) than online focus groups and bulletin board groups combined.

The key features that researchers need to know about online research are:

O   *Short-term communities are mostly relevant to specific research needs and stand as an alternative to other* ad hoc *techniques.*

O   *Long-term communities are essentially a different way of doing market research (with branded panels perhaps being the most similar). They are an ongoing discussion with customers and have a relatively high fixed cost (typically hundreds of thousands of dollars) but with an almost zero cost of marginal research – i.e. one more project is effectively free, and with very fast responses (days not weeks).*

O   *Research communities can be entirely qualitative or a combination of qualitative and quantitative. However, the paradigm that underpins the quantitative research offered by research communities is not the traditional quantitative paradigm of random probability sampling.*

○ *Many of the experts in the field of online research communities can be quite emphatic that their way is the best, or even the only, way. However, there is little evidence that one method is yet much better than another, and it should be remembered the best way to run a community in 2010 may not be the best in 2012.*

The key points for the future are:

○ *The world is still changing. Over the next few years other techniques will emerge and online research communities will either develop and change or be superseded by other innovations.*

○ *Text analytics software is potentially going to have a major impact on how open-ended responses in general and discussions in particular are processed.*

○ *Even if online research communities do not themselves change the face of market research, it is likely that ideas such as discussions and listening are going to be a major part of the future of market research.*

○ *The traditional model of market research, based on the random probability sampling assumption, is rapidly becoming discredited, leading to a search for a new paradigm, a NewMR, and communities are part of that broader change.*

12 Blog and Buzz Mining

"Why ask some of us when you can listen to all of us?" This was the shout from the early days of blog and buzz mining. Of course, it was always something of an exaggeration – most people are not blogging, posting, or commenting. However, the point that brands and organisations can learn an immense amount by simply listening to what people are saying to each other is an important one. Indeed, the shift of emphasis from questioning to listening is one of the key features of NewMR.

This chapter looks at techniques, such as blog mining, web scraping, and automated text analysis, that use software and systems to interrogate comments, posts, and conversations on the internet in order to derive meaning and insight. Two terms that are often used in this area are 'consumer generated media' (CGM) and 'buzz'. CGM is at the heart of Web 2.0 and relates to a wide range of things that people post on the web, such as blogs, amateur video (e.g. YouTube), and comments. Buzz is a term that relates to what topics are discussed on the internet. Another related term is 'word of mouth' (WOM), which relates to the power of messages that are passed from one person to another, both offline and online.

This chapter focuses on those techniques that depend on software and automation to investigate online comments and conversations. It does not look at the researcher-centric process of being a participant-observer in online communities and networks. That topic is addressed in the next chapter as part of the section on e-ethnography.

Blog and buzz mining includes interrogating blogs, forums, Twitter, social networks, comments – indeed anywhere where people post their views and comments.

The structure of this chapter is set out below:

- *An introduction to blogs*
- *The blog and buzz mining paradigm*
- *Finding material*
- *Extracting material*
- *Analysing material*
- *Full service solutions*

○   *Case studies*

○   *The ethics of blog and buzz mining*

○   *Summary of blog and buzz mining*

AN INTRODUCTION TO BLOGS

Blogs provide a method for anybody to have a platform for their views. Blogs are run by corporations, gurus, and the person next door.

WHO IS BLOGGING?

The status of blogs has changed substantially since the term first appeared on the scene in the late 1990s and then exploded into the wider consciousness in the early 2000s. By about 2004 it looked as though blogs were going to challenge conventional media and would become a popular voice for the masses. However, it soon became apparent that the level of effort required to maintain a blog means that most people will never own and run a blog.

Reports from organisations such as Technorati and comScore confirm the impression that fewer than 10% of internet users blog, probably many fewer. The Technorati 2009 State of The Blogosphere Report indicates that most bloggers are university graduates and tend to earn above average incomes, which is clearly a source of bias.

Another limitation of blogs, from a market researcher's point of view, is the difficulty in working out which country the blogger is based in. Similarly, when somebody posts a comment to a blog it is difficult to work out where they are from. Sometimes filters can be used to exclude/include a specific phrase or term that will help locate people to a country, but this tends to be hit and miss.

IS ANYBODY BLOGGING ABOUT YOU?

The original proposition about mining blogs was that customers are talking about brands and that if only brands would start listening they would be better informed and could also save money. However, only a handful of brands are actually talked about on a regular basis. Global juggernauts such as Nokia are talked about, strong and controversial companies like Australia telecommunications company Telstra are talked about, government agencies such as the UK's DVLA are talked about, but most companies, organisations, and brands are hardly talked about at all, certainly not enough to track and measure content and sentiment.

THE BLOG AND BUZZ MINING PARADIGM

The proponents of blog and buzz mining tend to contrast traditional market research with their NewMR approach, and emphasise a move away from asking questions towards listening.

Traditional market research, for example brand tracking, ad tracking, and customer satisfaction, is based on selecting samples of respondents and asking them sets of questions. The proponents of blog and buzz mining contend that the weaknesses of this are twofold:

1.   The respondents who agree to do surveys might not be typical of the broader customer base. For example, they might be more likely to agree with the propositions in the questionnaire, or be more satisfied with the brand, or be more aware of marketing in general (especially if they are members of an access panel, perhaps doing more than 50 surveys a year).

2.   The questions asked by organisations represent their own agenda; they do not necessarily represent the topics that customers and citizens find important.

By contrast, they assert, blog and buzz mining is based on listening to what real customers and citizens are saying to each other. People talk about what they find important, in their own language, and these conversations are not restricted to just those compliant or organised people who respond to surveys.

FINDING, EXTRACTING, AND ANALYSING

There are three steps that are essential to the blog and buzz mining process, which are:

1.   **Finding**. Using tools to find what is on the web, for example using search engines.

2.   **Extracting**. Using tools to extract the information found and store it in an accessible form, for example using web scrapers.

3.   **Analysing**. Using tools such as Leximancer to interrogate large amounts of text, to make sense of it and to produce the insight.

If a researcher intends to conduct blog and buzz mining themselves, then they will need tools to tackle each of these three steps. At the moment, most of the tools available tackle just one or two of the steps, so the researcher will usually need to combine tools. Free tools, such as the blog search tool Technorati and the web scraper OutWit, tend to be more limited than the commercial packages.

The alternative to conducting these three stages is to use one of the full service commercial solutions, such as TNS's Cymfony, an option that is covered later in this chapter.

FINDING MATERIAL

The first step in the blog and buzz mining process is to search for what people are saying about the topic of interest. The scale of the task is potentially so immense that thinking about it too much could almost be off-putting. The number of internet users is fast approaching two billion, with a large proportion of these using one or more social networks, forums, and blogs. Another indication of the scale of the tasks is that Technorati and BlogPulse both track over 100 million blogs.

Because of the scale of the job, computing power and algorithms are used to conduct the search for comments and conversations. Many of the tools and services available for finding information on the web are free, and these are highlighted in the sections below.

This section is divided into the following sub-sections:

- *Searching blogs*

- *Analysing Google's search terms*

- *Searching Twitter*

- *Searching social networks*

These sections all look at systems and services that assist market researchers to search the web for relevant comments and discussions.

SEARCHING BLOGS

One of the starting points for monitoring comments and conversations on the internet is to search blogs. Over the last ten years searching the blogosphere (the collective noun for all the blogs and comments on the internet) has become established as one of the key activities that allow brands to keep in touch with their customers' discourse.

Free blog search tools

There are a number of free tools available for searching blogosphere and a cross-section of them are explored below. Note that this list is not exhaustive and there are other options available; this list is simply intended as a starting point.

- *Google's Blog Search*

- *Technorati*

- *BlogPulse*

- *BlogScope*

- *IceRocket*

Although all of the tools listed here can be used to conduct a specific search, most of them are more powerful when used with either alerts or RSS feeds which automate a search so that the results are sent to the user rather than the user having to repeat a search. To find out more about alerts and RSS readers read the notes in Box 12.1.

Box 12.1 Using alerts and RSS feeds

Although a search can be conducted on a one-off basis it is sometimes more interesting to organise it so that it continues to operate and sends new results to the user. Many of the search options available to internet users have a facility to do this; indeed, they often have two ways to achieve this – email alerts and RSS feeds. This box outlines how both of these can be used.

In order to make the two routes clearer, we describe here how to use both techniques in the context of a Google search, but the method is very similar for a wide range of internet tools, i.e. these are not specifically a feature of Google.

Emails
Once a search has been created, the user can request that any future matches for the search are emailed to them. In Google Search these emails are called Alerts. On Google's results page there are two ways of creating an Alert: (a) a link on the left of the page to subscribe to Alerts, and (b) at the bottom of the page there is a link for creating an email alert.

When a user selects one of the two links they are taken to a form where they can specify the frequency they want to receive updates (for example, once a day or once a week). The user can also tweak other parameters.

If the user only creates one or two searches, then this is a very convenient way of monitoring a phenomenon on the internet. However, if more than one or two services are used to create emails, or more than one or two phrases are searched, then the user's inbox can soon be overloaded.

RSS feeds
An RSS feed (along with other similar feeds) is a method that websites have of broadcasting updates to people who want to follow them. However, these updates are not sent to an email inbox. The feeds are made available and the user needs to use a tool called an aggregator to pull the feeds together.

There are three different types of aggregators. Firstly, there are stand-alone packages such as Bloglines [http://www.bloglines.com/]. These are online services which users can access from anywhere. Secondly, many internet browsers have a method of integrating RSS feeds, for example Firefox displays a logo if a feed is available and clicking it creates a feed in the Bookmarks folder. The third option is to have an iGoogle account and to use Google Reader as part of that process.

Once feeds are organised via a reader they are tidier than emails and cause fewer interruptions. RSS feeds are widely used on a range of websites, especially news, search engines, and blogs.

Note, RSS is just one of many web feed formats, which can for most purposes be treated as interchangeable.

 In most cases the symbol for a web feed is an orange square with a broadcast symbol on it.

Google's Blog Search

Google's standard search engine can be run in a specifically blog oriented mode, accessed from the 'more' link or via http://blogsearch.google.co.uk/. Clicking on the 'Advanced Blog Search' link allows the user to specify a range of parameters about the search. On the Advanced Blog Search page the user can specify:

- *words that must appear in the blog, including exact phrases*
- *words that must **not** appear in the blog, useful for filtering*
- *specific words that must appear in the article title or blog title*
- *a specific URL or a specific author*
- *within a specific date range*
- *in a specific language*

Once the results are displayed they can be sorted by relevance (as defined by Google's algorithms) or by date (i.e. with the newest at the top).

Google Blog Search can be used for one-off searches, but it is more powerful when the user configures it to run in the background and to send the results to the user as and when they occur. This can be done either via email alerts or RSS feeds and is covered in Box 12.1

Technorati

Technorati [http://technorati.com/] is the most established name in reviewing the blogosphere and for a long time was the clear leader. In more recent times, Technorati has seen many of its advantages eroded, and there are claims that it has taken its eye off the blog searching part of its business. However, it remains a really useful resource.

One of the key features of Technorati's approach is that it has developed the concept of authority. It is a truism of the blogosphere that not all bloggers are equal. Some bloggers are widely read and have a major influence, others are very rarely read. Technorati rates blogs in terms of how many other sites link to them – the more links there are, the more 'authority' Technorati ascribes to it, on a scale from 0 to 1000. Technorati tracks over 100 million blogs and produces a ranking based on authority, producing both an overall rank and a category listings [http://technorati.com/blogs/directory/].

To check the authority of a particular blog, type its name into Technorati's search field and click on **Blogs** rather than **Posts** (to the left of the search field) then click **search**.

To use Technorati to search blogs, enter the search term in the search box, select **Posts** or **Blogs** (usually Posts) and then click **search**. Click on the 'refine options' to add more criteria to the search, for example to include all sites, or just those with medium and high authority, or just those with high authority.

BlogPulse

BlogPulse [http://www.blogpulse.com/] is a free service from Nielsen, a company that also provides commercial blog and buzz mining services. Like Technorati, BlogPulse tracks over 100 million blogs and has a search engine and the option of creating RSS feeds from the results of searches.

However, BlogPulse's interesting extra is the ability to produce a trend chart, showing the frequency of the appearance of three terms of your choice over the previous six months.

BlogScope

BlogScope [http://www.blogscope.net/] is a blog search engine being developed by the University of Toronto. Although BlogScope only claims to track 40 million blogs (compared with over 100 million for both Technorati and BlogPulse) this is not necessarily a major limitation.

One of the benefits of BlogScope is the way it provides additional information. For example, entering 'Market Research' into BlogScope (on 31 December 2009) produced 67 061 blog results, based on recency and at least some influence. It also listed the ten words most associated with market research, including: survey, product, customer, business, process, and online. The search also showed a popularity curve for the last six months, indicating that there had been a slight growth in the number of articles mentioning market research.

BlogScope's advanced search provides a wide range of parameters that can be configured to make the search more specific, including recency, influence, date, and some ability to filter by country.

IceRocket

IceRocket [http://www.icerocket.com/] is another powerful option in the blog search arena and, like the other options discussed above, it is free. It has a standard blog search option and also includes an option to search MySpace.

IceRocket has a trend tool that allows the frequency of the appearance of five terms of your choice to be graphed over a three month period. It has a section listing popular topics in the blogosphere, and also the most popular links between blogs and other media, such as news, videos, movies, etc.

Taking blog searches further

For anybody willing to spend some time and some IT resources it is possible to take blog searches a lot further. One great example of this is given by the work conducted for the CREEN project which is the subject of a case study later in this chapter.

Commercial services

There are a number of companies that offer a full service blog and buzz monitoring service, such as Nielsen's Buzzmetrics and TNS's Cymfony. These services grew up looking at the blogosphere, but have since developed to include communities, social networks, and anywhere else that people post comments and thoughts on the internet.

The limitations of searching blogs

Although monitoring the blogosphere is important for all brands, most users of blog searching techniques have been disappointed by how little their products or services are discussed. This topic is covered more fully in the summary of blog and buzz mining section at the end of this chapter. But the short answer is that monitoring the blogosphere is necessary, but not sufficient.

It should also be remembered that only a minority of people blog, and they tend to be people with higher levels of education and income. When brands listen to blogs they are not listening to everybody.

ANALYSING GOOGLE'S SEARCH TERMS

One simple and highly effective way to look at the level of interest in a topic is to see how many people are searching for that topic in a search engine, such as Google or Microsoft's Bing. Note, this section concentrates on Google, but other search engines can be used in similar ways.

Every time somebody uses Google search to look for something, the words they type into the search box are added to Google's database, having been flagged by date and by the estimated location of the person making the search. Because searches of Google's database of search strings can be targeted by location and time, they provide a powerful way of looking for trends.

There are a variety of ways of utilising Google's search database, including Google Trends, but currently the most powerful option is Google Insights [http://www.google.com/insights/search/]. Google Insights can be configured in a wide range of ways. For example:

- *conducting the search within one region*

- *comparing different locations, over time, for a specific search term*

> ○ comparing different time ranges for a specific search term, for example generating a graph where each year is a separate line, allowing the researcher to look for seasonal effects

The search can be made more targeted by choosing a specific country or region, by a category such as Games or Health, and by area of search such as web or news.

SEARCHING TWITTER

Twitter is a microblogging platform that has shown explosive growth since its launch in 2006, with millions of people posting their 140 character posts, or tweets as they are called. Because the Twitter database is so open there are some very powerful ways of searching it, and the searches can be easily tied to specific geographic locations. The options shown below are just three amongst a growing number, but they represent a good place to start:

○ Search. Twitter

○ TwitScoop

○ TweetDeck

Search. Twitter

Search. Twitter [http://search.twitter.com/] is provided by Twitter and has a very powerful advanced search mode. The parameters that can be specified include:

○ **Words** included in the tweets can be specified, with all the usual options of including exact phrases, words to exclude, and alternative words.

○ **Hashtags** are used to group tweets on a particular topic. For example, tweets with #mr as part of the message tend to be about market research, and tweets with #followfriday tend to nominate Twitter accounts worth following (as part of the follow Friday concept). Search. Twitter allows specific hashtags to be used in the search.

○ **Date** ranges can be specified for the search.

○ **Attitudes** is the term Search. Twitter uses to specify if a tweet contains a smiley (☺), a sad face (☹), or a question mark. However, most people do not use the emoticons, which somewhat reduces the usefulness of searching by attitude.

○ **Place** is perhaps the most powerful feature of Twitter Search. The search can specify a location, such as Paris, and ask for tweets that occur within a set distance of that location, for example 15 kilometres.

TwitScoop

TwitScoop [http://search.twitscoop.com/] has a range of uses, including acting as an alternative interface to the Twitter interface. However, in terms of finding out what is happening right at that moment, it is TwitScoop's Hot Trends that is relevant to this book.

Hot Trends shows a bar across the page with all the terms that are trending (becoming more popular) at the moment. Clicking on one of these trends then brings up a frequency diagram, showing how interest in the term built and decayed, along with a tag cloud of related terms and a list of key tweets.

TweetDeck

TweetDeck [http://tweetdeck.com/] is a popular alternative to Twitter's own interface, adding a wide range of extra functionality. From a searching/monitoring point of view, the key utility of TweetDeck is that it can be configured to have multiple columns, each displaying a different filter. For example, a user might have columns for the following items:

- *all feeds followed*

- *favourite feeds*

- *a specific search term, perhaps a band name*

- *a specific hashtag*

In addition to Twitter feeds, TweetDeck can also produce columns showing information from Facebook, MySpace, and LinkedIn.

SEARCHING SOCIAL NETWORKS, COMMUNITIES, AND FORUMS

Unlike blogs, many of the things said in communities, forums, and social networks such as Facebook and MySpace are not in the public domain, which makes searches harder to organise, less complete, and raises ethical issues. However, the situation is changing and evolving. For example, in December 2009 Facebook changed its default settings to make more information freely available.

In October 2009 Microsoft announced that its search engine Bing had entered into deals to provide a real-time search for both Twitter and Facebook. Similarly, in the same month Google announced a deal with Twitter. As noted earlier, IceRocket can be used to search MySpace and Twitter from its main menu.

However, for the foreseeable future it is likely that most searching within social networks, communities, and forums will be achieved by joining them and using their own search facilities, sometimes using tools such as web scraping which are covered later in the chapter.

Ethical issues

The ethics of searching closed and semi-open communities (i.e. a community that you have to join to read, but which anyone can join) is discussed more fully later in the book. However, it is worth highlighting the key issues at this point.

Warning

There is a general rule that covert viewing of subjects should be preceded by permission. In some cases this needs to be expressed permission, i.e. people signing a form, in others it can be implied permission. For example, if shoppers in a store are being observed in order to better understand shopping behaviour it might be sufficient to display a sign saying that observation is going on. Most codes of conduct (in both market research and social research) have an exception for when somebody might reasonably be expected to be observed. When people post a blog article or add a comment to the end of an online news story, they might reasonably expect to be observed.

However, when somebody writes something in a community or in a social network, they might expect to be observed only by other *bona fide* members of that community, they may not expect to be observed by others.

This has led to the general advice that, when joining a community or social network, a market researcher should announce their presence, i.e. they should not 'lurk'. If in doubt, they should ask permission before extracting information. Researchers should seek to protect the anonymity of subjects, even where those subjects do not appear to be taking any steps themselves to protect their anonymity.

EXTRACTING MATERIAL

The first step in blog and buzz mining is to find the information; the second step is to extract that information.

In some cases, extracting the information is very straightforward, simply requiring the found data to be visually inspected. For example, if an organisation is monitoring mentions of its brand name and a few associated terms in the blogosphere and Twitter, then it will be sufficient to set up RSS feeds and to manually review the aggregator, probably daily.

If the researcher only requires occasional and relatively straightforward trends and comparisons then tools like BlogScope and Google Insights often provide what is needed.

However, if the researcher wants to conduct text or content analysis of conversations, or if they want to conduct sentiment analysis or complicated and bespoke trend analysis, then the data needs to be extracted and put into a database. There are essentially two ways of converting found data into a database, and these are:

- ○ *RSS to database procedures*

- ○ *web scraping to database procedures*

These two approaches are covered in the next two sections of this chapter, first the RSS route and then the web scraping route.

IMPORTING RSS FEEDS TO A DATABASE

Aggregators such as Bloglines and Google Reader are great ways to pull information together from a variety of sources using web feed technologies. However, generally, aggregators are focused on the reader, presenting the information on the screen, usually employing multiple tabs, windows, or search facilities. To really interrogate the data the researcher needs the data in some form of database; this may be a fully developed relational database through to a simple Excel spreadsheet.

Whilst the web feed technology is relatively straightforward, there are no widely available tools that are being used 'off the shelf' to move RSS feed data into offline databases. Most people taking the RSS to database routes have created their own tools to achieve this.

Two factors that the researcher needs to keep in mind are firstly, that the amount of data could be very large, which could therefore put a significant load on servers and bandwidth. Secondly, there could be copyright and terms and conditions issues about using RSS feeds from websites to external databases.

WEB SCRAPING

Web scraping is the use of automation to extract information from websites by using software that emulates the behaviour of people using the web. For example, a user might set a search engine to show 100 results on a page and then use a web scraper to copy each of the results into a database, splitting the title, text, and link into separate fields.

Web scrapers can be quite sophisticated. For example, a web scraper can be programmed to work through a list of friends in a social network, selecting them one at time and recording their names, groups, and friends, profile information, and wall postings. Note, a web scraper can only see what the user of the web scraper is entitled to see. In the social network example, the only friends that can be scraped are people who are already friends of the person running the programme.

The term 'web scraping' can be an emotive one. Some see the practice as an invasion of privacy. It may also be seen as a breach of terms and conditions by the service being scraped. For example, at the beginning of 2008 web pundit Robert Scoble announced that his Facebook account had been suspended because he had used a web scraping application from Plaxo to capture the details of his 5000 Facebook friends and stored them in Plaxo. Facebook said they had detected that he had been viewing pages at a rate that implied he was using an automated script.

Many services ban web scraping, usually via their terms and conditions. For example, Google's Terms of Service ban any automated use of their system, which includes sending queries and scraping the results.

The specific meaning of web scraping and screen scraping is that software is used to access information that was intended to be read by a human. A web page is typically laid out using HTML, which is a mixture of formatting instructions and information. Scraping techniques make sense of the HTML and extract the information, depositing it in a file that can be further processed.

Compared with the more neutral phrase 'data mining', web scraping raises implications of extracting more data than the providers of the information might have expected. To an extent, when people post information on sites like Facebook they realise that 'friends' who they have allowed to read their profile can see what is there. However, they may not expect people to use software to extract all the information on the page and to store it in a database, allowing a wide range of their comments to be compared and analysed. Some people see a difference between having their comments scattered in a relatively public but unstructured way across the internet compared with somebody pulling all their comments together into one collection.

There is a wide range of software available for web scraping, some of it free and some commercial. In this section, two specific products are briefly reviewed: OutWit Hub and Screen-Scraper. OutWit Hub is a simple/free option and Screen-Scraper has a free option and two levels of premium service. This list is not exhaustive and does not represent a recommendation.

OutWit Hub

One relatively simple-to-use web scraping tool is OutWit Hub [http://www.outwit.com/]. OutWit Hub is free and is a downloadable extension to the Firefox browser.

OutWit Hub allows the user to take a page of search results, or a page of Twitter comments, or a page of posts from an online discussion and convert them into an organised set of headings. For example, the information might end up in a spreadsheet with separate columns for date, name, and content of the post. Once the data is in a convenient format (such as Microsoft Word or Excel), then the user can either analyse the text conventionally or via a text analytics programs such as Leximancer.

OutWit has a couple of automatic ways of analysing a page, such as List and Guess, but it also allows users to create a scraping template, using clues in the HTML of the page.

Screen-Scraper

Screen-Scraper [http://screen-scraper.com/] is a more fully featured web scraping program. Screen-Scraper (at the time of writing) came in three versions, Basic, Professional, and Enterprise. The Basic version is free, with the two premium services being charged for.

Some technical and programming knowledge is required to use Screen-Scraper, but it is capable of doing more than simpler programs. Screen-Scraper can incorporate a wide range of program language steps, including Java and Python, allowing multiple pages to be viewed and scraped.

ANALYSING MATERIAL

Analysis is the third stage of the find, extract, and analyse process. In most cases, the data that has been found and extracted is text, but it can also be images and video. When there is only a small amount of data, the best option is to analyse it manually, ideally using a theoretical basis for the analysis such as Grounded Theory.

As the amount of data grows there is an increasing need to use software. Because of options opened up by the internet, projects may acquire hundreds of thousands of comments, and potentially millions of individual words. Software designed to aid the analysis of text typically adopts one of two approaches:

1.   making the manual analysis more efficient, for example software designed to aid the coding of open-ended responses, or

2.   working with the data before human intervention, to provide information about what is already there

However, the more powerful commercial tools can, to a degree, offer both options.

TAG CLOUDS

One of the simplest analysis approaches is the creation of tag clouds (also known as word clouds and, in at least one service, tag crowds). In a tag cloud, the size of the words reflects how often they have occurred in the text that is being examined.

One popular web-based (free) service is Wordle [http://www.wordle.net/]. Wordle can produce simple tag clouds, but it also produces a range of engaging – if perhaps less informative – layouts, including a range of orientations, colours, and fonts. Figure 12.1 (created using http://www.wordle.net/) shows the Wordle output for the text of Chapter 11, Online Research Communities from this book.

Figure 12.2 (created using http://www.wordle.net/) shows an alternative Wordle output for the same information. This time the information is laid out with only 50 terms (Figure 12.1 showed the top 150 terms), all the words shown left to right, and sorted alphabetically.

The more sophisticated tag cloud options include the following abilities:

   ○   *to ignore common words, such as 'it', 'and', 'but', etc*

   ○   *to stem, i.e. join 'learn', 'learns', and 'learning'*

   ○   *a tabular word count*

   ○   *to click on a word in the cloud and be taken to a list of cases in the original text*

It should be remembered that a tag cloud (or its tabular cousin, the word count) is a very simple analysis. It might suggest words that should be inspected further, but it is not really analysis.

Figure 12.1

Figure 12.2

ADVANCED PACKAGES

There is a wide range of commercial packages available, which vary in cost from a few thousand dollars to many tens of thousands of dollars. Although these tools can greatly improve the efficiency of the researcher, none of them come close to replacing the researcher. A few of them claim they remove the need to read every word in the corpus (i.e. all the text collected), but that remains an opinion that few share.

As mentioned earlier, there are essentially two approaches that the researcher can seek to employ. The first is to use the software to make the researcher more efficient and, secondly, to use the software first and then to tweak the output.

Making the researcher more efficient

This approach includes packages such as Language Logic's Ascribe [http://www.languagelogic.info/] which helps with the coding of open-ended responses to surveys. It also applies to much more sophisticated products such as QSR International's NVivo [http://www.qsrinternational.com/], which allows the researcher to work with video, audio, and images, building a comprehensive analysis, allowing models to be built and validated against other cases in the data.

Text analytical software

The second approach is to start by letting the software interrogate the data, make initial findings and to create models. This stage is then followed by the user working with the findings and models to make them more coherent and applicable. Examples of software that do this are Leximancer [https://www.leximancer.com/] and PASW Modeller (which used to be SPSS's Clementine) [http://www.spss.com/software/modeling/modeler/].

Software overview

The more powerful options allow both the top-down and bottom-up approaches to be conducted, and some of them also have facilities to help find and gather the raw information from the internet. Generally, the better packages cost more, which is not the same thing as saying the more expensive products are better.

FULL SERVICE SOLUTIONS

At the time of writing, none of the free services were able to deliver the benefits that the early proponents of blog and buzz mining claimed it would. Although large amounts of information can be gathered, the process of turning that information into insight requires a substantial amount of effort.

This is where the commercial mining systems, such as TNS Cymfony and Nielson BuzzMetrics, come into the picture. They have powerful software tools, including intelligent bots (software programs), that search the internet, and advanced analytics. However, they don't just rely on their clever tools, they combine them with skilled analysts who work with the tools to produce insight.

One surprise to new users of commercial blog and buzz mining services is that the prices tend to be higher than they expect. The key reason for this is that the most expensive input to the insight process is analyst time, which is the same as for survey-based projects (given that the cost of surveys has greatly reduced over the last few years, with the growth in the use of online access panels).

Increasingly, the full service providers are also offering data-only solutions where clients can benefit from the bespoke tools that they have developed.

CASE STUDIES

This section looks at two cases studies, one from the world of market research and one drawn from a project in social research.

The RTL Nederlands case study highlights that blog and buzz mining can deliver results which can be used to change a product or service in ways that show a real improvement. However, the case study also shows the importance of having a product or service that people are actually talking about, of

 **Examples**

RTL Nederlands and InSites Consulting

This case study looks at how RTL Nederland (a Dutch broadcaster) and their agency (InSites Consulting from Belgium) explored the conversations in social media to provide guidance on how to manage and improve a popular TV programme, the internationally franchised 'X Factor' (a televised talent contest).

The nature of the 'X Factor' show is that it lasts several weeks, which lends itself to an iterative research process. The show starts with auditions, then a 'boot camp' stage, followed by several rounds, each of which result in a number of contestants being voted off the show. The series culminates with a single winner being chosen.

Rather than use the traditional research method of asking questions, the research employed web scraping technologies (an approach called e-ethnography and/or netnography), to explore the conversations that viewers were having about the show.

In the Netherlands, the show was broadcast on Fridays, therefore the agency conducted its 'web scraping' exercises on Mondays and fed information back to RTL Nederlands on Wednesdays, which allowed the information to inform the decisions being made for the Friday broadcasts. During the project the agency scraped 71 230 conversations from general sites such as http://www.Hyves.nl and www.forum.fok.nl, and from more specific sites. This quantity of online comment is a testament to how popular the 'X Factor' show is in the Netherlands. The collected and processed buzz showed that many people were very knowledgeable about many of the features of the show and were keen to talk about a wide range of aspects, including the music, the performers, and the judging.

(continued)

One specific issue highlighted by the research concerned one of the contestants, named Jamal. In the early discussions there was very little reference to Jamal, nothing very good, nothing very bad. His profile was simply too low. The show worked with Jamal to change his clothing, look, and provide him with coaching on how to make his personality stand out more. Jamal went from being a low-interest candidate to one of the three performers who appeared in the live final, and the discussion about him soared as his personality developed.

Other feedback that was acted on included viewer participation in the choice of songs for the contestants and providing more information about what happened backstage.

Without asking questions, the use of web scraping, a technique from the e-ethnology toolbox, allowed RTL to gain insight from a wide range of highly motivated viewers.

The study conducted by RTL Nederland and InSites Consulting covered more issues than are reported in this case study. For a fuller report of the project, and a similar project for the Dutch show 'So You Think You Can Dance', refer to the paper by Verhague, Schillewaert, and van den Berge (2009).

having the software tools and analytical experience to work with the buzz, and a client who is in a position use the information provided.

The CREEN case study (Thelwall, 2007, Thelwall and Prabowo, 2007) illustrates, again, that very interesting and potentially useful information can be gleaned from the blogosphere. Two specific points of

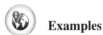 **Examples**

CREEN

The CREEN project, Critical Events in Evolving Networks [http://www.creen.org/], which ran from 2005 to 2008, was a project from the 6th EU Framework Programme.

At its broadest level, CREEN sought to use technology to identify events that might be early indicators of issues critical to public trust in science. The formal objectives of the project are listed on its website as:

1. to develop new methods to recognize emerging critical events in evolving complex networks, coupled networks and active agent networks

2. to apply these methods to the analysis of the emergence of new research topics (scientific avalanches) and possible crises in a social institution – the public trust in science.

One aspect of this project was a large-scale monitoring of a 100000 blogs, looking for posts that combined science-related words and fear-related words.

The project started by identifying the blogs it wanted to monitor and then monitoring the RSS feeds from these blogs. The key step was then to identify all the posts, amongst those 100000 blogs, that included both a synonym of 'fear' and a synonym of 'science'.

The analysis looked both at the total number of identified posts, allowing the researchers to find spikes, and the information within the spikes, allowing the researchers to look at the terms that were driving the spikes. For example, two of the search terms that caused spikes were 'Schiavo' and 'stem' – the first referring to a US medical case relating to turning off a life support machine for Terri Schiavo, and the second to stem cell research.

One of the partners in CREEN was the University of Wolverhampton and their Statistical Cybermetrics Research Group [http://cybermetrics.wlv.ac.uk/], who were responsible for the analysis described above. One by-product of this project was Mozdeh [http://mozdeh.wlv.ac.uk/], a tool for gathering and analysing RSS feeds.

This Statistical Cybermetrics Research Group produce an enormous amount of useful information in the area of searching the blogosphere. To find out more about the work of this group and to read about some cutting edge developments in the search of blogs the reader is referred to Mike Thelwall's book 'Introduction to Webometrics: Quantitative Web Research for the Social Sciences' (Thelwall, 2009).

interest from this study are firstly the scale of the exercise – i.e. very large – and secondly the way that a project can look at the topics people are talking about as opposed to the client's agenda.

THE ETHICS OF BLOG AND BUZZ MINING

Guidance and views about ethics in blog and buzz mining are changing and evolving as researchers and their representative organisations try to come to grips with what is a dynamic field. In addition to guidelines from organisations such as ESOMAR and local legislation, market researchers should pay attention to the terms and conditions that apply to material which has been posted on the internet. For example, before mining a closed network for information the researcher should check whether this would contradict the terms and conditions of that network.

 Warnings

When market researchers find themselves without any firm guidance as to what is appropriate, a good guiding principle is to consider what people generally would say if their project were to be made public. Remember that, in terms of the internet, most things do become public at some point.

Advice

In the absence of clear guidelines, the following (drawn from a variety of existing sources including the ESOMAR Guidelines on Passive Data Collection and the American Psychological Association) should be of some assistance.

1. Don't pretend to be somebody or something that you are not and when you join a group announce your presence (i.e. don't try to lurk under the radar).

2. Check whether the data constitutes personally identifiable information. If the data does qualify as personally indefinable information, ensure that the relevant data protection and security legislation is complied with.

3. Check whether any personal information gathered is sensitive. The EU (European Union) definition of sensitive is fairly useful here and includes data relating to: racial or ethnic origin, political opinions, religious or philosophical beliefs, trade union membership, and sexual preference or health.

4. The processing of personally identifiable data requires informed consent. In the case of blog mining and web scraping this is likely to hinge on whether the researcher can assume implied consent, because of the very large number of people involved.

5. Data for research purposes should be made anonymous as early as possible and certainly before being passed on to a third party.

6. Information that has been put in the public domain, for example posted on a public website (i.e. a site that can be read without joining, registering, or going through any other gate), is available to the researcher.

7. Information that is published in a 'walled garden' or in a 'members only' part of the internet is not the same as the public domain. Researchers should announce their presence and seek cooperation, either from the moderator of the community/forum/network or from the members.

8. Ensure that people are not exposed to harm, or at least not any greater harm than they had already put themselves in.

For further reading on this topic the reader is referred to an excellent paper by Neil Hair and Moira Clark (2007). One of the problems highlighted by Hair and Clark relates to Finn and Lavitt's (1994) study on computer-based support groups for sexual abuse survivors. Finn and Lavitt changed the names of the cases they quoted from, but used the exact names of the forums they were from and the exact dates, making it easy for anybody to identify the individuals.

The ethics of blog and buzz mining is an evolving field and researchers need to consider how their actions will appear to others, especially the owners of the views they are mining.

SUMMARY OF BLOG AND BUZZ MINING

Blog and buzz mining has made less progress over the last ten years than was predicted at the turn of the millennium, when some even predicted it might to a large extent replace brand, ad, and customer satisfaction tracking research.

The main reason for the shortfall in its performance has been the realisation that, unless a brand or service is a hot topic, it is probable that too few people are talking about it for it to be mined. Nevertheless, blog and buzz mining has proved to be an essential element of how brands and services should keep a finger on the pulse of what the public is saying. This is because of the essential asymmetry of word of mouth.

1.   People are not necessarily talking about you or the things you need to know.

2.   **But, if they are talking about you, you need to know it!**

STRENGTHS AND WEAKNESSES OF BLOG AND BUZZ MINING

This section looks at both the strengths and weaknesses of blog and buzz mining. Although some of the weaknesses are profound, the strengths are sufficient to make it an essential part of the market researcher's toolkit.

The strengths

The main strength of blog and buzz mining is that it takes the agenda out of the hands of the client and market researcher. Topics that arise from blog and buzz mining have an authenticity that originates from the fact that they are customers' own words.

By conducting blog and buzz mining, a brand or service can identify topics that are currently an articulated issue for customers. Blog and buzz mining can also be used to track bigger themes, such as what is in, who is in, and what people's fears and aspirations are.

If your customers are talking about you, then there is no longer an excuse for not listening.

The weaknesses

The main weakness of blog and buzz mining is that people might not be talking about you. Even if they are, the conversations they are currently having may not help you with the decisions you need to make now.

The tools for blog and buzz mining are still relatively undeveloped, and many of the interesting conversations (such as those on Facebook) are not easy to reach. This is likely to change in the future, but at the moment it does represent a weakness.

IS IT QUALITATIVE OR QUANTITATIVE, OR SOMETHING ELSE?

At one level it does not matter whether blog and buzz mining is classed as a qualitative or quantitative technique, it just matters whether it is useful. This view would say that the debate is purely academic, without a direct impact on how the research is conducted. However, it can also be argued that the debate about what constitutes qualitative or quantitative research enables us to realise where our existing approaches are deficient and need developing.

Qualitative methods are based on interpreting meanings. Qualitative methods do not seek to find formal mathematical links between conditions, and they reject the idea that they can produce 'value-free', objective findings. If qualitative analysis is ever computerised, it will not be because the rules have been quantified, it will be because the boundaries of artificial intelligence have advanced far enough to mimic the analysis done by the minds of qualitative researchers. By contrast, quantitative research is somewhat easier to define. Quantitative methods describe the data numerically and seek to find quantifiable relationships.

One of problems with many attempts to quantify qualitative analysis is that it often reduces the findings to just those very simple elements that can be counted. For example, researchers sometimes end up counting how many words were used and which words were used most often. Whilst these might be interesting, they are rarely the most interesting thing in the data.

Blog and buzz mining needs to avoid the temptation to be too easily satisfied with just those findings that can be quantified. It is likely that the really useful findings will be qualitative.

THE FUTURE FOR BLOG AND BUZZ MINING

The most immediate prediction is that blog and buzz mining is here to stay. If there is a method of hearing what customers are saying to each other about brands and services they have to be listened to, otherwise opportunities may be missed and potential problems not avoided.

The tools for blog and buzz mining are likely to continue to improve, with one of the drivers being the many research programmes being conducted in the academic sector.

The trend at the moment is for more and more information on the internet to be made generally available (at least in relatively open societies) – for example, the recent changes to Facebook's defaults and the open structure of Twitter. This trend will make more data available which, with improved tools, will increase the resolution of mining, i.e. smaller topics will become discernable.

It is unlikely that in the near future good blog and buzz mining will become cheap. The two key drivers are the cost of dealing with very large amounts of information and the need for human analysis in interpreting it.

13 Other Social Media Topics and Summary

This final chapter in Part III reviews several other social media market research topics, then looks at the ethical and quality-related issues, and finishes with a summary of social media-related market research and an assessment of the near future. The structure of this chapter is set out below:

- ○ *Community-enabled panels*

- ○ *Ethnographical research and social media*

- ○ *Researcher-to-researcher networking*

- ○ *Ethical and quality issues*

- ○ *Summary of market research and social media*

COMMUNITY-ENABLED PANELS

One development of the growth in panels and the interest in Web 2.0 has been the initiatives that some of the panel companies (and client panels) have been making to add a degree of community to their relationships with their panel members.

This has led to some confusion in the use of the term 'communities'. Researchers using online research communities make the point that collections of several thousand people, or tens or hundreds of thousands of people, are not a community in the sense that 100, 300, or 500 can be. This is similar to the difference between a community who might use a local pub or church and the concept of a city being a community.

The main driver for panels adopting a more community approach is to improve the engagement of their members with the panel, with the aim of improving respondent retention and cooperation.

COMMUNITY CHARACTERISTICS FOR PANELS

There is a wide variety of initiatives that the people running online panels have used to increase the sense of community within their panels. These initiatives include:

○   *the ability to post comments at the end of a survey, either passing messages to the end user of the research or to the people organising the panel*

○   *the ability of panel members to be able to post their own polls which other panel members can then answer*

○   *the ability of panel members to create their own discussions*

○   *the use of avatars and images*

○   *the ability to buddy and chat with other members*

○   *the use of innovative techniques such as online focus groups, blogging, and research communities.*

THE IMPACT OF CEDING CONTROL

One interesting result of panel companies creating more of a community focus is that they have had to cede some control to their members, which can be a potentially disconcerting experience. For example, when the online access panel company Toluna allowed its panel members to create polls and discussions, one of the first topics that members wanted to discuss was Toluna's remuneration/incentive scheme.

Australian online panel OpinionsPaid had a very similar experience when it created community elements for its panel members. The community aspects introduced to the panel included forums, blogs, and polls. The motivation behind the change, in addition to improving engagement, was to access a wider range of ideas and inputs from the panel members, and the first topics suggested by OpinionsPaid were on issues such as shopping patterns. However, before the panel members were prepared to engage in client-related topics they wanted to clear the air about the incentive scheme (a points-based system called Zoints) and bad surveys.

Over the course of the next three months the issues with the incentives were ironed out to most people's satisfaction. The problems with 'bad' surveys was harder to deal with, as surveys often have many stakeholders and may need to maintain comparability with other studies. One step that OpinionsPaid added was a post-survey forum to every survey, so that relevant feedback could be sent to the researcher, including views about the survey.

In terms of costs there were both plusses and negatives. The level of incentives went up which represented a direct cost per project. However, there were savings in overall project management costs. In the past anybody who complained about something did so by email and this initiated a potentially time-consuming process. Now most members with an issue post it to the forum. If other panel members agree, then the company gets the message pretty quickly and only has to respond in one place. However, if somebody posts a complaint and other members disagree, they say so, making the panel self-policing to an extent. This means the company is no longer dealing with things that are not actually a problem.

THE FUTURE OF COMMUNITY-ENABLED PANELS

The direction of travel of the internet and social media suggests that panels will increasingly adopt some elements of Web 2.0 to stay in step with member expectations and to engage and retain members.

Some panels will probably be ahead of the curve in the way that Toluna and OpinionsPaid are, some will be behind, but all the changes are likely to be in the direction of increased engagement and increased community characteristics. One of the largest providers of technology for community-enabled panels is Vision Critical and it is interesting to note that they are also a leader in providing researchers with tools to create engaging surveys; the two trends are likely to move together.

In terms of thinking about the future of community-enabled panels, it is useful to think about third-party/access panels and brand/client panels separately.

Brand panels

As the tools for managing communities become better, and as worlds of CRM, word-of-mouth marketing, and insight continue to merge, it seems likely that in the medium- to long-term future most brands will attempt to utilise a large brand community. In October 2008, Gartner expressed the view that more than 60% of the Fortune 1000 companies will have an online community by 2010.

However, in the short term there will be a growth in the number of brands and services looking to create community-enabled panels of 5000 to 20000 members. These panels are likely to be used for a wide range of conventional research and will probably put a high value on engagement, which will tend to mean both community features (such as blogs, forums, and polls) and more engaging surveys. It is likely that some of these brand panels will be managed in-house and some by external providers. It is also likely that some companies will oblige their research suppliers to use their brand panel for research, when appropriate.

Telstra: 'my Telstra experience'

A high profile example of this growth in brand panels is given by Telstra, the largest telecommunications company in Australia. In September 2009 it closed its longstanding (and controversial) customer forum NowWeAreTalking and announced that it was launching a new panel of 18000 members to help it understand the needs of its ten million customers. Telstra expect the new panel to be the largest customer experience panel in Australia. The intention is that members of the new panel will take part in surveys and some of them will be invited to take part in online discussions. Telstra's panel will be powered by Vision Critical's online research platform.

Third-party panels

The main driver for online access panels is the need to be profitable. Without being profitable they can't offer a service, they can't invest in the future, and very quickly they would cease to exist. At the moment, the online access panels are in the middle of a confluence of pressures:

- *clients want additional measures to improve reliability and validity*

- *agencies want lower prices, to help them deliver value*

- *respondents want a more engaging experience*

Whilst it is likely that the online access panels will increase the community features of their panels, their scope to make changes will in some cases be constrained by cost issues and the pressure from panel members for better surveys. This is why a number of panel companies are bringing in schemes which put more pressure on their clients to write better surveys.

ETHNOGRAPHICAL RESEARCH AND THE SOCIAL MEDIA

Some definitions of ethnography are so broad they could embrace the whole of market research, both qualitative and quantitative, without touching the sides. However, Caroline Hayter Whitehill achieves focus when she says '. . . *it is broadly accepted by academics and research practitioners alike that ethnography in today's world is about differing types of observation.*' (Hayter Whitehill, 2007). In order to make the definition clearer still, Hy Mariampolski refers to '*ethnographic and observational research*' in his textbook on qualitative research (Mariampolski, 2001).

In addition to the potential breadth of the term 'ethnography' there is a wide variety of new 'ethno' words which have been coined to discuss ethnography in the context of the internet in general and social media in particular. For example, we see references to netnography, e-ethnography, virtual ethnography, online ethnography, digital ethnography, and others.

Without making a specific case for one new term over another, this book uses the term 'e-ethnography' for those aspects of ethnographic and observational research that relate to the internet and particularly to social media. However, other authors have chosen different terms, and a good introduction to this area is provided by Robert Kozinets' book *Netnography: Doing Ethnographic Research Online* (Kozinets, 2010).

Other chapters in this book deal with specific examples of e-ethnography. For example, participant blogs are an example of e-ethnography, where participants report on their life via the medium of blogs. Online research communities are another example, particularly when the communities are used to allow members to report on their lives and experiences. Blog and buzz mining is very clearly an example of e-ethnography, with its observational search for what people are saying to each other.

The need for this type of ethnographical research was articulated by Stan Sthanunathan, VP, Marketing Strategy and Iinsights for Coca-Cola, when he said in *ResearchLive* in October 2009:

> 'We're too focused on understanding consumption behaviour and shopping behaviour. We need to understand the human condition, which you'll only know by observing, listening, synthesising and deducing.'

The previous three chapters do not cover all of the areas of e-ethnography that are currently being used by market researchers. This section reviews additional topics, including:

○　*WE-research, the rise of citizen researchers*

○　*Natural communities*

○　*Social graph research*

WE-RESEARCH, THE RISE OF CITIZEN RESEARCHERS

The idea behind the citizen researcher is that participants are recruited to work with market researchers as collaborators to explore lives, products, and services. This concept has been described as a shift from ME-research to WE-Research (Kearon and Earls, 2009).

The concept of citizen researcher is associated with the ideas and techniques of user-generated media, for example webcams, mobile phones, and personal video devices. Citizen research reflects a demand by people to be involved and recognition that the tools to make this demand actionable are now widely available.

The three examples below illustrate how citizen research is being deployed by a range of market researchers.

 Examples

UB case study: Real lives

This case study looks at using webcams, mobile phones, and remote usability to get inside people's lives to obtain a better understanding of their relationship with campaigns and competitions. The context was the UK snack food market and was conducted by United Biscuits, utilising their online research community Snackrs and their agency Virtual Surveys.

(continued)

The objective was to evaluate how people experience campaigns and competitions, particularly 'Bonkers about Biscuits' campaign that was run in 2009. It was an integrated campaign which included user-generated comments being posted on a microsite. United Biscuits wanted insights into how the campaign was understood, how it fitted into people's lives, and how it compared with other campaigns and competitions.

Ten participants were recruited from the community and, where necessary, provided with webcams. During the two week project they conducted a range of activities, including taking daily pictures of what was in their larders, recording their feedback from the project (including reporting back from shopping trips), and engaging in remote usability sessions where their use of the microsite was observed whilst they used an audio connection to talk to Virtual Surveys' usability researchers about what they were experiencing, an approach sometimes called Thinking Aloud.

The research provided both tactical and strategic insight to United Biscuits. The tactical insight allowed the company to tweak the 'Bonkers about Biscuits' campaign and site. The strategic research raised issues such as products that were still on retailers' shelves after the campaign or competition finished, particularly in smaller retail outlets.

One of the interesting features of this project is that none of the participants had any previous experience of this type of real life research, and activities such as remote session and recording personal video diaries needed to be explained to them; however, they were all able to complete the tasks and were highly engaged by the process.

 Examples

BBC Global News: Travellers' consumption of news

This example outlines how mobile telephones were incorporated into a citizen research project in order to explore the transient needs of busy travelling business people.

BBC Global News wanted to understand the relationship between business travellers and news while they were away. The challenge for the researchers (MESH Planning) is that interviewing travellers after they return home tends to be rather unsatisfactory. Travellers' recollections of their relationship with news services are normally dwarfed by all the other stimuli associated with flying to another country, business meetings, new locations, etc.

The solution implemented by MESH Planning was to use travellers' mobile phones to capture individual moments throughout the business trip, via a method they have branded TROI. The logistics of the research were as follows:

1. The company recruited businessmen and women who were planning to make a business trip in the near future (109 participants completed the whole research process).

2. Before the journey the travellers completed an online survey to provide profiling information and act as a benchmark for the later findings.

3. During the journey the travellers sent a text every time they encountered news services, describing the encounter, the channel, how it made them feel.

4. The participants were encouraged to fill in a daily online diary, expanding the comments they had made by text during the day.

5. After the participants returned home, twenty tele-depths were conducted to explore issues and queries that the pre-surveys, the texting, and the online diaries had elicited.

The research identified how important news became for business travellers. Not only were there practical needs, such as showing courtesy to colleagues by being in touch with news in their country, but news filled an emotional need to connect with home.

The research revealed that when these businesspeople are at home, news tends to be in the background, supplied by a variety of traditional channels, and typified by adherence to a routine. However, when they are travelling, their routine is removed, they lose contact with home and family, and surrender control to third parties; but they also often gain 'me time', e.g. when they are alone in their hotel room. They also show much greater use of the internet and mobile devices to access news in their hotel rooms and when on the move.

 Examples

Recruiting and training WE-researchers

In their 2009 ESOMAR Congress paper, John Kearon and Mark Earls outlined a citizen ethnography project, looking into the topic of binge drinking in the northern UK city of Newcastle. Kearon and Earls cite their approach as being informed by the cultural anthropologist and ethnologist Grant McCracken.

(continued)

The approach described by Kearon and Earls comprised two weekends. For the first weekend, the instructions to their citizen researchers was relatively light, which produced poor results. The second weekend was based on a better briefing and the use of example feedback. This second week was more successful and provided insight into the role of fancy dress in providing a focus for heavy drinking. For example, during that particular weekend there were people out and about in Newcastle dressed as Umpa Lumpas, a character from the popular book/film *Charlie and the Chocolate Factory*.

What these three case studies show is that the new technologies and a new mindset are combining to create accessible opportunities to see into people's lives and to gain insight in a way that touches the *'human condition'* referred to by Stan Sthanunathan.

Mass Observation project

Like many new ideas, the concept of the citizen researcher has a long history. One of the best examples is the UK's Mass Observation project, which ran from 1937 through to the 1950s (and was relaunched by the University of Sussex in 1981). The project was initiated by anthropologist Tom Harrisson, poet Charles Madge, and film-maker Humphrey Jennings who wanted to create an *'anthropology of ourselves'*.

Mass Observation consisted of about 500 volunteer observers who wrote notes about what they saw and heard, either as diaries or in response to open-ended questions. A representation of the life of a volunteer observer was captured by the UK TV drama 'Housewife, 49', which was based on the wartime diaries of Nella Last, which have also been published as two books, *Nella Last's War: The Second World War Diaries of 'Housewife 49'* in 2006, and *Nella Last's Peace: The Post-war Diaries of 'Housewife 49'*, in 2008.

To find out more about the Mass Observation archives and the current incarnation of the project, visit the Mass Observation website [http://www.massobs.org.uk].

EDL app – a tool for citizen researchers

Siamack Salari and EverydayLives launched a personal ethnography iPhone app in December 2009, available from iTunes, allowing anybody to turn themselves and their iPhone into a citizen researcher. The app allows citizens to capture video on their iPhone, annotate it, and upload it to a project sponsor's site.

The company describe the app as *'a sophisticated research tool designed by ethnographic researchers for ethnographic researchers, agency planners, marketers and research respondents'*. Although it looks as though most of the early users of the app will be professional researchers, this app will lower the barriers to entry and increase the prospect of self-employed citizen ethnographers.

NATURAL COMMUNITIES

Social researchers have been using online groups as a source of material since the mid-1990s. For example, as long ago as 1999 Peter Lyman and Nina Wakeford said *'the study of digital and networked technologies is one of the fastest growing fields of research in the social sciences'* (Lyman and Wakeford, 1999).

Natural communities is a generic phrase that includes all of the online phenomena where people combine for any common purpose, from discussions, to self-help groups, to mass games, to reviews, to social networks. Natural communities are where people choose to go, as opposed to research or marketing communities where they are persuaded to go.

Although market researchers may have been slower off the mark than social scientists, increasing use has been made of natural communities as a source of insight. A good example of this approach was provided by Steve August's (2004) study of attitudes towards digital cameras. In the project, August researched three communities: a Usenet group, a message board, and a moderated email group. One of the benefits highlighted by August was that they were able to study three to six months of archived discussions, which is clearly much faster than having to wait three to six months to generate research materials. August's study was also a good example of best practice in that permission was requested and notices posted in the communities to alert members to the researcher's presence.

This sort of research is very different from blog and buzz mining. This sort of e-ethnography is conducted on a human scale, involves people reading and analysing discourses, and can access the sorts of communities where automated techniques are either banned or deemed inappropriate.

SOCIAL GRAPH RESEARCH

Brad Fitzpatrick (2007) describes the social graph in the following way: *'What I mean by "social graph" is the global mapping of everybody and how they're related'*. Studying the social graph includes studying the way people in social networks are connected, how messages propagate, and how new connections are made.

This topic includes projects such as Guy Kawasaki's 'six Twitter types' (Kawasaki, 2009) and the University of Salford/Virtual Surveys study of why people join communities (Ferneley and Heinze, 2009). In these projects the aim is to understand why people join networks, what they do in these networks, and how they are connected.

One topic of particular interest to researchers and marketers is the question of how many connections people can sustain online. In the offline world people often refer to the 'Dunbar number', typically 150, named after the British anthropologist who first suggested that the human brain limits the number of people with whom one can have stable social relationship. Does the same number apply to online relationships? Seth Godin certainly seems to believe so (Godin, 2009).

A key area for further investigation via the social graph is the way that memes are transmitted and the way some ideas, videos, and messages 'go viral'.

RESEARCHERS USING SOCIAL MEDIA

As well as being a place to conduct market research, social media has become a place for market researchers to network, share ideas, look for jobs, and simply to have fun. Market researchers are active users of social networks, forming new and dynamic groups of friends and followers.

 Examples

The various types of social network activity engaged in by market researchers include:

General networks, such as Facebook. In these networks researchers are making friends, using their 'status' to talk about research, joining general research groups such as: 'The Big List of Market Researchers'; 'Market Research Rocks'; and joining specialist research groups (such as 'Big Conference'; 'International Journal of Market Research'.

In addition, most researchers use their Facebook accounts for 'normal' social networking, such as keeping in touch with friends and family, posting photos, and playing online games such as Farmville and Mafia Wars.

Professional networks, for example LinkedIn. LinkedIn is being used to form contacts, to engage in market research groups such as 'NewMR' [http://www.linkedin.com/groups?gid=2446402] and 'Next Gen Market Research (NGMR)' [http://www.linkedin.com/groups?gid=31804]), and for a range of job related issues.

Microblogging, which at the moment tends to means Twitter for most market researchers. As well as using Twitter to follow specific friends and opinion leaders, researchers are using hashtags to coordinate their interest in events (such as conferences), and Twitter to create Tweetups (events advertised and organised through Twitter, via services such as TwtVite [http://twtvite.com/]).

Specific communities, such as communities around a specific conference (for example the 2009 ESOMAR Congress organised a pre-attending community using the CrowdVine platform), or created for researchers (such as 'http://www.research-voice.com/'), exist but they may be losing ground to the three approaches described above, specifically to Facebook, LinkedIn, and Twitter.

The use of social networks by market researchers to network with each other is a dynamic area and no two researchers are using the various types of platform in the same way. New users may find the generalisations in Table 13.1 useful.

Perhaps there is an interesting study that could be conducted, comparing researchers active on social networks and those who are not. What are the implications for those who are networked and those not networked?

Table 13.1   Typical uses of social networks

Researcher-to-researcher networking	Facebook	LinkedIn	Twitter
Getting in touch with old friends	✓✓✓	✓✓✓	✓
Alerting contacts to your thoughts and activities	✓✓✓	✓✓	✓✓✓
Organising discussion groups	✓	✓✓✓	✓
Organising a research event	✓✓	✓✓	✓✓
Prospecting for new contacts	✓	✓✓	✓
Looking for/advertising a job	✓	✓✓	✓
Looking for services, such as consultancy, travel, insurance	-	✓	-

RESEARCH BLOGS

Many researchers and research companies maintain a blog and these blogs can complement the way researchers use social networks. Blogs are being used to express the views of the author, attract contacts, and initiate discussions.

Blogs can develop what is in effect their own social network. People who like the blog will tend to follow it via RSS feeds or similar, and will add comments to topics. Authors often announce new posts via Twitter and their Facebook and LinkedIn status. This social aspect of research blogs illustrates social media convergence.

ETHICAL AND QUALITY ISSUES

The explosion of social media has created a number of ethical and quality issues that are either new or differently nuanced. For example, in the past the ethical dimensions of the participant/observer method only applied to a small number of ethnographers, most of whom were well schooled in the issues. With the advent of social media, large numbers of researchers are suddenly finding themselves 'hands on' with large numbers of people, in participant/observer roles they are unfamiliar with.

This section first looks at ethical issues and then reviews quality issues, although it should be stressed that there is an overlap between the two in many cases.

ETHICAL ISSUES

This section looks at the key ethical issues that are facing market research as a consequence of social media.

Most market research codes of conduct and guidelines are based on some basic principles, and these principles have a direct impact on how researchers need to consider the ethical issues surrounding social media and market research. These principles can be summarised as:

○   ***Do no harm!*** *At the end of the research process respondents, researchers, clients, and bystanders should not have been harmed. The particular focus of most guidelines relates to respondents – for example, they must not end up with less money, confused, or with their health put at risk.*

○   ***Do not 'sell' stuff.*** *This rule has several reasons and implications. If research becomes involved in directly selling things then it will be subject to the same legislation as selling and direct marketing. If respondents think they are going to be 'sold to' then they might be less likely to cooperate with market research or to tell the truth.*

○   ***Do not mislead the client.*** *This is the principle that underpins that importance of quality, thereby firmly tying ethics and quality together.*

○   ***Respondent's cooperation is voluntary.*** *This relates to ensuring that 'informed consent' really means informed and that the respondent is aware they have consented.*

The ethical points discussed in this section all rest upon these basic principles as applied to market research in a social media context. The ethical issues that face market researchers include:

○   *Recognition*

○   *Safety and abuse*

○   *'Leading'*

○   *Harmful habits and products*

○   *Quality as an ethical problem*

○   *Not misleading respondents*

Recognition

In pre-internet and pre-social media research it was unlikely, other than at focus groups, that respondents would meet each other or that clients would meet or observe respondents.

However, social media research, especially asymmetric research techniques such as participant blogs and online research communities, changes that position markedly. The best practice is to encourage participants to disguise their real identities by adopting avatars that are not their real name and picture (it can help to supply images and suggestions for respondents).

Safety and abuse

The most basic step in protecting respondents, colleagues, and clients from abuse, is to preserve their anonymity wherever possible/appropriate. The next is to monitor the communications between respondents, and between respondents and clients, to ensure that nothing unsuitable is developing. Cyberbullying is one type of activity to watch for, but so are flirting and plans to meet offline.

Researchers should ensure that when they visit online communities and forums as part of their work they do not disclose information that would lead to the identification of people making comments, unless they clearly wish to be identified (e.g. high profile bloggers).

'Leading'

When an online community is used to promote brand affinity and brand advocacy the market researcher needs to ensure that they are not involved in the process of actively changing people's minds. This is especially important in areas of public policy and where a scheme has been advertised as consultation.

Harmful habits and products

Experience with online research communities has shown that when they are well run, with brands helping build engagement, the members tend to associate more closely with the brand, consume more of the brand's products or services, and become advocates for the brand. For 'normal' products and services this raises some ethical issues, since the research is clearly changing the customer in a predictable direction, in favour of the brand.

However, this raises the question about whether there is a bigger ethical issue about products or services that are considered harmful. Many researchers would have some concerns about running a tobacco community if they thought it was going to cause people to smoke more and to become advocates for a specific brand of tobacco product, or perhaps encourage people to become advocates for smoking. However, even for researchers who would worry about tobacco, where should the line be drawn? Are products that are implicated in obesity a problem? Are communities that promote 'must have' products, such as the latest sports trainers to low income demographics, a problem?

Quality as an ethical problem

The next section reviews quality issues. However, market researchers should remember that there are ethical issues that relate to quality. When new and interesting techniques are being used the researcher needs to ensure that the client is aware of the limitations and assumptions. With a conventional research project it is likely that the client will understand the caveats that apply, but this may not be the case with social media research.

Not misleading respondents

If respondents are to provide informed consent they need to be aware of the facts. If market research is to avoid future scandals it needs to be seen to be above suspicion. In order to not mislead respondents it is important not to mislead by omission, i.e. by failing to say things as opposed to saying things which are not true. For example, when joining online communities a market researcher should announce their presence and, where possible, ask permission to be there.

QUALITY ISSUES

Because social media research is so new there is limited guidance available about the quality implications, but reference to first principles suggests that the key issues are:

- ○ *reliability*

- ○ *validity*

- ○ *the absence of a theory or evidence about new techniques*

The use of online research communities and community-enabled panels is very different from market research's historical use of random probability sampling. If the people in the communities and panels are not similar to the wider population, will the results be valid? If the people in an online community become more engaged with the brand, more inclined to be brand advocates, will the same test conducted, say, 12 months apart even produce the same results?

The key challenge, however, for most aspects of social media is to establish a set of theories and evidence that support the use of techniques such as blog and buzz mining, online research communities, and participant blogs. Whilst this new body of knowledge is being accumulated, market researchers need to be careful about what they claim for these new techniques, ensuring that findings and theories are understood to be emergent.

SUMMARY OF MARKET RESEARCH AND SOCIAL MEDIA

The terms 'summary' and 'social media' are almost an oxymoron. The use of social media is growing rapidly around the globe, more people are coming online, more people are joining social networks, more people are leaving their comments, more people are sharing their photos and videos, and more people are tweeting. It is likely that the rate of change and the development of new features of social media will continue for the foreseeable future, although it is hard to guess what the next big ideas will be.

In this context, it is not surprising that the use of social media by market research is growing so quickly. The growth of social media research is being driven by two factors:

1.   The availability of many new ways of contacting people and of gaining insight into their lives.

2.   The growing awareness that traditional market research is failing to keep up with the needs of business to produce fast and actionable insight.

Social media-related research can be divided into two broad categories:

1.   Techniques that extend the canon of qualitative research.

2.   Techniques that challenge and which may even replace quantitative and qualitative research.

Techniques such as the ethnographic investigation of online forums and communities, of citizen researchers, and participant blogs all extend the range of tools available for qualitative research. However, online research communities, community-enabled panels, and blog and buzz mining are already competing for projects in both the qualitative and quantitative spaces.

THE FUTURE

In such a rapidly changing field as the use of social media for market research it is unwise to try to look too far forward. Perhaps the key issue is to identify the short-term challenges and issues.

Here are four predictions for what research will see happening in the next four years:

1. The development of brand panels used for an ever larger portion of companies' routine research, with a heavy emphasis on community engagement.

2. The development of citizen research, combining a range of techniques including participant blogs and the use of options such as EveryDayLives application.

3. The development of online research communities so that they can be created rapidly, answering specific questions, with a range of new tools for researching views and co-creating solutions.

4. Improvements to blog and buzz mining, in combination with the posting of questions to remedy the problem of it being so reactive.

PART IV

Research Topics

This part of the book moves the focus away from a modality-centric view and concentrates on the specific needs of the researcher and research buyer, for example looking at topics such as international research and business-to-business research, and at types of research such as website and DIY research.

The chapters in this part of the book are:

- Specialist research areas

- Website research

- Research techniques and approaches

- The business of market research

Specialist Research Areas

This chapter looks at key specialist research areas and reviews the implications of online and social media research in the context of these sectors. The areas covered in this chapter are:

○   *International research*

○   *Business-to-business research*

○   *Public sector research*

INTERNATIONAL RESEARCH

With the growth in internet penetration around the world and the emergence of online access panels in most of the developed and many of the developing markets, a growing share of international market research projects is being conducted via the internet.

The internet has, at least superficially, made international research much easier and potentially much cheaper. For example, projects can be scripted and hosted anywhere in the world, online systems support all the leading languages and writing systems, and there is no need to pay and organise local interviewers.

This section looks at the benefits and problems of using online and social media research as the medium for international market research. The topics covered in this section are:

○   *The international picture*

○   *The promise of the internet*

○   *Pitfalls in international online research*

○   *Online international quantitative research*

○   *Online international qualitative research*

○   *Social media and international research*

○   *Summary of online and international research*

THE INTERNATIONAL PICTURE

Nearly two billion people now have access to the internet, and the number is growing rapidly, with most of the recent growth being in Asia. Most of the world's market research is conducted in North America and Europe and in these markets online market research is already well developed, as it is in some other parts of the world, such as Australia and Japan.

The picture in terms of the adoption of online research and of other modalities is very mixed. For example, in Australia, Canada, UK, and the USA the figures for online survey research as a percentage of all quantitative research were 32%, 35%, 25%, and 21% respectively, which makes these four countries look fairly similar (in 2008, according to the ESOMAR Global Market Research Report 2009). However, the shares for surveys conducted face-to-face were 7%, 4%, 24%, and 2%, which suggests the UK is very different to the other three. This difference may well relate to the relative size of the countries, but it could also relate to cultural phenomena, particularly given the fact that Australia is the most urbanised of the four.

Even within regions there are large variations. The figures from ESOMAR show Germany and Netherlands as having 28% and 27% of their quantitative research online, whereas Spain has just 4%.

Different internet penetrations

Different countries have very different levels of internet penetration. In major developed nations, such as the USA and Japan, about three-quarters of the population has access to the internet, and in a few markets the penetration is much higher – Norway, for example, boasts a figure of over 90%. But different countries have very different figures. Table 14.1 shows a cross-section of internet penetration data, along with a number of other interesting characteristics.

Online access panels

The number of countries served by online access panels is growing. Table 14.2 lists some of the countries covered by the major panel companies in early 2010. However, it should be noted that the size and nature of these panels will vary from country to country. In some cases, panels in new countries are owned outright by the major panel companies; in others, one or more partnership arrangements are in place. As well as international panels there are, in most markets, local panel companies.

THE PROMISE OF THE INTERNET

At first glance, the emergence of the internet makes it appear that, at last, an international study can be conducted with identical fieldwork in each of several countries, with no reluctance by local agencies to implement the survey in the prescribed way, faster, and for a lower cost. It might almost seem that the internet has delivered that enticing trinity: better, faster, cheaper.

Whilst it is true that many international projects are now run successfully from a central location, especially when they are being run across a small number of reasonably comparable countries, the promise has not turned out to be so simple. Consequently, the market researcher needs to be careful of the pitfalls of international online research.

Table 14.1   Internet and population statistics[*]

Country	Population (Millions)	Internet Users (Millions)	Penetration	Median Age (years)	Urbanisation %	Adult Literacy %
Australia	21.2	17.0	80%	37	89%	99%
Brazil	198.7	67.5	34%	29	86%	89%
Egypt	78.9	12.6	16%	25	43%	71%
India	1,156.9	81.0	7%	25	29%	61%
Japan	127.1	96.0	76%	44	66%	99%
Malaysia	25.7	3.7	65%	25	70%	89%
Norway	4.6	4.2	91%	39	77%	100%
Poland	38.5	20.0	52%	38	61%	100%
South Africa	49.1	4.6	9%	24	61%	86%
USA	397.2	227.7	74%	37	82%	99%

Note, countries selected to produce a cross-section of characteristics and continents.

[*]Population and Internet figures from InternetWorldStats.com, download 18 November 2009. Demographic information from CIA World Factbook, downloaded 18 November 2009.

PITFALLS IN INTERNATIONAL ONLINE RESEARCH

Despite its promise, the internet's impact on international studies has been less clear cut, with a number of issues limiting the successes. The key issues are:

- ○   *Loss of the local partner*

- ○   *The identical survey myth*

- ○   *Different internet penetrations*

- ○   *Different demographies*

Table 14.2   Examples of countries covered by online panel companies

North America	South/Latin America	Europe	Africa & Middle East	Asia Pacific
Canada	Argentina	Austria	South Africa	Australia
Mexico	Brazil	Belgium	UAE	China
Puerto Rico	Chile	Czech Republic		Hong Kong
USA	Ecuador	Denmark		India
	Peru	Estonia		Indonesia
	Uruguay	Finland		Japan
		France		Malaysia
		Germany		New Zealand
		Greece		Philippines
		Hungary		Singapore
		Ireland		South Korea
		Italy		Taiwan
		Luxembourg		Thailand
		Netherlands		Vietnam
		Norway		
		Poland		
		Portugal		
		Romania		
		Russia		
		Slovakia		
		Spain		
		Sweden		
		Switzerland		
		Tunisia		
		Turkey		
		UK		
		Ukraine		

○   *Seasonality and calendar issues*

○   *Contextual and cultural differences*

○   *Languages and translation*

Loss of the local partner

The biggest single source of problems for an international online research project is the absence of local partners. With traditional data collection methods, both qualitative and quantitative, international research is conducted in partnership with people based in each country. These local partners will often help check translations, give advice about what works and what doesn't, warn about common mistakes and phenomena particular to the country.

With online projects there is not necessarily anybody in each of the countries to provide a current and up-to-date sense check of the research. Many of the other problems outlined in this section, particularly ones relating to language, culture, and inappropriate questions are made much worse in online projects because of the absence of a local partner.

The identical survey myth

One of the myths of online research is that it readily allows a single research instrument to be applied globally, and in a way that allows direct comparisons to be drawn. A slightly more modest claim is that comparable studies can be run in all those countries where a suitable online access panel is available, but this too is a myth.

The logic seems simple: an online questionnaire can be translated into however many languages are required and rendered in as many different language character sets as needed. The survey can then be sent to a matched sample of online panel members in each country. Surely the result is that the researcher has a survey that is being applied uniformly? Surely direct comparisons can be drawn?

One of the reasons that this is not so relates to differences in internet penetration, and this is explored below. However, in terms of implementing a global survey, most of the limiting factors relate to differences between the main characteristics of the countries, and these problems exist regardless of the data collection methodology. However, some of these problems are more pronounced when using an online modality. These issues are also explored below.

The sections below look at the main factors that limit the ability of a researcher to create a global study, with particular reference to online surveys.

Different internet penetrations

A multi-country online study is capable of reflecting large proportions of people in countries like Australia, Germany, Japan, and the USA (where internet penetrations are high), but it will only reflect a small minority of people from countries like India and South Africa. This is a fundamental imbalance in any global study using the internet, unless the relevant population is likely to be online, for example younger and more affluent consumers, or unless all the countries have similar internet penetrations.

Different demographies

When conducting a comparative study across a range of countries the researcher is faced with a largely irreconcilable problem. Should the sample from each country reflect the different demography of that country, or should it use the same sample specification across all of the countries?

Table 14.1 shows the median age, urbanisation, and adult literacy figures for a range of countries, and reveals some stark differences. In Japan, for example, 50% of the population is aged 44 years or older, whereas in South Africa 50% of the population is 24 years old or younger. Similarly, in Australia 89% of the population lives in urban areas, in Japan this is just 66% and in India it drops to 29%.

As an example, consider the issues created by the different age profiles across different countries. If a global study uses the same age quotas in each country, it will accurately reflect some countries but will give a distorted picture for others. If, by contrast, the sample for each country reflects that country's age profile, the overall results are likely to reflect age differences rather than just inter-country differences.

Seasonality and calendar issues

It is well known that many research topics are affected by the seasons. Talking to respondents about ice creams, swimwear, picnics, cold drinks, and days out will often produce different responses if they are conducted in a hot summer or in a cold winter. However, the Northern and Southern Hemispheres have opposite seasons, a global study conducted in December/ January could see Australian respondents suffering bush fires with smoke billowing over their cities, whereas respondents in New York, Beijing, or Moscow might be struggling through snow drifts.

Contextual and cultural differences

Researchers are well aware of the need to frame their questions in a clear context in order to be able to interpret the results. However, these contexts differ around the world. For example, a global study looking at gambling habits and preferences will have to deal with contexts that vary from deregulated, competitive markets, such as Australia, to highly regulated and less competitive markets such as the UK, through to markets where gambling is illegal. Similarly, in some markets soft drinks compete with alcoholic drinks, in other markets they don't.

The meaning of family, self, independence, or security all differ from culture to culture, which has implications for anybody looking at how these items might have been used or scaled in a survey. Indeed, even the way that scales are used varies from culture to culture. A satisfaction score of 75% in one country might mean the brand is doing really well, but in another (more 'polite') country, 75% might imply it was doing badly.

Languages and translations

Translating one language into another is not an exact science. A phrase translated from, say, French to German will have some subtle differences in emphasis. The same phrase translated into a language with few linguistic and cultural ties, such as Japanese or Tamil, will be even less precise.

Even quantities can create differences in the way they are perceived. A survey with its income boundaries in nice round numbers in US dollars will, in some other countries, either use odd-looking bands or require the values to be tweaked. An example of the problem is shown in Table 14.3.

Table 14.3   Currency band comparisons

Euros	US Dollars	UK Pounds	Japan Yen
Less than 10,000	Less than 14,857	Less than 8,948	Less than 1,325,870
10,000 to 50,000	14,857 to 74,285	8,948 to 44,740	1,325,870 to 6,629,350
More than 50,000	More than 74,285	More than 44,740	More than 6,629,350

Bands based on currency exchange rates 11:00 GMT, 19 November 2009.

However, the currency problem is even more nuanced, as the exchange rates chosen will only be true for a specific moment. If the fieldwork lasts a short time – for example, one or two weeks – it is unlikely that currency exchange rates will make a major difference. However, if a study is repeated later – for example, the following year – exchange rates may have changed considerably. If the rates have changed the researcher is in a 'lose–lose' situation. If the local amounts stay the same as the previous year, they have lost their link to the global report from the previous year. If the currencies are re-converted from the reference currency, the local prices may appear to have increased or decreased markedly. It is also worth noting that the value and meaning of $1000 varies enormously around the planet, in some countries it would be a typical weekly wage, in others a typical monthly wage, and in some it could represent or exceed the average annual salary.

If a study contains open-ended questions the costs of translations can be a considerable burden. If a project involved asynchronous qualitative research – for example, bulletin board groups or online communities – then the costs can be very high as translations will potentially be required several times a day.

Questions and concepts that don't translate

One regular complaint from survey respondents answering international surveys is that they are asked questions which are not applicable to them. One common example is the all-too-frequent experience of being asked which USA state they live in, even when they do not live in the United States!

A major source of problems relate to demographics. For example:

○ *In the UK social class combines economics with the social standing of a job; although this is a common feature of UK studies it does not translate in most countries.*

○ *A survey from Australia may include a* de facto *category in a marital status question. In other countries, this may need to be reworded as 'living together', 'living as married', or may simply be deemed too direct and personal a question to ask.*

○ *A United States survey may have an ethnicity question including the category 'African American'. This category makes little sense internationally. In the UK, the phrase 'African-Caribbean' would be much better understood. In some countries, any ethnicity question could be deemed too personal and in a few countries it is not legal to ask about ethnicity.*

○ *Zip/post codes can be another source of international confusion, particularly if software is used to verify the respondent's entry. A German postcode normally comprises five digits. By contrast, UK and Canadian codes include both letters and digits.*

None of these problems are unique to internet research, but the absence of the interviewer and a local partner can compound them.

How many languages?

Researchers from countries which have only a single language, or which approximate to a single language, such as Australia, France, the UK, Germany, and the USA, may be less aware that many countries have two or more languages. For example, Switzerland has three major languages (French, German, and Italian) and a minor one (Romansch), Belgium has two major languages (Dutch/Flemish and French) and one minor one (German), whilst in India there over 29 languages which are spoken by more than 1 million people.

There can be complexities even within a superficially straightforward country such as the UK, with many government-funded projects requiring the survey to be offered in English and Welsh (or English and Gaelic in Scotland).

Divided by a common language?

The ease with which the internet can be used to reach people and the fact that two or more countries appear to share a common language can obscure the point that usage and local variations require the survey to be modified to make it relevant to local respondents. For example, in the UK people refer to the bonnet and the boot of a car, but these become the hood and the trunk in the USA. Similarly, whilst France and the Quebec region of Canada both speak French, there can be important differences.

At a more subtle level, some words that appear identical have differences in meaning, for example a UK gallon is 20% larger than a USA gallon.

Incentives

Different countries have different laws, regulations, and guidelines which can make the handling of incentives more difficult. Some countries ban or restrict gambling (which can include prize draws), some countries' tax laws require many payments to be declared, and some have ethical guidelines that require some groups, such as doctors, to declare all payments.

ONLINE INTERNATIONAL QUANTITATIVE RESEARCH

International online quantitative studies are often easier to organise than either qualitative or social media projects. Closed questions, if correctly designed and translated, produce results which are more defined than either qualitative or social media projects. The main issues that tend to occur are missing key items from brand and product lists and the inclusion of items that do not apply.

The panel company can often be a useful partner in the research process and it makes sense for the researcher to find out what the panel company can do to ensure that the survey is likely to be successful.

ONLINE INTERNATIONAL QUALITATIVE RESEARCH

Online focus groups can create major cost and speed advantages in the area of international studies, both in terms of running studies where the moderator is in a different country to the respondents and also where the respondents might be in different countries to each other.

Bulletin board groups can also be a very powerful option for international studies. However, if translations are required, the costs can mount up very quickly if the moderators are not able to deal with the translations themselves. The key issue is that potentially translations are required several times a day for the length of the project. As members post things on the board, the moderator needs to be able to understand what they are saying and may need to respond to them.

SOCIAL MEDIA AND INTERNATIONAL RESEARCH

Although the use of social media techniques is a relatively new development, it has already proved its worth in international research.

One of the current trends in market research is the shift away from questions and towards listening, for example with blog and buzz mining. Blog and buzz mining's default mode is international, and steps have to be taken to restrict the languages being mined and the locations used. Trend tools can quickly show whether the same phenomena are happening in different countries.

Blogging and e-ethnographic approaches can create a powerful way of gaining insights into people in different circumstances, both within a country and across countries.

Online research communities can be a powerful way of conducting international research, but again the use of multiple languages raises issues. There is a general consensus that a community cannot be run in multiple languages, so multiple countries often results in either (a) running the community in one language (usually English), or (b) running different communities in different languages.

Running communities in one language

In some cases there is a genuine common language – for example, there are groups of countries that share a language such as English, French, or Spanish. Even though these groups can cause some mild amusement and confusion (Americans wear their pants over their underwear, whereas the English wear their pants under their trousers), they tend to work fine.

However, there are a number of examples of companies running their international communities in one language (usually English) across different language groups. This approach may be better than nothing, but is fraught with risks in terms of excluding points of view and discouraging non-native speakers from joining the discussions. The temptation to use English is that it is very often possible, even if not desirable.

Running parallel communities in different languages

Running parallel communities in different languages can be very rewarding, but it can consume a large amount of resources. There are essentially two ways of running the parallel communities:

1.   Run the communities from a single location, with translators retained to convert all the research comments into the target languages and to translate all responses back into

the researcher's language. This can be expensive, and if the translators have been away from the target country too long their use of online language may be too out-of-date.

2.   Delegate the running of the communities to local agencies/researchers, with the discussion guide being created at the centre, and the in-country researchers localising the guide and analysis.

SUMMARY OF ONLINE AND INTERNATIONAL RESEARCH

The internet has opened up a wide range of new and powerful options for conducting international research. The creation of online access panels in most markets was the most important factor in making this possible, along with improvements in the leading web survey systems to make it easier to run multi-country, multi-language studies, including languages such as Chinese and Japanese that require non-ASCII character sets.

The positives about using the internet are:

- ○   *lower costs and faster turnarounds*

- ○   *more comparable questionnaires (quantitative)*

- ○   *reaching more locations (qualitative)*

- ○   *international discourse (social media)*

The potential pitfalls are:

- ○   *lack of a local agency to check and localise the research*

- ○   *assuming the results are more standard than they really are*

- ○   *collecting the low hanging fruit, for example resorting to English or avoiding open-ended responses*

BUSINESS-TO-BUSINESS RESEARCH

Many business-to-business (or B2B as it is often called) market research projects have adopted the online modality for the same reasons as customer-focused market research projects, e.g. to obtain cost and speed efficiencies. However, there are some distinct differences between the B2B context and consumer market research and these are explored in this section, along with noting the key similarities.

This section on B2B covers the following:

- ○   *Types of research*

- ○   *Sampling issues with online B2B*

◯   *The recognition problem*

◯   *The future of online B2B market research*

TYPES OF RESEARCH

All of the types of research employed in consumer research can be used in B2B research, including online quantitative, online qualitative, social media, and e-ethnography.

SAMPLING ISSUES WITH ONLINE B2B

Business-to-business research works well online when the relevant population has access to the internet and where a suitable sample can be drawn. Samples are typically drawn from either client databases or online access panels, although more recently there has been growing interest in using other resources such as the business social network LinkedIn. There are also some specific lists provided by professional bodies – for example, in some countries there are (genuine) databases of doctors who are likely to cooperate with surveys (usually for a significant fee).

Client databases

When the research is focused on the client's customers and if the client has a database of those customers (including email addresses and the relevant permissions) then this can provide an excellent sample source.

In addition to all of the factors discussed in the earlier parts of the book one common phenomenon of B2B research is to use a copy of the report as an incentive for the respondents.

Online access panels

Online access panels can offer a method of obtaining B2B samples, but the method is notably different from the best practice procedure for offline B2B projects.

In a classic offline B2B study, the first thing the researcher typically does is to access a business structure, which will usually set out the number of businesses, the size of the businesses, and usually some information about how the business sector is structured. Once the business structure has been organised, companies are selected from industry lists or directories and approached for interviews, with the relevant decision makers in those companies targeted, for example stationery buyers, the person in charge of human resource services, or the decision maker for IT purchases.

B2B online access panels tend to be a mixture of B2B respondents directly recruited as B2B respondents and people who have been profiled from consumer panels to identify their relevant employment characteristics. Whilst many researchers have reported success with online B2B access panels, researchers should be aware that the online and offline sampling approaches imply differences.

All of the concerns that exist about consumer panels apply to B2B panels. Just because somebody says they are a CEO of a large corporation does not mean they are. When using an online access panel for B2B research it can be useful to have a discussion with the panel provider to find out how they have verified their panellists.

Table 14.4 illustrates the sorts of industries and roles that online access panels are able to supply.

Alternative approaches to sampling

In late 2008, LinkedIn, a leading social network for professionals, launched a service to help companies conduct market research with its members (in December 2009 LinkedIn had a claimed global membership of 53 million members).

Table 14.4   Typical industries and roles available from panels

Industry	Role
Advertising	Advertising
Agriculture	CEO/CFO/COO/CIO
Banking	Doctor
Education	Finance
Hospitality	Human Resources
Insurance	IT
IT	Legal
Leisure	Marketing
Media	PR
Medical	Research
Public sector	R&D
Telecommunications	Sales
Travel	Web tech/admin

THE RECOGNITION PROBLEM

In terms of research techniques, the full range of online approaches covered in this book are applicable, including online quantitative, qualitative, and social media approaches. However, one problem that occurs with offline B2B focus groups is an even bigger problem with online qualitative and social media research, namely the risk that either respondents will recognise each other or that a client observer will recognise one or more of the respondents.

The respondent–respondent and the client–respondent recognition problems are usually dealt with in one of three ways.

1. If there are a very large number of clients (e.g. thousands, tens of thousands, or more), then the normal customer-focused research protocols can be used, i.e. the respondent or the client observer leaving.

2. Take steps to minimise the risk of people recognising each other, for example by allocating each respondent their avatar (both name and image) and by getting them to agree at the outset to avoid behaviour that would reveal their identities.

3. The final alternative is to reframe the project as non-market research*. One typical non-market research approach is to use research techniques in a collaborative context to help the client and the customer co-create the future. This idea is central to much of the Wikinomics idea propounded by Dan Tapscott (Tapscott and Williams, 2006), i.e. that mass collaboration changes the rules.

THE FUTURE OF ONLINE B2B MARKET RESEARCH

For the foreseeable future there will continue to be some B2B market research conducted in the classic market research way, with respondent anonymity preserved, especially where the focus of the research is on non-customers or the whole market.

However, although it is too early to be sure, it may well be that the future of a large part of B2B research will be via the non-market research route. In this non-market research route, open collaboration would replace the 'cloak and dagger' approach of traditional B2B market research. In this scenario, many of the tools of market research would remain important, but the focus of the work would be collaboration between clients and customers working to create better products.

---

*The term non-market research (also mixed-purpose research) refers to the use of market research methods (for example surveys, depth interviews, and focus groups) but not regulated by the industry's professional bodies (such as ESOMAR, CASRO, MRS, AMSRS, etc). Because these non-market research routes are not regulated, most of the professional bodies prefer vendors not to describe the services as 'market research' as they feel this could cause confusion in the minds of respondents and make it more likely that legislative restrictions will be introduced that harm conventional market research.

PUBLIC SECTOR RESEARCH

The public sector is a generic term for services provided by governments (local, national, federal, and supranational) or on behalf governments. The term 'public sector' covers a wide range of organisations and a wide range of research needs, including:

○ *finding out whether users of a service are happy with it, for example users of public parks*

○ *finding out whether the people paying for a service are happy with it, for example taxpayers' views of policing*

○ *understanding the needs and priorities of a specific group, for example the travel priorities of a rural community*

○ *describing some social phenomenon or seeking to find the causes of it, for example exploring the factors causing a high incidence of teenage pregnancies*

○ *exploring the effectiveness of proposed actions, for example testing the effectiveness of anti-drunk driving campaigns*

○ *consulting with a group of people to find out what they want, for example changes in care schemes for the elderly*

○ *co-creating with a group, for example designing a new skate park in conjunction with the young people who are going to use it*

○ *collecting objective and subjective performance data, for example data on the punctuality and cleanliness of public transport*

○ *benchmarking one organisation, for example a council, against the performance of other organisations*

Most of the material in the rest of this book applies equally to public sector research, but there are a few areas where the public sector has additional requirements or where the normal requirements need to be adhered to more strictly. It is these differences that are addressed in this section. This section covers the following topics:

○ *In the public eye*

○ *Representativity*

○ *Geographical limitations*

○ *Social media and the public sector*

○ *Ethics*

○ *The future of public sector research*

IN THE PUBLIC EYE

Compared with the commercial sector, the public sector is much more likely to be inspected, audited, reported, or otherwise commented upon. Many countries also have freedom of information laws that require information to be handed over if requested.

One factor to keep in mind when dealing with public sector research is that there is usually somebody who thinks the service being researched is either spending too much or too little, or is doing too little or is too intrusive. If the research conducted is found to be defective, then it is likely that the weaknesses will be attacked, and if the research was paid for by the taxpayer it will often be attacked as a waste of public money. It is bad enough to be attacked when the research is good, but it is much more embarrassing when there really is a problem with it!

REPRESENTATIVITY

The issue of respresentativity, particularly in the context of quantitative samples, has been mentioned several times throughout this book, but the issue takes on a special relevance in public sector research.

Many public services are specifically targeted at people and groups who face extra challenges, often multiple challenges. For example, a research programme might be looking into the experiences and needs of groups such as disaffected youth, older citizens living on benefits, or adults with learning difficulties. Some of these groups are very hard to reach online. Sometimes, even if a hard-to-reach group can be reached online they may not be typical. For example, a study of housebound people using online surveys may well conclude that most housebound people use online shopping to get their groceries, ignoring the problems faced by the many housebound people who do not have access to the internet.

Another unusual factor about public sector research is that in many countries and many situations it is able to generate much higher response rates than are typically found in commercial research.

There are cases where online research will be acceptable, for example to test some types of general advertising, and there will be times when online is the best methodology (with students, for example), but the researcher should take extra care to ensure that the method could be defended in public or in front of politicians if necessary.

GEOGRAPHICAL LIMITATIONS

Much of the public sector deals with areas with very specific geographic boundaries. For example, regions, local government areas, river basin management zones, economic development areas, metropolitan areas, central business distrusts, and health authority areas. These tight geographical areas can provide a challenge for some online research approaches.

When using face-to-face or telephone modalities for quantitative research, choosing a restricted geographic area has little impact on the practicalities of the research, indeed it can even reduce complexity. However, producing a sample of, say, 1000 people from a restricted geographic area from an online access panel can be a problem. Even a large national panel may have only a few members for each tightly defined geographic area.

SOCIAL MEDIA AND THE PUBLIC SECTOR

Social media opens up a wide range of new options for the public sector, as it is doing for the other parts of market research. Indeed, the very newness of social media and its association with both youth and democratisation has led many public bodies to experiment with it.

However, social media also raises concerns for the public sector that are more pronounced than for most other research users. The public sector tends to have to meet higher standards than other sectors in terms of being seen to be fair to all parties, to use techniques that meet defined standards, and to be careful in terms of how it cedes powers.

This section looks at the following areas of special relevance to the public sector:

- O   *Consultation, engagement, and research*

- O   *Involvement versus representativity*

- O   *Key notes for social media and the public sector*

- O   *Reaching and missing key groups*

- O   *Assessing and managing risk*

Consultation, engagement, and research

One key task for any public sector researcher is to be clear about whether a specific project is focused on consultation, engagement, or research. This task is not always as easy as it might at first appear as these three terms are capable of being used in very different ways.

Consultation, for example can be any of the following very different exercises.

(a)   At one extreme a consultation by a public organisation might imply talking to users to explain what the organisation is planning to do and to answer any questions the public may have.

(b)   At another level, a consultation might be set up to learn about users' priorities, to allow the organisation to design improvements.

(c)   At yet a third level, a consultation might involve putting specific options to the public, so that the public can determine what they want, i.e. effectively handing the decision to the public or the service users.

When a public body looks to increase levels of engagement, it might mean that it wants more people to be aware of its service, it might mean that it wants to increase the number benefitting from it, or it could mean increasing the number of people who are supplying inputs (including ideas) to the service.

The term 'research' is much less ambiguous than 'consultation' or 'engagement', and implies that the public body is looking to learn from the people being researched.

Involvement versus Representativity

The more an exercise increases people's sense of involvement, the less representative it will tend to be. Projects that aim to increase involvement tend to be open to anybody who is relevant and who wants to take part. However, this sort of openness typically results in some groups being represented more than others. If an exercise does represent some groups more than others, then in theory it could be made more representative by weighting the data, but this is likely to alienate some people who will see their say being down-weighted.

If a public body wants their estimate of the public's view to be as accurate as possible, it should use a closed exercise, conducted with a carefully selected sample, and only disclose the process once the data has been collected. If the organisation wants to maximise involvement, then it should reverse all three of these rules, i.e. an open exercise, with the minimum constraints on who can take part, and it should publicise it before the exercise.

Key social media tools for the public sector

This section reviews the main social media tools and the way they are being used in the context of public sector research.

- *Online communities*
- *Online research communities*
- *Twitter*
- *Social networks*
- *Blogs and public discussions*
- *Virtual worlds*

Online communities

Online communities are increasingly being used to achieve a range of aims with a specific community, including information sharing, research, community building, self-help, and engagement. Examples of communities include general ones to help improve the service offered by an organisation or more specific ones, such as self-help groups.

Online research communities

An online research community is more focused than a general online community. The primary bene- ficiary of a research community is the public body itself, whereas the primary beneficiaries of a general online community are the community members. The use of online research communities by public bodies is very similar to the way these communities are used commercially. A typical online research community is a closed community, provided by a third-party agency. However, there are exceptions. For example, in late 2008 the UK's Identity & Passport Service used an open online research community (open to any 16–24-year-old UK resident who registered with the site and agreed to abide by its terms and conditions) as a consultation tool. The community was created to let the British Government hear young people's views about how the proposed ID Card scheme was to be implemented. Whilst the study undoubtedly delivered useful information, it also attracted a high level of negative comments from people opposed to the scheme.

Twitter

Twitter is being used in two ways by public bodies: to increase engagement with the body, and as a tool for research. The engagement role is typically achieved by a person or unit at an organisation tweeting. Once a following has been created Twitter can be used to have a dialogue with followers. Two good examples of this use are the Boca Raton Police Department, Florida, USA [http://twitter. com/BocaPolice] who use Twitter to keep in touch with their area and to highlight activities and supply advice, and Cumbria County Council in the UK who have used Twitter to distribute infor- mation, especially about the difficult traffic problems caused by the 2009 floods [http://twitter. com/cumbriacc].

The research use of Twitter by public bodies is very similar to its use in the private sector: firstly, to monitor specific references to the organisation itself; secondly, over the area it has respon- sibility for; and, thirdly, to monitor trends in the social discourse which might provide the body with insight.

Twitter is considered a relatively low risk activity for a public body. The main issue is to decide whether the body should follow people as this may risk some people complaining that 'Big Brother' is follow- ing them. Certainly, if a public body does follow people it should be very alert to any requests from people for it to 'unfollow' them. There also needs to be a clear policy about what should be tweeted and who is allowed to tweet.

One interesting example of how Twitter has been used is provided by the Australian Prime Minister, Kevin Rudd, who by the end of 2009 was being followed by almost one million people. One of the interesting things that Rudd has developed is a way of combining his personal tweets and those of his publicity team. When Rudd tweets personally, he finishes the tweet with KRudd, but when his team tweet on his behalf the tweet ends with #KevinPM.

Social networks

A large number of public bodies have a presence in social networks, for example having a 'page' on Facebook. However, concerns about what people might write or upload (and the costs of monitoring such sites) have resulted in many bodies using highly locked down presences. For example, many pages being run by public bodies do not allow photos, images, or comments to be uploaded by the public. For two examples of pages used by public bodies see:

Public Health Agency of Canada [http://www.facebook.com/pages/Public-Health-Agency-of-Canada/10860597051]

UK Merton Council [http://www.facebook.com/pages/Morden-United-Kingdom/Merton-Council/25892222184/].

At the time this book was researched there were relatively few methods of searching social networks, which meant that most people who were using social networks to research a topic were engaging in relatively manual, ethnographic, exercises. However, by late 2009 a number of social networks, such as Facebook, were changing their security policies which should result in a wider range of search options being available.

Blogs and public discussions

Blogs are a rich source of information and there is a wide range of tools available to search and mine the information in blogs and public discussions (covered in Part III). Blogs are also used by many organisations to provide an insight into what the organisation does. For example, Jim Dixon, Chief Executive of the Peak District National Park Authority in the UK, has a blog where he talks about his role, the authority, and the wonderful area he is responsible for [http://jimdixon.wordpress.com/].

For public bodies, it is important to monitor the comments that often follow news stories on the websites of newspapers, TV channels, and news portals. However, it should be noted that the public's comments on news stories are often drawn from a very small group of people who are posting frequently. This does not mean that they should be ignored, but equally they should not be assumed to be representative.

Virtual worlds

Just a few years ago Second Life was the talk of the internet and a wide range of organisations rushed to set up virtual stores to meet virtual customers. Second Life has peaked and the lead virtual world, World of Warcraft, is hardly suitable for most public sector research. However, virtual worlds still present some interesting opportunities.

One virtual world that has been used for consultation and engagement is Habbo (previously known as Habbo Hotel) [http://www.habbo.com/]. Habbo is a virtual world aimed at teenagers with over 100 million members around the world. In the UK, the NSPCC (National Society for the Prevention of Cruelty to Children) and Talk to Frank (a drugs advisory service) have both used Habbo to talk to young people, to find out about concerns and to engage them in conversations.

At the moment, and for most organisations, virtual worlds remain one of those techniques which seem quite close to being useful, but not quite ready yet.

Reaching and missing key groups

One of the key reasons that public sector organisations want to use social media is to reach groups that they are not able to reach in other ways, for example, young people and busy working people. However, the other side of this argument is that social media also misses many people, in particular those who are on low incomes or who are largely excluded from society.

When public bodies make extensive use of social media there is a risk of the organisation reaching the same people several ways, for example via Facebook, YouTube, and Twitter, rather than reaching an additional audience. If the costs, in time and money, of using additional social media channels are marginal then repeatedly reaching the same groups is not a major problem, but the duplication should be kept in mind when implementing plans and interpreting findings.

Assessing and managing risk

In designing a social media project a public sector researcher needs to assess the risk for the respondents, the client, and the research team. When using social media in the context of public bodies, this risk assessment is even more important. Key issues to consider are:

○ *Could the project be hijacked by an interest or lobby group?*

○ *If comments are going to be allowed, will they be pre-moderated or post-moderated?*

○ *What are the implications for the organisation if there is not much response?*

○ *What are the implications for the organisation if the response is very large?*

One reliable method of controlling risk is to limit the scope of the project and to make its role clear to the participants. For example, the UK Government's ID consultation community ran for three months, with all the members being aware from the outset that the project would only last that length of time. Similarly, a great deal of effort went into letting the participants know that their input would inform the decision-making process, alongside many other streams of information – emphasising that the consultation was not a referendum.

ETHICS

If the results of public sector research are going to be used in a public forum, for example in the press or in a decision-making body, then there is an expectation that the research will be reliable.

Historically, this has often meant the research was quantitative rather than qualitative, and the quantitative research has been traditionally based on conservative assumptions about random probability sampling and projectability. In most cases, online research cannot make assertions of random probability sampling and this needs to be taken into account when choosing a method.

One of the key areas of concern in public sector work is to preserve the perceived and actual independence of the researcher. This can be a very challenging process when conducting consultative or deliberative research. A project looking at new advertising for a soft drink can explore different ways of conveying information and developing loyalty without raising too many concerns. Similar methods when applied to a topic like climate change can easily be interpreted as 'leading' the respondent or 'spinning' the truth.

THE FUTURE OF PUBLIC SECTOR RESEARCH

There are three key strands in the way that public sector research has been developing over the last few years and all three are likely to develop further in the near to medium future:

1. Benchmarking and performance data to assess how organisations are performing against targets and other organisations. This area is mostly quantitative and is likely to see a gradual drift towards more use of online research.

2. Adoption of practices from the commercial sector, particularly in areas such as marketing, advertising, and concept development. This area tends to be for organisations' own consumption, so there is often scope to try a wider range of techniques and approaches.

3. The adoption of a more consultative and collaborative approach. This strand is already associated with Web 2.0 and social media and this is likely to continue.

15 Website Research

Website research is a branch of market research focused on the design and implementation of websites, and includes usability testing, visitor profiling, customer satisfaction, concept development, and more. It uses both quantitative and qualitative techniques and, in addition, several less traditional techniques such as automated metrics, expert reviews, and semiotics.

It is possible to think of websites as falling into one of two categories: websites open to everybody and those open only to registered members who need to login to access the site. In addition, there are hybrids, i.e. websites with some open sections and others that are only available to 'logged in' users. From a researcher's perspective, a website where all the users have to log in is a more constrained place and offers more options, as will be apparent in the sections below.

This chapter on website research starts by reviewing the various types of website research that are commonly conducted and then explores the various methods that are specific to website research. The chapter is structured as follows:

- Types of website research projects

- Popup surveys

- Website metrics and analytics

- Website reviews

- Accompanied surfing and observational research

- Other website research approaches

- Summary of website research

TYPES OF WEBSITE RESEARCH PROJECTS

This section lists the most common types of website research projects and their implications for clients and researchers:

- Website visitor profiling and satisfaction studies

- Usability testing

- ❍ *Website design and website concept testing*

- ❍ *Technical performance and ROI*

- ❍ *Search engine optimisation (SEO)*

- ❍ *Testing online advertising*

WEBSITE VISITOR PROFILING AND SATISFACTION STUDIES

Most website visitor profiling and satisfaction studies are normally conducted through quantitative surveys, typically delivered via popup surveys. Visitor surveys are normally run by, or on behalf of, the organisation that owns and operates the website.

Website profiling studies are used to investigate questions such as who is visiting a website? What they were looking for? How did they find the website? Have they visited the website before? Even a simple profiling survey will usually include some satisfaction-related questions, such as likelihood to re-visit, likelihood to recommend, whether the user found what they were looking for, and their overall satisfaction.

Website satisfaction surveys concentrate on the visitors' satisfaction, typically across a range of the services offered and across a range of criteria, for example, easy to use, reliable, up-to-date, etc. In many cases, a satisfaction study will also seek to deliver actionable information such as the drivers of satisfaction and the priorities for website improvements. A typical website satisfaction survey also includes profiling information.

The difference between a website profiling study and a website satisfaction study is more a matter of degree than anything else. Profiling surveys tend to be shorter (3–6 minutes) and to report the data as collected, i.e. without much additional analysis. Website satisfaction surveys are usually longer (8–12) minutes and include more processing, for example the use of analysis to explore visitor segmentation and the drivers of satisfaction. However, there are variations in survey lengths. One leading European provider of website surveys aims to design lengths of 2–4 minutes for profiling studies and 4–7 minutes for its website satisfaction studies.

Ad hoc versus tracking studies

Website profiling and satisfaction studies can be conducted as one off – i.e. *ad hoc* – studies or as part of a tracking or continuous project. Tracking projects can either be based on continuous or periodic waves of data collection. Like many other research topics, websites are often seasonal, so tracking studies should either cover the whole year or be held at the same time each year.

Website benchmarking studies

Website profiling and satisfaction studies are normally run for, or on behalf of, the organisation that owns and operates the website, but there is an exception to this, namely when conducting benchmarking studies. There are two common ways of approaching website benchmarking. The first is by forming a syndicate of sites who agree to use an identical survey and to share the results, usually aggregated. The second is to recruit a sample of respondents (for example from an online access panel), and ask them which sites they have recently visited (from a target list) and then to rate one or more of those sites.

Alternative sampling methods

Although most website profiling and satisfaction studies use popups (or some equivalent such as overlays or interstitials), there are alternatives which are sometimes used.

Website invitations. An invitation to the survey can be posted on a website. However, this normally attracts a very low response rate (low by comparison with a popup) and suffers from being entirely based on respondent self-selection. Invitations to a website's users to leave comments or take a simple survey can be a useful method of eliciting feedback, but they are not a reliable or representative method of market research.

Website banners. If a website offers advertising, then invitations to a profiling or satisfaction survey can be offered via banner (or other) adverts. The response rates from banners are typically very low and do not engender much confidence.

Emails to registered users. If a website's users have registered, then it may be possible to email them asking them to take part in a survey (depending on what permissions were collected). This can have advantages in terms of targeting groups of users and potentially asking a slightly longer survey (perhaps 15 minutes), but respondents' memories of the website will typically not be as sharp as people surveyed whilst actually visiting the site.

USABILITY TESTING

Usability testing focuses on assessing how suitable a website is in terms of its users and the functions that they, and the website owner, wish to accomplish. Usability testing can also include assessing whether a website is compliant with legislation, regulations, or guidelines, for example ensuring that it is accessible to people with specific challenges and needs.

Usability testing is a cross-over area between market research, HCI professionals (human–computer interface), and usability professionals. Because of the range of its multidisciplinary players there is a substantial body of information about website usability but with much of it residing outside normal market research boundaries. One of the most important thought leaders in the area of website design (in terms of users' requirements) is Jakob Nielsen, much of whose work is available at his website [http://www.useit.com]. This information is very useful when planning usability research.

Usability testing can be broadly divided into two categories. Firstly, usability can be defined in terms of making the site as suitable and effective as possible for its visitors. Secondly, usability can also be defined in terms of accessibility. Accessibility is a phrase that in general means determining how easy it is for a user with specific challenges (such as visual impairment or lack of limbs), but in more specific terms tends to mean compliance with the W3C WAI standards [http://www.w3.org/WAI/]. When conducting a usability project, it is important to be clear which of the two definitions applies, suitability or accessibility.

Usability testing employs a wide range of techniques, both qualitative and quantitative, including:

- *accompanied surfing*

- *eye tracking*

- *usability labs*

- *expert reviews*

- *user surveys*

- *automated testing*

These techniques are reviewed later in this chapter.

WEBSITE DESIGN AND WEBSITE CONCEPT TESTING

Website design and concept testing include website research that looks at the development of new sites, at changes to sites, and at the development of new features for a site. A wide range of market research techniques is used for design and concept testing research, including online and offline qualitative research, quantitative research, website analytics, and eye tracking.

Because the internet is such a fast developing medium, the review-design-implement-review cycle for a website is shorter and more aggressive than for most products and services. Typical elements in this cycle include:

1. Investigating the current website

2. Investigating what users/visitors want and need

3. Developing and testing new material

4. Implementing and testing revisions

As soon as Stage 4 is reached, it is time to revisit Stage 1. If there is not an existing website, i.e. if one is being created from scratch, then the process starts at Stage 2.

Stage 1: Investigating a current website

There are possibly more ways to research a website than almost any other phenomenon which market researchers are called upon to research. The ways of investigating a website include:

❍   *Visitor profiling and satisfaction (covered in the previous sub-section).*

❍   *Accompanied surfing, watching people as they surf the website.*

❍   *Professional reviews, assessing a website against defined criteria.*

❍   *Website analytics, metrics, and transactional data, i.e. information about what people do on a site.*

❍   *Semiotics, looking at what the language and symbols of the website imply about the company and people creating it.*

❍   *Eye-tracking, investigating which parts of the screen are viewed and which are not.*

❍   *Using blogs, bulletin board groups, and online research communities to follow users over a period of time to explore how a website fits into their wider lives.*

❍   *In-depth interviews (offline or online), exploring how the website fits into people's lives.*

❍   *Blog and buzz mining, looking at what people are saying to each other about the website (if it has a high enough profile).*

These approaches are covered later in this chapter. The objectives of investigating the website include finding what works and what does not, the way that visitors use the site, and exploring what messages the website conveys to visitors and users and assessing its effectiveness against specified criteria.

Stage 2: Investigating what users/visitors want and need

If the client already has a website, then the starting point for this phase of research is Stage 1, i.e. investigating the current website. In most cases understanding user/visitor wants and needs requires the researcher to look wider than just the website under review by, for example, exploring how the users/visitors use and relate to other websites.

In addition to the techniques mentioned in Stage 1, researchers might use one or more of the following:

❍   *focus groups (online or offline), often mixing both browsing tasks and discussions*

❍   *information architecture research, looking at how people group tasks and information together*

❍   *quantitative research, especially using marketing science techniques such as segmentation and conjoint analysis*

Stage 3 Developing and testing new material

The development of a new or changed website can use many of the research techniques outlined in Stages 1 and 2, particularly the qualitative and collaborative approaches. In addition, the 'develop and test' phase can include usability testing, professional reviews, and the quantitative testing of alternatives.

One popular device in website developments is the use of wireframes. A wireframe is a template for a new website, showing where the components (such as the navigation) will go and allowing different content to be shown as part of the design and testing process.

Eye-tracking can be used to assess whether new designs catch and hold the eye of visitors.

Stage 4 Implementing and testing revisions

Once a new website is launched, or changes to an existing website implemented, the users' experiences are measured, typically by quantitative testing implemented via popup surveys.

One phenomenon that many market researchers have reported when testing websites, is that frequently the satisfaction scores immediately after a change are lower than those before. It has been suggested this is because almost any change to a website has a short-term negative impact on regular visitors, requiring them to relearn some aspects of using the website. Also, it is very common for a new launch of a website to have bugs in it which normally get fixed during the first couple of weeks.

The key tests for a new design are the views after a few weeks and the metrics such as traffic levels, length of stays, and numbers of transactions.

Summary of methods for website design research

A wide range of techniques can be used in the different stages of the website review-design-implement-review cycle. Table 15.1 sets out the four stages of this process and the most commonly used market research techniques:

TECHNICAL PERFORMANCE AND ROI (RETURN ON INVESTMENT)

A website provides a wide range of opportunities for measuring its visitors, such as the number of visitors, the number of pages they visited, and how long they stayed. There are also tools that measure other technical aspects such as the download speed of a website, its appearance on different internet browsers, and the existence of faults, such as broken links and JavaScript errors. If the website is a transactional website (for example, if it is an e-commerce site) there is information about the revenue flows, the number of abandoned shopping baskets, and the link between spending money on adverts and search engine links and resultant sales.

This sort of research is normally performed by using website analytics and metrics, and tends to be carried out by web design companies and search engine specialists. Some research agencies offer these services, but the main impact for most market researchers is the growing requirement to combine the results of these technical measurements with the outputs of more traditional market research.

Table 15.1

	Investigate current site	Investigate needs/wants	Develop & test new material	Implement and test
Popup surveys	✓	✓	✓	✓
Focus groups		✓	✓	
Web analytics & metrics	✓	✓		✓
Professional reviews	✓		✓	✓
Accompanied surfing	✓	✓	✓	✓
Online research communities/ bulletin board groups		✓	✓	
Semiotics	✓			✓
In-depth interviews	✓	✓		
Usability testing	✓		✓	✓
Marketing sciences, e.g. segmentation or DCM		✓		
Eye-tracking	✓		✓	✓

SEARCH ENGINE OPTIMISATION (SEO)

One of the most important sources of visitors is via search engines, i.e. internet users typing queries into search engines such as Google or Bing and then being directed to the website. In order to get a large amount of traffic to a website from a search engine, it is necessary for that website to appear on the first page of results.

There is a large body of evidence about the best way to optimise a website to maximise the chance that it is found and ranked as highly as possible. This field of knowledge is termed SEO (search engine optimisation). There are also a large number of SEO specialists, with their own literature and conferences. Although a few market research agencies are engaged in SEO, the main contact between SEO and market researchers is in the form of joint working to produce overall optimisation and enhancement of the website.

An associated field to SEO is SEM (search engine marketing). SEO is the process of optimising the website so that the unpaid results of a search engine, i.e. the natural results, are as favourable as possible. By contrast, SEM is the process of obtaining the optimal results for the paid-for links, i.e. the sponsored links.

TESTING ONLINE ADVERTISING

The testing of online advertising, for example banner ads, is a specialised part of the general ad testing industry. The techniques used include:

- *qualitative testing, typically face-to-face (but online options exist) and using approaches common to the testing of other advertising*

- *eye-tracking, looking at whether people see the ad and whether their eyes pause on the ad*

- *web metrics, checking things like click-through rates and, if relevant, fulfilment rates (for example, which executions lead to the highest number of actions, such as sales)*

- *pre-post and control/test quantitative testing, which typically use popup surveys to compare people who have or have not seen the ad*

Online advertising is often described as the most accountable form of advertising (on a par with direct marketing techniques such as direct mail), because the advertiser can measure the number of clicks and sales that result from a particular advertising execution. However, this perception ignores any impact the ad may have in terms of brand building or increased intention to buy/use. Researchers need to make the case for considering the positive and negative brand-building effects of advertising. Also, some studies have indicated that people may return to a site as many as five times before they buy something, making it harder to link the ad that first brought them there to the sale.

POPUP SURVEYS

Popup surveys are surveys associated with a specific web page or collection of pages, which launch when a potential respondent visits the page or initiates some action on it. In a typical study, the survey appears in a new window, on top of the page the respondent is visiting. It should be noted that many surveys which appear to respondents to be popup surveys are technically overlays. However, this is a system technicality and should not distract the researcher from the core issues which are the same for both true popup surveys and for overlays.

The key issues for any researcher using popup surveys are:

- **Attracting respondents.** *The survey design needs to attract visitors' attention and secure them as respondents. The process of attracting respondents includes the design of the invitation and whether to use incentives.*

○ **Survey design**. *The survey design needs to deal with the objectives of the research, the reduced screen size, and needs to maximise the chance that respondents who start the survey complete it.*

○ **Analysis**. *In addition to conventional analysis, the researcher needs to consider invisible processing* and whether to integrate web metrics.*

○ **The logistics of popup surveys**. *The logistics of researching website visitors using popup surveys include: which visitors to invite, how long should they have been on the site when the survey is served, who to screen, and technology issues.*

○ **Ethical and quality issues**. *In addition to the general research guidelines there are a number of issues that relate specifically to popup surveys.*

ATTRACTING RESPONDENTS

Attracting respondents is the process of achieving as high a response rate as possible to maximise the representativeness of the research. The key elements in attracting respondents are the invitation and whether to use incentives.

Survey invites

There are two common approaches to the survey invitation process. The first is to pop up a small box that contains a simple survey invitation, such as in the mocked-up example in Figure 15.1.

The three underlined items in Figure 15.1 are all hyperlinks. The privacy link takes the potential respondent to a page explaining all the details about the study. The 'No thanks' link closes the popup. The 'Yes, I am happy to help' link takes the respondent to the first page of the survey.

The second approach to inviting respondents is to present the visitor with the first page of the survey, with the top part of the first page acting as the survey introduction/invitation, as in the example in Figure 15.2.

Figure 15.2 shows an example of how the first question of the survey can be combined with the invitation on the first page. The respondent is presented with the choice of starting to do the survey or rejecting it. In a popup survey, age is often asked as the first question, to enable children to be screened out. In the example in Figure 15.2 the study might be screening out people under 16 years old. Note that the age that needs to be screened out differs from country to country and may differ by product category and the subject of the research.

The small invite (as in Figure 15.1) will, in most cases, cause less offense but result in a substantially lower response rates. The first page (as in Figure 15.2) approach tends to result in higher response rates, and

---

*Invisible processing refers to collecting information about the visitor without asking questions, for example the browser they are using, their computer settings, and date and time of day.

The Acme Corporation

Please help us improve our website. Please take a few minutes to complete a short online survey.

The survey will only take 4-6 minutes. We respect your privacy and your details will remain anonymous.

Thank you.

Yes, I am happy to help │ No thanks

Figure 15.1

The Acme Corporation

X

Please help us improve our website. Please take a few minutes to complete a short online survey.

How old are you?
Please select the category that applies to you.
- ○ Under 16 years
- ○ 16 to 29 years
- ○ 30 to 49 years
- ○ 50 to 69 years
- ○ 70 or more years

Next

Notes about this survey
- The survey will only take 4-6 minutes.
- If you do not want to take the survey, just close this window or click here.
- We respect your privacy and your details will remain anonymous click here to find out more and view our privacy policy.
- The research is being conducted by Ope Full Research Agency, click here for more information or to contact us.

Figure 15.2

therefore more representative surveys. Pete Comley of Virtual Surveys suggests that the first page invite route can lead to response three times as high as the small box approach (Comley, 2000).

Successful invites usually follow some basic rules:

1. Make the invite look like it belongs to the website by using the same colours, logos, and fonts. People are more likely to do the survey if they can see that it is being run on behalf of the website to provide them, the user, with a better service.

2. Make it clear to potential respondents how long the survey is likely to take to complete.

3.   Keep the invitation short – the more you write, the less people read.

4.   Remember these are your customers, or your client's customers. You want their help, and you do not want to offend them or turn them off.

Incentives

Incentives can increase response rates. However, there is considerable evidence that offering incentives results in people completing the survey who would not normally have even visited the site, i.e. they have been attracted to the site in order to do the survey for the incentive.

If a site is available to the general population of internet users, the general advice is not to offer incentives. However, if people have to be registered users in order to use the website, a researcher may find that incentives can be used safely and appropriately.

It should be noted that different countries have different rules and laws about incentives. In particular, lotteries and prize draws are not always legal, and even where they are legal their use may be regulated.

SURVEY DESIGN

The survey design needs to deal with the objectives of the research, the constraints of the medium such as the reduced screen size (popup surveys do not normally take the whole page), and to maximise the chance that respondents who start the survey complete it. The design needs to take the nature of the site and its visitors into account. For example, music fans may respond to a different style of survey compared to people visiting a news service, and people visiting a transactional site, such as their bank, may be more cautious than people visiting a tourist information site.

Popup survey design issues

Any researcher designing a popup survey should firstly be aware of the general issues relating to survey design and specifically to the design of online surveys. These general design issues are covered in Chapter 3. However, there are additional issues that relate to popup survey design.

 Warning

The most important issue to keep in mind is that the popup survey has interrupted somebody. In most cases they have visited the site to achieve some goal, such as listening to a song, finding instructions on using a new product, checking services, or buying a product. The survey is standing between a website visitor and the completion of their task and therefore has to be appealing, engaging, and short.

Survey length

Advice varies, but a popup survey should probably take about five minutes to complete, and certainly no longer than ten minutes. The most important aspect of the length of the survey is that it needs to be short in terms of how long the respondent feels it is taking to complete.

Window size

A popup survey is typically designed to use a window smaller than the visitor's screen size. Seeing the original window behind the popup reassures the respondent about the survey and helps show they are in control. Researchers tend to want the popup survey to be 60–80% of the screen size, but different visitors will have different screen sizes. A good rule of thumb is to design the survey around the 20 percentile point, i.e. a size that assumes that 20% of users will have a smaller screen and 80% will have a larger size.

The server data for the website to be tested will reveal information about the screen size of its visitors PCs. For example, in November 2009, data collected from visitors to The Future Place blog [http://thefutureplace.typepad.com] showed that 20% of them had a screen width of at least 1200 pixels, and a screen height of at least 960 pixels.

Scroll bars

It is generally agreed that respondents should not have to use the scroll bars to see the whole survey page, especially the horizontal scroll bar, and especially on the first page of the survey. Because a popup survey tends to use a smaller survey window, there is less room available for questions, stimuli, and instructions. This means even more care is required to ensure that questions fit neatly on the page.

Forced completion

Opinions differ on whether popup surveys should employ forced completion, i.e. the survey refuses to move forward until the respondent gives a valid answer. The argument in favour of forced completion relates mainly to the analysis of the data. Missing data can make analysis difficult, especially if advanced techniques are to be used.

The counter argument is that a popup survey is asking for respondents' cooperation. If a respondent does not want to answer a specific question, should we force them? If the respondent would rather quit the survey than answer a specific questions, surely we would rather have their data. Researchers should also keep in mind the relevant research guidelines. For example, the ESOMAR guidelines on Conducting Market and Opinion Research Using the Internet say *'Beyond this, suitable technical measures should be implemented, where appropriate, allowing respondents not to answer particular questions (but to proceed with the rest of the interview). . . '*. Even in cases where the researcher chooses not to force completion, there will be individual questions that should be forced, for example the age question on surveys where children may have the chance to be served the invitation.

Progress indicators

There is considerable discussion about progress indicators, usually focusing on whether they improve data or completion rates. However, there seems little disagreement that respondents prefer to have an idea of how much of the survey they have completed, and how much remains. It is worth noting that the ESOMAR guidelines on Conducting Market and Opinion Research Using the Internet say *'The use of some form of metering device so that respondents can track their progress through the questionnaire is recommended.'*

Maximising response rates

Response rates tend to be a function of:

(a)   **Relationship**: how good the relationship between the visitors and the website is (if a site is very popular with its visitors the response rate will be higher)

(b)   **Invitation**: the appeal of the invitation process

(c)   **Length**: the length of the survey

(d)   **Engagement**: how engaging/boring the survey is

According to Virtual Surveys, a UK market research agency with a strong reputation in the area of website research, typical response rates in 2008/9 ranged from about 10% to 25%. If you are conducting a study with a lower response rate you need to consider why.

When talking about popup surveys, it is important to be clear about what is meant by the response rate. Best practice is to say how many people started and how many completed the survey, both as absolute figures and as a proportion of all those invited to take the survey. In terms of completion it is also useful to quote the figure as a percentage of those who started the survey.

Table 15.2 shows a hypothetical example based on a study where 10 000 popups were served.

It also shows that 2000 respondents started the survey, which equates to 20% of all invitations served. Of the 2000 people who started the survey, 1000 finished it, equating to a completion rate of 50%, and 10% of all those were served an invitation.

Of the four factors listed above (relationship, invitation, length, and engagement) there is little the researcher can do to change the degree to which people currently like the website, so that has to be taken as a given. The design of the invitation and the survey should leverage any goodwill the site has by being clearly branded as belonging to the site and by explaining that the reason for the research is to improve the service to visitors/users.

As mentioned in the design section, starting the first page of the survey as the invitation will increase response rates in most cases. The scale of this effect must not be underestimated; Runham (1999)

Table 15.2

Invitations served	10 000
Starts	2 000
Start % (starts / invites)	20%
Completes	1 000
Response rate (completes/invites)	10%
Completion rate (completes/starts)	50%

reported a response rate of 80% to a survey on the BBC website. This was deemed to be partly due to online research being newer in 1999, the use of an interstitial approach (more on this later), and because of the strongly positive relationship between the BBC and its visitors.

Shorter surveys (in terms of the actual and perceived time taken to complete them) have better response rates and better completion rates. The ideal survey is up to five minutes long and research suggests that up to ten minutes is reasonable. But beyond ten minutes will result in markedly fewer completed surveys being collected as a percentage of invitations. One tactic that some researchers have used to reduce the length of surveys, is to spread the elements across two questionnaires. This requires a larger sample size, but can make the survey much more acceptable.

Popup surveys are more at risk of being abandoned than surveys completed by access panel members because they are not normally incentivised and, to some extent, panel members have become accustomed to poor designs. This means popup surveys should be as engaging as possible, for example avoiding/minimising the use of grids, dropdowns, and other disliked survey features. For more information on the design of website surveys, see the earlier survey design section or refer to a textbook such as *Designing Effective Web Surveys* (Couper, 2008).

Transactional sites

Special care should be taken when researching transactional sites, for example, where people are making payments or conducting online banking. Internet users are constantly warned to watch out for breaches in security and to avoid dangerous activities such as spoofing and phishing. Therefore it would be unwise to pop up a survey whilst somebody is making a payment or transferring funds. In these cases, the most typical research process is to request that a respondent agrees to take part in the survey before the transactional part of the visit, and then completes it when the transaction is complete or abandoned.

ANALYSIS

In addition to conventional analysis, the market researcher needs to consider topics specific to popup surveys, such as whether to use completes only or include partial surveys, invisible processing, and web metrics.

Analysing completes only or completes and partial surveys

Most market research analysis is based on complete surveys, i.e. where all of the respondents have reached the end of the survey and in most cases have answered all of the appropriate questions.

However, some website researchers prefer to include partial responses. This preference relates to the context of the survey. Popup survey respondents have been interrupted from doing something else. If the researcher only uses the completed surveys they risk missing the messages from the busiest, and perhaps least satisfied, visitors.

Invisible processing

As well as the responses to the surveys, the researcher can collect a wide range of data about the PC and browser being used by the visitor. This process is called invisible processing and the data is called hidden data or sometimes passive data. Examples of information which is often collected in conjunction with the survey data in popup studies include:

○ *the screen size, height, and width, in terms of pixels*

○ *the operating system being used (for example Windows 7 or Linux)*

○ *the browser being used, including its version number (for example Firefox or Internet Explorer)*

○ *whether or not the user has enabled/installed JavaScript, Flash or other technologies*

○ *the date and time of the survey*

○ *the IP address of the respondent, which in turn can give an estimate of their country and location*

All of this hidden/passive data can be useful in the analysis. For example, the survey might show that people using smaller screens were less satisfied, which would have implications for the website's design. The operating system and the screen size will also provide a clue as to whether the visitor is using a smartphone, something which is becoming increasingly important to both researchers and website owners.

However, there are ethical considerations in collecting this data since the assumption underlying market research is that respondents must give informed consent, which is not possible if respondents are not told about the collection of this information. The ESOMAR guidelines make it clear that the respondent should be told about any invisible processing and any use of cookies. For example, the ESOMAR guidelines Conducting Market and Opinion Research Using the Internet say *'Invisible processing – clear statement of any invisible processing related to the survey that is taking place.'* and *'Cookies – clear statement that they are or are not being used, and if so, why.'* (ESOMAR, 2009)

Web metrics

Web metrics are data that is collected from the server about users' visits to the website. They are normally collected by third-party agencies, but they also include server logs. Web metrics can include where a visitor came from, what they typed into a search engine to find the site, which pages they visited, in which order, and how long they stayed on each page.

By linking cookies served by the web analytics software and the visitor survey it is possible to analyse the respondents' data in combination with their behavioural data. For example, web metrics data can be combined with visitor survey data to see whether certain paths through the website result in higher or lower levels of satisfaction. An analysis of the web metrics with the visitor survey data may reveal that people who visited the FAQs (Frequently Asked Questions) tended to have lower levels of satisfaction with the site compared with the average site visitor.

Linking the web metrics to the survey data raises additional concerns, especially if the information is personally identifiable. The relevant ethical and legislative guidelines should be consulted, but the key is to ensure that the research is based on informed consent and that all data is treated appropriately (for example, with the correct level of data security and privacy).

THE LOGISTICS OF POPUP SURVEYS

The logistics of researching website visitors through the use of popup surveys are considerably more involved than research using, for example, online access panels. The logistical issues involved in popup surveys include:

- *Screening people out*

- *Time on site*

- *Sampling methods*

- *Pages and locations*

- *Technology issues*

- *Alternatives to popups*

- *Alternatives to cookies*

Screening people out

Not everybody who visits a specific website is going to be eligible for the visitor survey. For example, employees of the website owner are not normally interviewed, nor employees of market research agencies. If people are going to be screened out, then it is good to do it as early as possible to avoid wasting their time.

In most countries and for most projects it is important to screen out children. The ESOMAR guidelines (as at November 2009) specify that young people aged under 14 years of age should not be interviewed without prior parental permission (but this age may be higher or lower in your particular market; for example, in the UK it is 16 years). Therefore you should normally find out the respondent's age on the first or second page of the survey, and certainly before finding out any personal information.

Other typical groups that a market researcher might want to screen out include:

- *employees of the company providing the website (ideally try to screen their IP addresses from being intercepted in the first place)*

- *people who live in other countries*

- *people who work in advertising, journalism, or market research*

Time on site

If the research is being conducted to explore people's experience or satisfaction with the website, there is no point interviewing visitors before they have had a chance to experience the site. Therefore, most researchers will specify a period of time on the site, such as two, five, or ten minutes. Efforts are then made to ensure that the visitor has been on the website for at least that amount of time before the survey is served.

The method of deferring the survey invitation will depend on the technology being used and the limitations created by the architecture of the website. One of the easier approaches is to pop up the survey early in the respondent's visit and to ask them to click on a button to hide the survey and for it to then reappear after a fixed period of time. When the survey does appear/reappear it is normal to ask the respondent whether this is a good time to conduct the survey, and to provide them with a method of deferring the survey further.

Sampling methods

Popup surveys use a sampling method in order to select a subset of visitors to the website. Even if it was decided that every visitor should be invited to take a survey, a sampling method is still needed to avoid asking people who had already completed or rejected the survey.

The sampling process comprises two elements. Firstly, a method of selecting a subset of the visitors. Secondly, a method of avoiding re-asking the same visitor.

One-in-N sampling

The selection of a subset of respondents is normally achieved by using a random selection process to invite an average of one-in-N respondents. The calculation of the one-in-N is based on the traffic figure for the website, the number of interviews required, the expected response rate, and the period of time that the survey is to run over.

Table 15.3 shows a hypothetical example of a popup survey being conducted on a website. The research is designed to last one month, perhaps to get a balance of types of visitor. The average number of visitors in a typical month is one million, and the number of completed surveys required by the study design is one thousand.

Table 15.3

Period of time for the survey	1 month
Number of Interviews wanted	1000
Visitors per month	1 000 000
Expected response rate	20%
Invitations required at 20% response rate	5000
Ratio of invitations (5000) to traffic (1 000 000)	1-in-200

The expected response rate is 20%. If this study is a repeat of an earlier one, then the response rate estimate may be fairly accurate. If the estimate is based on other factors then it might be very inaccurate, which would mean that the one-in-N ratio would need recalculating once the survey is running to ensure that the data collection period fits the one month time scale.

When designing a website survey, the researcher should consider the time-frame for the data collection. If the traffic to a page is very high, it might be possible to complete the required number of interviews within an hour, but that would run the risk of giving a biased set of answers. In most cases, people who use a website between 9am and 5pm will differ in some ways to people who visit during the evening or night. Similarly, many website surveys show differences in the views or characteristics between those who visit on a weekday compared to those who visit at the weekend. Therefore most market researchers prefer to collect their data over a period of not less than one week, and often longer, in order to sample as accurately as possible.

Once the one-in-N ratio has been assessed, the survey scripting team can use a random number generation routine to select visitors on a basis that means every visitor has a chance of being selected, and such that over the day the ratio works out correctly.

It should be noted that the response rate is initially an estimate (even when based on previous surveys on the same website), so it is normal for the response rate to be monitored to see if the one-in-N figure is correct. If the response rate achieved is higher than expected, then the rate of sampling is slowed down. If the response rate is lower than anticipated, the sampling rate is accelerated.

One potential area of discrepancy between the website's own estimate of traffic and the number of invitations served relates to how many people visit a page on a website, look at it and leave, a phenomenon sometimes called bouncing. Most popups rely on the visitor to do something on the site before they are served. If visitor does nothing except view the page they arrived on, they will be invisible to most popup methods.

Avoiding asking the same visitors again

From methodological, business, and ethical points of view the researcher does not want to reinvite people who have already taken the survey, nor those who have been asked and who declined. This is usually achieved by using cookies (although there are alternatives in some situations).

A typical research process runs as follows:

1.   Check to see if this visitor accepts cookies. Most people's browsers do accept cookies, but a small percentage (usually less than 5%) does not. If they do not accept cookies, do not consider sampling them, otherwise you run the risk of asking the same people over and over again.

2.   Check to see if they already have a survey cookie from your organisation (you can't check whether other companies have served them a cookie). If they already have one, do not consider sampling them.

3. If they accept cookies and do not already have one of your survey cookies, apply your randomised one-in-N sampling routine. If they are not selected for a survey, ignore them*.

4. If they are selected for a survey, serve them a cookie (so you don't bother them again) and serve them the invitation, asking if they will do the survey.

Sampling people or computers?

One issue with sampling visitors is that there is an implicit assumption that a person and a PC are the same thing. Indeed, in most cases, the implicit definition is that a person is the same as a specific browser on a specific PC. If somebody uses both Firefox and Internet Explorer on a particular PC, they will look like two people to most survey systems.

Cookie-based sampling tends to under-sample people who share a PC and may allow some people to do the survey twice, for example if they use more than one PC or use more than one browser on one PC.

This problem is often ignored, particularly if incentives are not being offered. The number of people excluded because they share a PC is usually not large, and unless the sampling rate is very high (e.g. one in 5) it is unlikely the same person will be sampled twice even when they use two or more PCs.

This weakness in sampling is worth bearing in mind when looking at a survey's verbatims. If one or two people say they were asked twice, it is possible they are people who (a) use two or more PCs, (b) use two or more browsers, (c) cleared their cookies down between the first invite and the second, or (d) were simply confusing different surveys on different websites. However, if more than 1% or 2% say they have been asked more than once, it is more likely there is a problem with the administration/implementation of the survey.

Pages and locations

Care needs to be taken to sample visitors in a way that fairly represents the users of the relevant parts of the website. For example, if all the sampling were conducted on the website's home page, those visitors who arrive directly at another part of the site will not be sampled or represented. Users clicking on links on other sites, using a search engine (such as Google or Bing), or who have bookmarked a page may arrive at a page other than the home page. People who have used those methods of finding what they want may well differ in a range of ways from people who typically arrive at the home page – for example, they may be more likely to be repeat visitors or more advanced users.

In order to fully understand the website's visitors, it is common practice to sample visitors from different parts of the site, often employing quotas. For example, a study might sample 100 interviews

---

*If the research design specifically wants to reduce the probability of sampling heavy users of the site, i.e. people who visit often, then a cookie can be served to everybody inspected at Step 3. This procedure means that the first time a visitor is encountered during their visit they are either invited to take a survey or permanently discarded.

from ten different parts of the website. The data can then be weighted in proportion to traffic data collected from web metrics or server logs.

Technology issues

The history of popup surveys has been a cat and mouse game between browsers and the people designing survey software and market research approaches. The reason for this is that many of the approaches used by market researchers are also used by advertisers and direct marketers and this has resulted in user resistance. An example of this technology war has been the appearance and development of popup blockers.

In addition, many websites have lengthy approval processes before software can be added to their site, for obvious security and performance reasons. This approval process can limit the sort of survey invitation technologies that can be used and can have implications for how long the setup phase of a project will take.

At the time of writing, there are technical solutions to most problems, and popups can still be used, as can a range of alternatives, such as overlays. Most third-party solutions use the overlay rather than the true popup. (Overlays and other alternatives to popups are considered a little later in this chapter.)

Installing code on the client's website

One issue facing any market researcher conducting popup surveys is implementing the trigger for their survey on the client's website. In some cases, all of the code for the triggering is installed on the client's website. However, more typically, a small amount of code is installed on the client's website and that code 'calls' a larger script hosted elsewhere. Even a simple project is likely to involve code to read and serve cookies, conduct a one-in-N sampling process, and cause the popup survey to appear.

 Warning

It is vital that the code added to the client's website does not cause a problem, either in terms of delays or, worse still, crashes. Adding the code to the client's website can sometimes be very protracted, depending on the processes that the site employs.

Triggering surveys on exit

Researchers would often like to trigger the survey on exit, i.e. when the respondent has finished their visit and is either moving on to another website or closing their browser. Sampling visitors on exit would allow the researcher to fully explore the respondents' experiences. In general, this approach is very difficult to implement because there are so many ways that people can exit a site, including closing their browser or even their PC.

Most situations require the researcher to achieve some degree of compromise and usually the cooperation of the respondent, for example by gaining their permission to do a survey and then closing the popup window until after they have left the site.

Alternatives to popups

Although most popup surveys are launched by using a scripting language, such as JavaScript, to create a new window on top of the one the potential respondent is visiting, there are alternatives, including:

- ○ *Pop-under windows*
- ○ *Overlays*
- ○ *Banner invitations*
- ○ *Static invitations*
- ○ *Interstitials*

These options are reviewed below.

Pop-under windows

A popup is a new window that sits on top of the website being visited. By contrast, a pop-under hides itself behind all the other open windows, and is revealed when the other windows are closed (or after a fixed period of time).

The key negative associated with pop-under windows is user resistance; people tend to like them even less than popups. The second problem is that they may be revealed a long time after somebody has left the site, making them less relevant.

Overlays

To most website visitors an overlay looks very much like a popup, but it is produced in a quite different way. A popup is a separate browser window, sitting in front of the original page. An overlay is part of the original page, scripted to sit as a semi-transparent layer in front of the other content.

Some researchers use overlays because they have heard that people do not like popups. However, the experience of an overlay is very similar to the experience of a popup, and it is usually the experience that visitors complain about, not the way the interruption is coded.

The positive side of using an overlay is that it is easier to ensure that respondents see the survey invitation. The downside is that it can require more code to be added to the client's website, something which can be a major issue. Most current third-party solutions are based on overlays rather than true popups.

Banner invitations

If a website serves advertising, for example banner ads, then this mechanism can be used to serve survey invitations. The mechanics of this approach can be very simple if the invitation is straightforward. However, it can be made more interesting by using a flash video or some other form of animation as part of the ad, to catch visitors' attention.

The main drawback is that the response rate to banner ads is typically well below 1%, i.e. very much lower than that typically associated with popup surveys.

Static invitations

The simplest way to invite visitors to complete a survey is to use part of the page to ask them, and include a link to the survey as part of the request. This approach is often used when seeking visitor feedback and typically is labelled 'Have your say' or 'Tell us what you think'.

As a method of encouraging feedback this sort of link can be useful. However, as a research method to investigate visitor profile or their satisfaction with different aspects of the site, it is a very poor method because of the very low rates of response. A popup invitation is a reasonable approximation to a random sample, whereas a static invitation elicits a self-selected group of respondents.

Interstitials

An interstitial is a page inserted between one page and another. For example, if a visitor on a website's home page clicks on a link for the News Page, an interstitial page might appear before the News Page – the term 'interstitial' refers to the idea of stitching a page in between two others.

The interstitial page is used as either an invitation to a survey or the first page of the survey. The potential respondent has the choice to take the survey or to decline it. If they decline, they proceed straight to the page they had requested. If they choose to complete the survey they first do the survey and are then forwarded to the page they had requested.

Unless a website proposes to invite every visitor to the page to take a survey, some form of sampling is required, in the same way as for popups.

Alternatives to cookies

As mentioned above, the most usual way to control survey invitations to avoid inviting the same person more than once is to use cookies. However, in some circumstances there are alternatives to using cookies. This section looks at three alternatives:

- ○ *Signing-in*

- ○ *IP address*

- ○ *Digital fingerprint*

Signing-in

If the website, or the section of the website being investigated, requires visitors to sign-in/log-in, then the database of registered members can be used to control survey invitations. The sampling routine keeps a list of all visitors who have previously been invited and samples from those who have not previously been invited.

The sampling process can be made more sophisticated by using screening or quotas based on data held in the website's database. This sort of sampling will normally need to be handled by the department or company handling the database, not by the research agency. (Note, unless the respondents have given their informed consent to any loss in anonymity, care must be taken to not store their identity or logon details with the survey responses.)

IP address

One piece of passive data that is easy for a website to capture is the visitor's IP address, a 12-digit number that uniquely identifies every device connected to the internet. A database can be used to recognise every IP address that has been served a survey invitation to avoid the same address being served two invitations. The use of IP addresses can be extended to screen out some groups of IP addresses altogether, such as those that appear to come from specific countries or from a specific company.

However, many internet providers allocate IP addresses dynamically, i.e. the users receive a different specific address each time they log on. Therefore, many researchers have rejected this route as too likely to annoy visitors who might be invited more than once.

Digital fingerprint

One technique that is increasingly used to indentify respondents is digital fingerprinting (also known as a device fingerprint and machine fingerprint). This technique captures information from the users' machines, such as their TCP/IP configuration and details of their computer's operating system, to create a composite picture unique to that computer/user.

At the time of writing, the main use of digital fingerprinting was to identify duplicate respondents in panel and cross-panel databases, but the same technique can be used to control website invitations.

The drawbacks and potential drawbacks of digital fingerprinting include:

○　*more technology and sophistication required than for cookies*

○　*it assumes that each person uses one PC, and each PC is used by one person, like cookies and any other PC-based system*

○　*the concern that digital fingerprinting may break data privacy laws in some countries.*[*]

ETHICAL AND QUALITY ISSUES

In addition to the ethical and quality guidelines that apply to all research and specifically to online research, there are a number of issues that relate specifically to popup surveys.

The advice in this section is largely framed around the ESOMAR guidelines, particularly 'Conducting Research Using the Internet'. However, a researcher should check the latest picture, in terms of ESOMAR's guidelines, local guidelines, and relevant laws.

---

*In November 2009 the UK's Research Magazine *reported that an opinion by Canadian technology and privacy lawyer Brian Bowman, published by the Canadian Marketing Research and Intelligence Association (MRIA), suggested that digital fingerprinting may not meet the 'reasonableness test' required under Canadian privacy laws. If this opinion proves to be true it could have a wider significance than just Canada, as the laws in Canada are, according to MRI President David Stark, similar to the laws in Europe, Argentina, Australia, New Zealand, and Japan.*

The ethical and quality issues can be divided into a few main themes:

- O   *Protecting respondents*
- O   *Protecting clients*
- O   *Informed consent*

Protecting respondents

Protecting respondents from harm is probably our prime ethical duty and it is the one that is most likely to involve legislative implications. The following all relate to protecting respondents.

Children. Given that most research guidelines require prior parental permission to interview children, popup surveys are not normally suitable for children. This means finding out if a potential respondent is a child early in the survey and screening them out. Note that children are defined differently in different countries and there are sometimes different age rules for different products. For example, in many markets the age restrictions for alcohol are different to those for chocolate.

Anonymity. If a study is supposed to be anonymous, researchers need to make sure that respondent anonymity is protected. This means, for example, screening verbatim responses to see if respondents have entered data that could reveal who they are, and looking at any linking of registration data, web metrics, and survey responses to make sure that they do not allow a person to be identified.

Security. A respondent taking part in a survey should feel confident that their communication with the survey is secure and adequately protected. If they are visiting a banking site, they will expect the survey to be similarly secure, for example by using https. Dealing with security also includes ensuring that the respondent does not download a virus and that their PC is not left less secure or less functional after completing the survey.

Inconvenience. The ESOMAR guidelines also mention protecting site visitors from annoyance and inconvenience. This means, for example, not serving the same invitation to the same person more than once and making it quick and easy for people to reject the survey.

Protecting clients

In terms of protecting clients there are two broad areas of concern. The first relates to the impact of the survey and the second to the interpretation of the results.

The first area relates to issues such as damage caused by the survey, for example by causing the client's website to crash or become insecure. Another possible issue for the client to consider is that a long and boring survey is likely to negatively impact on respondents, who are visitors/customers.

The second area of concern relates to misinterpreting the research. In addition to the normal concerns that research guidelines suggest, such as the projectability of the research, the researcher needs to ensure that the client understands the impact of the response rate, the completion rate, and any imbalance caused by sampling issues. For example, if a survey is only triggered from the home page it will miss those users who arrive directly at other pages, via search engines or previously stored URLs, and this excluded group could differ from those arriving via the home page.

Informed consent

The key elements about gaining informed consent are:

- ○ *telling the potential respondent how long the survey will take*

- ○ *saying who is conducting the research and how they can get in touch with you*

- ○ *providing a link to a privacy policy*

- ○ *saying whether invisible processing is being conducted*

- ○ *saying whether the research is anonymous. If it is not, explain what is happening, gain the respondent's opt-in, and provide a print-screen option showing what has been agreed to*

- ○ *say where the data will be stored and for how long*

 Example

Directgov: Website Customer Satisfaction Tracking Study

Directgov is the UK's official digital channel for public access to government information and services online.

Directgov brings together online government services all in one place, whilst at the same time cutting down the number of websites. The site can be browsed by topic – including money, travel and transport – or by audience group – such as disabled people or parents. It also has a search engine that finds content directly. It provides access to government directories as well as links to relevant third parties who can offer additional trusted advice and support.

The site, initially launched as UK Online in 2004, has utilised research from the outset to ensure that it meets the public's needs. In 2005 the site was relaunched as Directgov and research conducted by UK website research specialists Virtual Surveys has been used to monitor its users. The objectives of the website research have been to:

- ○ *understand who is using the website and its sub-sites*

- ○ *understand whether the website was meeting its visitors' needs*

- ○ *identify and prioritise the changes most likely to improve the visitor experience*

Directgov's programme of website satisfaction research comprises three waves of research per year conducted with website visitors, targeting those who are using the site for their personal use. The research is achieved via popup surveys, using advanced approaches and including interstitials and overlays in order to maximise the acceptability of the surveys and minimise inconvenience.

The key features of the website research being used by Directgov are:

(a)   Research is spread across about 30 areas of the website, including both information and transactional areas, with a minimum target of 250 interviews per area.

(b)   Both the survey invitation and the survey are clearly branded as Directgov. This reassures visitors that they are still dealing with Directgov and lets them know that the purpose of the survey is to improve the service to them.

(c)   The surveys are accessible to AA standard of W3C guidelines. Because this is a government website there is a need for it to be accessible. This includes being suitable for people using screen readers (for those who have a visual impairment) and for those with JavaScript turned off.

(d)   The surveys on the transactional sites are organised in a way that does not interrupt the transaction.

(e)   The surveys are anonymously integrated with Directgov's web analytics data to provide additional insight.

(f)   The surveys' questions include KPIs, open-ended responses, visitor characteristics (e.g. age, sex, education), and topics of special interest.

The analysis of the data looks at both the overall picture and the messages for each of the areas researched. It includes changes over time, visitor profiles, differing measures of satisfaction, and the ability of the site to meet visitors' needs. The research provides guidance on future improvements utilising direct approaches such as open-ended questions, and more advanced techniques such as MaxDiff.

One indication of the success of the Directgov website is the way that the public's use has increased over time. The purpose of the visitor satisfaction research is to help ensure that the volume of usage and the satisfaction of visitors both increase in the future.

Thanks are extended to Directgov and their website research agency, Virtual Surveys, for permission to use this case study.

The Directgov case study shows how a complex site with many stakeholders can conduct a rigorously structured benchmarking and tracking, customer satisfaction study. The key lesson for any researcher setting out on this sort of project is that there are going to be numerous technical and ethical issues to deal with before the final research can take place. This case study is also very relevant to the section on public sector research, where the need to meet higher standards, in some areas, than those that may apply in the private sector is discussed.

 Advice

BEST PRACTICE GUIDELINES FOR POPUP SURVEYS

This section summarises best practices in website visitor surveys and reflects a broad consensus but, as with all best practice guidelines cannot represent an absolute consensus.

1. Make the survey page about 60–80% the size of the smallest common screen size. If, say, 20% of visitors are still using a 600 × 800 pixel screen, use a survey page no bigger than about 480 × 640 pixels. This ensures that the original page is still visible and serves as a visible clue to the respondent as to what is going on.

2. Keep the survey short, ideally less than five minutes and certainly no longer than ten.

3. Tell people how long the survey will take, and make sure this is accurate.

4. Make sure there is an easy and obvious way for people to reject the survey.

5. Tell people what the survey is about, who is conducting it, and how they can get in touch with the people running the survey.

6. Ensure that a link to a privacy policy is available.

7. Make sure the survey matches the style and appearance of the website; there should be no doubt that the survey is on behalf of the website.

8. Make the survey as engaging as possible to maximise the response rate and the satisfaction with the survey.

Further advice on best practice in website surveys can be found in Pete Comley's paper 'What Works, What Doesn't Work and What Will Work in the Future' (Comley, 2000).

WEBSITE METRICS AND ANALYTICS

The largest activity and spend on website research lies largely outside of market research and is concerned with website metrics and analytics. Collectively, these tools are passive observational techniques that collect information about who visits a website and what they do there.

This section addresses three topics:

○   *Web analytics*

○   *Behavioural targeting*

○   *Measuring traffic volumes*

WEB ANALYTICS

Website owners use web analytics to measure visitor traffic and behaviour. There is a wide range of web analytics systems, including free services (for example Google Analytics) and a range of commercial packages. The website analytics sit behind the website and are, in most cases, invisible to the websiste's visitors.

In addition, the server itself produces a wide range of data, often referred to as server logs. These reports can be used separately from third-party analytics or in conjunction with them.

The sort of information that the web analytics collect are:

Visitation patterns. Normally this is collected on a per respondent basis. Typical information includes which page the respondent landed on first, where they came from, how long they spent on the page, which links they clicked on, where did they go next.

Visitor information. Information can be collected about each visitor, including their screen size, operating system, language, location (country and to some extent location within country), what browser they are using, and what features are enabled, e.g. JavaScript and Flash.

Interaction information. What information have users entered into the website, for example into search fields and forms?

Longitudinal information. Is a visitor new or a repeat visitor, how many times have they visited?

Collecting information

Web analytics gather information about a specific visit, but they can also link it to previous visits (subject to some limitations), producing a large database of visitor records. The specifics of how each web analytical package tracks visitors can differ, but they all tend to feature the following:

○ *Session cookies. A session cookie is a text file that the website passes to a visitor's browser when they arrive at the website and which only applies to that specific visit to that website. The session cookie can serve several purposes, one being to avoid the need to ask the visitor to re-enter their login details every time they change to another part of the site. Session cookies provide the mechanics for the web analytics to track the progress of the visitor around the website. A session cookie loses its relevance at the end of the session.*

○ *Persistent cookies. A persistent cookie is similar to a session cookie, but stays on the visitor's computer much longer, e.g. weeks, months, or even years (these cookies are also known as tracking cookies). One use of persistent cookies is to control advertising. Cookies tell the advertiser whether the visitor has already seen a particular ad, and potentially how many times. Web analytics use persistent cookies to track visitors to the website across different visits, over a period of time. Note, cookies only store text and they will normally have an expiry date.*

○ **IP addresses.** An IP address is a unique reference to a device connected to the internet, allowing information to be sent to and from it. Web analytics and other tracking software can record the IP address of the visitor. However, for many users their specific IP address is allocated dynamically when they connect to the internet, making IP addresses a less precise method of tracking people.

○ **Digital fingerprints.** The term 'digital fingerprints' refers to a group of characteristics about a visitor's PC and configuration, for example screen size, operating systems, software downloads, etc. Digital fingerprints provide another way of identifying people and tracking them as they visit and revisit a website.

One assumption that all of these data collection and tracking systems share is that each person only uses one computer (or internet-enabled device), and that each computer is used by only one person. If a PC is shared by a whole family then web analytics may treat that family as one person. Similarly, if somebody uses one PC at work and another at home, that person may appear as two people to web tracking systems.

Anonymous?

In general, people tend to describe the data collected by web analytics packages as being anonymous, but this is not strictly true and is not the view of some of the more aggressive regulators. Many data protection authorities, such as the German government, classify an IP address as a personal identifier (although IP addresses are shared for some users, they are unique for some people).

Web analytics tend to allocate a visitor's profile a unique, but superficially anonymous, ID code. However, the way that these anonymous ID codes can turn into identifiable data was revealed by a data reputation disaster that happened to AOL. In 2006, AOL accidently released the search records for about 650 000 anonymous profiles, covering searches made over a period of about three months. On 9 August 2006, the *New York Times* carried an article that reported how they had taken the contents of these searches and quickly tracked one profile (4417749) down to a real person (Thelma Arnold, from Lilburn, Georgia). Evidently Ms Arnold's searches included services in Lilburn, people with the surname Arnold, and some other key information. [http://www.nytimes.com/2006/08/09/technology/09aol.html]

The argument between the commercial companies with databases of anonymous profiles and the regulators tends to be the difference between 'actively identified' and 'potentially identified'. The main issue that market researchers need to keep in mind is that this area is going to be increasingly subject to investigation, regulation, and guidelines.

Linking web analytics and survey data

There is a growing trend to combine web analytics data with survey data, to create a richer picture by utilising the strengths of both approaches. The key steps in this process are:

1. When the respondent agrees to take the survey, obtain an ID for that user's web analytics profile.*

2. After the web surveys are completed, combine them with the tracking information, ensuring that the records are anonymous, i.e. anonymous for the research agency, anonymous to the analytics provider, and anonymous for the end client.

3. Analyse the survey data and the tracking data, for example to see if people who visited more pages had higher or lower levels of satisfaction.

4. A potential extension to this process is to map data from the combined analysis to the wider database of analytics data, to evaluate the relative frequencies of different categories of visitors.

BEHAVIOURAL TARGETING

Behavioural targeting (or BT as it is often called) is a method of using information about website visitors to tailor their experience, a process also referred to as personalisation. BT can be used to ensure that a website presents those features that a visitor is most interested in; it can also be used to present advertising that is judged to be most likely to be effective.

Although BT is used in the context of website visitors, it is even more associated with search engines, where the content of numerous searches are used to gain an ever richer picture of the user. For example, if somebody searches for hire cars, wedding flowers, hotels, and suit hire it is a fair bet that they are planning a wedding, and advertisers who sell wedding-related products and services will be keen to target their advertising at them.

As an example of how far BT might progress it is worth noting a 2007 interview with Eric Schmidt, CEO of Google. Schmidt said that Google wanted to increase the data they hold on people and the quality of their algorithms to such an extent that they could answer questions such as '*What shall I do tomorrow*' and '*What job should I take?*'. Shortly after Schmidt made this comment the European Parliament expressed renewed interest in controlling and limiting the activities of companies such as Google.

Deep packet inspection

A more recent development in the area of BT has been the attempts to launch business models based on an approach called deep packet inspection. When a user visits a website or uses a search engine, they feel as though they are connecting directly with the provider of the website. However,

---

Note, under the ESOMAR guidelines, respondents' consent must be sought before collecting their data in a way that allows their analytics and survey data to be combined. There is currently no consensus about the amount of detail that is required to be conveyed in order to comply with the concept of 'informed consent'.

in most cases what is happening is that they are sending a message (a key click, a search string, etc.) from their PC to their ISP (internet service provider) who then forwards it to the website. Similarly, what appears on the user's screen is sent from the website to the ISP which forwards it to the user. All these messages are sent as data packages via the ISP.

Deep packet inspection is a system where the ISP gives a copy of all these messages to a third party, who opens the packages and records information about the user, so building their profile over time. Most of the companies looking to exploit this approach claim that they ensure the data is anonymous and that they don't collect the more sensitive types of information, such as medical and sexual orientation.

Two high profile attempts at utilising deep packet inspection were Phorm in the UK and NebuAd in the USA (note that NebuAd has no connection to the web survey system company called Nebu). Both schemes were met by widespread protest, and as of December 2009 neither scheme had made much progress.

MEASURING TRAFFIC VOLUMES

'Traffic' is the term used to describe the volume of people visiting a website, or a page within a website. Website owners know the number of people visiting their site from their web logs (system data from their server and software) and from any website metrics they may be using. However, people also need/want information about other organisations' websites, either to assess the performance of their own website or in terms of evaluating whether they should pay for advertising.

In addition to simply asking website owners for audited web log data (something that potential advertisers with the site may do) there is a variety of ways of assessing relative volumes, including:

○ ***Explicit panels.*** *Companies such as Nielsen and comScore have created panels of people who have downloaded PC monitoring software which sends information about the panel members' browsing and associated behaviour back to the companies' servers. The panel members may also be sent surveys to enrich the raw data.*

○ ***Implicit panels***. *In this model, logging software is downloaded as a by-product of some other activity. For example, Alexa.com use this method with people who have downloaded their toolbar.*

○ ***ISP liaison***. *In the ISP liaison model, the traffic company (e.g. Hitwise), base their estimates of traffic on data from ISPs.*

The reason why there are so many systems is that none of them is perfect, and different approaches have different strengths for different types of sites and for different markets. The explicit panels provide the richest information, but they are dependent on the size of the panel, which in turn makes them more relevant to sites with heavier levels of traffic. The implicit panels tend to have larger panel sizes and cover more countries, but there are concerns about how representative the people who have downloaded their software are (and there are concerns about how informed the consent was from people downloading their tracking software). The ISP model depends on most of the ISPs being included and on most visitors using a regular ISP.

SITE REVIEWS AND PROFESSIONAL REVIEWS

Websites can be reviewed in terms of a number of criteria, such as: technical errors, technical requirements, complexity, accessibility, e-retailing, search engine optimisation, and usability. The reviews can be conducted using automated processes, manual reviews, or by a combination of the two.

TESTING TECHNICAL ISSUES

Reviewing a website for technical issues includes checking the following:

- O   *Does the website work with all the leading internet browsers?*

- O   *Does any aspect of the website crash when used?*

- O   *Are any of the links from the website broken (i.e. do they fail to link to a site they are supposed to link to)?*

- O   *What sort of computer and browser configuration does a visitor need? For example, do they need broadband, or a Java-enabled computer, or a large screen?*

- O   *How would the site function on a mobile device such as an iPhone?*

- O   *What are the implications for the maintenance and updating of the website?*

USABILITY ISSUES

Usability reviews typically employ a checklist approach where a number of factors that have been identified as important are assessed: for example, is the navigation intuitive?

One concern about professional usability reviews is that they tend to favour conventional designs, provided that they conform to known good practice. Professional reviews can struggle with truly innovative sites, with new metaphors, and truly new approaches.

ACCESSIBILITY ISSUES

In this context, accessibility means ensuring that people who have specific challenges – such as visual, auditory, physical, speech, cognitive, and neurological disabilities – can use the website.

Many governments have implemented laws or guidelines specifying steps that websites should take to make their sites accessible (for example, the USA has its section 508 of the US Rehabilitation Act). In addition, many companies have decided to implement a specific level of accessibility, even in markets where that is not required by legislation or regulation.

The international guardian of accessibility is the W3C (the World Wide Web Consortium) [http://www.w3.org/] and specifically the Web Accessibility Initiative (WAI) [http://www.w3.org/WAI/]. The WAI's website includes a wide range of notes and guidelines about implementing accessible websites.

Although there are software tools that will help review a website (and a list of them can be found on the WAI's website), it is generally agreed that a human expert view is also required. A few market research agencies have this review ability in-house. However, most reviewers are from outside the market research industry.

AUTOMATED WEBSITE TESTING

There is a wide range of software and tools available for evaluating websites. Broadly these can be divided into three categories:

- ○ **Accessibility**: *the degree to which the website conforms to the needs of people with disabilities; these tools are often referenced against the W3C WAI guidelines.*

- ○ **Performance**: *looking at issues such as whether the site has errors and what the download speed is.*

- ○ **Appearance**: *how the website will appear to users, particularly in the context of different settings and browsers.*

The range and nature of tools available change rapidly, so the packages mentioned below are presented as examples and a researcher is advised to check for updates and alternatives.

It should be stressed that automated tools make the job of the researcher much easier, but they cannot be used in isolation; there is still a need, in all cases, for human inspection. One important point to keep in mind is that none of the automated tools evaluate the content of the website, e.g. does it make sense and is it engaging?

A cross-section of software that looks at accessibility is listed below. The list is not exhaustive and does not imply that the author endorses them.

- ○ *WAVE [http://wave.webaim.org/], a free accessibility testing package, it can also be installed as a Firefox extension*

- ○ *AChecker [http://achecker.ca/checker/index.php], a free accessibility testing package*

- ○ *Accessibility Check [http://www.etre.com/tools/accessibilitycheck/], a free accessibility testing package*

- ❍ *Total Validator [http://www.totalvalidator.com/], a free website testing tool (accessibility and performance), also available as a Firefox extension, with a commercial 'pro' version available*

- ❍ *W3C Quality Assurance Tools [http://www.w3.org/QA/Tools/], a collection of free tools that include programs that check whether a website works in the way it should and whether it uses the appropriate definitions and rules*

- ❍ *BrowserShots [http://browsershots.org/], takes a URL and shows the user what the page looks like on a range of browsers and using a range of screen sizes; the basic service is free, but there is also a paid-for premium service*

- ❍ *Rational Policy Tester Accessibility Edition [http://www-01.ibm.com/software/awdtools/ tester/policy/accessibility/index.html], a commercial accessibility testing package*

- ❍ *Rational Policy Tester Quality Edition [http://www-01.ibm.com/software/awdtools/ tester/policy/quality/index.html], a commercial package looking at performance and quality issues*

As mentioned above, it should be noted that software will only take the testing process so far. To be sure that a site conforms to the relevant standards an expert assessment (often with somebody who registered with an appropriate body or qualification) is necessary.

ACCOMPANIED SURFING AND OBSERVATION RESEARCH

One of most powerful ways of evaluating websites is to watch people as they use the site. This sort of observational research is usually conducted by asking respondents to undertake specific tasks, such as making a booking, searching for a resource, or playing a game. Accompanied surfing is a combination of an individual depth interview and an anthropological observation.

There are varying degrees of complexity in the ways that this observational research is conducted. At one extreme, it can be as simple as the researcher sitting next to the subject as they complete their tasks, talking to them during the process to gain insight into problems and issues. In many cases, the PC the respondent is using will be fitted with specialist software to record the mouse movements and clicks. It is also common practice to use a video camera to record the subject during the process. The reporting of this sort of testing often employs a 'window in window' approach, where a small video of the subject is played in the corner of the screen whilst the rest of the screen shows the screen as the subject saw it.

More sophisticated research options include the use of web testing labs, where the screen and the subject are viewable from another room (or via the internet from other locations). Some of these labs have facilities to allow several people to test a website at the same time. Another approach is to conduct remote sessions, where subjects use their own PC, and software (or a telephone) is utilised to provide an audio link during the testing process.

Accompanied surfing is very powerful in revealing how users relate to a website and how they use it. Accompanied surfing also reveals to the market researcher the subject's relationship to any brands advertised on the site and to the owner of the website. Normally, when people surf the internet it is a solitary experience and accompanied surfing is a much more natural fit than a group activity.

Accompanied surfing can be combined with a focus group to create a hybrid method. For example, a group of 6–8 participants can be gathered for a focus group. During the group they spend some time at their own terminals, surfing, and being observed. They are then brought back together to discuss their experiences and observations.

OTHER WEBSITE RESEARCH APPROACHES

This section looks at some further techniques that market researchers have found useful when researching websites:

- *Eye tracking*
- *Semiotic analysis of websites*
- *Information architecture*
- *Social media research and websites*

EYE TRACKING

Eye tracking uses advanced technology to determine which parts of a website people are looking at by following their eyes. Although early eye-tracking devices were very intrusive (involving techniques such as special contact lenses or head-enclosing devices), modern eye tracking is much less so and usually uses non-contact methods.

The two most typical outputs from an eye-tracking project are a heatmap of the website – showing where people's eyes spent the largest amount of time (often the top left part of the screen) – and track paths (also known as gaze trails) – showing the different routes people's eyes took when viewing a page.

A number of specialist web testing market research companies provide eye tracking as a service, but it can also be purchased from non-research companies. Eye-tracking systems are normally too expensive to use routinely in evaluating web page designs, but they have shown that they can produce useful generalised findings. For example, most studies show that visitors focus on a triangular area at the top left of the screen only occasionally moving to the bottom of the screen. This means that eye tracking can be used to periodically evaluate major elements of a website's design.

In addition to website testing, eye tracking is used to test product placement in TV shows and video games.

SEMIOTIC ANALYSIS OF WEBSITES

Semiotics is the study of signs and symbols. In terms of website research, market researchers have mainly used semiotics in two ways. Firstly, to look at a website to evaluate the messages that it will create in the minds of the people using it. Secondly, to evaluate what might have been in the mind of the organisation which created the website, for example as a method of researching competitors' websites.

Semiotics can also be used to help create or modify a website, ensuring that the overt and implied messages are those that its owner wants to convey.

INFORMATION ARCHITECTURE

Information architecture relates to the way that a website is organised – for example, which items are placed together, which items should be at the top of a structure, and which should be further down. Information architecture research helps identify the clues that visitors to a website expect to find in order that they can locate what they are looking for.

The Information Architecture Institute says 'We define information architecture as the art and science of organizing and labeling websites, intranets, online communities and software to support usability.' [http://iainstitute.org/documents/learn/What_is_IA.pdf, viewed 21 December 2009]

At one level, every investigation of a website is an exercise in website information architecture. However, there are researchers who specialise in information architecture and there are approaches specifically associated with the field. These specialist techniques include:

○   *Feature sorting*

○   *Focus groups*

○   *Accompanied surfing*

○   *Web analytics*

These four techniques are covered further below.

Feature sorting

In feature sorting the respondents are presented with cards representing the various features that a website might offer. For example, on a news site there might be cards representing local news, business news, regional news, news archives, search, blogs, comments, weather and so on.

The task for the respondents is to put the cards into groups, and possibly to name the groups. When using a focus group approach, these piles of cards provide an input into further discussion of how respondents expect a website to be organised. If the sorting exercise was a quantitative one, then the data will typically be used in a cluster procedure, often a hierarchical one.

One useful resource for feature sorting is the SynCaps program from Syntagm [http://www.syntagm.co.uk/]. SynCaps produces routines and procedures to create cards, including the use of bar codes to make the recording of the information easier, and software to conduct the clustering and analysis.

Focus groups

One popular way of evaluating a website and for gaining insight into different ways of organising a site is the use of focus groups. Within a focus group there is time to use several techniques such as feature sorting and personas. When using personas the group adopts the point of view of a specific type of user – for example, a busy user or somebody looking for critical information – and explores what that person might do when confronted with a website and what alternative solutions would help that person.

Accompanied surfing

Sitting with a respondent as they visit a website, watching what they do and asking them about what they are trying to achieve can allow a theory to be developed. For example, a technique such as grounded theory would allow an information architecture to be designed that better met the needs of the users.

Web analytics

Maps of the routes taken by visitors to a website, as recorded by web analytics and server logs, can be used to define the different usage patterns of website users. This analysis then allows the existing structure to be described. This sort of research tends to be used as an indirect input to the design of an improved information architecture. It is an indirect input to a new design because it can highlight current successes and problems, but it cannot itself suggest new approaches.

SOCIAL MEDIA RESEARCH AND WEBSITES

The use of social media research for websites is still in its early stages. However, there are a few techniques that are beginning to make an impact on website research, particularly blog and buzz mining and online research communities.

Blog and buzz mining

If a website has attracted sufficient interest, then blog and buzz mining can be a useful tool to research what people are saying to each other about it. However, for most websites the level of discussion in places like the blogosphere and Twitter will be too small to be useful.

Online research communities

Online research communities have been adopted in two areas of website research: assessing how a website is currently being used and to help develop new and amended websites. Online research communities, when used for website research, tend to be short-term communities and more qualitative than quantitative.

In some research projects, these two phases of review and development are combined: firstly, by asking the community members to explore how a website is currently used; secondly, by working with them to develop changes; and finally assessing the changes.

 Example

The NUS case study illustrates how online communities are being used in conjunction with website development and research.

NUS case study: Using an online research community for website research

NUS Services is owned by Students' Unions and the National Union of Students (NUS), a confederation of 600 local unions representing some 95% of all students in further and higher education in the UK. NUS Services' mission statement is to: 'Create, develop and sustain competitive advantages for member Students' Unions – reducing costs and maximising commercial revenues'. To this end it provides three core services: purchasing, commercial development, and marketing services.

In 2008, the NUS decided to redesign its website (http://www.nus.org.uk/) from scratch and they wanted to put students at the heart of the process. Guided by NUS Services, the method they settled on was to conduct a short-term online research community (i.e. an MROC) provided by UK agency Virtual Surveys.

The community operated for two weeks and 57 young people contributed to the project. The members were a mixture of sixth form, undergraduates, and post-graduates (note 'sixth form' is a UK description of the last two years of high school).

The community started by exploring the sorts of sites that young people choose to use, from Facebook and MySpace, to eBay and Wikipedia, to BBC and Guardian. This phase explored best in class characteristics, in terms of preferred sites. The community then explored the various sites the students 'needed' to use, such as university, reference, and government sites, along with the existing NUS site. The final stage was to investigate new ideas for the NUS website, looking at design ideas from the NUS and their design agency Code Computerlove and receiving ideas from the community members.

(continued)

The outcome of the research was:

(a)   The NUS's new website was launched in September 2008 and is widely seen as being a major improvement, in both usability and its focus on what students actually want.

(b)   The students who took part in the project were enthused by the process and were willing to be quoted about their collaboration in designing the new site.

Amongst the comments from the participants were:

'I have really enjoyed taking part in this and I am happy that I had the chance to help develop the new site! So thank you for the opportunity!' and 'It has been really cool to be part of making the new site, and I think that it should be advertised that it was helped to be made by students so that everyone feels that it is something for them'.

The NUS case study highlights the ability of an online community to put site users at the heart of a redesign. In particular, the research helped focus the NUS on providing a best in class website for young people.

There is a lot more information on the use of social media in research, much of it appropriate to website research, in Part III Social Media.

SUMMARY OF WEBSITE RESEARCH

Website research provides an interesting lens on the wider market research process for two reasons:

1.   Website research uses a very wide variety of research techniques, including some of the more advanced topics in both qualitative and quantitative research.

2.   Website research attracts competition from a wide range of non-market research companies, such as HCI (human–computer interface) professionals, usability professionals, database companies, website design and management companies, web analytics companies, and community development companies.

Although a wide range of techniques are used for website research, the key approaches are:

   ○   *popup surveys to measure the profile and satisfaction of visitors*

   ○   *web analytics to investigate the volume and habits of website visitors*

      ○   *accompanied surfing to investigate users' perceptions of websites*

      ○   *focus groups to investigate website development ideas*

      ○   *professional reviews to assess usability, accessibility, and performance*

Perhaps the greatest challenge for market researchers working in the area of website research is to rise above the level of measurable phenomena, such as traffic levels, clicks, and fulfilment rates, and to investigate issues such as affinity, advocacy, and engagement.

16 Research Techniques and Approaches

This chapter reviews a range of research approaches and investigates how they are being developed and used in the context of online and social media. The following specific topics are covered:

- Marketing sciences
- Prediction markets
- Mixed purpose research
- Deliberative research
- DIY research

MARKETING SCIENCES

The last 30 years has seen a large number of developments in the area of marketing sciences, such as adaptive conjoint analysis, discrete choice modelling, what-if modelling, and MaxDiff scaling. These developments have been intimately associated with the development of computing, both in analysis and in data collection. In the early part of these developments the driving force was the widespread use of personal computers, but for the last 15 years the emphasis has shifted towards options created by the internet and distributed computing power.

This section looks at the following topics and the way that they relate to both marketing sciences and online market research:

- Evoked sets
- Adaptive scripting
- BPTO and other pricing techniques
- Conjoint analysis and discrete choice modelling
- MaxDiff scaling
- Choice models and NewMR
- Challenges created by the internet

EVOKED SETS

An evoked set is a list of items that is designed to be particularly relevant to an individual respondent. At the most trivial level this can be a list of brands that the respondent has ever bought or heard of. A more sophisticated evoked set might be a sub-set of attributes that are salient to each respondent's product choice. In terms of scripting online surveys, the process of evoked sets is often associated with the term 'piping'. For example, the list of brands heard of might be piped into a question asking which brands the respondent ever buys, and the list of brands bought might be piped into a question asking which brand the respondent buys most often.

The key benefit of evoked scripts is that they allow larger sets to be included in the study whilst helping to ensure that the respondent is answering questions about choices that are relevant to them. For example, evoked sets can greatly expand the range of things that can be accessed in choice models (York and Hall, 2000).

One weakness of evoked sets is that it produces smaller bases, particularly for those items that are less likely to be selected. Incomplete data sets can make it more difficult to use techniques such as cluster and factor analyses.

ADAPTIVE SCRIPTING

Adaptive scripting refers to the process of making a survey adapt to the answers entered by the respondents. Evoked sets are one example of adaptive scripting, but they are only the tip of the iceberg. Adaptive scripting can be used for the following:

○ *personalising surveys to talk about events specific to the respondents (for example their retail option, their mode of travel, their annual spend)*

○ *allocating people to cells, concepts, or sub-sets of questionnaires*

○ *using iterative techniques, such as hill climbing heuristics, to identify key characteristics of consumers; also see notes on BPTO and other pricing techniques below*

○ *constructing designs and evaluating utilities for techniques such as Conjoint Analysis, DCM, and MaxDiff; see notes below for more information on these*

BPTO AND OTHER PRICING TECHNIQUES

BPTO (Brand Price Trade-Off) is a technique which attempts to find the prices that consumers would pay for a set of products. This is achieved by increasing the prices that are offered each time a respondent selects a particular price/brand combination from a set of choices. Although there are problems with the classic BPTO, by utilising the power of adaptive scripting it can be adapted to create a more sensitive and reliable method (Poynter, 1997, 2006). The adapted BPTO uses computing power to vary the prices of products both upwards and downwards.

Adaptive scripting can also be used to breathe new life into other pricing techniques, such as Gabor Granger and Van Westendorp's Price Sensitivity Meter (PSM). For example, in Gabor Granger approaches, adaptive scripting can be used to create an iterative process which increases the price of a product if a respondent says they will buy it, and reduces the price if the respondent says they would not buy it. In a PSM study, the scripting can be used to ensure data consistency. For example, if somebody indicates that $40 is '*expensive but worth considering*' then the survey can check that they don't say that $35 is '*so expensive that you would not consider buying it*'.

CONJOINT ANALYSIS AND DISCRETE CHOICE MODELLING

Adaptive scripting can be used to create a wide range of conjoint analysis and discrete choice modelling (DCM) studies. Amongst the uses are:

1. **To create evoked sets of attributes and levels**. For example, to remove those attributes and levels not relevant to a specific respondent, and to express others in terms relevant to each respondent.

2. **To create designs for the test**. With most choice modelling techniques it is necessary to create tasks that rotate different attributes and levels so that they can be evaluated. The two common approaches are either to use computing power to create fixed designs, which can be used with conventional web interviewing systems, or to generate random designs at run time, which requires either specialist web surveying software or some form of dynamic scripting.

3. **To create adaptive surveys**, for example using Sawtooth Software's ACBC (Adaptive Choice Based Conjoint). In an adaptive survey the choice tasks are designed during the interview based on previous answers. The key benefit of adaptive scripting is that it reduces the size of the interview, because the interview focuses on the key tasks.

In the area of conjoint analysis and discrete choice modelling the internet has become such a dominant medium that there are few tools and conference papers that utilise offline modalities. For international studies this can be a problem as there are many countries where internet penetration is too low to make it a viable modality.

MAXDIFF SCALING

MaxDiff scaling is a technique developed by Jordan Louviere in 1987 to provide unbiased scaling (Louviere, 1991). Whilst paper and pencil designs are possible, adaptive scripting offers the advantage of more robust designs, in particular randomised designs, and of making the scaling process adaptive.

MaxDiff is particularly relevant to online techniques because it can be used to reduce the number of questions asked to each respondent, and the tasks can be made more engaging through the use of adaptive scripting and animation via techniques such as Flash. MaxDiff is also known as Best/Worst scaling and can be used to create Best/Worst conjoint analysis.

CHOICE MODELS AND NEW*MR*

New*MR* is a movement within market research to create new approaches that are not based on old-style market research and which are moving towards more collaborative and respondent-focused techniques. (New*MR* is covered in Part V Breaking News!) One of the key concerns highlighted by New*MR* is the realisation that many traditional research methods, such as scales and grids, are flawed. This results from experiments conducted in neuroscience and behavioural economics (Ariely, 2008, Lindstrom, 2008; Lehrer, 2009).

Concerns about the problems associated with traditional approaches have led more researchers to look towards the simplicity (at least in terms of the respondents' tasks) of choice models. In choice modelling, respondents are shown a choice set and they make a choice, a process analogous to what they do in real life (consumers are rarely asked to rate products in their everyday lives). However, whilst the tasks that are presented to the respondents are easier for them to answer, the data is harder to process and requires more design, more analysis, and more time.

Adaptive choice tasks may well be a model for how much market research will be conducted in the future, rather than asking respondents to rate large numbers of brands and attributes on five-point scales.

CHALLENGES CREATED BY THE INTERNET

The internet is associated with a wide range of innovations and improvements in terms of marketing sciences, but it has created some challenges, two of which are explored in this section. These are:

1.   Long and boring surveys

2.   Excluding developing markets

Long and boring surveys

There are several reasons why many market research surveys are long and boring, so it would be wrong to point too much blame at marketing sciences, but marketing sciences are certainly responsible for some of the problems. Some types of analysis require specific types of data and in order to collect this data surveys are often scripted with one or more of forced responses, long lists of scales and questions, and many repetitions of choice tasks.

Techniques such as factor analysis, principal components, and cluster analysis require that each respondent has rated all of the scales and that there are sufficient scales to cover the variance represented by the underlying factors.

In choice modelling, the fashion has been to use techniques that allow models to be approximated at the respondent level rather than at the aggregate level. This in turn requires that sufficient choice task data is collected at the respondent level to enable individual models to be estimated.

The contribution to long and boring surveys made by marketing science needs addressing in three ways:

1.   Making the surveys less boring. For example, tasks can be made simpler and newer scripting techniques such as the use of Flash can make them more fun.

2.   Not trying to achieve everything in one survey. For example, a long list of attributes can be used initially to create a factor solution, allowing a much smaller list of attributes to be used in the main study.

3.   Improving analysis techniques to remove the need for complete data sets. Perhaps the greatest innovation in recent years was the introduction of Hierarchical Bayes, which in some contexts facilitates the use of incomplete data sets instead of complete sets.

Excluding developing markets

Although the internet (and the rise of personal computers in data collection before that) has been associated with some powerful developments in marketing sciences, it has led to a growing gap between the techniques that can be applied in developed economies and those applied in less economically developed countries. Many of the improvements in approaches originate in North America where computer-aided data collection has been available for almost 30 years and, consequently, many modern techniques require computers to aid the data collection.

At first appearance it looks as though more effort should be used to develop marketing science techniques suitable for use in countries such as China and India, especially given the growing economic and research interest in those countries. However, it might take ten years to develop a modified set of tools, by which time the majority of consumers in India and China may have access to computing power and the internet, perhaps via a new generation of smartphones.

PREDICTION MARKETS

In a prediction market the respondents are asked to estimate how successful a concept is likely to be. The format of the interview is more like a stock market and less like a market research interview.

Prediction markets represent a radical departure from the traditional paradigm of market research (i.e. one based on random probability sampling of relevant consumers) and offer a very different method of evaluating new concepts. In the traditional market research approach to concept testing, a sample of relevant buyers is selected, ideally representative of the population of relevant buyers. The sample is shown the products (or asked to try the products, or view advertising for the products) and then asked how likely they are to buy the products.

In a prediction market test, a more general sample is recruited, with little or no effort to ensure they are representative of anything in particular. This general sample is then asked to 'gamble' on which concept or concepts they think are most likely to be successful, just as a stock market gambles on which companies are going to be successful.

IOWA ELECTRONIC MARKETS

The prime example cited by advocates of prediction markets are the Iowa Electronic Markets (IEM), a group of prediction markets which are operated by the University of Iowa, in the USA. Iowa Electronic Markets attempt to predict future events by allowing the people taking part to buy and sell 'positions' (similar to shares) in terms of events such as election results and economic indicators. The track record of the IEM in forecasting events has been very successful and is widely considered to compare well with opinion polling.

It should be noted that the IEM are just one example of prediction markets. The largest prediction market, in terms of turnover, is probably Betfair, a UK-based betting exchange. The Betfair model is, in turn, very similar to the way the markets for derivatives work in the financial arena. Another example of a prediction market is HSX, the Hollywood Stock Exchange, which has a good reputation in predicting movie-related successes.

WISDOM OF CROWDS

The underlying theory of prediction markets is expressed in James Surowiecki's book *The Wisdom of Crowds* (2004). Loosely, the idea of the Wisdom of Crowds is that getting a collection of people to make an estimate of something can be as good or better than asking for an expert view.

Surowiecki uses an anecdote about the late 19th-century British polymath Francis Galton to introduce and highlight his thesis. He tells how Galton visited a country fair where an ox was to be butchered. Those attending the fair were offered the chance to win a prize by estimating the butchered weight of the ox. About 800 fairgoers paid their sixpence and wrote an estimate on a piece of paper in the hope of a prize. Galton was surprised about two aspects of the results:

1. The average estimate of the weight was very close to the actual weight (1197 pounds versus 1198).

2. The average estimate of the visitors to the fair was closer than the estimate of any of the experts present.

The thesis developed by Surowiecki was that, under the right circumstances, the crowd can be wiser than the few. This thesis is also one of the underpinnings of the increasingly popular process of crowdsourcing (although crowdsourcing also includes collaboration and approaching the crowd in order to find an expert).

USING PREDICTION MARKETS IN MARKET RESEARCH

The person who has done the most to introduce prediction markets to market research has been John Kearon – the 'Chief Juicer' – of the UK agency BrainJuicer (although Kearon prefers the term 'predictive markets').

BrainJuicer's approach to prediction markets involves a streamlined methodology which enables the survey to be conducted in a shorter time frame than that used by exchanges such as the IEM. One of the benefits that Kearon puts forward for prediction markets is that they tend to differentiate between the products they are testing, something which traditional research often struggles to do.

There are also a number of examples of companies using prediction markets internally to assess innovations. For example, Google and Intel both have prediction markets where their staff can wager 'bets' on the likely successes of different innovations.

The key elements of using prediction markets in market research include:

○ *Recruiting a credible sample (the technique does not require the sample to be representative, but clients will often be more comfortable if they can see some link between the participants and their target customer groups).*

○ *Providing the participants with information about all of the products to be tested.*

○ *Utilising an online exchange, or some proxy, that allows each participant to buy or sell their interest in the products. The respondents hope to maximise their reward by ending up with more shares in the product that is the most successful.*

Further information about predictive markets can be found in papers by Kearon (e.g. Kearon, 2007).

PREDICTION MARKETS AND NEW*MR*

Prediction markets provide an example of some of the key benefits and tenets of NewMR. In particular, they are a response to the recognition that the samples used by most market researchers are not random probability samples, are not truly representative of the relevant population, and use questions that customers cannot answer accurately (for example, when respondents are asked to predict what they will do in some hypothetical future).

The question market researchers typically ask in a concept test is '*How likely are you to buy/try/use this product/service?*' There is a growing realisation, supported by research from behavioural economics and neuroscience, that people cannot answer these sorts of questions (Ariely, 2008; Earls, 2007; Lehrer, 2009; Lindstrom, 2008). According to this analysis, traditional market research asks questions that appear not to work, of a sample that is not representative, and consequently produces results that require benchmarks, norms, and post-processing to create useful market indications.

By contrast, prediction markets take a convenience sample, motivate the participants to try to win, and ask them to respond directly to whether the product will succeed rather than assess whether or not they would buy it.

The model that underlies traditional market research is based on the natural science model. Whilst this model has worked well in the physical sciences (after a couple of thousand years of development), its record in the social sciences is far weaker. By contrast, the prediction markets are based on a mixture of behavioural economics and pragmatism. The history of futures exchanges in commerce (upon which prediction markets are based) dates back to 1710 and the Dojima Rice Exchange in Japan.

MIXED PURPOSE RESEARCH

Traditionally market research was clearly demarcated from other activities, especially from marketing-related activities. This was done for several reasons, including not wanting to bias respondents, not wanting to alienate respondents, and because market research's 'non-marketing' status meant that in many countries it was granted partial exemptions to some regulations, for example from some 'do not call' legislation and some data protection rules.

However, over the last ten to 20 years this demarcation has tended to break down because of increased use of research techniques by non-market researchers, the growth in importance of databases and CRM systems, and the realisation by many brands that every interaction with a customer is a discussion.

The ethics of this topic, i.e. mixing market research and marketing, are covered elsewhere in this book. This section looks at the practical and research issues that are implied by mixed purpose research. The topics covered in this section on mixed purpose research are:

- ⚪ *Terminology*
- ⚪ *The orthodox view of research*
- ⚪ *Why companies want mixed purpose research*
- ⚪ *Why some respondents want mixed purpose research*
- ⚪ *Key areas for mixed purpose research*
- ⚪ *Best practice guidelines in mixed purpose research*

TERMINOLOGY

This chapter uses the term 'mixed purpose research' to describe the use of market research techniques for aims that are not solely market research, or indeed mainly market research. The classic example of mixed purpose research is to feed the results of a survey back into the client's database. Mixed purpose research is also referred to as 'Category 6' (a now defunct term used by the UK Market Research Society) and more quaintly as *'using research for non-research purposes'*.

Informed consent

The key concept that is central to all research, and especially mixed purpose research, is the one of 'informed consent'. Most legislation and regulation, in most countries, allows a very wide range of activities if they are based on informed consent. However, the debate often turns around what the words 'informed' and 'consent' mean.

A good example of how the term 'informed consent' can be given different interpretations is illustrated by a debate that took place in Europe in 2009. A new EU ruling meant that a site wishing to serve a cookie required informed consent (not just a market research site, all sites). To some people this meant alerting the user each time a site wanted to serve a cookie and requesting permission (something that might be impractical, and might render several types of service impossible). To others, it meant that any user who had not set their browser to reject or query cookies was giving 'informed consent', which is perhaps a wildly optimistic interpretation of both the word 'informed' and the idea of consent. This debate is ongoing and is likely to be a growing area of concern in the future.

Sugging

One phrase that opponents often use when talking about mixed purpose research is 'sugging', or 'selling under the guise of research', i.e. where people pretend to be conducting research but then try to sell something. Researchers, and most regulators, are unanimous in considering sugging to be wrong, and of course it fails the informed consent test. The term 'mixed purpose research' is based on telling people what is happening and gaining their consent, it is unrelated to sugging which is based on **not** telling people the object of the exercise.

THE ORTHODOX VIEW OF RESEARCH

Many researchers are moving into new areas and adopting techniques such as online research communities that appear to push or break official guidelines. However, there are also plenty of people who vigorously defend the traditional interpretation and remit of market research. For example, in a comment on the UK MRS's website Research-Live in October 2009, Geoff Gosling, the chairman of the UK's Market Research Standards Board, said:

> 'Want to build a client engagement panel, incentivising respondents with your own product and taking direct steps as a consequence of that engagement? No problem, researchers can help with that. Is that research? No. Is it using research techniques?'

Gosling makes the point that by sticking to a narrow definition of market research the industry is, in many countries, permitted to self-regulate, and is thereby exempted from many of the rules that restrict the activities of marketers and other users of data in the commercial sector.

WHY COMPANIES WANT MIXED PURPOSE RESEARCH

Two things have pushed many companies in the direction of saying they want, or that they need, to integrate market research results with their databases. The first is that they are now in a position to use the information, because technologies such as CRM have moved forward to the point where they are actually useful. The second is more philosophical; organisations have realised that every inter-action with a customer is a discussion, and every touch point should be used to enhance the service provided by the organisation. This second point means that every sales interaction should provide insight but, equally, every research contact should be part of the larger picture.

In those cases where market research is conducted in a way that implies that it is neutral – for example, when the sponsor of the research is not disclosed, as in a brand study – the issue of inte-grating the research information for mixed purposes rarely arises. Asking permission to send the respondent's information to brand X would make the respondent aware that the study was for brand X and might affect the results.

However, when the research is branded as being on behalf of the client and where the previous contact has been via the company's marketing database or via visits to their website, the case for the research being conducted for mixed purposes is much stronger.

In terms of market research permissions there is a difference between opt-out and opt-in. In opt-out the customer is deemed to have expressed informed consent if they have not said they disagree. In an opt-in system, informed consent derives from the customer actually saying they agree to whatever it is that is being requested. Best practice is to use opt-in based techniques. In many countries and under many research guidelines opt-in is required.

WHY SOME RESPONDENTS WANT MIXED PURPOSE RESEARCH

Any researcher who has looked at clients' databases should have noted that there are customers who tick the box saying they are happy to receive sales literature and sales calls, but who do not tick the box saying they are happy to take part in market research. One of the reasons for this is that there is a degree of altruism implied by the standard market research proposition. The research will help customers, but it might be irrelevant to the individuals taking part in the study.

By contrast, some respondents, when they take part in studies, want to become more involved: they want to directly influence the brand, or might want to buy the product they have just tested, or they may want the kudos of being the first to recommend it to their friends and colleagues.

One clear example of this phenomenon is in the area of online research communities. Although these are created as vehicles for market research, a well-run community usually results in its members being advocates for the brand and typically consuming more of the brand. Also, several researchers have found that the incentive the community members most value is the project sponsor's products – something which most market research guidelines have ruled as unacceptable.

As a consequence, most online research communities operate as mixed purpose research; because that is the way their members want them to operate.

KEY AREAS FOR MIXED PURPOSE RESEARCH

Several types of research are clearly mixed purpose research, such as database profiling and most mystery shopping, but most of these are not particularly relevant to the topic of online and social media research. Two areas of current interest in the mixed purpose research debate that directly relate to online and social media research are customer satisfaction and online research communities.

Customer satisfaction is frequently conducted as a communication between the organisation and its customers. The market research agency may be an independent third party, but it is often almost invisible to the customer, especially when the survey is conducted via the internet. The branding of the questionnaire, the covering message, and the style of the approach often reflect the client rather than the agency. For several years the research purity of customer satisfaction has been ebbing away, with increased facilities for respondents to pass on queries and complaints to the brand in an identi-fied way (if they ask to). Similarly, there is often pressure from respondents for incentives that are linked to the brand.

Some companies have already crossed the divide between customer satisfaction and identified research. For example, in 2006 the UK bank Egg reported how it was using identified research to benchmark individual employees in terms of identifiable online interviews, something that clearly falls outside traditional market research definitions (Jennick and Schwartz, 2006).

Online communities are often created as an opportunity for customers to talk to the organisation. Even though the community may be operated by a market research agency, the branding and the concept are often a two-way, collaborative conversation between the organisation and its customers. There is growing evidence that members of well-run communities become brand advocates, which in turn implies that the research process has itself directly improved sales, something that puts online research communities firmly in the mixed purpose category.

BEST PRACTICE GUIDELINES IN MIXED PURPOSE RESEARCH

The single most important step in a mixed purpose project is to check the current regulations and guidelines in the relevant countries and markets. This is a dynamic area and laws, regulations, and guide-lines are changing all the time.

As part of this key step the researcher needs to ascertain which laws, rules, and guidelines apply. For example a mixed research project may need to ensure that it conforms to direct marketing or distance selling laws or regulations. Researchers may be surprised to find that many of these rules are more onerous than market research ones. For example, in many countries a request from a subject to avoid all further contact is binding for a direct marketing company, but is only advisory for a company operating under market research rules.

The general trend, especially in Europe, is towards identifying whether a project is market research or not. If it is market research, the procedures for market research are adhered to. If the project is not market research, then steps are taken to ensure that nobody (not the client, not the respondents, and not any third parties) is given the impression that it is market research (since that would imply that the project is abiding by guidelines that do not apply). If a project contains elements that are market research and elements that are not, mixed purpose research may be the most accurate description, but from a regulatory point of view it is more appropriate to define it as 'non-market research'.

The following best practice notes are generic and should be revised in the light of the information collected in the first instance, i.e. the relevant rules in the relevant markets:

1. **Do no harm!** Even when a researcher works on a project that is not 'market research' they should not do anything that harms the respondent, the client, their organisation, or the standing and reputation of the market research industry.

2. **Avoid confusion.** If a project is not market research, for example because it links back to a marketing database, it must ensure that people do not think it is market research. This means avoiding reference to market research guidelines and organisations (including the avoidance of market research logos). Ideally, the words 'market' and 'research' should be avoided. Companies may find it useful to have two sets of documentation (along with two sets of privacy policies, and possibly sections of their website), to ensure that the whole company understands the difference between what is a market research project, and what is not.

3. **Understand what is considered a personal identifier.** The term 'personal identifier' is much broader than many people think it is. In many countries a personal identifier includes any of the following: name, address, telephone number, photo, IP address, digital fingerprint of their PC, postcode, email address, social network name, and Instant Messaging address. If a data set contains, or can readily be linked to, personal identifiers, it needs to be protected, and its use restricted by permissions.

4. **Informed consent.** Anything that happens with respect to respondents should be on the basis of informed consent, and the focus needs to be on the word 'informed'. This usually means making it clear why the information is being collected, where it will be stored, how it will be used, how long it will be stored, and how the respondent can avoid further contact or request the deletion of their data.

5. **Prior consent.** Consent should be sought before collecting information. Think about the sugging example: what makes it seem so 'wrong'? For example, somebody may ask you lots of questions about your house and your circumstances and then ask for your name and address so that a salesman can contact you to offer you a great deal. This process does have a sort of informed consent; before the key items, the name and address, are obtained there is information and a chance to decline or accept. But to many people this feels like they have been

taken for a 'sucker'. There was no informed consent about the time and effort contributed by the person in answering the earlier questions. A second, and very good, reason is that in many cases and many markets it is a legal requirement to obtain prior, not retrospective, nor delayed, permission.

6. **If it gets out?** When looking at the project, think about what would happen if the respondents or the media found out about the project. Would there be a fuss? Would there be negative publicity? Would it hurt the company's standing (remember rule 1 above)? In this internet linked, socially networked world, most things do get out, so projects and permissions need to be organised in ways that are not likely to cause embarrassment or worse.

7. **Agree all uses of the data before the fieldwork**. One of the greatest stresses that occur between a supplier and a buyer is when the buyer asks for something, say a copy of the videos from a project, that was not envisaged before the fieldwork was conducted. Because the use was not envisaged before the fieldwork it is unlikely that the respondent will have granted permission for that use, so the request may have to be turned down. In some countries it is OK to go back and ask each individual for their permission, but in others it is not acceptable.

8. **Liabilities pass with the data**. If data is passed to third parties, for example the client, or different parts of the company, the restrictions that apply to the data (i.e. anything for which explicit permission was not obtained) pass on to the third party, as well as remaining binding on the researcher. For example, if the respondent has been told that their comments will be deleted after 18 months, this has to happen for all copies of the information.

It is likely that increasing amounts of market research will be in the area of mixed purpose research and researchers will need to be vigilant in ensuring that they are conforming to both research and other guidelines and regulations.

DELIBERATIVE RESEARCH

Deliberative research is another example of research techniques being used in a way that many would not describe as market research and which can sometimes sit very uncomfortably with the profession's guidelines.

Deliberative research is a technique which explores how people's views change and mature when exposed to stimuli and when given the chance to discuss them and think about them. At one end of the spectrum the research simply presents the respondents with facts about the subject under inspection. For example, if a finance company was planning to launch a new and innovative product the research might take the form of explaining the product and then getting a respondent to keep a blog, listing all of those occasions when such a product might be of use.

At the other extreme, deliberative research can be based on showing the respondents alternative 'truths' to see which result in the respondents' developing specific views. From an ethics point of view this route is problematic because it potentially results in the respondent being 'changed' by the research in a way that may be beneficial to the organisation sponsoring the research and which may not be beneficial to the respondent.

One example of the problems that deliberative research can lead to was provided in October 2008 [http://www.research-live.com/news/opinion-leader-found-in-breach-of-mrs-code-of-conduct/3005328.article] when the UK's MRS found that the research agency Opinion Leader had breached its rules when conducting research for the UK Government in 2007. The MRS found that the agency had breached one of its rules, 'to ensure amongst other things that respondents would not be led towards a particular answer'. The complaint was that the choice of information given to the respondents led them towards accepting that nuclear power should be developed. The response of the agency was to assert 'We do not accept the MRS ruling, which we believe to be incorrect. We do not believe that the MRS – a market research trade body – is competent to assess these new forms of deliberative engagement.'

To some extent the argument about leading respondents is simply contextual. A test of twelve different TV ads that try to convey that a soft drink is more refreshing and trendy is not likely to raise much concern. Twelve ads that present climate change in different ways is likely to be seen as leading – there being an almost automatic assumption that is one of the ads is 'right' and the rest are 'wrong'.

Although the Opinion Leader example was from a face-to-face project, it is likely that online research communities will be a natural environment to exploit the opportunities presented by deliberative research, but the boundaries between 'informing' and 'leading' the members of such communities promises to be a tricky one.

DIY RESEARCH

DIY (do it yourself) research is a rapidly-growing area of online and social media research, despite the efforts of some market researchers to discourage it. There have always been some client-side researchers who have conducted their own focus groups, or executives who have engaged in 'meet the consumer' exercises, but these have been a very minor part of the total research picture.

The arrival of the internet has opened up a growing number of ways for brand managers, R&D teams, marketers, and even board directors to conduct their own research without going via insight teams or research providers. In business terms, these DIY researchers are disintermediating the research specialists, both the research providers and often the in-house insight teams.

In July 2009, on Research-Live, Tim Phillips told the story of a senior executive who described the process of conducting simple quantitative research as 'doing the monkey' because he tended to do this sort of research himself, using the Survey Monkey service (Phillips, 2009). This example is just a foretaste of a trend that could be a major factor in the research world.

DIY QUANTITATIVE SURVEYS

Survey platforms such as Survey Monkey and Zoomerang have made it very easy to create and administer simple surveys. Through the use of intuitive interfaces and well-designed templates, it is very easy, even for a novice, to create surveys that look and feel professional.

These DIY tools typically have multiple levels. The most basic level is often provided free. Higher levels are then offered for higher levels of fees, often using terms such as Professional or Premium. The highest level is offered at the highest price, but even these higher prices are typically much lower than the cost of using the large-scale products used by market research agencies.

Hard data on who exactly is using these products is hard to come by, but it is clear that these products have made major inroads into academia and amongst individuals and departments in companies wishing to do research without going through either agencies or their internal research departments.

The rise of these DIY tools has led to many market researchers counselling against them, but with others pointing out potential benefits.

The case against DIY quantitative surveys

Many professional market researchers, from both the vendor and buyer side of the industry, are dismissive of the use of DIY products by non-research specialists. Amongst the points they make are:

1. A questionnaire is a psychometric instrument. Writing a questionnaire that is likely to produce meaningful results (for example, one does not use leading or confounded questions) requires skills that the DIY user may not possess.

2. One of the key points about market research is ensuring that an appropriate sample is selected. Non-researchers may contact a convenience sample that might lead to misleading results being produced.

3. The indiscriminate use of these tools might lead to some potential respondents being inundated with survey requests. In the Research-Live article mentioned above, Sue Brooker, the deputy chair of the UK's MRS Standards Board is quoted as saying '*If people get too many surveys in their inbox which are badly designed, they're going to decide that all research is rubbish*'.

However, most of the pronouncements of market researchers on this subject have been in their own media, so it is unlikely that many of the users of these products will have heard or read them.

The case for DIY quantitative surveys

However, not all market researchers are opposed to the use of these DIY tools. The points they make include:

1. These tools have resulted in more people taking customers' views into account. Traditional market research is normally too expensive and time consuming for it to be used right across

an organisation. Where no research exists at the moment, surely it is better that people start to explore how to use it?

2. Many surveys from 'professional' market researchers are actually very poor. For example, there are many instances of surveys lasting 30 or even 40 minutes, with large attribute grids and batteries.

3. Is it that hard to learn how to conduct surveys? Many students have some exposure to the survey process at university, there are textbooks and workshops, and courses such as the University of Georgia's Principles of Marketing Research. Given the chance to conduct more research, many more people will learn how to conduct surveys, to help them find out what customers want and to provide better business insight.

4. If the tools become more popular they will become better.

Some researchers are more open-minded than the nay-sayers about change and progress. The Research-Live article quotes Kantar's social media knowledge leader, Tom Ewing, who believes that research needs to realise that the world is changing, and who says 'The people who are in the market for DIY research usually aren't in the market for bigger research. So, surely it is up to us to educate them how to use it?'

BYPASSING THE RESEARCH AGENCY

Some research buyers are bypassing the research agency by sending their questionnaire directly to access panel companies, who script and field the study and return the results. At the June 2009 Online Methods Conference in London, Unilever's Jaroslav Cir talked about how he uses panel companies to disintermediate the research agencies for simple projects. Cir's point was that if a project needs a simple survey, perhaps with a questionnaire that has been used several times before, then he tends to commission these projects directly with a panel supplier such as GMI.

This disintermediating approach is the logical conclusion to the commoditisation of some types of market research. Disintermediation has been a powerful force in commerce over the last 20 years, with functions that used to require people, like bank tellers, travel agents, and insurance agents, now being self-completed.

The key questions that a buyer needs to consider in deciding whether to bypass the research agencies are:

1. Do you know exactly what you want? For example, do you know who the sample should be and do you have the questionnaire?

2. Do you know a supplier who can be relied on? The buyer is probably looking for a one-stop-shop who can script and host the survey, supply the sample, and deliver the results in a suitable form.

3. Do you have the time and skills to extract the insight you need (or, perhaps aiming higher, the insight you want)?

4. Is the cost saving big enough to make it worthwhile?

When the answer to these four questions is yes, it makes sense for the research buyer to disinter-mediate the research agency.

By contrast, the main case for using an agency as a research supplier is where they can add value at one or more stages of a project. Areas where a market research agency might be able to add value include:

1. **Knowledge and specialisms**. Can the agency improve the scoping, design, construction, moni-toring, or analysis of the project? For example, by using learnings from other projects or buy applying specialist skills?

2. **Saving time**. If the booking and oversight of the project are going to take a significant amount of time, for example if several panel companies need to be contacted, then the agency can save the buyer time. The same point is true in terms of monitoring the project and conduct-ing the analysis – if a project needs monitoring and/or analysis.

3. **Capacity**. If the research buyer needs to complete several projects, it may be better to place the work externally to avoid being swamped.

4. **Independence**. The research will be more independent and may be seen as more credible if it is conducted by a specialist agency rather than being conducted internally.

5. **Risk reduction**. The project may appear simple, but an agency, especially a larger one, may have the resources to deal with unforeseen problems. Even having a second pair of eyes when creating the questionnaire will reduce the risk of making a major mistake.

The decision about whether to use an agency depends on whether value is being added. If value is being added, the second question is whether the value added is worth the premium an agency would charge.

COMMUNITIES AND OTHER SOCIAL MEDIA

In many ways the social media world is like the old Wild West, with few rules and with people staking claims all over the place. It is not surprising that at the same time as the research industry is coming to grips with the research opportunities and implications of social media, many organisations are roll-ing up their sleeves and starting to use a variety of new techniques themselves. Amongst the many activities that are being undertaken on a DIY basis are:

1. **Communities**. Software such as Ning allows anybody to create a community at almost zero cost and with few technical skills. In many cases, these communities are being created by business units such as the R&D team and are completely bypassing internal insight departments.

2. **Facebook groups and pages.** A large number of brands have created one or more presences on Facebook and have used them to have conversations with customers. These groups and pages are often looked after by marketing or brand teams rather than researchers. Indeed, many companies have created applications (for example Facebook applications) to both engage potential customers and to find out more about them.

3. **Co-creation.** There has been an explosion in the use of co-creation, often in the guise of a competition, to engage customers and to generate and evaluate new ideas. These projects are sometimes run by, or in association with, researchers, but they are typically run by marketing or e-marketing teams and often without any research involvement.

4. **Twitter and blog mining.** Most 'switched on' organisations are searching and monitoring Tweets and blog posts. At the very least this is done to monitor mentions of the brand, at the more sophisticated level it is done to gain insights into customers' lives.

The burgeoning world of social media is possibly the area where the need for DIY approaches will develop the most. The growth of social media is all about the concepts of free conversation and authenticity. The traditional research process of using a third party to carefully research a specific topic is likely to be too expensive, too indirect, and too slow for many situations.

The challenge for professional researchers is how to add an additional level of value to the interactions that brands are developing with their customers.

17 The Business of Market Research

As well as providing a medium for conducting market research the internet has also had a major impact on how the business of market research is being conducted. For example, the internet is creating new ways of connecting, sub-contracting, collaborating, and delivering value. In many cases these changes are resulting in reduced costs and increased capacity. The internet has also created new weaknesses and business concerns, such as security and reliability, which have in turn added extra costs to the way market research companies are run.

Many of the earlier chapters in this book have mentioned how changes are impacting on the business of market research, but those references were in most cases tangential to the topic being covered at that point. This chapter looks specifically at some of the key internet-related trends that are reshaping the way that market research conducts its business. These topics include:

- *Remote working*
- *Researcher networks*
- *New forms of research*
- *New competitors*
- *Changes to the research business model*
- *Outsourcing and offshoring*
- *Systems' security and reliability*
- *Online reporting*
- *Quality and ethics*

REMOTE WORKING

The internet has made a major difference to the ability of people involved in the research industry to work remotely. In this context, remote includes working from home, from satellite offices, from hotel rooms, and even working whilst attending conferences.

Over the last 20 years researchers who are on the road (between offices, attending groups, presenting to clients, and attending conferences) have transformed from being largely out of contact to being in almost continual contact via mobile phones, email, and Wi-Fi access to files and surveys. It is a moot point whether this change in connectivity has led to the shortening of project timelines for market research or has been a consequence of the shortening of timelines.

Whilst remote working has delivered cost savings to organisations, in terms of being able to utilise higher percentages of its employee time it has also introduced security problems and concerns. Although most of the horror stories are from outside the market research industry, there are many examples of lost laptops, lost data sticks, emails going astray, and remote access systems being hacked. One consequence of security concerns is that there is a growing divide between some research companies who maximise the benefits of remote working and connectivity and others who lock their systems down so securely (for example, banning their staff from synchronising their office iPhone diaries) that their staff are quite limited in what they can do remotely.

RESEARCHER NETWORKS

Traditionally, market researchers have been members of networks within their companies, and to a lesser extent with researchers they meet at conferences or on training courses. The internet has added many other methods of connecting, some of which appear to be creating networks that are becoming very significant and which may well change the way researchers share information and challenge existing power structures.

NETWORKING PEOPLE

A growing number of researchers are networking via social networks such as Facebook, LinkedIn, and Twitter. At market research conferences it is observable that there are two sorts of networking happening in parallel. The first is the traditional business card swapping sort of networking, where strangers meet, discuss a topic, such as the presenter in the last session, and then swap cards. The social network version tends to work the other way round: first, people make some sort of contact, perhaps by reading tweets or by joining in a discussion on some topic in LinkedIn, and then seek each other out at the conference.

One example of how people are networking is via the LinkedIn groups function. Some of the market research groups on LinkedIn now have over 10000 members, making them larger than national and international research associations. The key to how these groups provide engagement is via their discussions. Members post discussion topics and, if they catch the group's attention, a genuine discussion takes off. When people notice comments they agree with they are drawn towards 'friending' them and establishing more contact (in LinkedIn friends are called 'contacts').

Twitter is being used by a growing number of market researchers to create very *ad hoc* networks. Researchers such as Nigel Legg (@nigellegg), Susan Sweet (@SusanSweet), Diane Hessan (@CommunispaceCEO), and Kathryn Korostoff (@ResearchRocks) have created a significant presence on Twitter, putting them in touch with new people, and putting the people who follow them in touch with new people.

Another way that researchers network online is around the more influential market research blogs, for example the blogs written by Nigel Hollis (Millward Brown, http://www.mb-blog.com), Alison Macleod (The Human Element, http://mackle.wordpress.com/), Jeffrey Henning (Vovici, http://blog.vovici.com/), and Katie Harris (ZebraBites, http://zebrabites.com/) all regularly attract a number of comments. The people making these comments are in effect creating a network, and will often refer each other to new interesting ideas and posts.

Beyond the standard social networks there are a number of networks created specifically for market researchers, such as ResearchVoice (http://www.research-voice.com/) and Market Research Global Alliance (http://www.mrgasn.com/). These networks all add something that their organisers and members feel is missing from the more generic networks.

NETWORKING IDEAS

The use of social media by market research is doing more than connecting people together; it is facilitating the transmission of ideas and memes. For example, many of the ideas that underpin NewMR were developed in the discourse of these networks and online forums. In the future, many of the new ideas in market research may originate and be refined in this cyberspace, rather than inside individual companies.

The Further Information section at the end of the book has a list of some key social networks, groups, blogs, and researchers on Twitter who are all worth following, but it can only represent a small cross-section of everything that is on the net. *The Handbook of Online and Social Media Research* website has a more up-to-date list, and this will be updated.

NEW FORMS OF RESEARCH

As well as providing a new data collection modality for traditional research approaches, for example for survey research and focus groups, the internet has helped create new forms of research, particularly:

- ○ **Web analytics**: *measuring who is using which website, what they are doing, and how often they do it.*

- ○ **Website research**: *looking at what makes a good website, what the users think of it, and who the users are.*

- ○ **Asynchronous techniques**: *such as bulletin board groups and online research communities.*

- O **Blog and buzz mining research**: *listening to the conversations that people are having with each other.*

- O **Social and collaborative research**: *for example, using online research communities.*

- O **E-ethnography**: *exploring aspects of people's lives through online discourses.*

- O **WE-research**: *for example, allowing participants to help capture the stories of their own lives, using tools such as blogs, webcams, and mobile phones.*

Each of these new forms of market research is explored in greater detail elsewhere in the book, but it is useful to note the number of new forms that have been created by the internet, and then to recall that the world wide web is only about 20 years old. One result of all these new areas of research is that it is even harder for one researcher, or even one company, to be fully informed of what is happening and of how to utilise different approaches (which is one reason this book was written).

NEW COMPETITORS

The adoption of the internet as a data collection modality and as a method of answering insight questions has put market research in competition with a growing range of rivals, amongst whom are:

- O *e-marketing companies, who feel happy to include surveys in their mix of business services*

- O *website and database providers, who are happy to create online communities and run online polls*

- O *website and usability professionals who are happy to run popup surveys and qualitative research*

- O *online community specialists who see research as simply one part of the services they offer*

- O *web analytics companies, offering blog and buzz mining and user analytics*

- O *brands doing their own research either using the new DIY tools such as Zoomerang or by going directly to online panel companies.*

In addition, there is the 'now traditional' competitor, i.e. management consultants.

CHANGES TO THE RESEARCH BUSINESS MODEL

The internet has had a major impact on the business model of many market research organisations, moving the key cost element away from fieldwork and towards client service. An illustration of the cost ratios of different field costs was shown by the ESOMAR 2007 Prices Study, which indicated that, overall, telephone only costs about 60% of what face-to-face studies cost, and that online research only costs about 60% of what telephone studies cost.

In the days of face-to-face research, fieldwork was a major cost in the research process, often the single largest cost component. Indeed, it was not unusual for some agencies to simply mark-up the cost of the fieldwork to calculate their price to the client, and even some of the larger agencies monitored the ratio of field to other costs as part of their key management metrics. The competence of many research companies, particularly the larger ones, was partly assessed in terms of their ability to recruit and manage a field force of interviewers, spread around the country, to produce sampling frames, to print and distribute questionnaires, and to collate and punch surveys.

In the days of telephone research, the interviewing was still a major cost, even though not as large as face-to-face. The price of the fieldwork was still a major driver of the price of the research to the end client. The competences of agencies, especially the larger ones, included the ability to run call centres, employing large numbers of people on relatively low wages.

In the world of the internet as a data collection modality there are two main ways of obtaining the sample: online access panels and client databases. In the case of client databases, the marginal cost of one more interview approaches zero – for example, if a sample comprises 500 interviews from the client's database, the cost of interviewing 501 is very similar. (Note that large increases in the sample size do have an impact on the costs. For example an increase from a sample of 500 to 1000 creates more monitoring, potentially more coding, and opens up the opportunities for more analysis.)

In the days of face-to-face and telephone research it was usual for agencies to have their own field forces and call centres, but this is much less common with online access panels, where the large providers, such as e-Rewards and SSI, are used by a very wide range of agencies. When an agency works with an online access panel, the cost of one more survey is not close to zero, but it is much lower than it was with older data collection modalities.

A market research agency using internet data collection will typically have more IT and technical people than an agency using face-to-face or telephone interviewing. IT and technical people tend to be paid somewhat more than interviewers, and often more than the middle-ranking market researcher.

The net results of the changes that are implied by moving from face-to-face to internet data collection are:

○ *The same volume of internet research generates a smaller total amount of revenue compared with face-to-face and telephone projects, on average. Assuming that inter-agency competition will result in the savings in the fieldwork costs eventually being reflected in lower prices to the client.*

○ *Research agencies that mostly use online survey research tend to employ fewer people than agencies who employ field forces or telephone interviewers.*

○ *Average and median wages tend to be higher in agencies that are predominantly using internet data collection for survey research.*

     ◯   *The cost of the fieldwork is no longer the main driver of the prices charged to end clients.*

If the trend towards online research communities continues, then there will be further changes to the cost and employment structure of research agencies. Even when an online research community is being used to replace a quantitative study, its costs and its demands on researcher time tend to be much more like qualitative research than quantitative research. This trend would move the business model even further towards one based on researcher time, and even less on the cost of other inputs.

OUTSOURCING AND OFFSHORING

Outsourcing and offshoring have both become a much larger part of the business of market research over the last 20 years, and this change has been accelerated by the internet. This is partly because the nature of online research lends itself to compartmentalisation and partly because the internet is itself the medium for many forms of outsourcing and offshoring.

Outsourcing refers to the process of using a third-party company to supply a service that contributes towards the total service being offered to the end client. One major example in market research is the use of online access panels. Before the growth of telephone and online research modalities, many research companies had field forces, i.e. teams of interviewers who were responsible for the domestic interviews (international fieldwork has typically been outsourced for many years, for all but the largest multinational companies).

The term 'subcontracting' can often be used interchangeably with 'outsourcing', although it has perhaps more of an inference of a short-term arrangement, and outsourcing has more of an implication of an ongoing relationship.

'Offshoring' refers to moving a process from one country to another. The term covers both moving processes to a subsidiary in another country and moving processes to an outsourcer in another country. When people use the term 'offshoring' they may be thinking specifically about moving projects to countries with different quality and legal systems, or they might simply be referring to moving projects from one country to another. For most commentators, moving a project from USA to Canada is offshoring, as is moving a project from the UK to Ireland; however, there are some people who use the term differently.

One area of concern that is specific to offshoring, as opposed to outsourcing, is that the process may be moving outside the legal framework of the domestic market. If intellectual property or sensitive information is moved from one country to another, are the agency's and the end client's rights as protected as they would be in their home market?

In late 2009, an organisation called the Federation for Transparency in Offshoring (FTO) was created and this led to much heated debate in various market research online forums. The two main complaints about the FTO were that it did not call for transparency in outsourcing and that one of its two logos was a 'No Offshoring' logo. Taken together, these two factors led many to assert that the FTO was more about protectionism and less about transparency, a charge it vigorously denied.

The twin topics of outsourcing and offshoring are likely to stay at the fore of research discussion as there are several currents at play, including:

- *Data protection legislation*

- *Increasingly sophisticated contracts*

- *Protectionism*

- *Quality concerns*

- *Process integration*

- *Specialisation and cost savings*

These topics are discussed below.

DATA PROTECTION LEGISLATION

Many countries have passed legislation restricting the movement of some types of information across national borders. For example, the EU (the European Union) has strict laws about moving personal data outside the EU area, and within Germany the government has passed legislation restricting the movement of some types of data outside Germany. It is likely that the number of these laws and rules will increase, which will tend to inhibit offshoring.

INCREASINGLY SOPHISTICATED CONTRACTS

There has been a trend for the buyers of research to use increasingly sophisticated and all embracing contracts, which often require (amongst many other things) outsourcing and subcontracting to be specified in the proposal. These contracts also often include clauses about the movement of data and intellectual property that are more restrictive than the rules laid out by national legislation. This trend may reduce the drift towards outsourcing and offshoring.

PROTECTIONISM

During recessions, and periodically in response to popular political pressure, there tends to be a rise in protectionism, often supported by popular pundits such as Lou Dobbs (Dobbs, 2004). Protectionism may reduce the amount of offshoring.

QUALITY CONCERNS

As with all new processes, one bad experience can result in a major disinclination to use something. There are a considerable number of anecdotal accounts of problems with outsourcing, in particular call centres, especially to non-native speakers of the respondents' languages.

PROCESS INTEGRATION

The rise of multinational companies and the growth in the range of internet tools has made it harder to define exactly where some processes take place. One example of this is the growth in the use and size of the online access panel companies. A large panel company may have a local office, but its panel may be managed in another country, and its invitations may be emailed from that separate country. The respondents may be from the local market, but the servers for the project may be in a third country, and may be backed up in another. As the trend moves towards cloud computing this process will become ever harder to define.

SPECIALISATION AND COST SAVINGS

Research, especially online research, is being broken into specialities, for example scripting, creating Flash tools, panel provision, survey hosting, coding, and tabulation. One of the key drivers of this process is the cost savings that it generates. The reality of a competitive market is that it is very hard for one company to avoid using techniques such as outsourcing or offshoring if their competitors are offering lower prices, unless there is a quality difference that the client is willing to pay for.

THE FUTURE FOR OFFSHORING AND OUTSOURCING?

At the moment, the pressure of legislation, control cultures, and protectionism is pulling against outsourcing and offshoring. However, against that trend, the forces of process integration and economics are pulling in the other direction.

It may be that the final outcome will be increased levels of outsourcing and offshoring, but perhaps with increased levels of transparency and contractual rigour.

SYSTEM SECURITY AND RELIABILITY

The growth in the usefulness of the internet has been matched by a growth in the risk of IT systems being compromised, either in terms of unauthorised usage (e.g. hacking) or of not being available (e.g. system downtime). The net result of these risks is that an ever larger proportion of companies' budgets is being spent on making their IT systems more secure and more reliable. It has also resulted in more procedures and restrictions on what people are allowed to do in order to maintain the integrity of systems.

This section briefly looks at three areas where there have been changes and assesses the likely near-future implications for the business of market research.

- *System security*

- *System reliability*

- *Changes to procedures*

SYSTEM SECURITY

The main element of system security reviews is to look at all the entry points to a company's IT system and, where necessary, take measures to mitigate risks. The following list highlights some of the key areas of concern:

- *sending and receiving information to and from a client*

- *sending and receiving information to and from subcontractors and partners*

- *sending and receiving information to and from respondents*

- *sending and receiving information to and from employees*

- *the use of third-party systems, for example SaaS options such as survey systems and online focus group software*

- *avoiding any physical loss of data, for example on laptops or data sticks.*

The four sending and receiving issues mentioned above have many similarities, and there are some key steps that are common to all four in terms of improving security. This is because in most cases the sending and receiving relates to some usage of the internet.

Sending versus connecting

There are four main ways that information travels from the company to others (e.g. to clients, staff, and suppliers).

1. The information is sent via some medium (e.g. email or post).

2. The information is placed somewhere for the other party to pick it up (for example www. yousendit.com or a third-party portal).

3. The sender connects to the recipient's system and uploads it (e.g. the sender logs onto the recipient's extranet or ftp site and uploads the information).

4. The recipient connects to the system of the sender and downloads it (e.g. the recipient logs onto the sender's extranet or ftp site and downloads the information).

With options 1 and 2 the key security step is the encryption of the information, just in case the information ends up in the wrong hands. Another important process with options 1 and 2 is to use secure systems, which is why some companies will not let their staff use mobile devices such as iPhones or third-party cloud-based systems such as Google mail to convey company information.

With options 3 and 4 the key security steps are user authentication (e.g. strong and frequently changed passwords) and systems procedures to tightly limit the areas that can be reached when connected, i.e. the right data is available to the right people, but nothing else.

Internal security

One area that has increased dramatically over the last few years relates to the requirement to limit employees' access to data and systems on a 'need to use' basis. In the past, it was not uncommon for everybody on a team to have access to all the projects that the team worked on, to improve flexibility and to provide cover. The current trend is to authorise data access to the fewest number of people possible, on a project-by-project and system-by-system basis, to improve security.

SYSTEM RELIABILITY

As computing in general, and the internet in particular, has become more central to how market research companies operate, the issue of reliability has become more critical. Key elements in the search for reliability include:

- ○ *the company's servers and intranet*

- ○ *virus protection*

- ○ *the company's connection to the internet*

- ○ *the ability of interviewing systems to be available 24/7*

CHANGES TO PROCEDURES

For many years, some companies have used physical security procedures such as empty desk protocols (i.e. where researchers have to ensure that everything on their desk is locked away when they are not there). These procedures are becoming more common and are being updated to encompass the use of computer and the internet:

- ○ *bans or strict limits on the use of data sticks*

- ○ *bans on using mobile phones to access company mail servers*

- ○ *bans on storing and working on company files on laptops*

Client contracts and audits

Over the last few years, an increasing number of clients have sought to put tighter contracts in place, specifying security and reliability procedures. Additionally, some clients now ask their IT departments (or a third-party specialist) to audit their suppliers' procedures to ensure that they meet the client's specifications. These trends are likely to continue and could have a significant impact on some research companies and the way some researchers work.

ONLINE REPORTING

At one level, online reporting is simply a faster, more direct way of doing what researchers have always done in terms of gathering information and sending information and insight to colleagues and clients. However, online reporting is changing the client–supplier relationship from a set of discrete moments to a continuous process.

Online reporting has introduced flexibility and has the potential to reduce the cost per item reported. However, it also has the potential to increase costs with its increased capacity and 24/7 requirements. The business implication of online reporting tends to be high initial and fixed costs, with the prospect of speed, quality, and cost efficiencies in the medium term.

Online reporting has two dimensions: firstly, reporting on process information, and secondly, communicating research findings.

PROCESS REPORTING

Online data collection systems (including CATI systems), along with project management systems, produce a rich flow of project management information. The information that process reporting provides includes:

○   *the number of people invited to take part in a survey*

○   *the number of screen-outs, incompletes, and completes*

○   *errors and system messages*

○   *time-related information, for example, surveys completed by time of day*

○   *information about the respondents, including browser information, country, operating systems*

○   *top line results and quota details, for example, demographics and the results for key questions*

Process reporting has the potential to improve project management and help identify problems earlier than they would otherwise be identified. Process reporting creates the opportunity for the researcher to be much more hands on than was the case with more traditional business models. However, there is a time penalty to be paid if the researcher is more hands on, especially on those projects where nothing goes wrong.

RESEARCH FINDINGS

In this section, the term 'findings' refers to a wide range of deliverables, including presentations, reports, dashboards, aggregated data, cross tabulations, and raw data.

Traditionally, findings were communicated via paper and overhead transparencies or, occasionally, via photographs and 35 mm slides. Over the last 30 years there has been a continuing revolution in how findings can be communicated. The medium of storage and delivery has developed from floppy disks to email, ftp, and portals.

The findings can be reported using three different paradigms:

- ○ *Static*

- ○ *Interactive*

- ○ *Dynamic*

Static reporting

Static reporting can be thought of as '*view only*' reporting and is almost a definition of a 1.0 (as opposed to a 2.0) approach. Static reports are not dynamically linked to the data and cannot themselves be used interactively.

Examples of static reporting include PowerPoint presentations and cross-tabulations when they are delivered in Microsoft Word or PDF format.

One of the key advantages of static reporting is that everybody is looking at the same thing with the same information. Most projects have some key documents (for example, the brief, proposal, questionnaire, project report) which need to be stored in a reliable static form; dynamic is not always better.

Because static documents are less likely to be edited or changed they can be spread more widely through an organisation than either interactive or dynamic reporting.

Interactive reporting

An interactive report is one that allows the user to interrogate the data to create alternative perceptions or representations. Examples of interactive reporting include electronic tables (such as E-Tabs [http://www.e-tabs.com]), raw data interrogation systems (such as Quanvert [http://www.spss.com/

software/data-collection/quantime/quanvert.htm]), and what-if simulators (either bespoke systems or configured in Microsoft Excel).

The benefits of interactive reporting include the ability to specify different slices of the data and to model changes. The main business change is that the process moves from being focused on the moment of the delivery of the report to a more continuous process.

Dynamic reporting

Most web reporting systems offer some degree of dynamic reporting. A dynamic report is one that changes as additional reports are generated or additional information is gathered.

Some forms of dynamic reporting are designed for the researcher or the systems team, to help with the managing and analysis of the project. Other dynamic reporting options are designed to send information to the clients to improve their access to information. The automation of this sort of reporting offers the opportunity to reduce costs, but it can also increase costs, and can create a major change in the paradigm of vendor/buyer relationship, from discrete moments to a continuous feed.

One typical use of dynamic reporting for clients relates to tracking projects, for example an ongoing customer satisfaction project. In a traditional project, the client might have received monthly reports, with perhaps a two week delay. With dynamic reporting, the client can interrogate the data on a daily basis to see what the latest figures are, and potentially drill down to a specific product, franchise, or area.

Because the number and size of data sets available to clients have been growing ever larger there has been a growth in the development of dashboards. A dashboard is a simplified reporting system which highlights key items that require attention, often incorporating some element of colour coding (for example, flagging potential bad news in red).

Dynamic reporting can raise its own specific challenges for its users. If an analyst spots something interesting in the data then he/she needs some way of 'freezing' it before sending a report to clients or colleagues. If the analysis is not frozen it may appear differently for each viewer, for example, if they view the report at a different time and if new data have been added.

Another issue for suppliers of research is that if data is sent to clients periodically, they can operate a quality check process that is also periodic, which is usually more accurate, efficient, and cost effective than continuously monitoring the data. However, if the research buyer could be accessing the data continuously, the vendor needs to adopt a continuous process for checking the data and keeping themselves up to date, which is usually not the most efficient way of running a project.

DELIVERY PARADIGMS

There are two very distinct delivery paradigms for online reporting – Push and Pull. The paradox about these two delivery paradigms is that in general the Pull paradigm is the one that is more popular, whilst the Push is (in most cases) the more effective.

A **Push** delivery system is one where the research supplier sends the data to the research buyer. The main example of a Push system is where the data is emailed to the client, for example as an attachment or as a link to data on an extranet.

A **Pull** system is one where the data is made available to the research buyer so they can access it at their convenience, for example via a research or results portal.

Pull systems are generally considered very appealing since they help the research buyer organise the data, they avoid the buyer being overloaded with emails, and they can provide a method of combining reports from different projects.

However, in many cases data made available on Pull systems is accessed much less than data received via a Push method. Most research buyers are very busy and if they have to remember to go to a portal to fetch a report they may only do it when they really need to. Alternatively, if they receive a Push delivery, perhaps accompanied with a brief message saying something like *'Look at the sales in the South, they seem to be catching up at last!'*, they are more likely to look at it straight away.

The key driver about the effectiveness of Pull systems appears to be how essential the data is to its recipient. If the user needs the information in order to be able to do their day-to-day job, then a Pull system is great, and represents significant benefits for both the vendor and the buyer. If, however, the data is not regarded as essential, or only needed occasionally, then Push systems are more likely to result in the information providing benefit to the research buyer than a Pull system.

Delivery systems

For many years the default delivery system for reports, data, and other information has been email, but there are a number of other possibilities, in particular extranets, ftp sites, portals, desktop/messenger systems, and these are examined below.

Extranet

An extranet is an extension to an intranet. An intranet is a bit like the internet, but it exists within an organisation and is only accessible to people within that organisation. Normally, intranets are protected by a sophisticated set of security levels and permission-based access systems.

An extranet is where a company provides a third-party company access to a small section of their intranet, so that data can be transferred from the third party and made available to their organisation. For the research buyer, the key benefits are that the supplier carries most of the work and costs and that the structure of the data tends to match the buyer's preferred layout and systems.

An extranet reporting system is essentially a Pull system, but it can readily be made hybrid by ensuring that the research provider sends the buyer an email when the data becomes available, including links to it, and highlighting something interesting in the data.

FTP

FTP has become an old-fashioned method of moving data from one organisation to another, although it is one that is still loved by some IT departments (because it is low cost and can be made very secure). An FTP site is accessed via a special mode of internet browsing (using FTP, File Transfer Protocol). The data provider puts the data onto an FTP site (using appropriate passwords, security, and encryption), and tells the buyer that it is available. The research buyer then downloads the data after which the provider removes it from the FTP site.

FTP tends to be a Pull method. It also tends to be an indirect method because, these days, the downloading is normally not conducted by the research user but often by an IT, systems, or admin person.

Portal

A portal is typically provided by the research provider or by some third party (such as Confirmit's Reportal). A portal is a specialist location accessed via the internet. Research providers put the data on the portal and make it available to the research buyer.

The default paradigm for a portal is as a Pull system. However, this can be ameliorated by the researcher supplier sending links and messages to the research buyer to highlight points of special interest.

Desktop/messenger systems

Another approach to reporting is to supply the research buyer with either a desktop application or an online tool that delivers alerts to their screen when something interesting happens. The alerts can be triggered by the research supplier or they can be triggered from dashboard and/or exception reporting systems.

Instead of sending alerts to the user's screen they can also be configured to send messages to one or more of email, SMS, Instant Messaging, or other messaging systems.

QUALITY AND ETHICS

Quality and ethics have been discussed at various points in this book, in the context of the topics being covered at that point. In this section, quality and ethics are reviewed in terms of how they influence the business context for market research.

This section starts by looking at quality concerns, particularly reliability and validity, and the measures that have been taken to address these issues. It then goes on to discuss the ethical issues, including the risk of harm to respondents, the boundaries between marketing and market research, and the issues relating to data protection and security. Finally, it reviews the outlook for further changes in this field.

However, before embarking on a review of the quality and ethical issues and their impact on the business of market research, it is useful to take a high-level view of the quality and ethical issues. Because the internet in general, and social media in particular, is changing and evolving so quickly, official views, guidance, and legislation about quality and ethical considerations are likely to lag behind what is happening in commercial research.

This lack of formal guidance means it is useful for companies to have a set of guiding principles in the field of ethics and quality. For example, one such guiding principle is '*If something a market researcher is doing were to come to the attention of the public, to clients, or to colleagues, would it lower the reputation or standing of the researcher or of market research in general?*' If the answer is yes, then there is an ethical issue, whether or not it currently breaks a specific guideline or law.

EXTERNAL DRIVERS OF ETHICAL AND QUALITY ISSUES

It is important to acknowledge that many of the changes affecting market research come from the outside world, sometimes through the mechanism of government legislation or directives, sometimes through the actions of companies in other business sectors, for example the increased provision of popup blockers and spam lists and filters.

Government legislation and directives

Over the last 20 years, many governments (including the supranational EU) have been very active in passing legislation and issuing directives that affect market research in general, and often online research in particular. These laws and directives have included:

1. **'Do not call' and 'Do not email' legislation.** These rules tend to be aimed at telemarketing and email marketing, but sometimes they have had a direct effect on market research, and in other cases have required market research to define itself very narrowly to avoid being caught by the new rules.

2. **Distance selling legislation.** These rules are often focused on what can be done via mail, phone, and the internet, and again have required the market research industry to take steps to ensure that it could separate itself from marketing.

3. **Child protection legislation.** Some forms of this type of legislation restrict the way that children are contacted, for example the USA's Children's Online Privacy Protection Act (COPPA). In other cases, it restricts who can contact children, for example the UK requires moderators for children's research (including online) to undergo a Criminal Records Bureau (CRB) check.

4. **Age-related rules.** Beyond the issue of children, there are often laws or directives relating to specific products. For example, in the UK the minimum age for interviewing people about their alcohol consumption is 18, but in the USA it is 21.

5.   **Data protection and privacy legislation**. Many countries have passed legislation protecting personal data and restricting what can be done with it. For example, the EU has directives that greatly restrict the transfer of personally-identifiable information outside its borders. In many markets, companies have to nominate a senior employee who will be legally liable for what the company does.

6.   **Online accessibility legislation**. Various laws have been passed around the world requiring websites (which can sometimes include web surveys) to be suitable for people with disabilities or restricted access. This type of legislation often requires the existence of policies such as privacy or prior permission before serving things like cookies or gathering information about a respondent's computer.

7.   **Gaming and gambling**. Countries have very different rules about what constitutes gambling and on how gambling is regulated. An internet survey with a prize draw for $500 as the incentive may require quite different rules and procedures in different countries.

8.   **Employment protection, equal rights, and minimum wages** are all alleged to have increased the cost of employing interviewers and to have increased the attractiveness of the cost benefits provided by online surveys, contributing to the change in the balance of one modality versus another.

In general, these laws are the result of coercion from the public and pressure groups and the occasional scandal. The pressure for change has, in many cases, grown in response to how easy and how cheap the internet has made it to contact people.

There is a concern that if one country or region adopts legislation which is more restrictive than other areas, there may be a flight towards less regulated countries, given that some elements of market research, such as emailing, can be conducted from anywhere in the world.

Private sector initiatives

Whilst governments can pass legislation to change how the internet is used, the private sector (including volunteers) can change it by providing new software tools or services. The key ones that relate to market researchers are:

   O   *popup blockers*

   O   *spam filters*

   O   *HTML filters*

Avoiding being seen as a spammer

If a research organisation wants to stay in business it is almost essential that it avoids being labelled a spammer.

IT companies have responded to the deluge of spam in two key ways. The first is to make email programs smarter in the way they spot spam, for example by looking for specific patterns within the message. The second has been the creation of the DNSBLs. DNSBLs are lists of domain names thought to be involved in malware (e.g. sending viruses or tracking software) or spamming. If company's domain appears on this list it is very difficult for them to send emails, so it is important that market research invitations are not conducted in a way that results in them being added to one or more DNSBLs.

A white list is the opposite of a DNSBL, i.e. it is a list of domains that have signed up to specific procedures, and an increasing number of market research organisations are signing up to white lists to help ensure that their emails and invitations are received.

A SHORT HISTORY OF QUALITY, RELIABILITY, AND VALIDITY CONCERNS

Since bursting onto the scene in the mid-1990s, online data collection has been subject to concerns about its validity and reliability. The initial concerns were centred on the relatively low level of internet penetration and some concerns relating to methodological issues about moving offline studies online – for example from moving from an interview mode to a self-completion mode. The volume of quality, reliability, and validity concerns lessened between the years 2000 to 2005, but they never went away completely.

However, from 2005 to 2009 a number of concerns emerged, leading to a variety of initiatives by those with a substantial stake in online market research. An article by Reg Baker (*Research World*, June 2008) outlined some key milestones. In 2005, Jeff Hunter of General Mills reported conducting the same concept test using two samples from the same panel; the two studies provided different business recommendations. This was followed by similar results from others. The highest profile 'wobble' was created when Procter & Gamble's Kim Dedeker produced a similar finding at the Respondent Co-operation Summit in Chicago in 2006, and challenged the '*integrity and methodology*' of online research.

The discussion about online research quality crystallised around a number of topics:

○ *The ability of online panels to generate results that were reliable (i.e. the same from one use to another) and valid (projectable to the population).*

○ *The role of so-called professional respondents (respondents who do many studies and who appear to be highly motivated by the rewards).*

○ *Duplicate respondents, who join up to a single panel multiple times and also those who might be invited more than once when one panel uses a sample from other panels to meet requests too large to be satisfied from its panel alone.*

○   *Respondents who falsify the answers to screening questions in order to be classed as eligible for the study.*

○   *The growing tendency of some respondents to respond to longer surveys by simply 'clicking through' to the end, something that has been described by Jon Krosnick as 'satisficing'.*

The concerns raised about quality issues have led to a number of initiatives by trade bodies, providers, and buyers of market research. Three key initiatives are ESOMAR's Guidelines, the ARF Online Quality Research Council, and the growth in market research ISO Standards. These three topics are outlined below.

ESOMAR's Online Research Initiatives

From the earliest days of online data collection, ESOMAR has sought to provide guidance on the proper use of the internet in market research processes. Amongst these initiatives are:

○   **Conducting Research Using the Internet.** *These guidelines cover most of the issues that researchers using online processes will face, and provide several useful examples, such as an example privacy policy. Most national research bodies also have similar guidelines.*

○   **26 Questions to Help Research Buyers of Online Samples.** *This list of 26 questions was first introduced in 2005 and has been updated periodically. The questions are designed to help people who are buying research to question suppliers of panel research to help them make better informed decisions.*

Online Quality Research Council

The ARF has created the Online Quality Research Council to address the quality issues in market research and summarises its mission as being based on 'Knowledge driven standards and metrics'. The Council has spent over US$ 1 million on researching the nature of the quality issues and in making recommendations through its 'Foundations of Quality' programme. The Council launched its Quality Enhancement Process in September 2009.

Amongst the key findings from the Foundations of Quality, presented by Joel Rubinson to the 2009 ESOMAR Online Research Conference, were:

○   *Panels tend to replicate their own results (despite the Procter & Gamble experience quoted earlier). However, the same survey administered to different panels can generate significantly different results. (Note, this does not mean surveys will always replicate when given to the same panel, just as they would not necessarily replicate every time with any method or mode.)*

○   *Purchase intent for a product in a concept test is partly a function of panellist longevity. It seems the longer somebody has been on a panel the less likely they are to say they would buy the products being tested.*

○   *Taking multiple surveys a month (for example up to 10 a month) is good for respondent engagement.*

○   *Being on multiple panels turned out to be less of an issue than had been previously expected.*

The Foundations of Quality project included 17 panel companies and over 100 000 interviews.

ISO Standards

ISO (the International Organisation for Standardization/*Organisation Internationale de Normalisation*) is an international body that establishes standards for a wide range of activities (for example, car brake testing, crop production, and IT procedures). Over the last few years there has been a move towards creating ISO Standards for market research.

At present there are two ISO Standards that relate directly to market research:

- ○ *ISO 20252, Survey Research*

- ○ *ISO 26362, Access Panels*

There is ongoing liaison abut ISO standards for customer satisfaction and brand valuation.

In some circles, ISO standards are controversial because they require a company to spend money to sign up to a system that is assessed by external investigators. Some researchers have commented that the ISO standards favour larger companies compared with small companies.

The argument of people sceptical about ISO standards is that improved quality standards can save larger companies money, through eliminating errors caused by the size of their operation. By contrast, the argument goes, the increased bureaucratic and cost implications of the ISO standards do not necessarily generate cost savings or quality benefits for smaller companies. This view has been additionally fuelled by calls by some industry representative to make the adoption of ISO standards a prerequisite for tendering for contracts.

However, ESOMAR and many of the world's leading organisations believe that ISO is good for the research industry and for buyers of research.

Other initiatives

In addition to those listed above there are a large number of other initiatives from a variety of organisations, including research organisations and individual companies.

Most panel companies have conducted research on issues such as duplicate memberships and false answers to screening questions, in order to tidy up the membership of their panels.

ETHICS

Online research has raised a number of new ethical concerns and has brought some long-standing issues into greater prominence. Key ethical concerns include:

- ○ *Protecting respondents from harm*

- ○ *Protecting clients from harm*

○   *Protecting colleagues, market research, and ourselves*

○   *The boundary between marketing and research*

○   *Privacy policies*

Protecting respondents from harm

When thinking about respondents it is essential to think of the different ways that the market research process can lead to harm. Key areas for potential harm include sensitive data, children, and inappropriate communications.

Sensitive data

Any personally identifiable data is important, and should be treated with respect and in accordance with data protections laws and advice. However, some data is considered sensitive and should be subject to even more care. For example, the European Union's data protection definitions of sensitive data include religious beliefs, political opinions, health, sexual orientation, and race.

When respondents are entering sensitive data, such as financial information, their information needs to be protected. If the data is very sensitive or collected from a sensitive location such as an online banking site then this may mean ensuring that the data collection takes place in a secure environment, such as HTTPS. HTTPS is one of several secure environments which have been designed to keep transactions secure and to provide reassurance to the user. HTTPS is a combination of the normal internet protocol (HTTP) and Secure Sockets Layer (SSL).

Children

One key issue for market researchers is to ensure that children remain safe, something that is not always easy on the internet as it is not possible to be certain how old somebody is.

One problem for market researchers is that there are no agreed definitions of what a child is. Agnes Nairn (2009) has highlighted the inconsistencies between various definitions, for example those of ESOMAR, national governments, and the United Nations.

Inappropriate communications

In pre-internet research, opportunities for respondents to meet each other were marginal. They might have met at a focus group or in a hall test, for example, but this rarely resulted in issues. In online research communities, however, respondents may be engaging in a long-term project with real opportunities to develop relationships, and therefore for potentially negative consequences to arise.

Practice varies. At one extreme some researchers require all posts to be posted as 'anonymous' and do not allow respondents to form buddies or friends. At the other extreme, some researchers take the risk and do not impose rules on how people represent themselves in their communities – sometimes arguing that this is a part of treating the respondents as collaborating adults.

My recommendations are:

1. Encourage respondents to use an avatar or 'handle' rather than their own names and photos.

2. Have clear terms and conditions, and specifically mention – and ban – cyberbullying.

3. Monitor inter-respondent communications (after telling them that you will be doing it) and watch out for inappropriate behaviour.

Protecting clients

As well as protecting respondents from harm, market researchers have a responsibility to look after their clients' interests and ensure that nothing the agency does creates a security risk. Topics to consider include:

○ *Reliability and validity*

○ *Restricting access*

○ *Intellectual property*

○ *Reputation*

Reliability and validity

Most codes of conduct have strict guidelines on the need to ensure that the buyer of the research is aware of any limitations to the confidence they should have in the research findings. The two main categories that are specific to this book are the projectability of online quantitative research, and the as yet untested applicability of most social media research.

Restricting access

Most vendor/buyer relationships these days specify that any materials passed from the research buyer to the agency will only be accessed by appropriate employees, often specifying an 'empty desk' policy and a permissions-based security system on the supplier's computer system. If the client has provided extranet access, then the agency needs to ensure that access to it is kept secure.

Intellectual property

Intellectual property (also IP, and IPR – intellectual property rights) is a major concern with online and social media research.

In terms of conventional online research, the key issue tends to be trying to ensure that ideas and images used in surveys do not 'leak' into the wider world. This is a problematic area and the researcher needs to both minimise the risk of leaks and to make sure that the research buyer is aware that nothing is 100% safe on the internet. Even if an image is difficult to capture via the PC, people can always use their iPhone (or similar) to capture an image or video on the screen and immediately post it.

For example, in November 2009 a blogger called *pastapadre* (http://www.pastapadre.com/2009/11/28/ potential-features-for-ncaa-football-11#more-13775) posted an image from a survey page showing a computer game called NCAA Football. Another example was the way that a Burger King branded video game for Xbox 360 consoles was tested by Greenfield Online in 2006 and which appeared on the gossip and news website Kotaku.com (Stark, 2009). Typing the words 'Burger King' and 'Kotaku' into a search engine in December 2009 resulted in both the image from the survey and the text of a 'cease and desist' letter from Greenfield Online's General Counsel.

When using social media for market research there is an additional intellectual property right problem relating to co-creation. When using co-creation, it is necessary to ensure that the 'rights' of any ideas or products developed by the research reside with the research buyer.

Reputation

The researcher needs to ensure that any market research project does not damage the reputation or standing of the research buyer. Issues that might cause a loss of reputation include:

- *functional problems with website popups*

- *surveys that are too long, or which contain errors*

- *failure to respect the respondent – for example, in a social media project – and failing to respond promptly to participant posts.*

Protecting colleagues, market research, and ourselves

As well as looking after respondents and clients, researchers should also be aware of potential harm that could be experienced by their colleagues, themselves and, indeed, the market research profession.

Social media research raises two new issues that were fairly minimal in the pre-social media days. The first risk is that the personal identity of the researcher will be known to respondents, who may then start following them in other networks such as Facebook. The second problem leads on from the first: if researchers are identifiable, then the news that they are away on a family holiday is potentially a security risk.

The boundary between marketing and market research

The boundary between market research and marketing is one that has been jealously guarded from the earliest days of market research, although the reasons for the separation have shifted over the years.

In the early days of market research the profession was established by people who were looking to create something akin to an academic discipline and who felt that market research could be based on 'scientific methods'. The model for the market researcher was the independent, disinterested observer. It was felt that if marketing and market research were allowed to become entangled, some or all of the following may happen:

○ *the independence of the researcher might be compromised, changing the results of the research*

○ *respondents might start to become distrustful of market research; i.e. they might not be willing to be as open to a researcher if they thought the information would be used to sell them something*

There may also have been a wish on the part of the market researchers to be seen as being different from marketers.

More recently, an additional argument for maintaining the separation of market research and marketing has appeared. In most developed markets there are a variety of data protection and data security laws. In many of these markets there are exceptions or provisions in these laws to exclude market research from some of the more onerous rulings. If market research becomes more entangled with marketing, it is possible – or perhaps likely – that the laws will be reframed to further restrict market research.

Although the majority of the market research profession still appears to want to maintain the separation of marketing and market research – and this is the overwhelming view of the market research organisations – a growing number are challenging this view, and an even larger number are using the exceptions and workarounds in the market research rules in order to blur the marketing and market research boundary.

The people who challenge the traditional non-marketing mindset tend to argue that the separation is a relic of the Adult<>Child relationship of the past, and is less relevant in the current Adult<>Adult relationship that is now the norm. This argument suggests that the rules should be determined by the respondent rather than the researcher.

Privacy policies

A privacy policy is an online statement listing all the key things that somebody visiting a website (or taking part in an online survey) needs to know, or might reasonably want to know. At one level, a privacy policy is simply a courtesy to website visitors and respondents. However, in many countries it is also a legal requirement and, in terms of market research, many research organisations, such as ESOMAR, specify that all online research should be accompanied by a privacy policy. Normally, the privacy policy is provided via a link rather than being expressed in full on the face of the website or survey.

When designing a privacy policy, one of the most common approaches is to visit a number of other sites and learn from what their privacy policies look like and what they say. The ESOMAR guidelines

Conducting Market and Opinion Research Using the Internet [http://www.esomar.org/uploads/pdf/ ESOMAR_Codes&Guideline-Conducting_research_using_Internet.pdf] has a description of the use of privacy policies and advice on drafting them, including a draft privacy policy.

 Advice

In terms of privacy policies relating to market research, the following are all important items:

- O   *A note saying who is conducting the research.*

- O   *Who the research is for, unless there are good reasons for not disclosing this.*

- O   *A statement of what information will be kept confidential and what will not.*

- O   *What invisible processing is conducted – for example, are browser variables read, are cookies served?*

- O   *How to contact the researcher.*

- O   *Information about the security of the survey and its data.*

- O   *An explanation of what sort of data will be collected, where it will be stored, who will access it, what uses it will be put to, and how long it will be stored.*

- O   *A note of any standards that the researcher and the survey conform to, for example market research standards such as ESOMAR or third-party ones such as Trust-e.*

- O   *Explain how the respondent was selected. If it was from a third-party database (e.g. a client database) most countries require that this is declared*

In short, a researcher should '*Say what they are doing and do what they are saying.*'

PART V

Breaking News!

This (brief) part of the book looks at emerging trends and ideas that may form a major part of online and social media research over the next few years. By the time the book is printed, distributed, and purchased, some of these may have faded, some may already have becomes hits, most of them will probably still be in that stage between success and failure.

18 NewMR

'NewMR' is the expression being used to describe a large number of changes taking place in market research, in terms of both methods and the underlying theory and philosophy. It has been used several times throughout the book and this chapter looks specifically at NewMR and the way it is challenging existing paradigms and seeking to establish a new methodology. This chapter is divided in the following three sections:

○   *Introduction to New MR*

○   *Problems with the traditional research model*

○   *New paradigms*

INTRODUCTION TO NEW*MR*

NewMR is a term that groups together the new constituents of market research that have been emerging over the last few years and combines two core elements:

1.   The search for a new paradigm (or paradigms) which recognises that most commercial market research studies cannot assume random probability samples, and that some traditional research questions have been shown, by recent developments in behavioural economics and neuroscience, to be flawed.

2.   The adoption of social media as method of obtaining market research insight.

It should be noted that not all techniques described as NewMR possess both of these criteria. For example, prediction markets do not use social media and semiotics does not necessarily involve computers at all.

Amongst the many techniques that have been grouped under the heading NewMR are:

○   *blog and buzz mining*

○   *MROCs (also known as online research communities)*

○   *predictive markets*

○   *e-ethnography and netnography*

○   *semiotics*

○   *WE-research*

NewMR is based on a realisation that people's lives are untidy, that representative samples cannot (in most cases) be recruited, that asking questions can only reveal part of the picture, and that by working with customers and citizens we can find out more and provide better insight compared with traditional market research routes.

The debate about the need for a new way to conduct research is not universally agreed; indeed, there are still many in favour of trying to defend or repair the old model. However, there are some very influential voices in favour of change, including Stan Sthanunathan, Vice President of Marketing Strategy and Insights at Coca-Cola Co, who has said '*Random is not a scalable option any more*' (ARF ORQC meeting October 2009), and '*We are focusing our time on technicalities of research, whereas the expectation from clients is actually in a totally different space. The clients are saying, "Inspire me, help me to take some transformational action," and we're busy creating better mousetraps.*' (Research-Live interview, 22 October 2009).

'*We've hardly scratched the future!*' is the view of Angus Reid, CEO of Vision Critical. Talking about the issues covered in this book, Reid highlighted the speed of change, the potential of technology to improve the process of research and, perhaps most importantly, the need to protect and improve the quality of research. In the last three years, the number of custom or proprietary panels supported by Vision Critical's technology has grown from zero to around 350, with revenues rising from about US $5 million to US $70 million. Reid predicts that we will see not hundreds but thousands of these panels in the near future. For Reid, the future needs to include better tools for conducting research, better control of who is in the sample, enhanced relationships with the people being researched, and the benefits of longitudinal data.

PROBLEMS WITH THE TRADITIONAL RESEARCH MODEL

In order to appreciate NewMR it is important to understand the traditional research model and the problems that it may have begun to suffer from.

The heart of the traditional market research model is quantitative market research. This traditional quantitative research is typically conducted by selecting an appropriate sample of the relevant population and surveying them via questionnaires. When market researchers talk about 'the science' they are usually referring to quantitative research conducted with surveys. The science of traditional quantitative market research rests on two fundamental assumptions:

1.   The people who are surveyed approximate to a random probability sample.

2.   The people who are surveyed are able and willing to answer the questions they are asked.

However, an increasing number of market researchers are challenging these assumptions (although equally many would argue that both assumptions are being met to a sufficient degree). These two assumptions and the issues surrounding them are reviewed below.

THE RANDOM PROBABILITY SAMPLING ASSUMPTION

The random probability sample is the *sine qua non* of traditional market research. If we do not have random probability sampling, then we do not have a traditional model of quantitative market research that works. The problem is that most commercial market research does not approximate to random probability sampling.

A random probability sample is one where the population is known (for example, the population might be all men in France, or all buyers of a Nokia phone, or all viewers of the 'Big Brother' TV programme) and where each member of the population has a known and non-zero chance of being selected. If a random probability sample is contacted and measured on some characteristic, it is possible to project the results from the sample onto the whole population, subject to sampling error. The sampling error can readily be calculated and provides a method of expressing confidence in the results – for example, a researcher might quote the results of a polling exercise as being +/–3% with a confidence of 95%.

However, these days it is very rare for market research samples to approximate to a random probability sample, undermining the ability of the research to create projectable results.

Although expert views vary, and have tended to become more relaxed over the last 50 years, it is suggested that if 30% or more of the population have a zero chance of being selected, the process cannot deliver the benefits of random probability sampling. In other words, the sample needs to represent at least 70% of the population for it to deliver results that are projectable to the whole population.

There are three key reasons why commercial market research samples tend not to achieve the required 70% level:

○ **Coverage error**. *Coverage error expresses the degree to which market researchers are not able to reach the whole population. For example, if a research project uses CATI, those without a landline are not likely to be sampled, nor are those who are very rarely home. If the internet is used to conduct the interviews, then those who do not have access to the internet are not likely to be sampled. Similarly, in-street interviewing is unlikely to sample those who do not visit the high street.*

○ **Non-response error**. *Non-response error occurs if some of the people asked to take part in the research decline the invitation. In many commercial market research projects the proportion who agree to take part in the study can be well under 50%.*

   ○   **Non-completion error.** *If people fail to finish the survey then in most cases their data won't be included in the final data set, further reducing the link between the sample and the population.*

 Examples

Figure 18.1 shows a simple example which illustrates the cumulative effect of these three phenomena. This example illustrates that a method that is often assumed to be one of the more representative techniques, namely telephone, can be flawed in terms of its assertion to approximate to a random probability sample.

Example of representation errors
A survey uses RDD (Random Digit Dialling) to contact people via telephone, with a sampling algorithm in place to select both households and people within those households with multiple occupants. In this market, the proportion of the population who live in a house with a landline is 80%.
Of the people contacted, 25% were available and agreed to take part in the study.
Of the people who started the interview, 10% terminated the interview before the end, i.e. 90% completed the survey.
The net response rate is therefore 80% × 25% × 90% = 18%.
The net effect of these three effects (coverage, response, and completion) is that the sample reflects just 18% of the relevant population, far below the level that is reasonably assumed to reflect a random probability sample.

Figure 18.1

One of the challenges for telephone research in many markets is that the proportion of households with a landline is falling. In some Western countries fewer than 60% of households have a landline. At the same time, the presence of mobile phones (i.e. cell or cellular phones) has boomed globally, with many developed countries having more mobile phones than people (with many people having two or more phones). However, mobile phones are often considered unsuitable for RDD telephone research, due to respondent resistance and in some cases legislation (for example limiting the use of autodialers). However, the position remains dynamic and many researchers report success in including mobile phone users in their samples.

In much of online research, the random probability sampling model is further corrupted by the use of online access panels. An access panel typically comprises less – usually much less – than 5% of the population. In terms of the logic above, this means that the coverage error becomes dominant. More than 95% of the population are not on panels and therefore have a zero chance of being selected.

ARE PEOPLE WILLING AND ABLE TO ANSWER RESEARCH QUESTIONS?

The second of the two assumptions underlying the traditional market research model is that people are willing to answer market research questions, and that they are able to answer them. In an ideal world market researchers would be able to ask respondents questions like:

'When this product is launched next year, how many times will you buy it?'

'How attractive do you find this pack?'

'Does this TV commercial make you think more highly of the brand?'

'If we change the colour of the glass from brown to blue, will you drink this sherry more often?'

'What factors "drive" your choice of bank?'

From the early days of market research, it was understood that these questions were difficult for respondents to answer. The problem had previously been tackled by psychometricians such as Thurstone and Spearman, and various strategies were employed to improve the process, such as the use of Likert scales and semantic differential scales rather than numbers. Another improvement was the development of marketing science methodologies to reveal relationships, for example the calculation of implied drivers through the use of techniques such as regression.

However, more recently, the process of asking direct questions has been challenged by information gathered from other disciplines such as neuroscience, behavioural economics, and social anthropology. Increasingly we are beginning to realise that market research respondents are unreliable witnesses about themselves (Kearon and Earls, 2009).

For example, in *Buyology* (Lindstrom, 2008), Martin Lindstrom uses neuroscience to illustrate that we do not know why we do things. In *Herd*, Mark Earls (2007) discusses how our mirror neurons result in us buying what other people buy, not what we plan to buy. In *How we Decide*, Jonah Lehrer (2009) talks about how asking people to rate a product before making a choice changes the choices that are made, and that these choices are less good than those made when the subjects are not asked to rate products. In *Predictably Irrational*, Dan Ariely (2008) shows that the context of the question changes the choices that are made in ways that appear to be both irrational and predictable.

Taking this new body of information into account, the net position is that many of the methods used by traditional research are deeply flawed as a method of understanding people's individual intentions and of revealing their likely future actions. To paraphrase Lindstrom, we are asking people who can't remember where they left their car keys to remember what they were thinking and feeling when they bought that packet of toilet tissues a month ago! To borrow a term from Ariely, we can think of real consumers as being the 'irrational consumer'.

RESPONSES TO PROBLEMS WITH THE TRADITIONAL RESEARCH MODEL

Although the problems detailed above may seem almost insurmountable, various measures have been developed by market researchers to tackle both the sampling problem and the 'irrational consumer' problem. In many ways, these could have been framed as part of New*MR*; however, they have tended to be used in conjunction with the language of 'the science', and should be considered at the moment as old market research. These responses include:

- *Quota samples*

- *Sophisticated reweighting*

- *Norms and modelling*

- *Measuring relativities, not absolutes*

Whilst all of these strategies have proved useful, there is a concern that the companies offering these solutions have not made it sufficiently clear that the samples they are using do not approximate to random probability samples. Most of these solutions could have been more clearly positioned as post-random probability sampling, and essentially the precursor to New*MR*.

The sections below give a brief overview of each of these approaches.

Quota samples

The most common way of dealing with the sampling problem has been to recruit a sample that resembles the population on a number of key characteristics. In general, this approach is based on an assumption that if a sample shares specific characteristics with the population it will operate as a reasonable proxy for the population. At a pragmatic level this assumption appears to often hold true, but there is no science or theory to support it.

Sophisticated reweighting

There are more sophisticated approaches to the random probability sampling problem, such as the propensity score weighting utilised by Harris Interactive (Terhanian, 2008) and the use of CHAID by Brian Fine (Fine et al., 2009). However, these approaches are not in general use, partly because of their requirements for high quality reference information and the increased processing implications. The strength of these techniques in producing results that relate to the real world is highlighted by Harris Interactive's record of success in predicting the election results in the USA.

Norms and modelling

The results of concept tests are rarely directly predictive of market shares; similarly, the raw scores from voting intention studies are rarely predictive of the results of elections. However, the companies that specialise in this field have developed methods of using the results of previous studies to create more accurate estimates.

Measuring relativities, not absolutes

This approach is often adopted by brand and advertising tracking studies. The absolute scores are considered to be largely irrelevant, the focus of the attention and the analysis are the changes over time. The implicit assumption is that the change that occurs in the sample is likely to reflect similar changes in the population.

STATISTICAL SIGNIFICANCE TESTING AND PANELS

Traditionally, market researchers have used significance testing to imply validity – the implication being, for example, that a particular result is true, plus or minus x% with a confidence of 95%. However this figure relates to the sampling error of a random probability sample, and assumes no measurement error. Clearly, in the case of most commercial market research this is nonsense; the samples are not random probability samples and there is measurement error.

However, the same calculations can be used to provide information about reliability. For example, when an online access panel sample is described as not being a random probability sample, what is meant is that it is not a random probability sample of the target population. However, it will, in all likelihood, be a random probability sample of the population of samples that could have been generated from that particular panel. Taken in that context, the calculation of the sampling error becomes a useful way of estimating how different another sample from the same panel might have been.

The implication is that sampling statistics should still be calculated when using convenience samples such as online access panels. However, the descriptions used should imply that they are an estimate of reliability, not validity; i.e. of consistency, not necessarily projectability.

OTHER PROBLEMS WITH TRADITIONAL MARKET RESEARCH

In addition to the structural problems outlined above, buyers and users of market research have raised a number of other issues.

Speed. An increasing number of conference presentations and magazine articles are produced by clients saying that they find market research too slow. Clearly, some of the speed issues relate to client-side problems, such as commissioning the research too late. However, in many organisations the gap between wanting to know something to needing to know it to 'it is too late to worry now', is very short, often a few weeks, sometimes a few days or hours.

Cost. The cost of market research is often highlighted as a problem. However, perhaps the main problem is not the cost of the research that is conducted; it is the research that is not conducted because costs were too high. Because of its many phases and procedures the minimum price for a research project is often relatively high, discouraging many clients from doing some projects and increasing the temptation for companies to conduct DIY research.

Lack of insight. There are complaints that too many research debriefs and presentations simply describe the process and enumerate the responses. Clients are often looking for clear business advice, i.e. they are looking for recommendations, not just further information.

SO, WHY DOES MARKET RESEARCH USUALLY WORK?

If the sample is usually the wrong sample and the questions often don't reveal why people do what they do, why does market research usually work?

The claim that market research usually works can be supported in two ways. Firstly, there are those occasions where the research can be tested. Probably the best example of this phenomenon is election polling, where the polls are usually correct, in an area where sampling would appear to be critical, and where respondents might not only not know their intentions but also might not be prepared to disclose them. The second illustration is the scale of shock and public discussion when market research really does get it wrong, such as the New Coke fiasco in 1985.

A second factor that needs to be considered is what we mean when we say market research works. At best, market research can only be a probabilistic risk reduction system. It seeks to reduce the number of Type I and Type II errors (as statisticians call them). A Type I error is a false positive, i.e. a bad business decision is not spotted and allowed to go ahead. A Type II error is a false negative, i.e. a good idea is flagged as a bad one. For market research to work, its cost needs to be sufficiently below the benefits generated by the reduced chance of Type I and Type II errors. Nobody should suggest that market research removes the risk of either Type I or Type II errors, it works by reducing the risk.

 Author's View

Note that this section is written in the first person to highlight that it is my conjecture, supported by 30 years of working with data and extensive research, discussion, and attending conferences.

I think that there may be many reasons why market research tends to work, but I feel the key reasons are as follows:

- *Homogeneity*
- *Wisdom of crowds*
- *The 'art' of market research*

I explore these three reasons below.

Homogeneity

As Mark Earls has illustrated (Earls, 2007), people tend to do what other people do. People who manage to function in society tend to be like other people. If we show three TV commercials for breakfast cereal to 100 men aged 20 to 35 years old and to a sample of 100 females aged 36 to 50, then the commercials will have to be very unusual for them to be rated differently, at least in terms of the relativities between the three commercials. If Ad A is seen as the most fresh and modern by the men, then it will usually be seen as the most fresh and modern by the females. If three ads were about female sanitary protection, then the response might well be different. A random probability sample protects against the sample creating bias but, in the real world, in most cases having the wrong sample does not create biases that change the relative results between items being assessed.

Note, there is no rule that says the wrong sample will work OK, but it often does, based on empirical data.

Wisdom of crowds

Many years ago I worked with an automaker that had a very large, very extensive database of what cars people said they would buy next and what they actually bought next. The interesting thing about this data was twofold:

(a) The car somebody said they would buy next was a really bad predictor of what that person did buy.

(b) However, the aggregate total of what people said they would buy was a good predictor of the aggregate total that people bought.

What this data showed was that people were bad at predicting their own behaviour but really quite good at predicting what groups of people will do. If we consider the prediction market methodology, this is exactly what the respondents are being asked to do, i.e. estimate what other people would do.

My conjecture is that when a market researcher shows somebody an ad and a concept for a new type of beer and asks them how likely they are to buy it, the respondent is unconsciously conflating some mixture of their own likelihood with some estimate of what 'people like them' might do.

The 'art' of market science

Market researchers have been taking what respondents say and interpreting it for years. Few market researchers would simply take what a respondent says and report it as a finding. When Lindstrom and others show that what people say is not a good guide to what they will do they are not saying anything new. Dealing with this issue has been part of market research's stock-in-trade since its infancy. For example, sales estimates from respondents are based on what the respondents say, but they are typically converted using algorithms based on the sort of changes necessary to convert a set of respondent scores into metrics that have some link with the real world.

Traditional market research has looked at response rates as an indication of whether a sample represents the population, but the key issue is whether there are any systematic biases between the sample and the population. If there is no bias between the sample and the population, then coverage error and non-response error will not matter. The skill (or art) is in identifying cases where there is likely to be bias.

Summary

My net position is that market research often works, but not in the way that it is often claimed. However, by not focusing on the real reasons that market research works, people run the risk of being surprised when it does not work.

THE ABSENCE OF THEORY

NewMR is not just a collection of new methods; it represents a different methodology, based on different assumptions about the nature of truth and evidence. At the moment, most of the NewMR techniques that are being adopted – such as online communities, community panels, and blog and buzz mining – are not based on any formal theory and there is a need for these techniques to establish a proper basis for their use.

ALTERNATIVE PARADIGMS AND METHODS

This section looks at some of the NewMR techniques and reviews where they are most likely to find either a theory or pragmatic support.

Qualitative NewMR

Qualitative approaches such as discussions in MROCs, e-ethnography, netnography, WE-Research, blogging-based research, and some blog and buzz mining need to look to the theories of qualitative research for their underpinning.

Quantitative NewMR

There are several routes that quantitative NewMR can take in terms of developing theories.

Learning from qualitative sampling

Quantitative approaches – such as community panels (indeed online access panels as well), quantitative exercises in MROCs and the automated parts of blog and buzz mining – can learn from the theory of sampling used in qualitative research. Concepts such as confirming and disconfirming samples, maximum variation sampling, and archetypes need to be developed and articulated. Some of the current approaches already fit this pattern, for example a quota-controlled sample to collect the views of heavy and light users, young and old, male and female, is based on good qualitative sampling principles.

Modelling the data

Given a consistent method of taking measurements and of measuring outcomes, models can be constructed that link the method of measurement with market outcomes. This is the approach that is used when sophisticated re-weighting is used (Terhanian, 2008; Fine et al., 2009); it is also the method used by concept and ad testing companies when they generate market forecasts from their data.

Behavioural economics' models

At the moment the best example of a NewMR technique that borrows from behavioural economics is that of prediction markets. This model requires more data to establish the parameters through which pseudo markets can tap into the wisdom of crowds, and to more clearly define when wisdom of crowds might apply and when collective ignorance is more likely to be a group response.

TRIANGULATION

NewMR researchers are unlikely to be able to operate with the (unfounded) certainty of a researcher who felt that their methods and conclusions were founded on scientific methods and Newton's laws. Regardless of whether a NewMR researcher is using a quantitative or a qualitative methodology, they are likely to benefit from one specific approach from the qualitative toolkit, namely triangulation.

Triangulation is a method of identifying and verifying some phenomena by looking at them from different angles. For example, if buzz mining suggests brand X is in trouble, have a look at their share price, have a discussion in a community, perhaps look at the company's profile on LinkedIn to see if more people seem to be leaving than arriving.

THE NATURE OF TRUTH TELLING

People find some sources easier to believe than others; a source that is more widely believed is said to be more credible. In the past, experts and authority figures were likely to be believed because of their standing, but as issues like the climate change debate have shown, experts are no longer automatically believed, nor are politicians or priests so widely believed.

NewMR researchers need to look at how and why different people are able to build credibility and to be believed. Why is it, for example, that a market researcher finds it so much harder to be believed than a journalist? A market researcher is less likely to have their own agenda and speaks to more people than a journalist. A journalist, however, can claim credibility on the basis of being able to identify the right people to speak to and to ask the right questions (but that sounds like what market researchers should be doing, too).

19 Trends and Innovations

This chapter looks at specific new trends and innovations currently taking place in market research and which relate to online and social media research. This chapter includes:

- ○ *Listening*
- ○ *WE-Research*
- ○ *Social networks and market research*
- ○ *Twitter*
- ○ *New power structures, new networks*
- ○ *Collaboration and co-creation*
- ○ *Innovation communities*
- ○ *Collaborative quantitative research*
- ○ *Mobile research*

LISTENING

One of the key memes from late 2009 onwards has been listening. This theme has been used both in its general use that we must listen more to people, but also specifically in the context of moving away from asking questions and towards listening, for example when using blog and buzz mining, or any other observer/listening type research.

WE-RESEARCH

WE-Research is a fashionable term coined by Mark Earls and John Kearon (Kearon and Earls, 2009) that brings together a variety of approaches which use respondents (or perhaps participants, volunteers, or collaborators) to research with and on behalf of brands and market researchers. As well as papers and presentations on the topic, there is a rush to create tools to enable WE-Research, for example Revelation's blog and qual-friendly research platform [http://www.revelationglobal.com/] and the iPhone ethnography tool that can be downloaded from iTunes [http://www.edlapp.com/].

SOCIAL NETWORKS AND MARKET RESEARCH

Over the last few years social networks such as FaceBook, Cyworld, and Mixi have become one of the largest phenomena on the internet. In November 2009 Alexa.com listed Facebook as the second most visited site on the internet, behind Google.com, with Chinese network QQ.com coming in at 11th and MySpace at 12th. By November 2009, Facebook was quoting 300 million members, about one in six of all the world's internet users.

As customers and citizens moved into social networks, market researchers followed them to gain new insights. Given that this field is still very new (Facebook was only launched in 2004), it is likely that the use of social media by market researchers is in its infancy and that there will be rapid developments over the next few years.

WHAT IS A SOCIAL NETWORK?

Definitions are fluid and developing, but there appear to be a few characteristics that help distinguish whether a service is a social network. These characteristics include:

- ○ *A personal presence*. *A social network needs to provide a method where a user can locate their interactions (posts, comments, lists of friends). In most cases this is achieved by requiring users to be members and allowing them to create a profile.*

- ○ *'Special' connections*. *In social networks special connections may be called friends, followers, or contacts. In a typical network the connections that a member has are a subset of the network's total membership.*

- ○ *Posting*. *A social network provides the members with a chance to post something (pictures, comments, blogs, art, etc) and to associate these with their personal presence.*

- ○ *An administrator role*. *The social network is normally 'owned' by a person, a group, or an organisation. The owner normally reserves some powers to itself that it does not grant to all members, such as the power to ban a member.*

Optional, but common, features include:

- ○ *Avatars*. *An avatar is an online persona or identity. In many social networks people can choose a name they want to be known by and an image. The name and image can be their own name and their own photograph. But their name can often be anything they like and likewise their image (subject to any bad taste and legal constraints imposed by the social network).*

- ○ **Discussions**. *A discussion or a forum is a place where members (and possibly non-members) can discuss a topic. In a discussion the comments persist (i.e. they are there the next time you log in) and they are organised in some logical order (e.g. oldest to newest, newest to oldest, or next to the comment that a reply relates to).*

- ○ **Messaging**. *Most social networks have some way of sending messages to other members.*

SOCIAL NETWORKS AND OBSERVATIONAL RESEARCH

Observational research in social networks is typically divided into two categories. The first category is large-scale mining, accessing large amounts of information and processing it with the aid of sophisticated systems. This approach is described in Chapter 12, Blog and Buzz Mining.

The second use of observational research is a much more intensive process of visiting sites, reading the comments and following threads. This approach is ethnographical and is variously described as e-ethnography or netnography.

SOCIAL NETWORKS AND PARTICIPANT/OBSERVATIONAL RESEARCH

The e-ethnographical approach can be extended from the observational model to a participant/observer model, where the researcher posts questions and discusses topics with members of the communities. It should be noted that this approach raises a number of ethical issues that need to be addressed before undertaking any participant/observer research in social networks.

SOCIAL NETWORKS AS A SAMPLE SOURCE

From the early days of social networks there have been some researchers who have attracted respondents by using advertising in social networks to attract respondents. More recently, companies such as PeanutLabs [http://peanutlabs.com/] have developed more sophisticated models for attracting respondents across a wide range of social networks.

It is likely that there will be further innovations in the use of social networks for attracting respondents for market research. One frequent 'thought experiment' that conference speakers like to play with is the concept of a company like Facebook becoming a vendor of online samples itself.

BUSINESS-TO-BUSINESS (B2B) NETWORKS

There are a number of social networks targeted at business and professional people, with one leading example being LinkedIn [http://www.linkedin.com/]. LinkedIn has already created a B2B sample service, and this phenomenon is likely to expand.

THE ETHICS OF SOCIAL NETWORKS AND MARKET RESEARCH

Because social networks is a rapidly developing field, the ethics and guidelines are also rapidly developing, and market researchers are recommended to be very careful about how they use these networks in a market research context.

There is a growing consensus that comments posted in social networks are not 'in the public domain' and researchers should seek permission to use them. Researchers should also remember that, because the internet is so readily searchable, they should avoid using literal quotes from social network discussions (in most cases), as this could potentially reveal who the respondent is.

In many codes of ethics and in a growing number of laws, the intention/expectation of the person making a post is important in determining what can be done with that post. In terms of privacy there are two issues. The first is that if a researcher has to join a network to see the post, then the person making the post is doing so in the expectation that they are talking to genuine members of the community, not to professional researchers or journalists. The second issue is that when somebody makes, say, 200 posts over the course of a year, they did not necessarily have the expectation that all their quotes would be brought back together as a single corpus for investigation.

TWITTER

Twitter is normally classified as a microblogging site, but that rather understates its impact and its currently unique position in social media. Twitter was launched in July 2006 and by February 2009 the number of users had reached almost ten million; by June 2009 this had rocketed to over 40 million, and nearly 60 million by August 2009.

Not surprisingly, Twitter caught market researchers' eyes and there was a rush to investigate how it could be integrated into research and potentially used to explore new types of insight.

This section reviews the key elements of Twitter, especially from the researcher's point of view and then considers where Twitter may go next.

TWITTER – THE BARE ESSENTIALS

At its most basic, Twitter allows users to post 140 characters in response to the prompt 'What's happening' and people who follow that user will see that post in their feed (others can find it by searching for it). The posts in Twitter are called tweets, and the process of posting is called tweeting.

It is necessary to sign up to Twitter in order to be able to post tweets but, because the database is open, it is not necessary to be a member in order to search the tweets and members.

The following headings outline the main elements of Twitter.

Celebrities

One of the drivers of Twitter's popularity has been the prominence of celebrity tweeters, such as Ashton Kutcher, Britney Spears, Ellen DeGeneres, and Oprah Winfrey (all of whom gained at least 2.7 million followers in less than 16 months – Kutcher gaining over 4 million in just 11 months).

The attention being paid to celebrity tweets highlights the phenomenon that different people use Twitter in different ways. Some people use it to follow people, some to gather news, some to communicate with friends, some to advertise their stuff, and some just to show off.

Retweet

Retweeting is one of the ways that key ideas, comments, or links expand beyond one group of people and into other networks. When a Twitter user sees a tweet that they think is worth passing on they Retweet it and it passes on to all the people who follow them. The more an idea catches people's eyes the more it is Retweeted and the further it reaches, creating viral patterns for some messages to spread. This sort of phenomenon is especially clear when a particularly newsworthy event occurs, such as the death of Michael Jackson.

Direct messages

A direct message is simply a message from one Twitter user to another, without it being available for others to see or search. Twitter direct messages are another symptom of the death of email, particularly amongst younger people who are fleeing email in favour of other methods of messaging and communicating.

Third-party applications

There is a wide and growing range of third-party applications, which extend the functionality of Twitter. For example, TweetDeck provides users with a wide range of extra functionality and TwitScoop provides a way of examining what is trending in Twitter.

Hashtags

Hashtags are a method of grouping tweets together. For example, people tweeting about the 15th United Nations Climate Change Conference in Copenhagen in December 2009, used the hashtag #COP15 as part of their tweet (all hashtags start with the hash character #). This meant that people could use #COP15 in Twitter (or in whatever third-party applications they might be using) to see all the tweets relating to Copenhagen.

Market researchers who tweet have used hashtags to group tweets about a topic, about market research (see #mr), or about specific conferences.

Searching Twitter

There is a wide range of tools available to search Twitter, including Twitter's own search [http://search.twitter.com/]. Twitter search allows tweets to be filtered by text in the post, geographic location, language, and hashtags, making the search very powerful.

Twitter backchannel

The backchannel is a collection of tweets on a subject, usually organised via a hashtag, which can be used to provide an alternative flow of information. For example, during a TV show, viewers' tweets about the show and the issues raised by it may create a backchannel of information, quite separate from the official channel.

Tweetups

A tweetup is a meeting or event organised via Twitter, typically using a third-party service such as Twtvite [http://twtvite.com/]. Market researchers have started creating tweetups around larger events such as conferences. Although largely fun events at the moment, tweetups are another example of the way that the power structures in companies are changing.

Tweetferences

A tweetference is an enhancement (at least in many people's eyes) of a conference, using Twitter. Twitter-using attendees group their tweets together by choosing a specific hashtag (for example, the ESOMAR Online Conference in 2009 had the hashtag #esoc). The tweets typically cover the pre-conference period, the conference, and the post-conference discussion. A number of attendees have started tweeting during presentations, sometimes including photos of the presentation or presenter.

Non-attendees are able to follow the conference and presentation in real-time and get a disjointed sense of what is happening, and indeed to add their thoughts to the session.

Tweetups are a typical feature of tweetferences and are often used to allow market researchers who are local to the location of the conference, but who are not attending, to join in social and informal events.

Another standard component of a tweetference is a tweetwall. A tweetwall is a large screen showing a constant stream of updated tweets, using hashtags to select the relevant topics. Some conferences have displayed a tweetwall alongside the main presentation, showing the backchannel alongside the main presentation. However, there have been unpleasant events where audiences have effectively turned into a sort of mob, using the backchannel to abuse the speaker.

WHERE NEXT FOR TWITTER?

There were some signs towards the end of 2009 that Twitter's exponential growth was slowing. Although a global total of some 100 million users is a substantial number, it only represents approximately one in every 200 000 internet users.

One of the challenges for Twitter (and third-party applications providers like TweetDeck) will be to develop methods for its users to deal with the signal-to-noise ratio. As the number of tweets escalates, it grows ever harder for users to find the interesting ones and exclude the rest. New tools such as filters and lists become ever more necessary.

Twitter has been largely blocked in China and has been slow to take off in Japan. So there is plenty of scope for one or more rival products to spring up, especially in Asia.

One of Twitter's big successes may also have sown the seeds of its eventual downfall, namely its use of an open database. The open database has made it very attractive to Web 2.0 evangelists and to developers of third-party software. But it may also have reduced the barriers to entry of new competitors. If other services that might emerge on the scene are able to 'borrow' much of Twitter's activity but add some key functionality, such as long tweets (say 200 characters), or allow a user to have differentiated lists of followers, then Twitter's early lead could evaporate in the way that Yahoo! lost ground to latecomer Google, and MySpace lost ground to latecomer Facebook.

From a market research point of view, Twitter has opened many eyes to a range of possible benefits in the future, including the ability to follow people and to target information to a narrow geographic area. At the same time, Twitter has shown market researchers how little has so far been achieved in automating the processing of open-ended text, even when it is just 140 characters long.

NEW POWER STRUCTURE, NEW NETWORKS

It is increasingly obvious that the growth of social media is changing power structures and networks inside market research companies. In the past, the people in the top few positions were the most knowledgeable and often the most skilled, a combination of experience and Darwinian evolution.

Individual researchers tended to have a limited number of networks: firstly, their colleagues at work; secondly, colleagues from previous employers; and, if they were lucky enough to attend conferences and courses, then these too could produce networks.

However, Web 2.0 and the growth of social networks have changed the picture. Facebook came into most organisations in 2006–2007 because new graduate employees brought it with them, having developed their usage whilst at university. Social media is much easier, in general, for the so-called 'net naturals' to get their heads around than it is for some of their more senior colleagues (although it is interesting to note that Twitter users tend to be older).

New networks are being formed in ways that cross company and country boundaries. When re searchers are looking for advice or support, they are increasingly doing it via networks, looking outside their company. If this trend continues, the market research profession could end up with a two-speed workforce, those who are networked and those who are not. Potentially the networked researchers will have the balance of their loyalties shifted away from their employer and towards their networks.

COLLABORATION AND CO-CREATION

When the term 'Web 2.0' first burst on the scene, much of the talk was about the 'four Cs': Collaboration, Crowdsourcing, Ceding control, and Co-creation. All four of these Cs relate to the proposition that, instead of ideas being generated by the organisation, they could also be generated by people outside the organisation.

Collaboration is about moving from 'the brand knows best' to a recognition that customers, suppliers, and staff can all be sources of great ideas. Collaboration has been a part of many focus groups for many years, but new tools such as communities, blog groups, and wikis allow research to tap into the ingenuity of the wider community.

Crowdsourcing refers to companies seeking solutions from outside the company, for example by putting out a call for ideas, solutions, or input, with well-known examples being Lego and the many companies who have organised votes on new flavours, names, packs, etc.

Ceding control refers to moving from a '*ME*' paradigm to a '*WE*' paradigm. Ceding control can be a scary process for research agencies, who tend to be used to controlling all the variables.

Co-creation refers to creating new products or ideas with customers. Co-creation is closely associated with User-generated Material, for example when customers are challenged to create and submit their own commercials.

As well as creating opportunities for market research, the four Cs can also generate new business models, which may reduce the need for market research in some cases, as in the Threadless.com case outlined below.

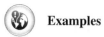 **Examples**

Threadless.com

Threadless.com is a manufacturer and retailer of t-shirts. It has pioneered a new form of business, one that is based on crowdsourcing and on integrating design, feedback, and marketing, thus creating a model that is a perfect example of Wikinomics (Tapscott and Williams, 2006).

The Threadless.com model can be thought of as comprising three steps:

1. Anybody who wants to be a t-shirt designer uploads their design to the Threadless. com website. One reason they might upload a design is to win prizes (at December 2009, $2000 in cash, $500 in t-shirt vouchers, and a chance to win $22 500). However, many of the people submitting designs are doing so because they want to 'be discovered' (some have gone on to be professional designers) or just to gain egoboo (the good feeling people get when their work is recognised). This means the design process has been crowdsourced, Threadless.com do not create designs.

2. Users of the Threadless.com website rate the designs that have been submitted, indicating on a score out of 5 whether they would buy it as a t-shirt or a print, and with an opportunity to make a comment. Threadless.com is collaborating with its customers to determine which t-shirts it should sell.

3. The winning t-shirts are then manufactured and sold via the website.

The business loop for Threadless.com is a closed consumer/consultative loop. All the designs come from the community, they are assessed by the community, and they are bought by the community.

INNOVATION COMMUNITIES

Innovation communities are created specifically to leverage innovation from outside an organisation. These communities have a relatively long history, for example Franke and Shah published a study looking at innovation communities and the nature of the suggestions being generated, refuting the notion that ideas from customers tend to be merely incremental (Franke and Shah, 2003).

Richarme and Ishmael, writing in ESOMAR's *Research World*, highlighted four steps that can increase the productivity of an innovation community (Richarme and Ishmael, 2009).

1. Ensure community members have everything they need to be productive, including training and specific information.

2. Keep a track of which members contributed what.

3. Remove non-productive members, letting members know there is a minimum standard of involvement.

4. Keep the community busy.

Amongst the detailed points that Richarme and Ishmael make are many that echo the points made in Chapter 4, Working with Panels and Databases. In particular:

- ○ *have a clear purpose in mind*

- ○ *set clear guidelines for what the community is to do*

- ○ *develop a collaborative mentality, not a competitive one (something to keep in mind when designing incentives)*

- ○ *don't rely on extrinsic rewards*

COLLABORATIVE QUANTITATIVE RESEARCH

Most aspects of a collaborative and co-creational research are qualitative in nature, but there are also collaborative quantitative research techniques, and these may grow over the next few years, partly driven by the need some research buyers have to produce numbers.

One example of a collaborative quantitative research is the collaborative poll. In a collaborative poll the researcher seeds the list with a plausible list of words and then enables the respondents to expand the list. For example, if a researcher wants to find out which word best expresses the character of a specific brand, they could seed the poll with, say, 'Happy', 'Sad', 'Exciting', and perhaps 'Sexy'. The poll is then opened to the respondents who see the answer list plus an 'Other' option. If the respondent chooses *Other*, they are then invited to type in the text of their choice.

Subsequent respondents are then shown the expanded list. The list is then either allowed to grow to a specific size, for example 20 items, or a randomising system is used to show a subset of the total list. These interviews are sometimes referred to as collaborative surveys.

The output from a collaborative poll is based on the views that occur after the list has become stable, the quantifying phase. This approach assumes a reasonably large sample size as it would be normal to expect at least 200 – and ideally more – collaborative surveys to be conducted before the quantifying ones are assessed.

A collaborative poll can also be used with a smaller sample, for example fewer than 100, simply to produce a set of characteristics to use in some other study.

One example of collaborative polls running as a public experiment is Grupthink [http://www.grupthink.com/]. Grupthink is a free standing community where people can join and either post their own poll, vote in an existing poll, or add an option to an existing poll.

MOBILE RESEARCH

Although not strictly speaking online, the connection technology that has developed the fastest over the last 20 years has been the mobile phone (cell or cellular phone in some markets). By the end of 2009 the International Telecommunications Union was estimating that there were about 4.6 billion mobile phones in use (compared with a global population of about 6.8 billion); this means that nearly as many people have a mobile phone as have access to a television.

For the last few years the trend in mobile phones has been towards 3G and internet connectivity, with the cutting edge being the growth in smartphones such as Apple's iPhone and Google's Nexus.

Given that far more people have access to mobile phones than computers and given that people tend to have their phone with them all the time, is there a major possibility that online data collection will be replaced by mobile data collection, or perhaps supplanted by mobile online surveys?

Whilst it would be foolish to say never, mobile research has been the 'next biggest thing' for a long time now, with only a tiny impact on the research industry.

THE SLOW ADOPTION OF MOBILES BY MARKET RESEARCH

Despite the phenomenal growth in their use, mobile phones have only had a marginal impact on global market research. A 2008 study by Confirmit illustrates this point well, with only 4% of global market research using mobile (mostly SMS) studies (Macer and Wilson, 2009). This result shows mobile as showing no growth in number of companies using it during the period 2005–2008. By research value, mobile dropped to 0.1% of the global total.

When the Confirmit study asked research agencies about their predictions for increases and decreases in their utilisation of different modalities, the results showed strong growth for web and mixed mode (e.g. CATI and web), with major declines for paper, and smaller declines for CATI. The data for the use of mobile showed an increase, but only a small increase and from a small base. The study shows that, whilst there is considerable interest in mobile research, its actual use remains a tiny percentage of the research whole.

The key to understanding the slow adoption of mobile phones can be understood by revisiting the well-established view that a new methodology needs to show a market advantage in at least one of the three criteria: faster, cheaper, or better.

When telephone made large inroads into the world of market research it raised quality concerns, but it was both faster and cheaper. The quality concerns mirrored many of those aired more recently by the use of the internet. Not everybody had a telephone and the range of stimuli that could be used were much more limited than with face-to-face.

When the internet became adopted as a common method of data collection, it too offered advantages of being faster and cheaper, but at the expense of quality concerns.

By contrast, mobile research struggles to offer a solution that is generally faster, or cheaper, or better. One of the reasons for this is that online research has already created a service which is fast and cheap. Although mobile may have the potential to offer a service that is faster it is likely to only be hours faster, rather than days faster.

At the moment, mobile surveys tend to be more expensive than online surveys, often offering prices comparable with other forms of telephone surveys. In most cases, mobile surveys are not able to compete in terms of 'better'. Using a technique such as SMS, only very simple surveys can be conducted; when the mobile phone is used for voice the surveys need to be shorter. Where mobile tends to have an advantage is when it can be better in the sense of being closer to the moment – for example, when the mobile phone is used to record events during the day, or where the survey is triggered by a specific event, such as making a visit to a store.

Given the near ubiquitous nature of the mobile phone, the increased convergence of communications technology, and the increasing sophistication of mobiles (for example, the web usability of the iPhone), the consensus assumption appears to be that mobiles will make a break through at some stage in the future, but not necessarily this year or next year.

THE FUTURE OF MOBILE RESEARCH

There are three forecasts about mobile that are relatively sound and based on current trends. There are also two that are more speculative.

Clear trends

These three trends are already in place and appear to be continuing to unfold.

1. **SMS and simple mobile surveys**. For the right tasks these surveys work well, but the projects tend to be limited to those that only use very simple questionnaires, often with just three to six questions and one or two open-ended questions. One of the key benefits of this type of research is that it can be organised to work with particular events, such as a visit to a specific location.

2. **Web surveys on smartphones**. Respondents are already filling in some of their surveys on their smartphones and a number of the web survey software providers are beginning to offer tools for rendering web surveys on phones such as the iPhone.

3. **WE-Research tools**. A number of research companies have been using respondents' mobile phones to capture aspects of their lives, through the use of texting, pictures, and video. The launch of the iPhone ethnography app from EveryDayLives is just one initiative amongst many that will allow researchers to work with respondents, participants, and volunteers to co-create the research and insight.

Possible trends

1. **Take off**. Most pundits expect mobile research to take off at some stage but, because it has not happened already, they have been guarded about saying when it might happen. It could very well happen in Asia or Africa first, where computer access is low and the mobile phone is the connection point between so many people.

2. **Voice**. Given that most quantitative research now uses panels and increasingly large numbers of qualitative projects use panels, perhaps there will be a faster growth in panels of people with mobile phones who will answer screener questions on the mobile and, if qualified, do a CATI survey using their mobile, at a time of their request.

20 An Overview of Online and Social Media Research

Well done to everybody who has stuck with the book from beginning to end, through online quantitative and qualitative research, through the emerging disruption that is social media research, and finally through the research topics and breaking news.

The upside of your journey is that you should now possess the framework to help understand an ever-widening research area. The downside is that in the time it has probably taken you to read the book, some of it will be out of date; indeed, some of it may even have changed from being right to being wrong!

This final chapter reviews the material covered in the rest of the book, highlighting the main themes, pointing up the key principles, and alerting the reader to issues that they may want to stay on top of. It also makes a number of suggestions for steps the reader may wish to take in order to stay up-to-date.

This chapter reviews and comments on the following topics:

- Online quantitative research

- Online qualitative research

- Social media and market research

- Applying online and social media to research problems

- New MR

- Staying in touch with developments

- Final thoughts about quality and ethics

ONLINE QUANTITATIVE RESEARCH

Online research has changed the face of quantitative research, partly by facilitating change and partly by accelerating discussions about changes that were happening anyway.

The three key changes that online quantitative research has created are:

1. A shift from interviewer-mediated surveys (for example, face-to-face and telephone) to a self-completion mode.

2. A shift from fresh sample to access panels.

3. A shift away from most functions being completed in-house towards more functions being provided externally (for example, most panels are run by third parties and most web survey systems are written by third parties).

Each of these three changes is explored in more depth below.

Online market research has also accelerated concerns about changes in the nature of market research. There are now concerns about all forms of commercial market research being unable to generate samples that approximate to random access samples and about the abuse that respondents are being subjected to, for example by the use of longer surveys and boring question formats.

THE LOSS OF THE INTERVIEWER

The loss of the interviewer is one of the biggest differences between online research and both face-to-face and telephone.

On the plus side, the removal of the interviewer has saved costs and resulted in many surveys being answered more honestly because the tendency for respondents to provide socially-acceptable answers has been reduced.

However, without the interviewer it is harder to know if the respondent understands the questions, harder to motivate the respondent, and harder to know whether the respondent is who they claim to be. Without an interviewer, the layout of a questionnaire is much more important than it was with either face-to-face or telephone, and the need for researchers to be better trained even greater.

Readers who wish to know more about the best way to create only questionnaires are referred to Mick Couper's book *Designing Effective Web Surveys* (2008).

THE SHIFT TO ACCESS PANELS

Before the advent of online surveys the use of access panels was rare, especially outside North America (where they tended to be mail/postal panels). However, the absence of alternative methods of sourcing online respondents and the search for lower costs and faster speeds have led to the majority of online research, in most countries, to be based on online access panels.

The shift to access panels represents a shift from traditional sampling to an almost exclusive reliance on what is in effect a set of convenience samples.

Another result of shifting to online access panels is that for most projects the total field cost is now a much smaller proportion of the total costs compared with 10 or 20 years ago.

THE USE OF OUTSOURCED SOLUTIONS

Another change wrought by the shift to online is the growth in outsourced solutions. Whilst some of these changes may have happened anyway (since they are a general trend across a range of industries), the shift to online research has facilitated some very specific changes to workflow practices. Specific functions that are increasingly being outsourced are:

○ *the provision of the sample, e.g. the online access panels*

○ *the provision of web survey systems, either by acquiring them from the likes of Confirmit or Nebu, or through using the SaaS (Software as a Service) options they provide*

○ *the scripting of surveys*

THE CHANGING NATURE OF MARKET RESEARCH

As a consequence of the changes outlined above, the very nature of market research has altered. The costs of projects are less determined by the cost of fieldwork. Project turnarounds tend to be much shorter, consequently with less time for analysis and thought. The researcher in many cases is much less in control of the process, with many of the decisions being taken at an IT level or even outsourced.

The acceptance that it is impossible to conduct random probability sampling via online access panels has created a need to establish new theories and practices that support the use of panels. One consequence of the growing comfort with non-random probability sampling approaches has been the growth of in-house panels. These panels appear set to grow rapidly, driven by the need for speed and costs savings.

ONLINE QUALITATIVE RESEARCH

Although some very interesting and powerful tools have been developed for online qualitative research, such as online focus groups and bulletin board focus groups (OLFGs and BBFGs), online qualitative has only had a modest impact on the total qualitative business.

Perhaps the biggest change to be introduced by the use of online qualitative research has been an increased awareness of the difference between synchronous and asynchronous techniques, for example between online focus groups and bulletin board focus groups. Asynchronous techniques allow access to elements such as consideration, reference, and maturation and the usefulness of this approach is one of the features that have underpinned the success of online research communities/MROCS. Asynchronous approaches are also more convenient for most respondents.

To a large extent the debate about why online qualitative has not had the success that online quantitative research has enjoyed is an academic one. It is clear that many researchers claimed that the online medium was too restrictive and did not enable them to utilise such things as non-verbal clues. However, most of the side-by-side studies found that online qualitative often produced the same business recommendation as face-to-face qualitative.

Perhaps the reasons for the slow uptake of online qualitative have more to do with the researchers than the technique. Many qualitative researchers have traditionally been slower adopters of technology and many enjoy the process of getting out and about, meeting clients and consumers. However, in the future, as the so-called 'net naturals' start to populate the ranks of market research, things may change.

SOCIAL MEDIA AND MARKET RESEARCH

Social media is a disruptive change which is having an impact on many aspects of society and market research. Its impact is as yet too new and too pervasive for its current and likely ongoing impact on market research to be adequately analysed. What can be done, and what this book has set out to do, is to look at some of the main changes which are taking place at the moment, and to make a few tentative guesses about what might come next.

Key aspects of social media and market research include:

- *Online research communities/MROCs*
- *Community-enabled in-house panels*
- *Participatory blogs*
- *Blog and buzz mining*
- *E-ethnography*
- *Social networks and beyond*

ONLINE RESEARCH COMMUNITIES/MROCS

One of the fastest growing areas of market research over the last couple of years has been that of online research communities, or MROCs as they are also known (Market Research Online Communities).

MROCs differ from other online communities in that they are set up specifically to support a company's research function, i.e. they are 'purposed' communities. These research communities come in a wide range of forms, from short term (from three days to three months) to long term (six months or longer). Their size varies from just a few members (such as 30) through to relatively large communities of 1200 or more.

The key to online research communities is the concept of discussion and even the larger MROCs are more qualitative than quantitative. Communities are not intended to be a representative sample of customers; they are a way of accessing the views, thoughts, and potentially the creative powers of customers. The workload with communities tends to be high, with members and moderators expected to be active daily on the very short-term communities and weekly on the longer-term communities.

One of the challenges of MROCs is to turn the discussions into insight in both a timely and cost-efficient way. At present, most communities are analysed in fairly traditional ways, which can result in quite high costs.

Although MROCs are the biggest hit so far in the use of social media it is likely that other forms will become at least as successful over the next few years.

COMMUNITY-ENABLED IN-HOUSE PANELS

Community-enabled panels are in some ways the quantitative big brother of the MROCs and the natural descendents of traditional in-house panels. These panels tend to range from a few thousand members up to 20000 or 30000 members (and may grow further in the near future).

These panels do not have the same sense of community that the MROCs are able to leverage, but they can develop a sense of common purpose, for example, working together to improve the services or products offered by a brand.

The key drivers for these in-house community panels are to be able to conduct cost-effective and rapid quantitative studies. Other types of research are possible, for example online focus groups, discussions, or blogs, but the key tends to be quantitative studies.

Many research buyers have taken onboard the argument that online access panels are not approximating to random access panels. They have taken the next logical step and decided to maximise the cost and speed benefits, deciding on a case-by-case basis whether a research project can be conducted via the in-house panel or whether it needs a more independent sample.

Examples of projects that need an independent sample tend to be market sizing and structure studies and comparative analyses.

PARTICIPATORY BLOGS

Participatory blogs are one of a growing number of research techniques that enable citizens to become researchers, something that Mark Earls and John Kearon have termed WE-Research. In participatory blogs respondents, or perhaps participants, are recruited and shown how to use the blogging platform created for the project. The participants then capture some aspect of their life or daily experience via the blogs.

Examples of the sorts of experience include when the participant feels tired during the day, when they notice advertising for a deodorant, when they use news services when travelling, and even when they feel sweaty. The basic blogs can be enriched by allowing users to upload video, use their mobile phones, and browse each other's blogs.

Participatory blogs are a qualitative technique and one of the many ways that market research is beginning to engage with the ethnographic process.

BLOG AND BUZZ MINING

Blog and buzz mining refers to the process of using automated tools to gather and listen to the millions of discussions happening on the web, in blogs, social networks, Twitter, forums, and in the chat and comment sections of new services.

Blog and buzz mining appeals strongly to the meme of the moment – at least in 2010 – of listening, of asking fewer questions, and spending more time observing what people do and finding out what they are saying to each other.

The plus side is that the conversations about brand, services, and products are real conversations between real customers, talking about their priorities and concerns.

Although this form of passive research holds great promise and some interesting projects have been run there are two main limitations:

1.   Most brands and services are not talked about enough to produce the level of information brand managers need in order to make their decisions. For high profile brands like Apple and Nokia there is a large amount of buzz on the net, but for most everyday products, such as washing powder and breakfast cereal, there is not enough spontaneous discussion, at least until something special happens. This means that whilst listening is essential, it is rarely enough.

2.   The second limitation is that the analysis techniques are still relatively primitive. The difference between an opinion former and a follower is not an easy decision to automate. The difference between a comment and an ironic comment is not easy for a machine to interpret. The majority of analysis tools used at the moment are either very simplistic or heavily dependent on human operators.

However, despite both of these limitations the importance of listening is growing. Even in markets where there is often not enough material about specific brands and products (for example, the sliced bread market), there is often a tremendous amount about the human condition: what do people think about bread in general, what are their key health and taste issues, what are people saying about shelf life versus the use of additives?

The growth of interest in blog and buzz mining has spawned a new debate about ethics which centres on what is in the public domain and what is not, and what uses of material are acceptable and what is not. Whereas listening to the buzz sounds good, blog mining sounds more neutral, and talk of web and screen scraping worries many people.

E-ETHNOGRAPHY

The term 'e-ethnography' is just one of many derived from ethnography, such as netnography and virtual ethnography. The use of ethnography can be broadly divided into three categories.

1. **Observational techniques.** These in turn can be subdivided into macro techniques such as blog and buzz mining, and human-scale projects such as reading and following specific people on the web (for example, in a social network such as Facebook, or via Twitter, or via their blog) to understand more about some aspect of people's lives and interactions.

2. **Interactive approaches.** In these approaches the researcher combines observation with questioning. These techniques include online research communities at one end of the spectrum through to joining online communities and engaging people in conversation as part of the observational process.

3. **WE-Research.** In this approach the research is being conducted by customers and citizens; capturing slices of their own lives and working with the researcher to gain a greater understanding of whatever is being researched. Participatory blogs fit this model as does the use of the new iPhone ethnography app from EveryDayLives.

E-ethnography, by whichever name, matches the desire to listen more and to rely less on asking questions. However, ethnographical approaches require both more time (usually) and skills that are not currently commonly available in the market research industry.

The new options created by social media have also created and amplified a wide range of ethical issues and considerations. What does informed consent really mean in this new socially connected world, what steps should the researcher take to ensure that participants are adequately aware and to protect the people being observed? For example, when visiting online discussions the researcher should probably avoid using literal quotes as the text of a quote (thanks to search engines) identifies its source and that will often identify an individual.

SOCIAL NETWORKS AND BEYOND

The largest single phenomenon of social media to date, at least in the West, is the social network Facebook. Between social networks such as Facebook and local variants such as Mixi and Cyworld, the way people connect, share information, and send messages is being revolutionised.

To date, market researchers have only made marginal usage of social networks as a resource for market research. These uses have included:

○   *as a source for buzz mining, including the use of web scraping techniques, to find and follow large numbers of public and semi-public conversations and comments*

○   *a place to engage in e-ethnography, to observe people in depth and possibly to engage them in discussion*

○   *as a supply of contacts, solicited via adverts, attracting people to take part in research events such as communities or surveys*

○   *as a source of sample for market research surveys, for example, via companies like Peanut Labs*

○   *the creation of artificial social networks for research purposes, such as MROCs*

Given the scale of social networks, and the growth of new variants such as Twitter, it is likely that the future will provide many new ways for them to be integrated into the market research process.

Social networks have also had an impact on the way that market researchers communicate and network with each other. On Facebook, Twitter, and especially LinkedIn, market researchers are forming networks and sharing ideas and information in ways that promise to restructure how power and influence are exercised in the research industry.

APPLYING ONLINE AND SOCIAL MEDIA TO RESEARCH PROBLEMS

The internet, and more recently social media, has become ever more central to people's lives, especially in the Western economies, and it is natural that market research has adopted it as a primary way to observe, listen, and communicate with customers and citizens. Most forms of quantitative research have started to make use of online data collection, usually via the services of online access panels or some other form of database. Indeed, it is probably easier to list those areas where online is not a suitable medium rather than list the cases where it is suitable.

Key areas where online research tends not to be considered suitable are:

○   *where the stimulus material needs to be experienced physically, e.g. touched, sniffed, handled, driven, etc*

○   *studies aimed at people less likely to be online, for example the very poor or the very old*

○   *studies which seek to provide market sizing information, especially in topics that relate to the medium itself (e.g. usage of press and TV).*

In addition, many qualitative researchers choose not to use online equivalents, preferring to stick to face-to-face methodologies.

In contrast to online, social media's history is much newer and far fewer types of project are currently considered suitable. The sorts of projects that tend to use the social media medium include:

○ *ethnographic approaches*

○ *co-creational research*

○ *ideation and alternative/additional customer feedback*

NEW*MR*

New*MR* refers to two major strands in market research. The first is market research that is adopting the techniques and mores of social media, research that is more collaborative, less command and control, and which seeks to work 'with' customers rather than 'on' customers.

The second strand that underlies New*MR* is the search for a research paradigm that is not based on random probability sampling, since it is now generally agreed that online research does not permit this, and there is growing agreement that face-to-face and telephone are no longer able to meet the stringent requirements of random probability sampling.

The new paradigms appear to be coming from two quite distinct directions. The first is based on finding new support for traditional techniques, for example a better understanding of when quota sampling produces reliable results, or where modelling the results of a concept test can provide useful forecasts of likely sales. The second direction is to use entirely new paradigms such as that of prediction markets, which leverages a 'wisdom of crowds' approach to forecast outcomes, in a model closely aligned to the successes of the Iowa Electronic Markets.

There are no hard and fast definitions in this area, but the key New*MR* techniques that are available at the moment include:

○ *blog and buzz mining*

○ *online research communities/MROCs*

○ *community-enabled panels*

○ *prediction markets*

○ *participant blogs*

○ *e-ethnography*

STAYING IN TOUCH WITH DEVELOPMENTS

Whilst this book provides a primer for anybody who wishes to get involved in online and social media research, a book alone cannot keep a researcher in touch with the changes that are happening all around the industry.

For the lucky few, attending conferences and workshops is probably the best way to stay in touch with the leading edge. Particularly useful are those events that provide a mix of theory, case studies, comparative studies, and interaction. However, even if a researcher is unable to attend a conference in person, it is increasingly possible to get a taste of what is happening via both Twitter and the blog posts of those attending.

Beyond the luxury of attending events, the best way to stay in touch is to follow the blogs of key thinkers in this space, to follow the tweets of opinion leaders, and to join LinkedIn and get involved in the better conversations. (**Hot tip!** If you are looking to avoid wasting your time on LinkedIn, only take part in conversations that already have at least five comments. Most discussions never reach five comments and these can usually be ignored.)

The appendix to this book lists a wide range of resources and the website that accompanies this book, http://hosmr.com, lists many more. However, the two best (at the moment) are probably the Vovici blog written by Jeffrey Henning (for its sheer volume of good material) and the 'Bad Research, No Biscuit' blog for highlighting much that is currently wrong with online market research.

FINAL THOUGHTS ABOUT QUALITY AND ETHICS

The extra speed and reach created by the internet have generated new challenges in the areas of quality and ethics, with research organisations and legislators having to run just to keep standing still. As well as being aware of both laws and regulations, the market researcher needs to establish their own moral compass that will help when confronted with issues which are as yet undocumented and regulated.

The key things that the researcher needs to keep in mind are:

1.   Ensure the client is aware of the benefits and limitations of what they are buying. Clients have had 70 years to understand the traditional research model; it will take time for the new ideas to be so widely understood. Also, the new rules and tools are not established, so the message to clients will change as the situation unfolds.

2.   Help the client to assess and manage the risk. For example, if a product is widely loved and very open, then a social media project might be a good idea. However, if a brand is widely disliked, then it may be more prudent to use a more controlled form of research, such as a closed community with tight terms and conditions.

3.   Things said on the internet, stay on the internet. This makes the internet very different to most casual conversations and even most survey responses. Respondents, researchers, and clients need to be aware that what they say may be around for some time, as may its consequences.

4.   Respondents may need protecting from themselves and each other. Respondents should normally protect their anonymity, for example, by using non-photo and constructed avatars.

They should be dissuaded from 'hooking up' with other respondents via the introductions made as part of the market research.

5.   Just because it looks like a public comment does not mean that it is a public comment. Nor has the person making the comment consented to their copyright or intellectual property being used for the researcher's purposes, especially when conducting blog and buzz mining.

AND FINALLY . . .

Many thanks to all of you who have made it to the end of the book. I hope you have found it useful. We would like to update the book in the future and I am already gathering material on the book's website at http://hosmr.com. If you have any comments or suggestions, please feel free to visit the website, and perhaps be listed as a contributor in the next release.

Glossary

This glossary covers the key terms used in the book. However, it is not a comprehensive glossary of all the terms used in the world of online market research.

Activity cycle The activity cycle of a participatory project, such as an online research community, is the frequency that tasks occur within a project. If the moderator sets a new task daily, and participants are expected to contribute daily, then the activity cycle is daily.

Adaptive scripting Adaptive scripting is where the survey is written so that each respondent sees a survey that is tailored to their responses. At one end of the spectrum this might be as simple as defining a list of products regularly used and then only asking about these. At the other end would be a product like Sawtooth Software's Adaptive CBC, which creates questions specific to each respondent and to their earlier answers.

Aggregator An aggregator, such as Bloglines or Google Reader, collects together feeds (for example RSS feeds) so that the user has information (for example from blogs or news sites) gathered in a single convenient location.

ASP (application service provider) An ASP is an application accessed over the internet rather than having the software on the local computer. ASP is essentially the same as SaaS (see below).

Asynchronous research Asynchronous research refers to forms of research which do not require the researcher and the respondent to be online at the same time (forms of research that do require this are known as synchronous research). Online quantitative surveys, online research communities, and bulletin board groups are asynchronous techniques. By contrast, face-to-face interviewing, CATI, and online focus groups are all synchronous.

Avatar An avatar is an online identity. In some environments an avatar is simply a name, in others it is a name and an image, and in places such as Second Life the avatar is a rendering of a character. An avatar can be somebody's real name and photo, or can be a made-up name and any image they choose to use.

Bandwidth Originally the term related to the capacity of a channel to carry a signal and was often expressed in terms of units such as bits per second. More recently it is often used more generally to describe the capacity of a system to handle more users or requests rather than just the capacity of its wiring.

Banner ad A banner ad is an advert displayed on a web page. The most typical type of banner ad is one that runs across the page, but there are a wide variety of shapes and positions that can be used.

Most banner ads are clickable, which means that when a user clicks on them something happens, such as being taken to a page containing further information.

The response rate to banner ads is normally very low, with fewer than 1% of the people being shown the ad clicking on it.

BBG/BBFG See Bulletin Board Group

Behavioural targeting Behavioural targeting (also known as BT) is a method of using information about an individual to target services or advertising to them. For example, if somebody uses a search engine to look for flights to France and cottages in Normandy the service might target advertising relating to holidays in Northern France to them.

Blog Short for weblog – a website organised as a chronological set of posts, for example an online diary or a collected set of thoughts and musings.

Blog mining Blog mining is the process of searching blogosphere for information. For example, a brand might search for all mentions of their brand name and seek to understand the context for those mentions, e.g. positive versus negative.

Blogosphere The blogosphere is a collective noun for the sum total of all the blogs being written and all the online comments made to those blogs. The term is sometimes used more widely to describe all online discussions and posts, for example including bulletin board discussions.

BPTO Brand Price Trade-Off is a method of assessing the price sensitivity of products. A respondent is presented with an array of priced products and asked to select the one they are most likely to buy. After they make their choice the prices are systematically adjusted and the question repeated. This process is repeated a number of times to provide the input into analyses that determine the price value and elasticity of each product in the test.

Brand Price Trade-Off See BPTO.

BT Could be the UK telecommunications company, but in social media more likely to be behavioural targeting (see above).

Bulletin board group A bulletin board group (also known as BBG, BBFG, and bulletin board focus group) is a method of conducting online qualitative research. A BBG is conducted over a period of time using bulletin board software. A BBG is an asynchronous qualitative technique.

Buzz Buzz is a jargon word for the hot topics of conversation. The term is sometimes used in connection with mining, for example buzz mining, which means searching the internet to find out the latest topics and to understand what people are saying to each other.

As of early 2010, Buzz is also the name of Google's new social network (they already own Orkut).

CATI CATI means Computer Aided Telephone Interviewing. Strictly, CATI means using a computer system to administer surveys, typically by dialling the respondents, showing the interviewer the questions to ask, with the interviewer entering the responses back to the computer. Occasionally, the term CATI is used interchangeably with telephone surveys (because most telephone surveys are CATI).

CEO blog A blog written by the leader of a company, combining their personal perspectives and the official view of the organisation, for example Mark Cuban's 'Blog Maverick' [http://blogmaverick.com/].

CGM See consumer generated media.

Choice model Choice model is a generic term that relates to modelling behaviour through the use of data captured from respondents completing tasks, where each task requires the respondent to make a choice, as opposed to, say, rating or ranking. DCM and MaxDiff are both choice-based approaches.

Closed communities Most MROCS (online research communities) are private, only people who are invited to join them can see them and take part, i.e. they are closed. Open communities, by contrast, are ones where either a wide range of people can ask to be members and have a reasonable expectation of being granted membership or are visible/available to everybody.

Cloud computing Cloud computing refers to networks of large clusters of computing power, each cluster capable of replicating each other so that the service they provide is less likely to be interrupted and workflows can be balanced. Common examples of services provided by cloud computing are Google and Amazon. As cloud computing becomes more common, the concept of 'where' a piece of data is becomes more and more redundant, in a sense it is everywhere, at least it is everywhere with an internet connection.

Community plan The community plan is the community's equivalent of a focus group's discussion guide, setting out the prompts, tasks, polls, etc.

Conjoint analysis Conjoint analysis is a method of working with a set of attributes, which are each comprised of a set of levels (e.g. Colour might be an attribute and Red, Green, and Blue might be the levels). Typically, the data collection makes the respondent trade off one set of levels against another. The objective is to estimate a numerical value for each level of each attribute, indicating its contribution to consumer choice.

For example, a very simple laptop study might have five attributes: weight, screen size, processor speed, brand, and price. The weight attribute might have 1Kg, 1.5Kg, 2Kg, and 2.5Kg as its levels.

Many types of conjoint analysis are also called trade-off analysis and if the respondent chooses (as opposed to rating or ranking) then conjoint can also be known as discrete choice modelling (DCM).

Consumer generated media (CGM) CGM refers to the change from a publish culture to a mass contributory culture. The photos on Flickr and the home-made videos on YouTube are both examples of CGM.

Cookies Cookies are small text files stored on a website visitor's computer. Cookies allow a website to tell whether somebody has been to the site before. One use of cookies is to avoid asking the same person twice to do the same popup survey.

Crowdsourcing This is a method of solving a business problem through an open invitation to solve the problem. One type of crowdsourcing is a competition for a prize, where the winner potentially takes all, such as the 1823 British Admiralty competition to find a reliable chronometer to use at sea. Another type of crowdsourcing is where many people each add part of the solution, such as the model underlying Wikipedia and Threadless.com.

Cyberbullying Cyberbullying is a generic phrase for all electronic methods of making other people feel worse. A good source on cyberbullying is http://yp.direct.gov.uk/cyberbullying/.

Cyber-skive A phrase which describes people who are at work, but who are not working and are using internet access for their own purposes. One form of cyber-skiving is to use Facebook when at work, and answering online surveys is another. Researchers should keep in mind that they ought not encourage respondents to complete surveys at work as it could result in the respondent losing their job if caught.

Cyworld Cyworld is the leading social network in South Korea.

DCM DCM, Discrete Choice Modelling, is a form of conjoint analysis that allows the utility of different attributes and levels to be estimated.

See also Conjoint analysis.

Deep packet inspection A method of finding out what an internet user is interested in. Traffic on the internet is typically sent as small packets of data from the user to the ISP to the website. In deep packet inspection the ISP sends a copy to the inspection company who opens the packet and adds the information to a database. The most typical use for this approach is to help make advertising more targeted, i.e. as part of behavioural targeting.

Discrete Choice Modelling See DCM.

DIY research DIY (do it yourself) is a term which applies to services that allow people with no research training to easily conduct surveys. It includes easy-to-use survey platforms such as Survey Monkey, and one-stop sample/survey options such as AskYourTargetMarket.com.

DNSBL DNSBL stands for DNS Blackhole List (and DNS stands for Domain Name Service, which is how addresses on the internet are organised). A DNSBL is a list of sites believed to be responsible for spam and which many ISPs and systems therefore block.

eDelphi Delphi is a research technique based on collaborative thinking, often with experts or people interested in a field. eDelphi is an internet-based version of this, where ideas and thoughts are shared by the moderator, for example by using email or some other form of internet collaboration.

e-ethnography e-ethnography is a catchall phrase for ethnography conducted via the internet. It encompasses everything from large-scale observation through blog and buzz mining, to small-scale observation such as visiting online communities, to working with participants as collaborators, for example in WE or citizen research.

Email groups Email groups, also called moderated email groups or MEGs, are a form of focus group conducted via email. The moderator sends questions to the group members who reply to the moderator, who then summarises the responses and uses them to inform the next questions.

Evoked sets An evoked set is a subset which is tailored to be specific to a respondent. For example, a survey may cover 30 brands of cereal, but a respondent might only be asked detailed questions about the brands they sometimes buy; this subset is the respondent's evoked set.

Extranet An extranet is an extension to an intranet to let external organisations have access to sections of an organisation's intranet. One key use of an extranet, in market research, is to allow vendors to supply results to buyers by depositing the findings into the buyer's intranet.

Eye tracking Eye tracking is a method of recording where somebody is looking and is particularly useful in assessing websites. Until a few years ago eye tracking required intrusive devices such as headsets, but there are now non-intrusive options which can passively record where people are looking.

Factor analysis Factor analysis is a statistical method of assessing whether a set of attributes can be replaced with a smaller set of underlying factors – for example, in the way that weight, height, and waist size could all be thought of as versions of the underlying factor 'size'.

FAQs FAQs, or frequently asked questions, are a method for a website to help users by providing a collection of answers to the questions that users tend to ask.

Flash Flash is a technology from Adobe which allows websites to be dynamic and allow interactivity. Flash is the main technology used by companies who are trying to provide more engaging surveys.

Friending Friending is a term used in social networks to signify that two people have identified a connection between them. The term 'friend' tends to be used in the more overtly social networks, such as Facebook (other networks have other phrases). The term 'connection' is used in LinkedIn, and in Twitter people 'follow' each other. 'Buddy' is another term used. The term does not signify that people are necessarily friends in the real world.

Grounded theory Grounded theory is a formalised method of interpreting qualitative information. The process includes reviewing the information to create codes, then concepts, and finally categories, with a view to generating overall theories explaining the data.

HB See Hierarchical Bayes.

Heuristics A heuristic is an iterative technique for solving a problem. A heuristic can be as simple as deleting all interviews that are conducted too fast, or it can be a complex system for automated analysis of online discussions.

Hierarchical Bayes Hierarchical Bayes, often referred to as HB, is an advanced statistical technique which allows data sets with large amounts of missing data to be processed. The basic idea is a two step process. (1) the respondent data is used to create an overall distribution. (2) Alternative, but complete, results are generated for each respondent (normally hundreds of thousands of times) to create a set of scores which reflect the overall distribution of the scores.

HB has become very important to conjoint and Discrete Choice Modelling where it removes the requirement to ask so many trade-off questions of each respondent.

Hill climbing Hill climbing is a type of procedure that seeks to find the answer to a problem by repeating an exercise and each time getting a bit closer to the result. Hill climbing is often used to solve mathematical or statistical problems.

HTML HTML, Hypertext Markup Language, is a method of turning text into a graphical page and is the basis of most web pages. HTML can be used to make emails more attractive and interactive.

Hybrid communities Hybrid communities are online communities used for more than one purpose, such P&G's Tremor panel which can be used for word-of-mouth marketing and market research.

Intellectual Property Also referred to as IP and IPR (Intellect Property Rights). Intellectual Property describes ideas, knowledge, designs, and concepts, things which may have value, or which may have value in the future. A research buyer's IP often includes product ideas, designs, advertising, logos, etc. A vendor's IP could include questionnaire and methodological designs. One concern about research, especially online research, is the risk that IP will be leaked by respondents. Social media raises a concern about who owns the IP of ideas developed collaboratively.

Internet service provider An internet service provider (an ISP) is the method by which most people access the internet, connecting to their ISP which then acts as a bridge to the internet.

Interstitial An interstitial is a method of inserting a web page between the page a visitor is on and a page they request. Interstitials can be used as a mechanism for website surveys as an alternative to popup surveys.

Intranet An intranet can be thought of as an internet that exists within an organisation. The term 'intranet' is somewhat flexible, but the core idea is one that uses a browse-like approach to organise information and to provide access to it.

Invisible processing Invisible processing is a collective term for the many forms of information that can be collected without asking an explicit question. For example, during a web survey the system can capture some or all of the following: date and time of the survey, browser being used, IP address, operating system, and language.

IP address Every device connected to the internet has a specific address, which allows it to send and receive information; this address is its IP address. Some devices and users have a permanent IP address (i.e. it never changes), other users have a dynamic address (i.e. it can change from one session to another), assigned by their ISP each time they log on.

ISP See Internet service provider.

JavaScript A scripting language often used with websites to add functionality. Most internet browsers (for example Firefox and Internet Explorer) can interpret and run JavaScript commands that have been encoded within a page. However, some users turn JavaScript off, which is why accessibility guidelines suggest that pages should be able to work without JavaScript.

Legacy issues Legacy issues are created over time, and refer to things that have to be done now in order to take care of issues such as compatibility. For example, new versions of Microsoft Word need to be able to read older formats, that is a legacy issue. Questions that are asked on face-to-face surveys are sometimes asked the same way online in order to maximise continuity, an example of legacy.

MaxDiff MaxDiff is a choice-based method of assigning numerical values to a range of features or attributes. In a typical deployment, the list of attributes is broken into subsets of four or five and shown to the respondent, who then says which is most important and which is the least.

One of the key strengths of MaxDiff is that it makes very few assumptions about the nature of the data and produces results from different groups, countries, and cultures that are directly comparable.

MEGs See Moderated email groups.

Memes Memes are ideas or concepts passed from person to person. The term 'meme' dates back to Richard Dawkins' book *The Selfish Gene* and the word itself become a meme, especially in terms of the way ideas are passed along in social media.

Microblogging Microblogging is a form of blogging where the posts are very short. The most popular example of microblogging is Twitter.

Mixi The leading social network in Japan.

Moderated Email Groups (MEGs) See Email group.

Moderator In a focus group, the moderator is the researcher who is leading the group and conducting the research. In an online community, the term moderator has two meanings: (1) the researcher who is leading the discussion and conducting the research; (2) the person responsible for the orderly conduct of the community, providing advice to people with problems and checking that the terms and conditions are being observed.

Monetise The ability to turn a service into money. In social media, this method does not necessarily depend on charging a fee for the main service. For example, the service may be funded by advertising, by charging for a premium service, or by merchandising.

MROCs Market Research Online Communities is another term for Online Research Communities. The term MROC was first coined by Forrester.

Natural communities A natural community is an online community which has not been created for a specific commercial purpose, for example communities of special interest groups, but also communities such as Facebook and Bebo. By contrast, brand communities, MROCs, and word-of-mouth communities are not natural communities.

Netnography Netnography is a form of ethnography that looks at the behaviour of people on the internet, a term associated with Robert Kozinets. In market research, it is often used to describe looking at large amounts of community or blog behaviour to draw conclusions about what people are saying or thinking. As with e-ethnography and virtual ethnography, definitions are somewhat fluid at the moment.

New*MR* New*MR* is a term which describes new market research associated with two key themes: (1) social media, and (2) to create methods that do not depend on assumptions of random probability sampling.

Non-market research Where market research techniques are used for non-research purposes, for example to collect data for marketing databases, also known as mixed-purpose research.

Online focus group A focus group conducted online using modified chat software.

Online research communities A community created specifically to provide market research insight, as distinct from either a natural online community or a marketing-related online community. An online research community is also known as an MROC or as an insight community.

Orkut Orkut is a social network provided by Google.

Overlays An overlay is part of a web page which is scripted so that it can be made to sit in front of the rest of the page. An overlay is an alternative to a popup window. To most internet users there is little difference in the appearance of an overlay and a popup; however, most popup blockers do not block overlays, hence their use as an alternative to popup surveys.

Paradata Paradata is data about the process. In online market research this refers to data such as the speed of the survey, the type of browser the respondent is using, the length of open-ended responses (Jeavons, 2001).

Parallel IDIs Parallel IDIs (in-depth interviews) is a method of conducting interviews with a group of people without the individual members being aware of each other. The typical way of conducting these IDIs is with bulletin board group software. Parallel IDIs are an asynchronous technique; the researcher and the respondent do not need to be online at the same time.

Platform In the context of this book, platform is an IT word referring to the combination of software, hardware, and systems which make an online service available. In blogging, Wordpad and Typepad are platforms that allow people to create blogs. In online surveys, Confirmit and NEBU are platforms that allow people to script and host surveys. Vision Critical, for example, provide a platform that can be used for communities and community enhanced panels, whilst Itracks provides a platform for online qualitative research.

Pop-under A pop-under is a web page created by a site (for example for a survey or for advertising) which is placed below currently open windows. The pop-under either becomes exposed when all the other windows are closed (which implies the visitor has left the site) or after a predetermined period of time. Pop-unders are generally considered unpopular with internet users.

Popup A popup is a window launched by a website which sits in front of the website that a visitor is looking at or using. Popups can be used for advertising or for popup surveys. Popups are generally considered unpopular and most internet browsers include 'popup blockers', a method of reducing the number of popups that are launched.

Popup survey A popup survey is a survey launched via a popup. The main use of popup surveys is for visitor surveys, as part of a website research programme.

Portal A portal is a generic phrase for website that acts as a gateway to a range of services, often from different providers.

Post-moderation When people are allowed to post comments to a website they tend to be pre-moderated or post-moderated. Post-moderated is where comments are initially published and then removed if they prove to be unsuitable.

Prediction markets Prediction markets are a research tool where predictions are formed by allowing the participants to buy and sell 'positions' on what they think will happen in the future (in a similar way to futures markets). The most well-known example of prediction markets are the Iowa Electronic Markets which have been successfully predicting the results of USA elections for many years.

Pre-moderation When people are allowed to post comments to a website they tend to be pre-moderated or post-moderated. Pre-moderation is where comments are not published until they have been checked to ensure they are suitable. Pre-moderation is the safest option, but it can use more resources and slow discussions down.

Private communities A private community is one where only people who have been invited to join can see it and make contributions. Most MROCs are currently organised as private (or closed) communities.

PSM Van Westerndorp's PSM (price sensitivity meter) is a method of conducting pricing research, based on respondents stating their expectations for the price of a product being tested.

RDD RDD, random digit dialling, is a method of recruiting a sample for a telephone survey in a way that can approximate to a random sampling approach. Software is used to generate random telephone numbers, which are then dialled. The process can be structured so that it represents different area codes to improve the sampling algorithm.

Render Render describes the process of converting something so that it appears on a screen. For example, a questionnaire may consist of simple text questions, but a routine may be used to 'render' it as a Flash-enhanced page.

Research 2.0 Research 2.0 was a term used to describe how the paradigm shift implied by the term 'Web 2.0' was being applied in market research. Research 2.0 implies a move away from research done **to** people into research that was done **with** people, such as blogs and communities. By 2009 it was deemed by many researchers to have become dated and has become subsumed by the term 'NewMR'.

River sampling River sampling is a process of attracting respondents as and when they are needed, as opposed to drawing them from a resource such as a panel (to extend the analogy, panels would be seen as ponds or reservoirs). The use of popup survey invitations and online advertising to attract respondents are both examples of river sampling.

ROI ROI (return on investment) relates to the (usually financial) return that results from doing a project. In a perfect world a $100 000 research project might be shown to have saved $500 000 of advertising costs, a ROI of $400 000.

RSS feed An RSS feed is a method of spreading information. A website can be configured to send a message out in a standardised format every time a new entry is added to the page. This standardised format is called a feed and the best known feed format is the RSS feed. People who want to follow the information use a feed or news aggregator to collect and organise the information.

SaaS SaaS (software as a service) is a process where users access the software over the internet and in effect rent it instead of buying it. Many of the survey systems are available as SaaS.

Satisficing Satisficing refers to the phenomenon where some people try to reduce the cognitive load on them by only doing sufficient to satisfy the process (hence satisfice). More recently, the term has taken on a wider meaning in market research to include people who are simply clicking through a survey without making any effort to answer the questions properly.

Screen scraping Screen scraping is a method of using software to collect information from a web page and store it in a database. For example, a screen scraper could be used to collect all the comments from a community discussion and store it in a form where it can be processed. The terms 'screen scraping' and 'web scraping' can be emotive as they imply the user is not 'playing fair' with the website and, indeed, scraping is against the terms and conditions of some sites such as Google and Facebook.

SEM Search Engine Marketing is a partner activity to SEO (see below). SEM refers to optimising the performance of sponsored links. A sponsored link is displayed by a search engine (such as Google or Bing) in addition (and usually ahead of) to the links found by the searching process. Note, in marketing sciences SEM also means Structural Equation Modelling.

SEO Search Engine Optimisation, the process of modifying a page to maximise its chances of being found and ranked highly by search engines such as Google and Bing.

Serve In web-speak, serve is the process where the server sends something to a browser. For example, if a new page is created, it is 'served'. If a popup appears on the user's screen, it is 'served'. When a cookie is sent to the browser it is 'served'.

Skype Skype is a popular method for people to use VOIP to give them free or low-cost telephone calls. The calls from one Skype user to another Skype user are free and are usually heavily discounted to regular telephones. To use Skype, the user has to have an internet connection and audio, for example a PC with microphone and speakers, or a portable device such as an iPhone.

Social bookmarking A method of tagging something useful and then sharing that tag with other internet users. Leading systems include Delicious, Digg, and Redit.

Soft launch A soft launch is the process of starting a survey by only inviting a few respondents, aiming to collect perhaps 20 to 50 completes, in order to check the survey and indeed the whole process.

Status (social networks) Many of the popular social networks, such as Facebook and LinkedIn, have a method for users to say what they are currently doing or thinking. The sharing of status information is currently one of the most effective ways of people being aware of their networks of contacts.

Tag cloud A tag cloud is a visual representation of a set of text, either normal text or tags. The tag cloud is the result of a two-step process. First it counts the frequency of all the words in the collection, then it produces a picture where the most frequent words are displayed such that the more frequently they appear in the text, the larger they appear in the picture.

Tags A tag is a short description of something, for example a picture, a piece of text, or a clip from a movie. For example, in Flickr the most popular tags for photos tend to be: wedding, nature, travel, party, and Japan. In market research the process of coding can be considered a form of tagging.

Tagging is useful because it allows items to grouped and to be searched.

TCP/IP TCP/IP is the way that the internet passes information around, it is what is known as a protocol, allowing different devices and systems to talk to each other.

Thread A thread is a discussion, especially on a bulletin board. A thread starts with a post, i.e. comment or question, and is then followed by other people posting their comments.

Tweet A post in the microblogging system Twitter is called a Tweet. A ReTweet is the process of reposting somebody else's Tweet so that it reaches a wider audience.

Twitter Twitter is a microblogging system, where people post blog items with fewer than 141 characters.

UGM User-generated media (UGM) refers to media created by the public rather than by professionals. The best known example in the West is YouTube, where millions of people have uploaded their own videos.

Virtual worlds Virtual worlds are sites such as Second Life and World of Warcraft where people can spend time interacting with other people, either playing games or just socialising.

VOIP Voice Over Internet Protocol is a method of routing telephone calls via the internet to massively reduce the costs of telephone conversations. There are a large number of commercial operations, but the best known public use of VOIP is Skype, which provides free calls to other Skype users and discounted calls to telephones. The voice features of services such as GoToMeeting or in online focus groups are also examples of VOIP.

W3C W3C is the World Wide Web Consortium, the main standards-setting body for the web.

W3C WAI Standards The W3C WAI standard (the World Wide Web Consortium Web Accessibility Initiative) are the guidelines on how websites should be written that they enable everybody to use the web, especially those with special challenges such as visual impairment.

Web 2.0 The term 'Web 2.0' encompasses a wide variety of phenomena such as: social networks (FaceBook and LinkedIn), blogs, forums and chat, product review sites, user-generated content (e.g.

YouTube and Flickr), citizen journalism, and co-creation (such as Wikipedia). Compared with earlier publishing models, Web 2.0 is bottom-up. The term was first coined by O'Reilly Media in 2004 as a way of describing how people were starting to contribute their own content on the internet rather than simply downloading what was already there.

Web analytics Web analytics is software that measure the volume of activities of people who visit a website. It can be provided by the website software or via third-party software. Google analytics is an example of a web analytics service.

Web bug A web bug is a method of tracking activity, for example to tell if an email has been opened. It is typically a reference to a small image (e.g. a single pixel transparent image) and when the email loads the image from a server the email is recorded as being opened.

Weblog See Blog.

Web metrics The terms 'metrics' simply refers to things that can be measured and recorded. Web metrics refers to metrics that can be collected about the web. There are a range of uses of the term, such as information about a website, the nature of its visitors, traffic levels for websites and indeed countries. When somebody uses the term 'web metrics' it is often necessary to check what in particular the metrics they are talking about relate to.

Web scraping Web scraping is very similar to screen scraping, i.e. the use of software to harvest information from the web. The main difference between the two terms is that screen scraping implies manually finding a page and then capturing the information, whereas web scraping is often used to describe a more general process where the software can be used to both find pages and capture the information.

Web scraping is considered emotive by some people and against the terms and conditions of many services such as Google and Facebook.

Web survey systems A web survey system, such as Confirmit or NEBU, is a method of creating and implementing surveys on the internet. In terms of complexity they can vary from the DIY-focused tools such as Survey Monkey and Zoomerang through to fully featured systems which incorporate tools such as panel management, reporting, and analysis.

Wiki A wiki is a collaborative website where users can post and edit contributions in order to create the result. The best known wiki is probably Wikipedia, an online encyclopaedia created by hundreds of thousands of volunteers editing and re-editing the entries. Wikis are often used within companies as part of creating products, manuals, or project plans.

Wireframes Wireframes are often used in the design of a website. The wireframe is the basic template for a website which then allows different content to be inserted in the sections and tested.

WOM Word-of-mouth, often abbreviated to WOM, refers to passing messages, e.g. marketing messages, from person to person as opposed to broadcasting it via mass media. Word-of-mouth has always been important, but the internet makes it easier to spread and therefore of more interest to marketers.

WYSIWYG Acronym for What You See Is What You Get, a method of editing a document where the users see it on their screen the way it will be seen on the internet when in use.

Further Information

There are many free ways to find further information and to stay up-to-date, but only a few can be listed here. Below are listed some of my favourite blogs, references, and a cross-section of networks.

The website that accompanies this book, http://hosmr.com/ has a list of resources that will be regularly updated.

BLOGS

Probably the most important resource at the moment for researchers wanting to stay in touch with developments, are the blogs written either by the industry's thought leaders or by people keen to annotate the developments going on around us. The list below is simply a cross-section of the blogs available.

Title	Description	URL
Blackbeard	The blog of Tom Ewing, British thought leader in the social media space.	http://blackbeardblog.tumblr.com/
CRO-ing About Research	The blog of Joel Rubinson, the Chief Research Officer of the ARF (Advertising Research Foundation).	http://blog.joelrubinson.net/
Forrester	Forrester's blog on consumer market research professionals.	http://blogs.forrester.com/consumer_market_research/
FreshNetworks	The blog of FreshNetworks one of the leaders in the use of MROCs.	http://blog.freshnetworks.com/
Kumeugirl	The blog of Singapore based Lee Ryan, a regional qual director.	http://kumeugirl.com/
Nigel Hollis	Blog of Nigel Hollis, Chief Global Analyst at Millward Brown.	http://www.mb-blog.com/
The Future Place	Blog of Ray Poynter, Managing Director at The Future Place.	http://thefutureplace.typepad.com/
The Human Element	The blog of UK consultant Alison Macleod.	http://mackle.wordpress.com/
The Survey Geek	Blog of Reg Baker, COO of Marketing Strategies.	http://regbaker.typepad.com/regs_blog/
Virtual Surveys	A blog from UK online pioneers Virtual Surveys, written by a team.	http://www.virtualsurveysdiscussion.com/vslblog/
Vovici	The blog of Jeffrey Henning, Vice President Strategy Vovici.	http://blog.vovici.com/
Zebra Bites	The blog of Katie Harris, an Australian director of qualitative research.	http://zebrabites.com/

OTHER RESOURCES

The only two characteristics the sites below have in common are that I find them useful and that they are free.

Title	Description	URL
Australian Bureau of Statistics	A great online collection of demographic and economic information.	http://www.abs.gov.au/
CIA Factbook	Contains a wide range of country details, including population, telecoms, economic data, languages, etc.	https://www.cia.gov/library/publications/the-world-factbook/
ClickZ	A collection of reports and statistics about the Web and its users.	http://www.clickz.com/
ESOMAR Professional Standards	In addition to national guidelines researchers will often find the international guidelines on the ESOMAR site useful.	http://esomar.org/
Handbook of Online and Social Media Research	The website accompanying this book.	http://hosmr.com/
International World Stats	A collection of data about internet statistics, by region and country.	http://www.internetworldstats.com/
MRWeb	MRWeb is a market research portal and hosts the DRNO (Daily Research News).	http://www.mrweb.com/
Quirks	Large collection of MR articles (requires registration).	http://www.quirks.com/
Research Live	News service of the UK's MRS and linked to *Research* magazine.	http://www.research-live.com/

GROUPS AND NETWORKS FOR RESEARCHERS

Probably the most important network for any market researcher, IMHO, is LinkedIn, but there are many others that are useful, fun, or both.

LINKEDIN GROUPS

Name	Description	Location
ESOMAR	General market research group, focused on ESOMAR.	http://www.linkedin.com/groups?gid=2755
Future Trends	A large group, wider than market research looking at trends.	http://www.linkedin.com/groups?gid=145854
Next Gen Market Research (NGMR)	General market research group.	http://www.linkedin.com/groups?gid=31804
NewMR	Market research group focused on NewMR.	http://www.linkedin.com/groups?gid=2446402
Market Research Bulletin	One of the largest market research groups.	http://www.linkedin.com/groups?gid=1772348
Market Research Global Alliance	This group is very international and linked to the independent research group MRGA.	http://www.linkedin.com/groups?gid=41051
Marketing Science	Relatively small group, looking specifically at marketing science.	http://www.linkedin.com/groups?gid=147581

FACEBOOK

Facebook has become a less popular place for market researchers to meet and talk about work, but plenty of researchers still meet there socially, and a surprisingly large number take part in Farmville and Mafia Wars.

Title	Description	URL
Market Research Rocks! (hell yeah it does)	General market research group.	http://www.facebook.com/group.php?gid=9035511510
The Big List of Market Researchers	General market research group.	http://www.facebook.com/group.php?gid=18095664464

(continued)

Title	Description	URL
Quantitative Research Counts	Focused on quantitative research.	http://www.facebook.com/group.php?gid=18007030944
Qualitative Meaning	Focused on qualitative research.	http://www.facebook.com/group.php?gid=4547384484
Research 2.0	Focused on research 2.0.	http://www.facebook.com/group.php?gid=3406470409
International Journal of Marketing Research (IJMR)	Group devoted to the *IJMR*, a leading journal of market research.	http://www.facebook.com/group.php?gid=47554954831

RESEARCHER NETWORKS

These networks are created specifically for market researchers.

Name	Description	URL
MRSpace	General network of market researchers.	http://mrspace.ning.com/
Research Voice	General network of market researchers.	http://www.research-voice.com/
Market Research Global Alliance	General network of market researchers.	http://www.mrgasn.com/

TWITTER

There are too many people whose tweets are worth following to list them here and the picture changes very quickly. So I will restrict my advice to searching with the hashtag #mr or #esomar and then following those people who seem to be saying something relevant to you.

Oh, and my tweets can be found at http://twitter.com/RayPoynter.

References

Ariely, Dan (2008). *Predictably Irrational: The hidden forces that shape our decisions*. Harper Collins, USA.

August, Steve (2004) Community Involvement: Using online ethnography to explore the digital camera market. *Quirks Marketing Research Review*, July 2004.

Baker, Reg (2008) A Web of Worries. Research World, ESOMAR, June 2008.

Brace, Ian (2008) *Questionnaire Design: How to plan, structure and write survey material for effective market research*. 2nd Edition, Kogan Page Ltd, London.

Brüggen, Elisabeth and Willems, Pieter (2009) A critical comparison of offline focus groups, online focus groups and e-Delphi. *International Journal of Market Research*, Vol. 51, Issue 3, pp. 363–381.

Capeling, Theresa. Co-Moderating in an Online Environment. Itracks Newsletter, [http://www.itracks.com/LinkClick.aspx?fileticket=GygUvma_wyE%3D&tabid=99], Downloaded 14 February 2010.

Cheng, Colin C., Krumwiede, Dennis and Chwen, Sheu (2009) Online audio group discussions: a comparison with face-to-face methods. *International Journal of Market Research*, Vol. 51, Issue 2, pp. 219–241.

Cierpicki, Steve, Alexander-Head, Daniel, Rubie, Lou, Poynter, Ray and Alchin, Stephanie. (2009) It works for us but does it work for them? How online research communities work for consumers invited to participate. ESOMAR Online Research, 2009 Online Panels and beyond. Chicago, USA.

Comley, Pete (2000) Pop-up Surveys: What works, what doesn't work and what will work in the future. ESOMAR Net Effects 3 The Worldwide Internet Conference. Dublin, Ireland.

Comley, Pete (2002) Online research will take off in the UK in 2003: The case for and against. *Research Magazine*, October 2002, UK.

Comley, Pete (2006) The Games We Play: A psychoanalysis of the relationship between panel owners and panel participants. ESOMAR Panels Research Conference 2006. Barcelona, Spain.

Comley, Pete (2007) Online Market Research. In: Van Hamersveld, Mario and de Bont, Cees (eds) *Market Research Handbook*, 5th edition. John Wiley & Sons Ltd. Chichester, pp. 408–409.

Comley, Pete (2008) Real-time research. Market Research Society Annual Conference, UK.

Couper, Mick P. (2008) *Designing Effective Web Surveys*. Cambridge University Press, Cambridge.

Derval, Diana and Menti, Mario (2008) *The virtual sofa: Wait marketing in Second Life*. ESOMAR, Innovate! Conference, Copenhagen.

Dillman, Don, Smyth, Jolene D. and Christian, Leah Melani (2009) *Internet, Mail, and Mixed-Mode Surveys: The Tailored Design Method*. 3rd edition. John Wiley & Sons, Inc., New Jersey.

Dobbs, L. (2004) *Exporting America: Why corporate greed is shipping American jobs overseas.* Warner Business Books, New York.

Drolent, Jennifer, Butler, Alice and Davis, Steve. (2009) How Important is the Respondent's Perception of Survey Length? The survey burden factor. *Quirks Marketing Research Review*, November 2009.

Earls, Mark (2007) *Herd: How to change mass behaviour by harnessing our true nature.* John Wiley & Sons, Ltd., Chichester.

Eke, Vanessa and Comley, Pete (1999) Moderated Email Groups. *Computing Magazine*, UK.

ESOMAR Global Market Research (2006) *ESOMAR Industry Report.* ESOMAR.

ESOMAR Global Market Research (2007) *ESOMAR Global Prices Study 2007* ESOMAR.

ESOMAR Global Market Research (2009), *ESOMAR Industry Report.* ESOMAR.

ESOMAR Global Market Research (2009) ESOMAR Guidelines: Conducting market and opinion research using the internet. Downloaded November 2009.

ESOMAR Global Market Research. ESOMAR Guidelines: Passive data collection, observation and recording. downloaded November 2009 [http://www.esomar.org/uploads/pdf/professional-standards/ESOMAR_Guideline_on_Passive_Data_Collection_November2008_.pdf]

Ferneley, Elainie and Heinze, Aleksej (2009) Research 2.0: Improving participation in online research communities. European Conference in Information Systems (ECIS), Verona, Italy.

Fine, Brian, Menictas, Con, and Wang, Paul (2009) Remedying the Differences due to Multiple Online Panel Sources. ESOMAR Online Research 2009 Online Panels and Beyond. Chicago, United States.

Fitzpatrick, Brad (2007) 'Thoughts on the Social Graph', blog post, http://bradfitz.com/social-graph-problem/, 2007, accessed 2 January 2010.

Franke, Nikolaus and Shah, Sonali (2003) How Communities Support Innovative Activities: An exploration of assistance and sharing among end-users. *Research Policy*, Vol. 32, Issue 1, pp. 157–178.

Friedman, David (2001) What are the Arguments in Favor of Online Qualitative Research and When it is Best Applied? *Alert!*, April, United States Marketing Research Association.

Godin, Seth (2009) Dunbar's Number isn't just a number, it's the law, blog post. Available at: http://sethgodin.typepad.com/seths_blog/2009/10/the-penalty-for-violating-dunbars-law.html, accessed 2 January 2010.

Gordon, Wendy (1999) *Goodthinking: A guide to qualitative research.* Admap UK, Henley-on-Thames.

Greenbaum, Thomas L. (2001) Online Focus Groups Are No Substitute For The Real Thing. *Quirk's Marketing Research Review*, June.

Hair, Neil and Clark, Mora (2007) The Ethical Dilemmas and Challenges of Ethnographic Research in Electronic Communities. *International Journal of Market Research*, Volume 49, Issue 6.

Hayter Whitehill, Caroline (2007) Has Ethnography become a "Fat" Word? *International Journal of Market Research*, Volume 49, Issue 6.

Herbert, Michael (2001) Comparing Online and Face to Face Qualitative Research: From teenagers to third agers. AQR/QRCA International Qualitative Research Conference, Paris.

Ishmael, Gwen and Richarme, Michael (2009) Enhancing the open model through the use of community. *Research World* (ESOMAR), December 2009.

Jeavons, Andrew (2001) *Paradata*. ESOMAR Net Effects 4 (2001): Worldwide internet conference and exhibition, Barcelona, Spain.

Jennick, John and Schwartz, Gary (2006) Playing the Egg Game. Increased value in the customer experience. ESOMAR Annual Congress, London.

Kawasaki, Guy (2009) *The Six Twitter Types*. http://www.openforum.com/idea-hub/topics/the-world/article/the-six-twitter-types-guy-kawasaki, viewed 14 February 2010.

Kearon, John (2007) *Predictive Markets: Is the crowd constantly wise*. MRS Annual Conference, London, UK.

Kearon, John and Earls, Mark. (2009) Me-to-We Research – From asking unreliable witnesses about themselves to asking people what they notice, believe and predict about others. ESOMAR Congress 2009, Leading the Way: Ethically, Responsibly, Creatively, Montreux, Switzerland.

Kozinets, Robert V (2010) *Netnography: Doing ethnographic research online*. Sage, USA.

Last, N. (2006) *Nella Last's War: The Second World War diaries of 'Housewife, 49'*. Profile Books Ltd., UK.

Last, N. (2008) *Nella Last's Peace: The post-war diaries of Housewife, 49'*. Profile Books Ltd., UK.

Lehrer, Jonah (2009) *How We Decide*. Houghton Mifflin Harcourt, New York.

Lindstrom, M. (2008) *Buyology: Truth and lies about why we buy*. Doubleday, New York.

Louviere, Jordan (1991) Best-Worst Scaling: A Model for the Largest Difference Judgements. Working Paper, University of Alberta, Canada, 1991.

Lyman, Peter and Wakeford, Nina (1999) Going into the (Virtual) Field *American Behavioral Scientist*, 43, pp. 359–376.

MacElroy, Bill and Malinoff, Bernie (2009) Changes Needed in our Surveys to Improve Quality. The Market Research Event, San Diego.

Macer, Tim (2007) Online Research Tools: Some purchasing consideration. *Research in Business*, September, 2007.

Macer, Tim and Wilson, Sheila (2009) *The 2008 Confirmit Annual Market Research Software, Report and Key Findings*. http://www.confirmit.com/pdf/2008ConfirmitAnnualMRSoftwareSurvey.pdf, accessed 20 January 2009.

Malhotra, Naresh K. (2007) *Marketing Research: An applied orientation*, 5th edition. Pearson, USA.

Mariampolski, Hy (2001) *Qualitative Market Research: A comprehensive guide*. Sage Publications, Inc., Thousand Oaks.

Nairn, Agnes (2009) Protection or participation? Getting research ethics right for children in the digital age. ESOMAR, Congress 2009 Leading the Way: Ethically, Responsibly, Creatively. Montreux, Switzerland.

Oxley, Martin (2006) Centaur Insight Conference, London.

Phillips, Tim (2009) World of Temptation. Research-Live, July (http://www.research-live.com/features/world-of-temptation/4000459.article, downloaded 4 November 2009.

Poynter, Ray (1997) An Alternative to Brand Price Trade-Off. Sawtooth Software Conference 1997, Seattle, USA.

Poynter, Ray (2006) The Power of Conjoint Analysis and Choice Modelling in Online Surveys. Market Research Society, Annual Conference, UK.

Poynter, Ray (2007) Can Researchers Cede Control? What Web 2.0 means for market research. *Research World Magazine*, ESOMAR, July.

Poynter, Ray (2008) Whatever Happened to Letting Go? *Research Magazine*, MRS, UK, September,

Poynter, Ray, Cierpicki, Steve, Cape, Pete, Lewis, Andrew, and Vieira, Shizue (2009) What does Research 2.0 Mean to Consumers in Asia Pacific? ESOMAR Asia Pacific 2009 Competing On A World Stage, Beijing.

Quigley, Patricia and Poynter, Ray (2001) Qualitative Research and the Internet. ESOMAR, Qualitative Research, Budapest.

Rand, Yardena (2003) Worth Another Look. *Quirk's Marketing Research Review*, January.

Runham, M. (1999) IIR Internet Research Conference, UK.

Schillewaert, Niels, De Ruyck, Tom, and Verhaeghe, Annelies. (2009) Connected Research: How market research can get the most out of semantic web waves. *International Journal of Market Research*, Vol. 51, No. 1, pp. 11–27.

Stark, David W. (2009) From Social Engineering to Social Networking: Privacy issues when conducting research in the web 2.0 world. ESOMAR, Congress 2009 Leading the Way: Ethically, Responsibly, Creatively. Montreux, Switzerland.

Surowiecki, James (2004) *The Wisdom of Crowds: Why the many are smarter than the few and how collective wisdom shapes business, economies, societies and nations*. Doubleday, USA.

Sweet, Casey (2001) Designing and Conducting Virtual Focus Groups. *Qualitative Market Research: An International Journal*, Volume 4, Number 3, pp. 130–135.

Tapscott, Don and Williams, Anthony D. (2006) *Wikinomics: How mass collaboration changes everything*. Portfolio, USA.

Terhanian, George (2008) Changing Times, Changing Modes: The future of public opinion polling? *Journal of Elections, Public Opinion and Parties*, Vol. 18, No. 4, pp. 31–342.

Thelwall, M. (2007). Blog Searching: The first general-purpose source of retrospective public opinion in the social sciences? *Online Information Review*, 31(3), pp. 277–289.

Thelwall, M. (2009) *Introduction to Webometrics: Quantitative web research for the social sciences.* Morgan & Claypool, San Rafael.

Thelwall, M. and Prabowo, R. (2007). Identifying and Characterising Public Science Related Fears from RSS Feeds. *Journal of the American Society for Information Science and Technology,* 58(3), pp. 379–390.

Towers, Matthew (2005) There Are Benefits to Both: A comparison of traditional and online focus groups. *Quirks Marketing Research Review,* January.

Turner, Sonya (2008) Choosing the Right Approach Comes Down to Serving Each Project's Needs: Navigating the online qualitative landscape. *Quirks Marketing Research Review,* July.

Verhaeghe, Annelies, Schillewaert, Niels, and van den Berge, Emilie (2009) Getting Answers Without Asking Questions: The evaluation of a TV programme based on social media. ESOMAR, Online Research, Chicago.

Yoffie, Amy (2002) Qualitatively Speaking: Online focus groups . . . here today, not gone tomorrow. *Quirk's Marketing Research Review,* June.

York, S, and Hall, G. (2000) Using Evoked Set Conjoint Designs. Sawtooth Software Conference 2000, Hilton Head Island, USA.

Acknowledgements

The following people and companies have all made contributions or suggestions towards the creation of this book. Some helped by answering a query, some by helping with research or by supplying industry insight. Many of the people on this list helped via a LinkedIn group where earlier versions of sections of the book were reviewed and improved, and others by adding comments to my blog, still others by contributing to conversations on my blog. The scale of contributions that people have made towards this book vary between those who have reviewed thousands of words through to those who have supplied a single hard-to-find nugget of information or insight.

Without this co-creation the book would have been harder to write, less fun, and not nearly as useful as I hope it will prove to be. However, none of the people listed here can be held responsible or accountable for anything that is wrong in the book; any such errors of omission or commission belong to the author alone.

People I'd like to acknowledge and thank are listed below.

Name	Country	Company
Daniel Alexander-Head	Australia	Colmar Brunton Research
Steve August	USA	Revelation
Lynd Bacon	USA	Loma Buena Associates
Reg Baker	USA	Market Strategies International
Tamara Barber	USA	Forrester Research
Helen Bartlett	UK	Consultant
Doug Bates	Canada	Itracks
Jon Beaumont	UK	Virtual Surveys
Fiona Blades	UK	MESH Planning
Jim Bryson	USA	20/20 Research
Andy Buckley	UK	Virtual Surveys
Pete Cape	UK	Survey Sampling International
Steve Cierpicki	Australia	Colmar Brunton Research
Paul Child	UK	Virtual Surveys
Dr Nick Coates	UK	Promise Corporation
Richard Collins	UK	Confirmit

(continued)

Name	Country	Company
Pete Comley	UK	Virtual Surveys
Andy Dexter	UK	Truth
Zoe Dowling	USA	Added Value
Mark Earls	UK	Author, *HERD: How to Change Mass Behaviour by Harnessing Our True Nature*
Tom Ewing	UK	Kantar Operations
Dan Foreman	UK	ActiveGroup
Di Gardiner	Australia	Latitude Insights
Alastair Gordon	New Zealand	Gordon & McCallum
Mike Gray	UK	Virtual Surveys
Prashant Hari	Australia	Colmar Brunton
Katie Harris	Australia	Zebra Research
Peter Harris	Australia	Vision Critical
Chris Haydon	UK	Virtual Surveys
Jeffrey Henning	USA	Vovici
Shana Hugh	Canada	Vision Critical
Paul Hutchings	UK	Kindle Research
John Kearon	UK	BrainJuicer
Debbi Kleiman	USA	Communispace
Dan Kvistbo	Denmark	Norstat
Graeme Lawrence	UK	Virtual Surveys
Nigel Legg	UK	Katugas Research Services
Brian LoCicero	USA	Kantar
Tim Macer	UK	Meaning
Bernie Malinoff	Canada	element54
Pat Molloy	UK	Confirmit
Bryan Orme	USA	Sawtooth Software
Jonathan Puleston	UK	GMI
Angus Reid	Canada	Vision Critical
Joel Rubinson	USA	ARF
Meg Rudman-Walsh	UK	Virtual Surveys
Lee Ryan	Singapore	TNS
Siamack Salari	Belgium	EverydayLives
Pablo Sánchez Kohn	Bolivia	IQ 2.0

Name	Country	Company
Derek Sawchuck	Canada	Itracks
Karen Schofield	UK	Virtual Surveys
Duncan Southgate	UK	Millward Brown
Chris Stetson	USA	OpinionPath
Susan Sweet	USA	Doyle Research Associates
Christine Walker	Australia	Alliance Strategic Research
Karlan Witt	USA	Cambia Information Group
Brandon Walls	USA	U30
Sue York	Australia	Consultant

If I have missed you out please accept my apologies – there have been so many people contributing so much. Let me know and I will add you to the list on the website.

In addition I would like to thank the following companies for allowing material to be used: CDW, USA; Colmar Brunton Research, Australia; Communispace, USA; Directgov, UK; easyJet, UK; InSites Consulting, Belgium; NUS Services, UK; RTL, Nederlands; United Biscuits, UK; Virtual Surveys, UK; Vision Critical, Canada.

I would also like to thank all the people at John Wiley & Sons and ESOMAR who have helped pro-duce the book, especially Claire Plimmer who has been with project from proposal to completion.

Index

abuse 218, 255
access control 361
  bulletin board groups 135
  surveys 63
  accessibility issues 313–14
  legislation 356
  online surveys 60
  software tools 314–15
accompanied surfing 315–16, 318
activity cycle 141–2, 170, 179–80, 205, 209
adaptive scripting 323–5
adaptive survey modality 102–3
advanced graphical interfaces 23
advertising, testing online 289
aggregators 231, 232
alerts, email 225, 230
analysis options
  online focus groups 119
  paradata 98
  popup surveys 295–7
  web surveys 24
anonymity 138, 305
  participant blogs 169
  and web analytics 310, 311
answer lists, improving 49–50, 51
appearance of bulletin board groups 133–4
ARF online quality initiative 75, 358
Ariely, Dan 371
asynchronous techniques 111–12, 393–4
  email groups (MEGs) 110, 151–2
  see also bulletin board groups; online research
      communities; parallel IDIs; participatory blogs
audio in online surveys 57–8
August, Steve 251
auto-advance facility 38, 40
automated website testing 314–15
avatars 196, 207, 217, 379–80

B2B see business-to-business research
back button 32
  allowing use of 38
back filling, online surveys 97
background information, panel members 69–70
Baker, Reg 357
banner invitations 284, 302
Bates, Doug 121
BBC Global News: travellers' news
      consumption 248–9
behavioural targeting (BT), web analytics 311–12

benchmarking 74
  website studies 283–4
best practice guidelines
  for avoiding abuse 218, 255
  constructing an email invitation 62
  mixed-purpose research 332–4
  popup surveys 308
  for protecting real identities 217, 254
Black, Gordon 157
blog and buzz mining 108, 221–2
  case studies 237–9
  classification of 242
  essential steps in 223
    analysing material 234–7
    extracting material 231–3
    finding material 224–31
  ethical issues 239–41
  future for 242
  paradigm 223
  strengths and weaknesses 241–2
Bloglines, aggregator 231
BlogPulse 226
blogs 163–4
  in communities 193–4
  definitions of 172
  familiarity with 173–4
  other varieties of blogging 165–6
  research blogs 253
  search tools 224–7
  Twitter and microblogging 164–5
  see also participatory blogs
BlogScope 226
BPTO (Brand Price Trade-Off) 323
Brace, Ian 31
brand panels 245
Bruggen, Elisabeth 121
bulletin board groups 110, 132–3
  anonymity 138
  in B2B research 138
  benefits of 137
  characteristics of 133–6
  future of 150
  group dynamics 137
  and online communities 138–9
  product placement 138
  running projects 139
    closing the group 145
    creating discussion guide 143
    designing the group 140–3

bulletin board groups (*continued*)
    extraction of insight 145
    moderation of group 144–5
    recruiting participants 143–4
  software and services 148
business of market research 340
  changes to the research business model 343–5
  new competitors 343
  new forms of research 342–3
  online reporting 350–4
  outsourcing and offshoring 345–7
  quality and ethical issues 354–64
  remote working 340–1
  researcher networks 341–2
  system security and reliability 347–50
business-to-business (B2B) research 270–1
  future of 273
  recognition problem 273
  sampling issues 271–2
Buyology (Lindstrom) 371
buzz mining see blog and buzz mining

capacity issues
  panel companies 69
  web survey systems 27–8
Capeling, Theresa 122
CAPI (Computer Aided Personal Interviewing) 102
CATI (Computer Aided Telephone Interviews)
    systems 38, 350, 388
CDW, long-term, B2B research communities 214–15
ceding of control 188, 244–5, 385
CGM (consumer generated media) 221
Cheng, Colin 129–30
Child, Paul 193
children's surveys, parental permission 42, 297, 305
choice modelling 324, 325
citizen researchers 247–50, 378–9
Clark, Moira 240–1
cleaning data 96–7
client databases 8, 61, 76, 82
  B2B research 271
  dealing with complaints 79–80
  drawing samples 78
  factors that limit use of 77–8
  inviting respondents 78–9
  mixed-purpose research 80
  response rates 80–2
  types of databases 77
client panels 9
client protection 305–6, 361–2
client role, online vs. real focus groups 127
closed vs. open communities 180–1
closing an online survey
  key steps involved in 95–6
  options for 44
co-creation 86, 339, 362, 385
codes of conduct 80, 230, 254, 361

collaborative quantitative research 387–8
Comley, Pete 39, 76, 151, 157, 161, 187–8, 291
comments
  discussions and forums 190–1
  at end of survey 43, 156
  negative 205
  tagging 208–9
communities
  hybrid communities 184–6
  innovation communities 386–7
  natural communities 251
  reasons people join 210–11
  see also online research communities
community-enabled panels 243
  community characteristics 244
  future of 245–6
  impact of ceding control 244–5
community plans 204
complaints, dealing with 79–80
complex weighting 73
conformity to a plan 114
conjoint analysis 324
cookies 296, 309
  alternatives to 303–4
  and informed consent ruling 330
  sampling issues 299–300
cost issues 373
  online access panels 68–9
  online focus groups 125
    finished package vs. raw tools 123
    geographical factor 125–6
  specialisation reducing 347
  web survey systems 19–20
counting and voting in groups 114–15
coverage error 369
CREEN project 238–9
crowdsourcing 327, 385–6
cultural differences 112–15, 266
currency conversions, international research 266–7
customer satisfaction study 306–8
cyberbullying 218, 255

data collection modalities 99–100
  determining suitability of online 88–91
  interviewer presence or absence 100
  multi-modal survey options 25
  random probability sampling 100–1
  stimuli that can be used 102
  and survey adaptiveness 102–3
data permission types 77–8
data protection and security 28, 78, 153–4, 169,
    240–1, 346
databases
  importing RSS feeds to 232
  marketing 8–9
  see also client databases
dating metaphor 207

Decisive Moment, The (Lehrer) 371
Dedeker, Kim 74–5, 357
deep packet inspection 311–12
deliberative research 334–5
delivery paradigms 352–4
demographic issues, comparative studies 265
depth interviews *see* parallel IDIs
design issues
    bulletin board groups 140–3
    online research communities 197–202
    online/web surveys 31–65
    popup surveys 292–5
Designing Effective Web surveys (Couper) 31, 35,
    65, 295, 392
desktop/messenger systems 354
Dexter, Andy 17
digital fingerprinting 304, 310
Dillman, Don 46, 65
disclosure of client 78
discrete choice modelling (DCM) 324
discussion guides
    bulletin board groups 143, 146
    community plans 204
    conforming to 114
    online focus groups 118
    research plans 171
disintermediation 337–8
DIY research 335
    quantitative surveys 336–7
Dobbs, Lou 346
downloadable surveys 6
Dunbar number 251
duration of projects
    bulletin board groups 141, 142
    online focus groups 121–2
    online surveys 47, 48–9, 283
    participant blogs 168
    popup surveys 292
dynamic components, online surveys 59
dynamic reporting 352

e-ethnography 108, 246–7, 397
    citizen researchers 247–50, 378–9
    natural communities 251
    social graph research 251
Earls, Mark 175, 249–50, 371, 374–5, 378–9
easyJet Online Research Community 213–14
eDelphi 147, 406
EDL app for citizen researchers 250
email groups (MEGs) 110, 147, 151–2
email invitations 61–2, 78–9, 81, 284
email surveys 5–6
emerging trends and ideas 365
    changing power structures and networks 384–5
    collaboration and co-creation 385–6
    collaborative quantitative research 387–8
    innovation communities 386–7

    listening 378
    mobile research 388–90
    New MR 367–77
    social networks 379–81
    Twitter 381–4
    WE-Research 378–9
engagement, online community members 206–8
engaging surveys, creating 23, 29, 45–6
entertainment, online communities 197
ESOMAR
    26 Questions 68, 75
    guidelines 240, 363–4
    Online Research Initiatives 75, 358
ethical issues 354–5, 359–60
    blog and buzz mining 239–41
    boundary between marketing and market
        research 362–3
    legislation and directives 355–6
    online qualitative research 157–8
    online research communities 216–18
    online survey design 62–4
    participatory blogs 174–5
    permissions 77–8, 229–30, 334
    popup surveys 304–6
    privacy policies 363–4
    private sector initiatives 356–7
    protecting clients 361–2
    protecting researchers 362
    protecting respondents 360–1
    social media/networking 253–5, 381, 397
ethnography *see* e-ethnography
evoked sets 323
extranet reporting 353
eye tracking 316, 407

face-to-face versus online surveys 99–103
Facebook 229
    market research groups 419–20
    marketing teams 339
feature sorting 317–18
Ferneley, Elaine 210–11
fieldwork
    cost of 344
    launching 93–4
    monitoring 94–5
Fine, Brian 372
Fitzpatrick, Brad 251
Flash
    dynamic & interactive components 59
    for 'engaging' online surveys 53–4
    providing advanced graphical interfaces 23
focus groups 108
    feature sorting 317–18
    remote viewing of 110, 152–4
    size of, country differences 114
    using personas 318
    see also online focus groups

focus groups (*continued*)
forced completion 38–9, 293
forwarding at end of survey 45
Franke, Nikolaus 386
Friedman, David 129
friending 196, 217–18, 341
FTP (file transfer protocol) 354
Future Place, The, blog 164, 216, 293

Godin, Seth 164, 251
Google, behavioural targeting 311
Google Insights 227
Google Reader 231, 232
Google's Blog Search 225
Gordon, Wendy 114
Gosling, Geoff 330
Greenbaum, Thomas L. 128–9
grounded theory 234, 318, 407
guidelines
    ESOMAR 240, 363–4
    see also best practice guidelines

habits, promoting harmful 255
Hair, Neil 240–1
Hayter Whitehill, Caroline 246
headings, web surveys 39, 41
Heinze, Aleksej 210–11
Herd (Earls) 371
heuristics 323, 408
hidden data, analysis of 296
hierarchical bayes (HB) 326, 408
hill climbing, iterative technique 323, 408
home/personal page, community platforms 196
homogeneity, in people's responses 374–5
honesty
    online focus groups 129
    online surveys 47, 63, 79
    online vs. offline 13, 100, 113, 212, 392
HTTPS secure protocol for sensitive data 360
Hunter, Jeff 357
hybrid communities 184–6
hybrid survey options 25

IceRocket 226
identical survey myth 265
identity theft 217
IDIs (in-depth interviews) see parallel IDIs
images in online surveys 55–7
incentives
    bulletin board groups 142
    country differences 268
    fairness/value of 48
    online research communities 181–3
    popup surveys 292
incomplete surveys, dealing with 97
information architecture 317–18
informed consent 42, 63, 153, 306, 330, 331, 333–4
in-house panels 82–3, 86–7

additional options 85–6
management of 85
sophistication level 83–4
tips for using 86
innovations 378
    collaboration and co-creation 385–6
    collaborative quantitative research 387–8
    innovation communities 386–7
    listening 378
    mobile research 388–90
    social networks 379–81
    Twitter 381–4
    WE - Research 378–9
insight extraction
    bulletin boards 145
    online communities 208–10
    parallel IDIs 147
    participant blogs 171–2
InSites Consulting 237–8
intellectual property 361–2
interaction framework, bulletin board groups 143
interactive approaches, e-ethnography 397
interactive components, online surveys 59
interactive reporting 351–2
international research 112, 261
    adoption of online research 262
    internet penetration 262, 263
    key country and cultural differences 112–15
    online access panels 262, 264
    pitfalls in 263–8
    promise of the internet 262–3
    qualitative research 268–9
    quantitative research 268
    social media techniques 269–70
    summary 270
    web surveys 24–5
internet
    challenges created by 325–6
    internet-related surveys 4–6
    penetration 12, 90
        cross-country differences 262, 263, 265
    usage studies 12
Internet, Mail and Mixed-Mode surveys (Dillman) 65
interstitials 303
interview respondents see respondents
interviewers
    advantages of using 100
    loss of 392
introductions, online surveys 39
invisible processing 296
invitations
    client databases 78–9
    online surveys 61–2
    popup surveys 290–2
    website profiling 284
Iowa Electronic Markets (IEM) 327
IP addresses 304, 310
ISO Standards 75, 359

ISP liaison 312–13
IT skills 27, 29–30
Itracks 109, 121–2, 123, 130, 138, 148

Kawasaki, Guy 165, 251
Kearon, John 175, 249–50, 328, 378–9
Kozinets, Robert V 246
Krumwiede, Dennis 129–30

language issues 267–8
  international research
    country differences 268
    multi-lingual countries 267–8
    online research communities 269–70
    translation of survey questions 266–7
  online focus groups 122, 124
    loss of non-verbal 126–7
  online surveys 50–1
Last, Nella 250
layouts
  online surveys 51–3
  tag clouds 234–5
legacy issues 11, 409
Lehrer, Jonah 371
length of projects see duration of projects
Lindstrom, Martin 371
LinkedIn 381, 400
  groups function 341, 419
  researchers using 252, 272, 341
local partners, international research 264
long-term bulletin board groups 134
long-term communities 179–80
  CDW, B2B research communities 214–15
look and feel
  bulletin boards 140
  online research communities 199
  standards 60
Louviere, Jordan 324–5
Lyman, Peter 251

Macer, Tim 18
Malhotra, Naresh 31, 96, 121
management information systems (MIS) 119, 144–5
Mariampolski, Hy 114, 246
market research
  business model changes 343–5
  changing nature of 393
  and marketing 362–3
  problems with traditional 373–4
  qualitative vs. quantitative 107–8
  and social networks 379–81
marketing and market research, boundary
    between 362–3
marketing databases 8–9
marketing sciences 322
  adaptive scripting 323
  challenges created by the internet 325–6
  choice models and New MR 325

conjoint analysis and discrete choice modelling 324
  evoked sets 323
  MaxDiff scaling 324–5
    modules in web survey systems 26–7
  pricing techniques 323–4
Mass Observation project 250
MaxDiff scaling 324–5
McCarthy, Zoe, blog author 164
MEGs (moderated email groups) 110, 151–2
microblogging 164–5, 252
missing data 97
  and forced completion 38–9, 293
mixed-purpose research 80, 329
  best practice guidelines 332–4
  key areas for 332
  orthodox view of research 330
  reasons companies want 331
  terminology 329–30
  why some respondents want 331–2
mobile research 25, 388–90
modelling 14, 74, 324–5, 372, 376–7
moderation process
  bulletin board groups 144–5
  focus groups 120–1, 122
  online communities 183–4, 202–8
modes
  bulletin boards 135–6
  online focus groups 117
monitoring a survey 71–2
MROCs (Market Research Online Communities)
    see online research communities
multi-modal survey options 25
multi-page surveys 36–8
multimedia options 22–3, 102
  audio in online surveys 57–8
  bulletin board tasks 136
  images in online surveys 55–7
  online focus groups 118, 124
  photo and video uploads 194–5
  using Flash 53–4
  video in online surveys 58–9
multiple rooms, online focus groups 119
MyStarbucksIdea, brand community 185

natural communities 188, 251
negativity, dealing with 205
Netnography: Doing Ethnographic Research Online
    (Kozinets) 246
networking by researchers 252–3, 341–2
NewMR 205, 367–8, 399
  and choice models 325
  prediction markets 328–9
  problems with traditional research model
    368–9, 373–4
    responses to 372–3
  random probability sampling assumption 369–70
statistical significance testing and panels 373
why market research usually works 374–6

non-completion error 370
non-market research 273
non-response error 369
NUS case study, website research 319–20

observational market research 108, 315, 380
offshoring 345–7
one-in-N sampling 298–9
online access panels 7, 66–7
  choosing 67–70
  community-enabled 243–6
  countries covered 262, 264
  creating 76
  improving response rates 72–3
  management facilities 23
  and online surveys 60–1
  the panel paradigm 73–4
  and quality 74–5
  shift to 392–3
  statistical significance testing 373
  working with providers 70–2
online chat 194
online focus groups 110, 116–17
  analysis options 119
  arguments for and against 125–9
  choosing a solution 122–5
  discussion guide 118
  evidence about 129–30
  management information systems 119
  modes 117
  multimedia 118
  multiple rooms 119
  participant handling 118
  polling software 119
  resources for 130
  running a group 120–2
  webcams 119
online qualitative research 107
  growth and scale of 109
  international projects and differences 112–15
  reasons for lack of growth 109–10, 393–4
  synchronous and asynchronous
    approaches 111–12
  techniques 110–11
Online Quality Research Council, ARF
    75, 358–9
online quantitative research 3–15
  changes in 391–3
  client databases 76–82
  data collection modalities 99–103
  designing online surveys 31–65
  in-house panels 82–7
  online access panels 66–76
  post-survey qualitative explication 156
  running an online survey 88–99
  web survey systems 16–30
online research communities 176–8

agency versus client moderated 183–4
balance between research and member agendas 187–9
designing 197–8
  community tools 199–200
  look and feel 199
  recruiting members 200–1
  terms and condition 201–2
  type of community 198–9
examples of communities 212–15
future of 218–19
incentives 181–3
link to bulletin board groups 138–9
long-term communities 179–80
moderating and managing 202–3
  community moderator/manager 203–4
  community plan 204
  creating a sense of community 207–8
  creating member engagement 206–7
  dealing with negativity 205
  finding and delivering insight 208–10
  handling lulls in client engagement 208
  managing a short-term community 204–5
number of members 186–7
open versus closed communities 180–1
quality and ethical issues 216–17
research or hybrid communities 184–6
resources 215–16
short-term communities 178–9
summary 219–20
theoretical perspectives 210–12
tools 189
  blogs 193–4
  collaboration tools 195
  discussions/forums 189–92
  entertainment 197
  member personalisation 196
  offline activities 197
  online chat 194
  photo and video uploads 194–5
  polls and surveys 192–3
website research: NUS case study 319–20
online survey design see web survey design
online survey process 3–4
online surveys, running 88
  analysis and reporting issues 96–8
  closing the job 95–6
  designing the survey 91–2
  launching fieldwork 93–4
  monitoring fieldwork 94–5
  real-time reporting and monitoring 95
  reasons not to use online 88–91
  scripting and testing survey 92–3
  sourcing the sample 91
  summary 98–9
open-ended questions 13, 155
  coding of 97, 234, 236
  final comments at end of survey 43

using to spot problems 34, 94
open vs. closed communities 180–1
Opinion Leader research agency 335
outcome measurement 53–4
outsourcing 345–7, 393
OutWit Hub, web scraping tool 233
overlays 289, 302
Oxley, Martin 161

pages
  definition of 33
  interstitials 303
  online surveys
    first page 40–2
    going back to earlier page 38
    last page 43–5
    multi-page surveys 36
    questions per page 36–7
  and screens 35
    pages too long for 37
  website visitor sampling 300–1
panel providers, working with 70–2
panels see in-house panels; online access panels
paradata 94, 98
parallel IDIs 110–11, 132, 145–6
  differences in terminology 149
  future of 150
  logistics of 146
  resources 147–8
  running 146–7
partial responses, including in analysis 295
participant handling tools, online focus groups 118
participants, recruiting see recruitment of participants
participatory blogs 163, 166–7, 175
  issues to consider 172
    definitions of a blog 172
    ethical concerns 174–5
    participants' familiarity with blogs 173–4
  running a blog project 167–72
passive data, analysis of 296
permissions 77–8, 229–30, 334
persistent cookies 309
personal identifiers 310, 333
personalisation 196, 311
Phillips, Tim 335
politeness, online surveys 48
polls
  collaborative 387–8
  online research communities 192
  polling software, online focus groups 119
pop-under windows 302
population effects 11, 12
popup surveys 42, 289–90
  analysis 295–7
  attracting respondents 290–2
  best practice guidelines 308
  design issues 292–5

Directgov example 306–8
  ethical and quality issues 304–6
  logistics of 297
    alternatives to cookies 303–4
    alternatives to popups 302–3
    pages and locations 300–1
    sampling methods 298–300
    screening people out 297
    technology issues 301
    time on site 298
portals 156, 354, 411
post survey discussions and portals 156
postal versus online surveys 99–103
Predictably Irrational (Ariely) 371
prediction markets 326–7
  Iowa Electronic Markets (IEM) 327
  and New MR 328–9
  using in market research 328
  wisdom of crowds 327, 375
pricing techniques 323
prior consent 333–4
privacy issues 202, 356
  online research communities 217
  privacy policies 41, 363–4
  remote viewing of focus groups 153–4
  and web scraping 232–3
private communities 180, 412
prize draws 41, 44, 183, 356
product placement 138
products, promoting harmful 255
profiles
  anonymity issues 310
  online research communities 196
  website profiling studies 283–4
programmable scripts, web surveys 27
progress indicators 39–40, 293
project management tools 22
project reporting, web surveys 24
protection issues 28, 169, 240–1, 305–6, 346, 359–62
protectionism 346
PSM (price sensitivity meter) 64, 324, 412
public discussions 279
public sector research 274
  ethics 280–1
  future of 281
  geographical limitations 275–6
  in the public eye 275
  representativity 275
  and social media 276–80

qualitative explication of quantitative surveys 111, 155
  post-survey qualitative explication 156
qualitative research 105–6
  bulletin board groups 132–45
  future of 158
  growth of online 109–10
  international projects 112

qualitative research (*continued*)
  key ethical and quality issues 157–8
  online focus groups 116–31
  parallel IDIs (in-depth interviews) 110–11, 145–50
  pre-social media context 156–7
  qualitative explication of quantitative surveys
      111, 155–6
  reasons for lack of success 157
  remote viewing 110, 154
  versus quantitative research 107–8
  virtual worlds 110, 154–5
Quality Enhancement Process (QeP) 75, 358
quality issues 357–8
  ethical issues relating to 255
  initiatives 358–9
  key points 400–1
  online access panels 68, 74–5
  online focus groups 126–8
  online research communities 256
  online surveys 62–4
quantitative New MR 376–7
quantitative research 3
  changes in 391–3
  collaborative 387–8
  finding respondents to interview 6–10
  internet-related surveys 4–6
  moving surveys online 11–15
  online survey process 3–4
  reasons for success 157
  versus qualitative market research 107–8
questionnaire creation tools 21–2
questionnaire testing facilities 22
questions
  apparent repetition of 47
  on first page of survey 42
  on last pag of survey 44
  layout on a page 35–40
  moving a survey online 13–14
  number per page 36–7
quotas 72, 73–4, 95, 303, 372

Rand, Yardena 129
random probability sampling 90–1, 100–1
  drawing samples from databases 78
  problems with assumptions of 369–70
  sophisticated reweighting approaches 372
  statistical significance testing and panels 373
RDD (Random Digit Dialling) 370
reach concept 128
  missing key groups 280
real life research 247–8
real-time reporting and monitoring 28–9, 95
real-time (river) sampling 9–10
real-time (synchronous) techniques 111–12, 133, 146
recognition problems 254, 273, 310
recruitment of participants 6–10
  bulletin board groups 135, 143–4

citizen researchers 249–50
  Europe-North America differences 113
  online focus groups 122, 126
  online research communities 200–1
  parallel IDIs 147
  participant blogs 171
reliability issues 15, 256, 361
  online access panels 74, 75, 373
  systems 347–8, 349
remote viewing 111, 152–4
remote working 340–1
reporting 350
  delivery paradigms 352–4
  focus groups 124
  online research communities 209–10
  process 350–1
  real-time 28–9, 95
  of research findings 351–2
  web surveys 24, 98
representation errors 370
reputation 362
Research 2.0 143, 161, 412
research agencies
  bypassing 337–8
  changes to business model 343–5
  managing communities 183–4
  sending email invitations 79
  value of 338
research communities see online research communities
research-only communities 185–6
research plans, blog projects 171
research techniques and approaches 322
  bypassing the research agency 337–8
  communities and other social media 338–9
  deliberative research 334–5
  DIY research 335–7
  marketing science 322–6
  mixed purpose research 329–34
  prediction markets 326–9
researcher networks 341, 420
  networking ideas 342
  networking people 341–2
researchers
  networking 340–2
  protection of 362
  using social media 252–3
resources
  blogs 417
  bulletin board groups 147–8
  free websites 418
  online focus groups 130
  online research communities 215–16
  parallel IDIs 147–8
respondents
  attracting, popup surveys 290–2
  children as 42, 297, 305
  invitations to potential 78–9

irrationality of 371
methods of contacting 6–10
misleading 255
protecting 305, 360–1
rogue respondents 97
views of communities 211–12
views and opinions of 46–8
see also recruitment of participants
response rates
client databases 80–2
online panels 72–3, 75
popup surveys 294–5
river sampling 9–10
rogue respondents 97
routing at end of survey 44, 45
RSS feeds 230–1
importing to a database 232
RTL Nederlands and Insites Consulting case study 237–8
Rudd, Kevin 165, 278
Runham, M. 294–5

SaaS (Software as a Service) 18, 20, 28, 123
sampling 100–1, 103
from client databases 8, 78, 91
from panels 9, 73–4
from social networks 380
other sources 10
popup surveys 298–301
alternatives methods 284
river sampling 9–10
sample effects, online surveys 12
statistics 373
satisfaction studies, websites 283–4
scalability 27, 218
scope of blog projects 167–8
screen
definition of 33
size for popup surveys 293
versus form and page 35
Screen-Scraper 233
screen scraping 233
screening issues 46–7, 297
scripting online surveys 92
scroll bars 35–6, 37, 293
search engine optimisation (SEO) 288–9
search tools
analysing Google's search terms 227
for blogs 224–7
for Twitter 228–9
Search.Twitter 228
seasonality and calendar issues 266
Second Life, virtual world 110, 154, 279
security issues 305
and anonymity/privacy 153–4, 169
and remote working 341
sensitive data 360

of system information 28, 348–9
web survey systems 25–6
self-completion paradigm 34
SEM (search engine marketing) 288–9
semiotics 317
sensitive data 360
session cookies 309
Shah, Sonali 386
Sheu, Chwen 129–30
short-term bulletin board groups 134
short-term communities 178–9
managing 204–5
significance testing, panel samples 74
signing-in, sampling method 303
single-page versus multi-page surveys 36–8
size of groups
bulletin board groups 134, 140–1
focus groups 114
in-house panels 82–3
online focus groups 121
online research communities 180, 186–7, 199
skill base of organisation, assessing 29–30
smartphones, web surveys using 25, 390
SMS and simple mobile surveys 389
social graph research 251
social media 159–60
applying to research problems 398–9
DIY research 338–9
and market research 256–7, 394
blog and buzz mining 318, 396–7
community-enabled panels 243–6, 395
e-ethnography 246–7, 397
online research communities 319–20, 394–5
participatory blogs 395–6
social networks and beyond 397–8
and the public sector 276
assessing and managing risk 280
blogs and public discussions 279
consultation, engagement, and research 276–7
involvement vs. representativity 277
online communities 277–8
social networks 279
Twitter 278
virtual worlds 279–80
used by researchers 252–3
user-generated media 160
'Web 2.0' 161
social networks 379
as a sample source 380
characteristics 379–80
ethics of using for research 381
future of 397–8
and observational research 380
software and services
bulletin board group 148
parallel IDIs 148

software and services (*continued*)
  tools for evaluating websites 314–15
  for web surveys, buy vs. develop 17–18
spam filters 356–7
speed issues 373
  online focus groups 128
Stark, David 217, 218
static invitations 303
static reporting 351
statistical significance testing and panels 373
stimuli, comparison of survey modalities 102
sugging 330
Surowiecki, James 327
survey experience
  improving 45–6, 325–6
  quality initiatives 53
surveys
  linking web analytics with data from 310–11
  moving online 11–15
  online research communities 192–3
  see also web survey design
Sweet, Casey 120, 121, 122
synchronous techniques 111–12, 133, 146
  see also online focus groups

tag clouds 234–5
Tapscott, Dan 273
tasks, bulletin board groups 136–7
Technorati 225–6
telephone versus online surveys 99–103
Telstra, community-enable panel 245–6
terminology problems 149
terms and conditions 41–2
  bulletin board groups 142
  online research community 201–2
  participatory blogs 170
testing
  online advertising 289
  online surveys 64, 92–3
  usability testing 284–5
  website design and concept 285–7
  website tools 314–15
  websites for technical issues 313
thanking respondents 43, 48
third-party panels 246
Threadless.com, crowdsourcing example 386
timelines, panel surveys 71
tracking studies 283
traffic volumes, web analytics 312–13
transactional sites, popup surveys 295
translation issues 266–7
triangulation 377
truth telling 377
TweetDeck 229
TwitScoop 228
Twitter 381–2
  backchannel 383

celebrity tweets 382
direct messages 382
future of 384
Hashtags 383
low usage of 173, 174
and microblogging 164–5, 252
retweeting 382
searching 228–9, 383
Tweetferences 383–4
tweetups 383
use by market researchers 242
use by public bodies 278
Type I and Type II errors 374

United Biscuits, real life research 247–8
unnecessary information 63
unprompted lists 13
usability testing, websites 284–5, 313
user-generated media (UGM) 160

vertical scrolling in surveys 36–8
video in online surveys 58–9
video-casting focus groups 152–3
video uploading 137
virtual qualitative research 154–5
virtual worlds 110, 154–5, 279–80
VocalPoint, community 185
voting in groups 114–15

Wakeford, Nina 251
WE Research 247–50, 378–9, 390
'Web 2.0' 161, 414–15
Web Accessibility Initiative (WAI) 314
web analytics 309–11, 318, 415
web bugs 81, 415
web metrics, popup surveys 296–7
web scraping 232–3
  RTL Nederlands and Insites Consulting study 237–8
web survey design 31–2
  accessibility issues 60
  client databases 61
  drafting invitations 61–2
  multimedia use 54–9
  online access panels 60–1
  quality and ethical issues 62–4
  self-completion paradigm 34
  structural issues
    first and last pages 40–5
    question layout on a page 35–40
  summary and key points 65
  survey experience, enhancing 45–6
    being better with people 46–8
    improving surveys 48–53, 325–6
    measuring outcomes 53–4
    quality and engagement initiative 53
  terms used 32–4
  see also popup surveys

web survey systems 4–5, 16–17
  buying versus developing 17–18
  capacity 27–8
  cost-related issues 19–20
  creating engaging surveys 29
  data protection and security 28
  data reporting and monitoring 28–9
  deciding whether or not to have 17
  features of 20–7
  integrations with other tools 29
  skills required, assessing 29–30
  software versus SaaS 18–19
webcams
  post-survey qualitative explication 156
  used by online focus groups 119
  used in WE-Research 247–8
website research 282
  accessibility issues 313–14
  accompanied surfing 315–16
  automated website testing 314–15
  eye tracking 316
  information architecture 317–18
  popup surveys 289–90
    analysis 295–7
    attracting respondents 290–2
    best practice guidelines 308
    ethical and quality issues 304–8
    logistics of 297–304
    survey design 292–5
  reviews 313–14

semiotic analysis 317
social media research for websites 318–20
summary of 320–1
types of projects 282–3
  search engine optimisation 288–9
  technical performance 287
  testing online advertising 289
  usability testing 284–5
  visitor profiling and satisfaction studies 283–4
  website design and concept testing 285–7
website metrics and analytics 308
  behavioural targeting 311–12
  measuring traffic volumes 312–13
  web analytics 309–11
website visitors 9
  measuring traffic volumes 312–13
  profiling and satisfaction studies 283–4
  sampling issues 300–1
weighting of data 73, 95, 98, 277, 372, 377
welcome message, online surveys 40–1
WePC.com, ideas community 185
Willems, Pieter 121
Williams, Anthony D. 273
wireframes 287
wisdom of crowds 327, 375
Wisdom of Crowds, The (Surowiecki) 327
WOM (word-of-mouth) 221
Wordle, tag clouds 234

Yoffie, Amy 130